ORIGINS AND REVOLUTIONS

What changed in the three million years of human evolution? Were there tipping points that made us more recognisably human? In this innovative study, Clive Gamble presents and questions two of the most famous descriptions of change in prehistory. The first is the human revolution when evidence for art, music, religion and language appears. The second is the economic and social revolution of the Neolithic. Gamble identifies the historical agendas behind research on origins. He proposes an alternative approach that relates the study of change to the material basis of human identity. Rather than revolutionary stages, Gamble makes the case that our earliest prehistory is a story of mutual relationships between people and their technology. These developing relationships resulted in distinctive identities for our earliest ancestors and continue today.

Gamble challenges the hold that revolutions and points of origin exert over the imagination of archaeologists. He opens the door to an inclusive study of how human identity, in concert with material culture, has developed over the past three million years.

Clive Gamble is Professor in the Department of Geography at Royal Holloway University of London. He is one of the world's leading authorities on the archaeology of the earliest human societies. His many groundbreaking books include *The Palaeolithic Settlement of Europe*; *Timewalkers: The Prehistory of Global Colonisation*; the 2000 winner of the Society of American Archaeology Book Award, *The Palaeolithic Societies of Europe*; and most recently *The Hominid Individual in Context*, edited with Martin Porr. In 2005, he was awarded the Rivers Memorial Medal by the Royal Anthropological Institute in recognition of his outstanding contribution to the field. He was elected a Fellow of the British Academy in 2000 and in 2003 became co-director of the Academy's prestigious Centenary Project, *From Lucy to Language: The Archaeology of the Social Brain* that seeks to find out when hominid brains became human minds.

Origins and Revolutions

Human Identity in Earliest Prehistory

CLIVE GAMBLE

Royal Holloway University of London

CAMBRIDGE
UNIVERSITY PRESS

CAMBRIDGE UNIVERSITY PRESS
Cambridge, New York, Melbourne, Madrid, Cape Town, Singapore, São Paulo

Cambridge University Press
32 Avenue of the Americas, New York, NY 10013–2473, USA

www.cambridge.org
Information on this title: www.cambridge.org/9780521860024

First published 2007

Printed in the United States of America.

A catalog record for this book is available from the British Library.

Library of Congress Cataloging in Publication Data

Gamble, Clive.
Origins and revolutions: human identity in earliest prehistory / by Clive Gamble.
   p. cm.
Includes bibliographical references and index.

ISBN-13: 978-0-521-86002-4 (hardback)
ISBN-10: 0-521-86002-4 (hardback)
ISBN-13: 978-0-521-67749-3 (paperback)
ISBN-10: 0-521-67749-1 (paperback)

1. Human beings – Origin. 2. Social evolution. 3. Tools, Prehistoric. 4. Art, Prehistoric. 5. Neolithic period. 6. Agriculture – Origin. 7. Material culture. 8. Technology and civilisation. I. Title.
GN281.G28 2007
599.93′8–dc22

                                                          2006023259

ISBN   978 0 521 86002 4   hardback
ISBN   978 0 521 67749 3   paperback

Contents

Figures and Tables List

Figures

Tables

Acknowledgements

It is a great pleasure to be able to record my thanks to the many people and institutions that have contributed towards this book. The award of a British Academy Research Readership was essential to enable both travel and reading and the time to rethink the questions of why agriculture happened and the appearance of people like ourselves. As important was the opportunity provided by Dr Julie Hansen, who invited me for a semester as a Visiting Professor to research and teach at the Department of Archaeology, Boston University, funded by a Humanities Foundation Fellowship. My seminar class at Boston were among the first to hear the ideas in this book and set me right on a number of points; Ben Vining, Susan Mentzer, Satoru Murata, Menaka Rodriguez, Rita Pelosi and Sophie Telgezter. I should also like to thank Curtis Runnells, Priscilla Murray and David Stone for all their hospitality and good conversation. Across the Charles River a special debt goes to the staff of the Tozzer library and to Ofer Bar-Yosef at the Peabody Museum, Harvard: his encouragement is infectious and his generosity with data and ideas helped this project immensely. Unexpected travel opportunities came through C5 and the filming of a documentary series 'Where do we come from?' broadcast in 2002. The production team of Michael Proudfoot, Jessica Whitehead, Jim Sayer and James Routh made light of remote destinations and in six months I saw more than I could have bargained for. I was also able to meet with many friends and make new ones both off and on camera. To all of them, thank you for your patience and your knowledge.

During the writing of the book I have moved from an Archaeology to a Geography Department. At Southampton, I would like to thank many of the staff and students who have helped me in working out the arguments of this book. From the Centre for the Archaeology of Human Origins: John McNabb, James Steele, Martin Porr, Annabel Field, Jenni Chambers,

Anne Best, Fiona Coward, Rob Hosfield, Fotini Kofidou, Dmitra Papagianni, Vicky Elefanti, Gil Marshall, Matt Pope, Phil Kiberd, Farina Sternke, William Davies, Erica Gittins, Sonia Zakrewski and Yvonne Marshall. From the Department of Archaeology: Elaine Morris, Andy Jones, Yannis Hamilakis and Jo Sofaer. At Royal Holloway special thanks are due to Felix Driver, Rob Kemp, David Wiles, Matt Grove, Dora Moutsiou, Rob Imrie, Rebecca Sheldon, Scott Elias, John Lowe, Karen Till, Jim Rose, Danielle Schreve, Nick Branch and many Landscape Surgeons.

In 2003 with Robin Dunbar and John Gowlett of Liverpool University we began directing the British Academy Centenary Project *From Lucy to Language: the archaeology of the social brain*. Much of this book would not have been possible without the stimulation of this project and the invitations from Wendy James, Hilary Callan and Nick Allen to consider kinship and from Steven Mithen to re-evaluate music in human evolution. These are exciting times for human evolutionary studies and I would like to record the stimulating discussions I have had with Robert Proctor, Robin Dennell, Rob Foley, Marta Lahr, Trevor Watkins, Carl Knappett, Chris Gosden, John Robb, Chris Knight, Camilla Power, Steve Shennan, Alasdair Whittle, Brian Graham, Andy Garrard, Richard Bradley, Marcia-Anne Dobres, John Chapman and the late Andrew Sherratt whose judgement on the final version I would very much have valued.

I have been greatly assisted in the production of the book by Fiona Coward who critically edited earlier drafts and Penny Copeland who skilfully drew all the figures. I am very grateful to Patrick Kirch, Chris Gosden, Tom Minichillo, Olga Soffer, Angela Close, Andrew Garrard, Chris Henshilwood, Nikolai Praslov and Francesco d'Errico for supplying and allowing me to reproduce their original illustrations.

Although every effort has been made to trace the owners of copyright material, in a few instances this has proved impossible and I take this opportunity to offer my apologies to any copyright holders whose rights I may have unwittingly infringed.

My greatest thanks, as always, go to Elaine.

Note: All radiocarbon dates in this book are calibrated using the CalPal programme and given as years Before Present (BP).

PART I

Steps to the present

The longest of long revolutions

You don't need a Weatherman
to know which way the wind blows
Bob Dylan *Subterranean homesick blues* 1965

To begin with ...

One revolution invariably led to another. Fire drew some of our earliest ancestors into the circle. Stone tools made them hunters and these handy artefacts later became symbols, embellished by language and art. A life on the move was eventually exchanged for a settled existence that promoted agriculture, and the first civilisations followed. Then came the ancient Empires with their bookkeeping, literacy and the institutions of state power. The momentum they established led to industrialisation whose global ramifications define the contemporary world.

There, as I see it in an extreme digested read, lies the familiar contribution of three million years of prehistory to the larger human story. The investigation of the past is based around the origins of great advances such as technology, language, farming and writing; the where, when and why of becoming human. The origin points for these questions are investigated across the globe and are presented by archaeologists as step changes. Origins and revolutions are sought after as both the source of evidence and the causal device that, in the long corridors of prehistoric time, transformed hominids into humans.

I embarked on this book to question this familiar approach and to challenge what archaeologists regard as change. I cannot say exactly when I grew dissatisfied with the search for origin points and the identification of revolutions, but with hindsight I can see two points of departure early in my career. The first came from archaeologist David Clarke who launched his blistering attack on the cosy foundations of archaeological knowledge more than thirty years ago. He shook his prey like a terrier.

> Even those most complete and finished accomplishments of the old edifice – the explanations of the development of modern man, domestication, metallurgy, urbanisation and civilisation – may in perspective emerge as semantic snares and metaphysical mirages. (Clarke 1973:11)

But Clarke only had archaeologists in his sights although, judging by the rash of new revolutions that have been identified since his tragically early death three years later, not many were listening. What was lacking from his critique was the broader framework, which I discuss in Part I, where revolution is accepted as an apt analogy in many disciplines across the humanities and social sciences, and it is from this broad base that it derives its staying power as a convenient concept.

Archaeology has made one long-lasting contribution to this historical device through Gordon Childe's Neolithic Revolution, formulated in the 1930s, that drew an analogy with the Industrial Revolution. More recently there has been much discussion among archaeologists of a Human Revolution and I spend some time unpacking these concepts in Part I, together with origins research more generally, since they address what many see as fundamental changes that need explaining. The two revolutions, Human and Neolithic, have a cast of characters; among them farmers, hunters, anatomically modern humans and *hominins*. The last is now the widely used term to describe us, *Homo sapiens*, and all our fossil ancestors. The more familiar *hominid*, that it replaces, includes us, our fossil ancestors and the great apes.

That broader context of approval for the idea of revolution, and my second point of departure, is apparent in the writings of another Cambridge figure, Raymond Williams, occasionally glimpsed by undergraduates in the early 1970s on his way back from the radio studio, and whose books *Culture and Society: 1780–1950* (Williams 1958), and *The Long Revolution* (1965) were required reading. Williams spoke of 'genuine revolutions' that transformed people and institutions, and he wove together the democratic, industrial and cultural revolutions to show that they could only be understood in relation to each other. His time-frame was short, 200 years for the most part, but importantly his Long Revolution was an unfinished project of continuous change that made us who we are. He pointed out (1965:13) that we devote a great deal of our cultural and intellectual life to criticising these revolutions in an attempt to understand ourselves. Williams was therefore quite content with the shallow time depth of history to understand change: the process conveniently structured by the ruptures of revolution. But in 1970 I was an infant archaeologist interested in the long-term contribution of our evolutionary history to what we are. Quite simply, why were the devices of recent history suitable analogies for understanding the much longer sweep of social and economic change that was available to prehistorians? My own seed of change had been planted and now you have the harvest.

Human identity and change

Archaeologists will tell you that they were put on this earth to explain change. What they usually mean by that is their unflagging search for the evidence of origins; the fieldwork quest for the oldest. And once found these origin points, like well driven tent pegs, secure the ropes to explain the changes that led in the first place to the point of origin.

In this book I will not be looking for the origin of anything. Neither will I be examining existing nor proposing new revolutions as devices for understanding why change happened. Instead I will present a study of human identity in earliest prehistory. My basic point is that the study of change, and I do not deny that it has taken place, has to acknowledge the material basis of human identity. The construction of the self and personhood, what I understand as human identity, was always local rather than universal. Identifying what needs to be explained in the change between such apparently universal categories as hunter to farmer or archaic to modern human mis-represents the ways in which material culture is woven into our identities. Hence my emphasis on how artefacts, the archaeologist's bread and butter evidence, act as material metaphors for that hidden, inner identity. Metaphors in earliest prehistory need to be especially well anchored and I will argue in Part II that this was achieved through the hominin body since it provided at all times and places the reference for sensory and emotional experiences about the world. Major turning points such as language and art must have affected these hominin experiences. Notwithstanding, I will argue that such developments, however significant we regard them, were not origin points for a radically new hominin identity from which we can trace the beginnings of our own humanity. Artefacts are much older than words. Tools and techniques have always had a metaphorical relationship with the hominin body and identities have been formed from this interaction.

These relationships between artefacts and bodies are examined in Part II. In particular I set out a scheme for the study of material culture through the categories of instruments and containers that are proxies for parts of the body, and from which they derive their symbolic force. Material metaphors of this kind are comparable to the more familiar linguistic rhetorical devices by which something is understood in terms of something else. I set these material proxies in a framework where identity is created through social practices that enchain and accumulate and actions that consume and fragment.

Finally, in Part III I apply my concept of change to the prehistory of a social technology that spans almost three million years. I will show that change in this vast time period can be understood without recourse to either revolutions or the identification of specific, singular points of origin. There were no step-changes, only gradients in the respective authority of commonplace material metaphors that organised the world of experience. The dominant archaeological approach that seeks to establish rational associations in order to explain the variety of artefacts is supplemented in my account by a relational perspective that brings the body as well as the mind into consideration. What we regard as change depends on how we view artefacts as material proxies for identities derived from the active body and the inner self. The former is hidden to the archaeologist, the latter to ourselves.

I also tackle in Part III the question of whether agriculture did in fact change the world. Here is a historical tipping point not only for archaeologists but for all those seeking an origin for the modern world. My answer to the question is a negative in terms of the material basis of human identity. To make my point I concentrate on a neglected category in archaeology enquiry, children. I use the concept of the childscape, which I define as the environment of development, to provide a context for understanding how such an apparently fundamental change as growing crops and raising animals occurred. To assist this undertaking I examine two primary metaphors, the giving-environment and growing-the-body, that impacted on the childscape and the material project we call agriculture. I question the view of a number of archaeologists that humanity is no older than the earliest evidence for cultivation.

Rational and relational approaches

The difference that exists between my approach to change and the more familiar framework of the Human and Neolithic Revolutions is captured in the opposition of mind and body. The tension provides another tussle between rational and relational accounts of the ways in which people engage with their material worlds.

Two examples will help to set the scene. Phenomenologist Maurice Merleau-Ponty (1962:147) contended some time ago that 'bodily experience forces us to acknowledge an imposition of meaning which is not the work of a universal constituting consciousness'. Yet evolutionary psychologist Robin Dunbar (2003:163) has recently declared that 'what makes us human is not our bodies but our minds'. A theme of my book is to bring these positions together using material culture as the focus.

The start of Williams' Long Revolution furnishes two famous Latin sound bites in support of these opposite views about the authority of mind and body, rational and relational, for understanding the on-going global project of Modernity. Both come from the seventeenth century; '*Cogito ergo sum*' (I think therefore I am) and '*Habeas corpus*' (You should have the body).

Improvement of the mind

Cogito ergo sum, in the hands of the mathematician and philosopher René Descartes (1596—1650), privileged the mind over the body by dividing the world into oppositions that included subject and object, nature and culture, individual and society, structure and process. In Descartes' paradigm, the internal mind understood and interpreted the external world in a rational manner. The rewards of this way of thinking have been immense and included scientific and medical advances. Applied to the past, the rational paradigm sees our improving minds as driving history forward while below the neck our bodies stayed the same, merely executing orders from above. The benefits of progress can be measured by material items such as ploughs, steam engines, longevity, digital watches and the release from toothache. It is therefore un-surprising that the systematic study of the past followed, rather than preceded Descartes, and that the step-changes which archaeologists have used to structure their accounts of prehistory since the early nineteenth century embraced a progressive view of our history. For instance, when trained by a rational education the mind could be improved to the benefit of the individual and wider society. By analogy, the story of the past became one of improvement as our species changed from a natural into a cultural being. The perception of such a transition in part explains the interest in the skulls of our earliest ancestors and the importance attached to their size, shape and by inference their contents.

The archaeological contribution to this story has been to provide tangible proof of the pace of change in the classrooms of human evolution. For the most part the record card of material evidence is filled with phrases such as 'slow progress', 'could do better' and 'nothing to report'. This state of affairs changes with the first of my two revolutions, the Human Revolution. The period starts 300,000 years ago with several hominin species found in the same geographical localities. It ends with a single global species, *Homo sapiens*, ready to move on alone and turn its back on hunting and gathering. During this time the curriculum has been expanded from an early emphasis on survival and natural history to include advanced crafts, religious studies, music, languages, global geography, multi-culturalism and art classes. The Neolithic Revolution, beginning some 15,000 years ago, quickens this pace further, suggesting to some that this was the time when we truly appeared, as if woken from a very long daydream at the back of a stuffy classroom.

Archaeologists see two of their goals as deciding on the temporal and geographical origins of the expanded curriculum, outlined above, and commonly called modern behaviour. It was certainly a revolution as judged by the almost three million years of stone tool use that preceded it. But compared to say the American or French revolutions of the eighteenth century the terminology sits awkwardly. It is the significance *for us* of the origins of these modern humans, rather than the time it took for them to appear, that is truly revolutionary.

A whole body

The Cartesian system has of course had side effects. Scientific and medical advances have not all been beneficial. But rather like the NRA slogan 'People, not guns, kill people' this is seen neither as the fault of the technology nor the system that produced it (Robb 2004:131). Instead, it is people who are the weakest link. The rational mind both identifies and provides material solutions to problems. For example, our bodies wear out and are susceptible to disease. With this problem in mind solutions can be sought. The result is the treatment of the body as another piece of technology, 'machines of meat' as the novelist Kurt Vonnegut once described them. 'My body let me down' just as 'My memory is going' beg for an applied solution that will make them better instruments for serving the mind. Both depend on the mind making a judgement about ourselves that curiously distances one set of faculties from another as in the opposition between subject and object, internal and external states.

This is why *Habeas corpus* extends the argument in important ways. The move from a philosophy of the mind to the legal imperative of the body reminds us that to be a person we not only need to think but also to be seen and heard. *Habeas corpus* enshrined, in an Act of Parliament of 1679, a much older common law principle that there could be no imprisonment without legal hearing. Physical presence before witnesses recognised the materiality of being a subject of flesh and bone rather than just an object animated by thought. Or at least that is how I see these oppositions in the seventeenth century as philosophers and lawyers now defined what it was to be an individual in a rapidly changing European world (Williams 1965:Chapter 3).

The Long Revolution therefore gives the on-going project of hominin evolution a choice of starting point, mind and body, rational as well as relational. My intention is to re-unite the mind and the body in our understanding of the past by showing, through the study of two so-called revolutions, that they bring different perspectives to the central archaeological issue of change. This standpoint involves both the description and explanation of change from material evidence. This body-whole perspective is not new and draws on critiques in many disciplines, including archaeology, of the Cartesian system of how we understand the world. The unification is necessary to achieve what I hope will be a fresh understanding of why things changed in the past, based on a different appreciation of the material evidence. The point I do carry forward from the Cartesian system is that our bodies are a social technology. But they are also, as the anthropologist Marcel Mauss insisted, techniques. Bodies are material projects comparable to those of building a house or planting a field of barley. They are always cultural as well as biological artefacts, just as artefacts are similarly social and natural things. I will argue that to understand change we need to dig beneath the surface and view our evidence through other prisms than origins research and by analogies other than that of revolution.

CHAPTER 1

The Neolithic Revolution

The Neolithic took place in the grey night of remote prehistory
Gordon Childe *What happened in history* 1942

Changing trains

In 1934 the archaeologist Gordon Childe made a short trip to the Soviet Union. For twelve days he visited colleagues in museums and archaeological institutes in Leningrad and Moscow. He saw the country from the train and he returned laden with books and information about the origins of the Indo-Europeans. He also learned first-hand about theoretical upheaval. The Soviet archaeology he encountered was a fully fledged state instrument charged with the investigation of pre-capitalist societies and the history of material culture. Indeed, the word archaeology was prohibited and the names of the major institutes had been changed accordingly (Trigger 1980:93). By coincidence the leading archaeologist prior to the Russian revolution of 1917, N. Y. Marr, died in the year of Childe's visit. Marr's brand of Marxism as applied to prehistory stressed that social development was a staged process that took place independently, and therefore in parallel, in different geographical areas. There was little room for diffusion and migration as explanations for change until Marr was denounced by Stalin in 1950 (McNairn 1980:154, 165).

The movement of peoples was Childe's preferred mechanism for the archaeological variety he had already seen first-hand in museums across Europe. In this device at least he shared common ground with another of his contemporaries that he outlived, the ultra-German nationalist Gustav Kossinna who had died in 1931. Kossinna's views of Aryan racial superiority led him to propose a homeland for their origin among northern

Nordic peoples. From there, he argued, sprang all that was progressive and valuable about a European past (Barkan 1992; Härke 1992; Malafouris 2004; Veit 1989). Kossinna's agenda was to find archaeological evidence that would demonstrate this. Childe was opposed to Kossinna's programme on political, moral and scientific grounds. While he shared the view that as peoples moved so prehistoric cultures ebbed and flowed, he neither subscribed to racial superiority as a motive force nor to a northern home-land as a significant origin point, arguing rather for the importance of the east. Europe, he claimed, fell under the light from the east, *ex oriente lux*. He was to later write of his early syntheses that 'the sole unifying theme was the irradiation of European barbarism by Oriental civilisation (Childe 1958b:70)', and he directed his considerable powers of archae-ological synthesis and philological analysis to showing this was indeed the case.

Kossinna's legacy is well known and infamous (Klejn 1999). Two years after his death the Third Reich was founded, and his agenda was enthusiastically taken up by the *Deutches Ahnenerbe*, or German ancestral heritage, an organisation whose purpose was to use history and science to justify German superiority. The *Ahnenerbe* was a major National Socialist project, established by Heinrich Himmler in 1935 and generously endowed at Wewelsburg Castle, the ritual headquarters of the SS. Archaeology figured prominently in the justification of invasion and suppression of the free nations of Europe.

Childe would have been familiar with such overt nationalism as he criss-crossed Europe during the 1920s and 1930s. His travels linked archae-ological provinces together in great chains of historical connections based on the similarity of their prehistoric artefacts, although instead of railways it was the great route-ways of the Danube, the Rhine and the shores of the Mediterranean that tied the prehistory of the continent together. He strengthened these chains by binding them ultimately to chronologies derived from the text-aided archaeology of the Near East and Egypt. He was not the first archaeologist to do this but he was the most successful.

So it is interesting to think about what else Childe might have glimpsed through the train window during his visit to the Soviet Union in 1934. Almost certainly he would have seen the effects of Stalin's programme of agricultural collectivisation. Beginning in 1929 the working practices of generations of farmers had been bulldozed aside according to the dictates of centralised state planning. Collectivisation, exacerbated by drought, is largely held responsible for the famines of 1932–3 when five million peasants are believed to have died. Although an archaeological justification for such programmes was never sought, the idea that the movement of peoples, whether by choice or by force, was an inevitable process that drove history cannot be escaped.

Childe's two revolutions

It was immediately after his return from Russia that Childe began to re-work his synthesis of European prehistory. He started in 1935 with his Presidential address to the newly formed Prehistoric Society. Entitled 'Changing methods and aims in prehistory' he re-visited the tri-partite division of the past that had existed ever since C. J. Thomsen, in 1836, had ordered the collections of the National Museum in Copenhagen into cabinets containing stone, bronze and iron objects (Gräslund 1987). Subsequently these three ages had been much refined and subdivided, and in 1865 Sir John Lubbock, in his book *Pre-historic Times*, had separated the earliest into an Old and New stone age, or Palaeolithic and Neolithic. These terms now marked the difference in technology between hunters and farmers (Brown 1893:66).

Childe was as enthusiastic as the next archaeologist for refining the contents of those cabinets and adding geographical as well as chronological detail through excavation. But by 1935 he had lost patience with mere cataloguing. 'What then', he cried to the Prehistoric Society (1935a:7), 'is to become of the hallowed terms Palaeolithic, Neolithic, Bronze Age, Iron Age?' His answer now looks simple, but at the time it was radical. 'I should like to believe that they may be given a profound significance as indicating vital stages in human progress. I would suggest that the classifications Old Stone Age, New Stone Age, Bronze Age and Iron Age draw attention to real revolutions that affected all departments of human life' (Childe 1935a:7).

For Childe these revolutions were primarily functional-economic stages where the Neolithic meant food-producing, an interpretation apparently backed by the first appearance of artefacts such as polished axes, pottery and weaving as well as evidence of domestic animals and crops. However, his insistence that revolutions affected all departments of human life opened the door to considerations not just of economy but also of language, religion, politics and science. Although he did not specifically refer to a Neolithic Revolution in his 1935 address, the groundwork was laid so that by 1942 in his best-selling *What happened in history*, where the lack of a question mark should not go un-noticed (Whittle 2003:163), revolution had arrived. In this book Childe set out the evidence for two prehistoric revolutions, Neolithic and Urban, which by analogy to the Industrial Revolution of the eighteenth century resulted in population growth (Childe 1935a:11). The analogy was primarily justified by the spectacular archaeological evidence for Neolithic village settlements and the first cities, what Childe referred to repeatedly throughout his subsequent career as representing an 'upward kink in the population graph' (Childe 1958a:71). This analogy was first applied by Childe to his Urban Revolution and only later to the earlier Neolithic Revolution (Greene 1999:99). However, the Industrial analogy also suggests a further link to the development of democracy and systems of self-government that, as Williams (1965:11) showed, is never a simple relationship.

In *What happened in history* Childe used the terminology for social development put forward by Lewis Henry Morgan in *Ancient society* (1877), a book based mainly on the author's anthropological knowledge of North America. Morgan's three stages were savagery (hunters), barbarism (farmers) and civilisation (urban life). Barbarism was the turning point for human society because according to his scheme agriculture appeared at this time.

Morgan was Karl Marx's anthropologist, the source of his views on pre-capitalist societies, and his influence is obvious in Frederick Engels' 1884 (1902) writings on the origins of the family and the state. But even though Childe (1935b:152) pronounced Morgan's ethnography 'antiquated', the influence of Engels' writings, and the result of those twelve days of conversations with Soviet archaeologists, made him realise that the three terms were helpful for historical analysis (Trigger 1980:95).

Locomotives of change

Before describing Childe's two revolutions in more detail, I think it is worth asking why the concept of revolutions has such a historical appeal, spanning all aspects of the modernist project from the paradigm shifts that create scientific revolutions (Kuhn 1962), to the barricades thrown up by the intertwined democratic, industrial and cultural revolutions that challenged and changed political authority (Williams 1965).

The standard answer for archaeologists is that Childe was a Marxist (Trigger 1980), albeit an ambiguous one on occasion (McGuire 1992; McNairn 1980). Peter Gathercole (1994) has argued that books such as *Man makes himself* (Childe 1936) reflected the desire of the Left in the inter-war years to make a significant contribution towards scientific progress and hence the flagging cause of socialism. However, if Childe's Marxist beliefs were the reason, then why did someone who published so copiously and across so many disciplines – 22 books and more than 200 articles between 1923 and his death in 1957 – take so long to come up with the idea? The analogy to the Industrial Revolution is, let's face it, un-subtle; especially when, as Kevin Greene (1999:99) reminds us, the term was coined by Arnold Toynbee as long ago as 1884.

While Childe gained something from his trip to the Soviet Union, seventeen years after its own historic revolution, the trip can hardly be described as his road to Damascus. Indeed such conversions do not characterise Childe's academic career, which developed themes but never emulated the stadial models of change that he favoured.

And what bigger theme than 'what happened in history?' If Childe was either going to describe what occurred or take up the challenge of answering the question, then he needed a driving force. Prehistory did not supply him with one but European and North American history certainly did with its emphasis on revolutions as indicators of fundamental political change.

Revolutions come in all shapes, sizes and degrees of success, from gunpowder plots to bloodless coups, civil wars, popular uprisings and palace revolutions. They can be approached as universal stages in development or seen as the result of contingent factors tied to a particular time and place (Stone 1966). They can be analysed either for their timeless variables by social scientists such as Childe or for their particular personalities by historians proper. So useful are revolutions in accounting for change that many historians regard them as the locomotive of history (Clark 2003:33).

But where exactly is the engine headed? Jonathan Clark (2003:42) suggests that revolutions are merely convenient historical concepts for explaining the formation of the nation-state. Consequently they are a much-needed force for driving forward the modernist project. From this perspective revolution is the engine that explains how our current political systems came into being and how an older European past, composed of tradition, was transcended. Science, the state and a global economy resulting from both imperialism and colonialism are all pillars of modernism, and much of history and social science is devoted to understanding how they arose.

The target becomes clearer if we focus on the big revolutions that have been most discussed and picked over. At the highest level there are the twinned Industrial and Agrarian revolutions (Toynbee 1884 (1969)).

These were well underway by the eighteenth century in Europe and are fully entangled with the Enlightenment and rampant imperialism. If these revolutions formed the superstructure then imagine them as a canopy above an elaborate mosaic floor where their effects are picked out in decorative motifs that would include the notion of capital and the development of markets, technology and metropolitan growth. And beneath all the best mosaic floors there is always a hypocaust blowing out hot air, fuelled in this instance by the four big northern revolutions that drove industrialisation. Here Britain leads the way although there is a dispute (e.g. Stone 1965) over the identification of *the* revolution: was it the English civil war, that executed one king in 1649, or the Glorious Revolution, that switched dynasties in 1688 but kept the *status quo* of the monarchy? Less contentious are the other three revolutions; the American in 1776, the French in 1789 and the Russian in 1917. All four apparently led directly to the modern nation-state just as day follows night, or modernism succeeds tradition.

However, Clark's (2003:37) point is that the use of the term *revolution* has been a cheat, suggesting that we can control what we cannot. Christopher Hill (1986) has shown that in the seventeenth and eighteenth centuries *revolution* had a very different meaning. It was applied to the cyclical movements of astronomical objects rather than political rupture, and the term *révolution* expressed disorder rather than a programme of action to achieve a goal (Clark 2003:45). For Hill it was the English revolution, which he identified as the Civil War, that transformed history from a cyclical to linear narrative. Clark (2003:50) is less convinced, claiming that it was not until 1789 that Frenchmen were able to console themselves with the idea that political chaos was really a process with a history and one that could be typologised into stages.

It was at this time that social scientists, or rather their philosophical precursors, began their analysis of universal developments that historians have repeatedly challenged (Stone 1966). Three age systems were not invented by Morgan in 1867. They have a long history dating back at least to the Scottish philosophers of the eighteenth century (Meek 1976) and in France, Turgot's treatise on universal history (Meek 1973; Turgot 1751 (1973)). Deeper roots can be found among Classical authors and in particular their grading of materials — mud, wood and stone — into a system of historical value (Pagden 1986:72–3). Such is the hold of the concept of three ages that anthropologist Ernest Gellner (1986:78) impishly described this thinking and classifying in stages as the doctrine of Trinitarianism: that mankind passes through three and only three fundamental stages in its development. He was of course targeting Morgan and Marxism, but the roots of such thinking go much deeper still.

Where does Childe fit in? He was concerned with the workings of the modern state (Childe 1923) and the rise of its ancient counterpart (Childe 1934 (1952)). He was interested in process and the power of the economy to transform. His philosophy and values were Marxist and his *metier* was the grand narrative. His theme was change and in his address to the Prehistoric Society he argued that each prehistoric revolution made room for a larger population than the last.

But Childe's use of revolutions can take on a further dimension. When placed in the context of Kossinna and Marr, and the political developments in Europe of the 1920s and 1930s, we can see how his entire output is opposed to nationalism and the inevitability of totalitarianism. In his personal Retrospect (Childe 1958b:73), published after his suicide in 1957, he recalled that *What happened in history* was written in 1942 to convince himself that European civilisation − Capitalist and Stalinist alike − would recover from the Dark Age into which he saw it heading. The prehistoric revolutions he described in that book therefore sounded an optimistic note in desperate times. But how? He wrote later of his insistence that an agricultural surplus had to be concentrated for the Urban Revolution to take place, and by doing so he recognised 'the Hegelian rationality of the political and religious totalitarianism that characterized the ancient Oriental States' (Childe 1958b:72). The hope he wanted to convey was therefore based on Europe's historical ability to transform rather than to slavishly copy an older model of civilisation. On European soil, the Urban Revolution did not lead to Oriental despotism but to a positive transformation of the economic and scientific principles upon which those ancient states were founded. Europe had benefited by not being the first to attempt an Urban Revolution. Change brought progress in the eventual form of political systems of democratic self-government which required revolution to succeed, and this was an acceptable price to pay to escape the shackles of Oriental absolutism. Childe's message in 1942 to his less convinced contemporaries was therefore 'wait and see'. Europe had always risen above the Orient and would do so again, even though totalitarianism and fascism were now within its borders in Russia, Germany, Spain and Italy. For Childe, revolutions were indeed locomotives of change, drawing ever longer and heavier trains behind them. Before they provided the mechanical horsepower for written history he also used them to spin the wheels on older, prehistoric carts.

The Neolithic Revolution as an imaginative archaeology

Of course Childe was not working alone. He was quick to recognise the earlier contribution of Grafton Elliott Smith (1930 (1934)), who had welcomed the end of hunting and gathering as follows:

> The creation of civilization was the most tremendous revolution in the whole course of Human History. Within a few centuries so profound a change was effected in the mode of life, the aims and occupations, and in the size of the population and in the areas affected by the changes, as to open a new chapter of Man's career with new standards of values and new social conditions and aspirations.
>
> (Smith 1930 (1934):267)

There was no doubt in Smith's mind that this was a revolution. 'Agriculture is like the use of fire – the invention was a sudden inspiration and not the result of a gradual process' (Smith 1930 (1934):295). Contrasted with the aeons of Palaeolithic hunting when people lived 'just like an animal' (Braidwood 1948 (1957):122), the 'brilliant success' (Childe 1944:112) of the Neolithic Revolution was to 'escape from the impasse of savagery' (Childe 1942:55), enable sedentism and so pave the way for urban civilisation and ultimately the present world.

It was Childe's genius to make historical sense of a classificatory scheme. He took prehistoric artefacts out of the display cases and put them to work on the stage of world history. He inspired fieldwork to recover more precise information about the Neolithic Revolution (e.g. Braidwood and Howe 1960) and the worldwide testing of different models of how and why it all happened (e.g. Cohen 1977; Ucko and Dimbleby 1969). These models have included the factors that pushed people into agriculture, or at least magnified the consequences of any early experimentation. These factors were usually external prime movers including climate change, food shortage and propinquity to the right kinds of crops and animals. Then there are models which favour internal re-structuring, sometimes independent of such outside changes. Consequently, society is often portrayed as a complex organism concerned with honing its adaptive behaviour in order to achieve reproductive success. Population pressure figures strongly in many of these internal explanations as do the territorial packing of social units and technological advances such as axes, ploughs and storage vessels. For many archaeologists, creative ideologies mark the Neolithic mind as cognitively different while for others the changes are the products of natural selection leading to enhanced adaptive success.

TABLE 1.1.   *A three-tiered approach to the study of long-term change found in many disciplines (after Dark 1998:76)*

Unit of analysis	Explanatory factors	Interdisciplinary modes of analysis
Individual	Politics	Ecological
Social group	Economics	Evolutionary
Polity (state, chiefdom, nation, etc.)	Social organisation and structure	Economic
Network(s) of interactions between any or all of the above	Cognitive and psychological factors	Cognitive
	Ecological factors including human demography	Interactional (contacts and communication)
	Ideology	Structural
		Historical particularist
		Mathematical/formal

It is not surprising then that the Neolithic Revolution has become the catch-phrase for change in both academic and public conceptions (Cole 1959; Tudge 1999). However, I am not interested here in reviewing all the competing ideas, although some will be touched upon in more detail in Part III, and for excellent overviews I recommend Lewis Binford (1968), Andrew Sherratt (1997b) and David Harris (1996a) as well as more recent and contrasting accounts by Ofer Bar-Yosef (2001), Marc Verhoeven (2004) and Brian Byrd (2005). I would note, however, that archaeologists share many procedures in common with a wide range of other disciplines that tackle questions of change in human societies (Table 1.1), suggesting that our endeavours are part of much bigger projects, both modern and post-modern, and not just structured by deep time and fragmentary data from pre-literate societies.

As a result I am more concerned with what we can learn from the Neolithic Revolution about our archaeological imagination (Gamble 2001; Thomas 1996), the process by which we have an under-standing of the past and from which we go about the business of constructing imaginative archaeologies, than in merely cataloguing and dating the past.

The concept of the Neolithic Revolution is an excellent example of an imaginative archaeology. It exists because of the connections spun by masters such as Childe. The concept alters due to the social contexts that use such knowledge and incorporates new information and ideas on a daily basis. The best way to view an intellectual project as complicated as the Neolithic Revolution is as a network that brings into focus concepts, arguments, data, personalities and contexts for the production and consumption of the past in the present. The network includes myself while writing this book as well as archaeological ancestors, such as Childe, whose ideas I am drawing on. A network, as Marilyn Strathern (1996:521) has pointed out, is an interpretation. It can represent an argument as it flows between people through time and across geographic space. But as she also observes, networks have to be cut if they are not to end up including everything and everybody and hence becoming unwieldy to the point of suffocation.

This is another function of the Neolithic Revolution. It acts as a pair of scissors to cut the conceptual network, taking the continuum of archaeological time and snipping it into a big, but manageable, problem. Then our archaeological imagination can get to work. Such cutting is particularly suited to an approach that looks for the origins of elements in the Neolithic Revolution such as villages, weaving, polished axes, pottery, crops and domestic animals. These were the diagnostic elements in Childe's (1935:7) package, but an even better example came with his later Urban Revolution. Here a ten-point checklist (Table 1.2) allowed an archaeologist to recognise when civilisation had been achieved in his or her region (McNairn 1980:92−103).

The Neolithic Revolution and Orientalism

I mentioned briefly how Childe, and many others, juxtaposed the power of the East against the nationalist agenda of Kossinna and his northern homeland for European civilisation. Certainly the archaeological data point to the importance of Southwest Asia for both the earliest agriculture and cities. However, celebrating proof of evidence is to miss the point because an acknowledgement of the role of the Orient easily becomes Orientalism, Edward Said's (1978) concept of how familiar and unfamiliar spaces are created by what he termed imaginative geography. Orientalism is an exercise in cultural strength where the peoples and places of the East are contained and represented by the dominant frameworks of the West (Said 1978:40). This process has a very long history, as Said shows,

TABLE 1.2. *The list of traits identifying the Urban Revolution (Childe 1950)*

1. *Size*: an increase in settlement size towards urban proportions
2. *Surplus*: the centralised accumulation of capital resulting from the imposition of tribute or taxation
3. *Monumental public works*
4. The invention of *writing*
5. Elaboration of exact and predictive *sciences*
6. The appearance and growth of long-distance *trade in luxuries*
7. The emergence of a *class-stratified society* based on the unequal distribution of social surplus
8. *Composition and function of an urban centre*: freeing part of the population from subsistence tasks for full-time craft specialisation
9. *State organisation* based on residence rather than on kinship and involving territorial definition
10. The appearance of *naturalistic art*

but a benchmark event in the creation of modern Orientalism was Napoleon's occupation of Egypt in 1798 and the surveys of ancient monuments, history and culture that followed. Through such means the empires of Europe, and principally those of Britain and France, affixed the Orient to their continent as a theatre packed with opinions and assumptions as much as facts. And in this theatre, this contained space, the Orient and Islam are always represented as outsiders but with a special role to play inside Europe (Said 1978:71). These imaginative geographies persist as Derek Gregory (2004) has shown in his analysis of contemporary American understanding and interpretation of the Middle East, in what he terms the colonial present. His study bears out Said's perceptive comment that, 'it is finally Western ignorance which becomes more refined and complex, not some body of positive Western knowledge which increases in size and accuracy' (Said 1978:62).

The use of the Orient as a theatre is particularly evident in Childe's work. His interest was almost totally focused on understanding Europe. For example, one of his last books *The prehistory of European society* (1958a) had its rationale plainly written on the dust jacket: 'how and why the prehistoric barbarian societies of Europe behaved in a *distinctively European way*' (emphasis added). In other words, they were not just pale imitations of the civilisations of Egypt and Mesopotamia. Furthermore, as we saw earlier, in Childe's view prehistoric Europe made a better fist of the Urban Revolution than Oriental despotism, benefiting from the mistakes by fostering liberties founded on the freedom of its craftsmen (Sherratt 1997b:60). While Childe's view contrasted with that of Elliot Smith's, 'thus the civilisation of the whole world was derived from one original source' (1933:232), namely Egypt, he shared more with the high champion of cultural diffusion than is normally allowed. For example, he described the geographical theatre for the Urban Revolution as follows:

> it is bounded on the west by the Sahara and the Mediterranean, on the east by the Thar desert and the Himalayas, on the north by the Eurasiatic mountain spine...and on the south, as it happens, by the Tropic of Cancer. The geological, physiographical, and climatic conditions of this zone proved propitious to the revolutionary development. It provided the raw materials for the decisive discoveries. It offered inducements to intensive social organisation and rich rewards for large-scale cooperation. It gave facilities for communication by which new knowledge might be pooled and essential materials collected and concentrated. Finally its cloudless skies presented nightly the impressive spectacle of the uniform motion of the heavenly bodies that in other latitudes is too often veiled.
>
> (Childe 1942:77–8)

Even the aridity of Mesopotamia was an advantage since it forced people to live along the rivers and realise their potential as described earlier. In addition, the mountains that lie to the north, east and west formed a 'fertile crescent', as the Chicago-based Egyptologist James Breasted called it in 1926, and within whose boundaries the drama of agriculture and social transformation would be enacted. Here would be found the wild progenitors of wheat, barley and goats (Zohary and Hopf 2000) and for a while the oldest villages in what archaeologist Robert Braidwood (1960) described as nuclear zones.

Edward Said would recognise this process. Rather than celebrating the Orient, as it might at first appear, the archaeologists were instead setting up a separate place isolated in this instance by time and geography. And the reason for making such an imaginative archaeology was their interest in Europe rather than the Orient. The light from the East that they often write about, where the Neolithic Revolution burns particularly brightly, is not so much a celebration of historical difference as an example of an eternal asymmetrical relationship. Europe took the idea of civilisation and transformed it in its 'distinctively European way'. And why? Because empires and colonial projects require both imaginative archaeologies and imaginative geographies to feed the asymmetry of recent and contemporary political power. Europe, and the United States more generally, have an appetite for the identification of origins and this has characterised their colonial and national histories. For example, in his declaration of 1690 that, 'In the beginning all the world was America', the philosopher John Locke (Meek 1976:343) was engaged in an imaginative archaeology that would fold the peoples of an ever-expanding colonial world into the ambitions and identity of its self-proclaimed centre. Such imaginative archaeologies of political development depend on creating a distinct difference, a temporal realm where the *other* resides out of time and where we can go to reflect upon our historical position.

The concepts of the Palaeolithic and Neolithic are two such imaginative archaeologies which, to extend Said's analogy to another area of academic inquiry, hold the same relationship to each other as the Orient to Europe. The Neolithic dominates this power structure as farmers lord it over hunters and barbarians over savages. The Palaeolithic is a theatre with some nice painted scenery attached to the economic muscle of a Neolithic shopping mall. Consequently, our understanding of Palaeolithic people is very often phrased in terms of the farmers they are not, rather than the hunters they were. And to emphasise this asymmetry we find the invention of a third space, the Mesolithic, which has a particular function in mediating the transfer of Neolithic political power to the European continent. The term appeared in 1872 (Westropp 1872) and was later applied to evidence that showed Europe was not deserted after the Ice Age (Binford 1968:316). This archaeological space inhabited by the Mesolithic 'folk' was the drum upon which the revolutionary roll of agriculture was beaten out.

The Neolithic Revolution, a snippet from the potential archaeological archive, is one of those times and spaces that pull into focus those wider cultural practices that organise and sanction the production and consumption of knowledge about our complex world. It is a network that comes with a pedigree in understanding humanity in terms of a particular set of values and achievements and, most crucially, presents them as original.

Continuity backlash and transitions

We have seen that at least one historian, Jonathan Clark (2003), thinks that the concept of revolution is a bit of a cheat because it implies an ordered progression that in fact never existed. Following Childe's death in 1957 the commitment by archaeologists to prehistoric revolutions has been mixed for similar reasons. Several more revolutions have been proposed, as we shall see later in this chapter, and the most important has been the Human

Revolution, the subject of Chapter 2. However, between the 1950s and 1970s when large field projects in the Near East, Europe and Mesoamerica were amassing evidence concerning the origins of agriculture, and using the scientific revolution of radiocarbon dating to establish historical conjunctures that Childe (1958a) could only dream of, loud voices were raised in support of continuity.

For a short time, two of the loudest, backed by the Cambridge prehistorian Sir Grahame Clark, were Eric Higgs and Michael Jarman. In several papers (1969; 1972) they made the case for repeated experimentation in crop and animal husbandry rather than a single invention. Their guiding tenet was that from the Neanderthals of the Middle Palaeolithic onwards there had been a general trend in economic developments to increase control over resources and produce more per unit of land (Higgs and Jarman 1972:12). Cambridge exam papers of the time invited students to discuss 'that agriculture was neither Neolithic, nor a revolution' (Sherratt 1997a:271), and the smart answers concluded it was a 'continuously developing natural process of great selective value' (Higgs and Jarman 1972:13). Subsistence practices such as husbandry fluctuated during the long term that they advocated as the correct time scale for a meaningful economic prehistory. Furthermore, they successfully questioned Childe's Neolithic Revolution by showing that key artefacts such as ground stone axes, pottery and stone blades that could have been hafted to make sickles were found at earlier times at sites with hunting and gathering economies. Once expanded to a global scale the concept of the Neolithic Revolution, based primarily on the archaeology of Southwest Asia, started to leak like an archaeological sieve.

These archaeological challenges to Childe's Neolithic Revolution are examples of the gradual approach to change that is best summed up as a study of transitions. Here there are no locomotives to hurry change along and usher progress in. Instead change takes the form of future-creep. In future-creep there are no crisp divisions, only some gentle shunting that moves things forward until difference is inescapable. Such differences are expected to happen eventually and can be explained simply by the passage of enough time, a commodity with which human prehistory is abundantly blessed.

One of the best illustrations of archaeological future-creep are the seriation studies of artefact types and their agglomeration into archaeological cultures (Figure 1.1). These archaeological icons take the form of battleship curves describing the levels of occurrence through time that start thin, grow fat and end by tapering away to nothing. The explanation for

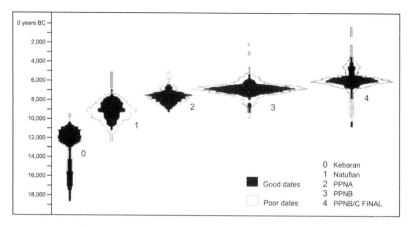

FIGURE 1.1. A chronological fleet of battleship curves. The data are radiocarbon dates that have been assessed for their reliability. They chart the timing of the origins, rise and fall of five Near Eastern archaeological cultures (after Aurenche et al. 1987).

their changing shape might be functional differences and improvements in a single artefact type, the replacement of one people's cultural inventory by another's in a site or across a region, or perhaps the transition from hunting to farming.

These battleship curves, as opposed to the step-like progression of revolutions, show archaeologists concentrating not on change but on the transition between well-defined points. These origin points are established in advance; for example, we might begin with a time with wild animals, small settlements and no pots and finish with one that had pots, domestic animals and large settlements. Transitions then become the passageways between two very different conditions, which of course we have previously defined as significant. Stone to Bronze and Bronze to Iron Ages would be another instance. Then the point of interest becomes the speed of the transition and whether it conforms to a model of slow gradual replacement, the incremental addition of novel traits and the loss of existing ones, or a more punctuated, sudden change. With a concept of transitions, even the most static archaeological evidence can become part of the long-term process of change and the 'revolution' rolls on over the millennia.

The paradox of change

But now we encounter a paradox. If archaeologists like myself regard the explanation of change as their main task, why do we spend so little time establishing what we mean by change?

Explanations abound for the appearance of literacy, urbanism and plough agriculture. They deal with the magnitude of change as well as the tempo, fast or slow. Competing explanations, be they social, functional, ecological or ideological, are fully debated (Table 1.1). And this is the problem. We think we know change when we see it, which is why the Neolithic Revolution has made sense for such a long time. However, when is a change really a change and not just variation on an existing theme? That is precisely the criticism directed by Higgs and Jarman at the list of traits and the timings of their appearance used to identify the Neolithic Revolution. Rather than a neatly bounded package of first appearances for items such as pottery, ornaments, villages, domestic animals and cemeteries there now exists a picture blurred by both time and geography. We shall see in the next chapter that the criticisms are even louder for the Human Revolution.

This was the unique perspective of Childe: by concentrating on the entwined historical relations between Europe and the Near East, he provided one of the few explicitly drawn contexts for understanding change as the transfer of political power between two different continents. His terminology and analytical approach to prehistoric evidence was directed towards uncovering this evolving international relationship. The context he set is rarely acknowledged beyond his interests in the Neolithic and Urban Revolutions and the distinctive contrasts between Europe and the Orient. Those who have followed have concerned themselves more with the transfer of elements, most notably livestock and crops, the regional variations on village and urban settlement plans and the local development of metallurgy and other craft skills. These are changes in the sense of novelties that appear for the first time but they are not changes in that bigger political sense which should be commanding our attention.

The archaeology of change personified by Childe is therefore the subject of international relations. Here political change has been defined by archaeologist Ken Dark as:

the origin, growth, decline, cessation or reorganization of political systems, structures and units at any level of analysis from the intra-state group to the global system. I also mean the generation, modification or cessation of those events and processes which cause these changes . . . I refer to that which is 'fundamental', in that it affects the very character of polities and of international relations.

(Dark 1998:4–5)

I would agree with Dark's insistence on the 'fundamental', in Williams' (1965:10) terms a 'genuine revolution, transforming men and institutions', which elsewhere I have identified as social life. Therefore, I understand change as organisation based on novel social premises. By contrast, variation is the accommodation of novel conditions within existing social premises (Gamble 2001:174). Dark's examples of change deal with non-state to state societies and the emergence and collapse of international systems. Consequently, he contends that millennia as well as decades are appropriate time scales to study change.

As Dark (1998:8) points out, change can be analysed, using this definition, in terms of temporally discrete *events*, *structures* (frameworks of action) or as a *process* with different modes and types of change. It can also be studied contemporaneously (synchronically) or through time (diachronically) in terms of continuities and dis-continuities. But there is no predicting the when, where or magnitude of change, especially at the vast scale of the big question of human origins.

But Dark's political definition of change raises a further dilemma for archaeologists. Re-creating the past in the form of the present has quite rightly worried us for the last forty years (Chapter 3). If our understanding of change is, as Dark shows, part of the modernist project, expressed in a variety of guises under the banner of international relations, then how does the study of change in the past escape from the concerns of the present? My short answer is that it can't and shouldn't. Our continuing reluctance to discuss what we understand by change means we have already fallen into the presentist trap. We have produced imaginative archaeologies that only make sense when related to the structures regulating the interaction between different cultural worlds. The way to avoid such pitfalls is to understand better the cultural context in which this archaeological knowledge has been produced. The paradox of change in the past is that nothing changes unless it has significance for the present.

Three current revolutions

Where does this leave the Neolithic Revolution? The concept remains shorthand for a widely recognised turning point in human prehistory but has been replaced as an analytical device based on Childe's analogy with the Industrial Revolution. The terms now used are deliberately broad — food production, plant and animal exploitation, for example — to allow the worldwide investigation of transitions in subsistence economies (Byrd 2005; Gebauer and Price 1992; Harris 1996b; Harris and Hillman 1989; Price and

Gebauer 1995; Sherratt 1997b). The term 'Neolithic' only has relevance to archaeologists working in Europe and Southwest Asia. The Americas, Australia and the Pacific do not use it, and increasingly African and Asian archaeologists prefer the historically more neutral alternatives. In a sense everyone now participates in the study of the Neolithic Revolution, and as a result the term is no longer required.

The secondary products revolution of 1981

The continuity backlash has become the new orthodoxy. Kent Flannery declared in 1969 that it was erroneous to believe that early cultivation was either an improvement or a drastic change (1969:74). This seemed to settle for good any return to the great leap forward that Childe and many others had envisaged.

However, revolutions are still alive and retain the rhetorical power to grab the headlines and set the agenda. Andrew Sherratt (1997b:156) owned up to this strategy when he decided in 1981 on an 'ugly title' with revolution in it as a necessary evil to give his concept legs. His 'secondary products revolution' (Sherratt 1997b:158–98) stressed the character of the transition to farming in the Old World where the interaction between plant and animal domesticates was crucial. In the Americas some herd animals became important pack animals but none of them were ever ridden or pulled ploughs and carts. Similarities between the Old and the New Worlds existed in that wool for textiles and milk were secondary products, meat being the primary one. Sherratt showed how the use of animal traction, and its importance for further agricultural intensification, came much later than the initial domestication of cattle and equids. These secondary products revolutionised the societies of Europe as they spread from a zone that stretched from southern Russia to the Nile delta and eastwards to Mesopotamia. 'Plough and pastoralism', the more handsome handle to the same article, summed up the transformation and re-positioned the impact of domestication and the resulting transformation of society at about five thousand years ago. Sherratt concluded that the axis of Old World development from Europe to India was a direct result of the diffusion of these new forms of energy by exchange and contact. And where they touched existing cultures these were transformed, 'their character was completely altered by the secondary products revolution, which created many of the basic features of the modern world' (Sherratt 1997b:198).

Sherratt's revolution has been criticised by Alasdair Whittle (2003:83) for lumping too much together as it searches for those broad historical patterns.

Instead Whittle (2003:166) favours a retreat from such grand narratives (Sherratt 1995), with their predilection for the single story of directed change, and argues for a move towards different kinds of history in which varying patterns of local diversity and density produce the complexity and layered nature of Neolithic ways of life.

The broad spectrum revolution of 1969

Two recurrent themes have followed accounts of the origins of agriculture: climate change and environmental circumscription (Sherratt 1997b). Childe (1934 (1952):25) had favoured an oasis or propinquity theory that brought potential domesticates and people together, while Braidwood (1960) had argued on the basis of his fieldwork in Iraq that nuclear zones, or hearths of domestication, existed (see also Sauer 1952). Desiccation had the effect of concentrating people in these favourable habitats where in Sherratt's phrase 'agriculture was an accident waiting to happen' (Sherratt 1997a:283). More recently the detailed climate curves that now exist for the period have been interpreted by archaeologist Ofer Bar-Yosef (Bar-Yosef and Belfer-Cohen 1992; Bar-Yosef and Meadow 1995) as evidence that the transition to agriculture was a punctuated event. The Younger Dryas cold phase that occurred between 11,500 and 12,650 years ago saw temperatures plummet across Europe (Renssen et al. 2001). For those Near East populations that had already become sedentary, Bar-Yosef argues, the local effect of the Younger Dryas was to select for an intensification of food production. Selection for change was felt most strongly in those settlements in the highly diverse but geographically compact habitats of the Levantine corridor (Bar-Yosef 1998). Sherratt has argued that such punctuation – and one thousand years qualifies in prehistory as a true revolution – has to be matched with centricity, where it happened. The Near East, he claims, in the tradition of Childe, offers a rare mix of opportunities that:

> gives the region its reticulate aspect: not just stark environmental contrasts but their intimate admixture, providing refuges and opportunities for unusual conjunctions – all subjected to rapid and large-scale climatic changes.
>
> (Sherratt 1997a:284)

But such a re-affirmation of climate change and environmental circumscription have only recently re-surfaced. Climate change was discounted in the 1960s following large-scale fieldwork. Instead the locus of change was placed among the hunters of the Upper Palaeolithic

(Flannery 1969:74) and the question asked was framed by human ecology: why do cultures change their modes of subsistence? In an influential paper Lewis Binford (1968) combined a more sophisticated appreciation of what hunting entailed with an account of how intensification leading to agriculture might have occurred. He put forward a demographic argument to counter environmental determinism and asked what selective pressures led to changes in the structural organisation of cultures to their environments. His answer, greatly elaborated since (Binford 2001), took into account the changes that arise from an increased packing of social units into the same geographic space. Binford's concern is to understand why, by settling down, hunters lost their key adaptive tactic, mobility, that helps solve the problem of uncertain supplies.

Binford directed attention to the geographical margins rather than the centre as the places archaeologists should look for these changes. These ideas were elaborated very effectively by Kent Flannery (1969), who applied a cybernetic model in which stable populations situated below carrying capacity evolved mechanisms to counter disequilibrium. This allowed him to answer the question from human ecology about why subsistence practices changed. Flannery outlined a model of transitions that invoked intensification through a process he termed the broad-spectrum revolution (1969:79) in which the environment remained constraining, but the key was an increase in diet breadth that raised carrying capacity and hence population. On ecological and energetic grounds Flannery argued that broadening the subsistence base to include smaller prey and plants, while at the same time domesticating larger species, would have had a revolutionary effect. His choice of revolution takes the emphasis away from the selective forces operating on a small group of field and farmyard staples and shows how harvesting from the full array of wild resources can produce dramatic results. No one set out to invent agriculture. Instead they followed ecological rationality by broadening their resource base and this led to unintended consequences.

More recently Mary Stiner (Stiner et al. 2000) has shown when this broad-spectrum revolution might have happened. It is not so much the size of resources that is important as the work involved in their capture that is in turn conditioned by their speed of flight. Furthermore the resilience of species to predation, the pace with which their numbers bounce back, is critical in conditioning patterns of predation. Tortoises and hares, for example, demonstrate very different flight strategies and resilience. So when and in what order do we see them become a regular part of the diet?

The effects of broadening the subsistence base starts with the Neanderthals and their predation on tortoises. But their predation pressure, as revealed by the large sizes of the animals they caught, was never very high, and Stiner (Stiner et al. 2000:56–7) interprets this as indicating small, dispersed human populations well below the environmental carrying capacity. It was during the Upper Palaeolithic that the reduction in size of these slow-moving prey starts to reflect heavier harvesting. As the easy-to-capture prey declined through the period so more difficult-to-catch species such as hares and birds are found among the food remains. Human numbers had increased and selection for a greater diet breadth now proceeded. The broad-spectrum revolution is therefore deep-seated and provides an example of continuity that would gladden Higgs and Jarman and other supporters of gradual change.

In his comment on Stiner's paper, Flannery (2000:64) reminds us that the 'broad-spectrum revolution was essentially a change in ethno-scientific classification by hunters and gatherers'. What had to happen was that some foods, such as wild cereal grasses that were ignored because they were costly in terms of time and effort to harvest and process, had to be promoted up the desirability list so that by the time they finally got to first choice, 'they had paved the way for a truly profound change' (2000:65).

The symbolic, sensory and sedentary revolution of 2001

The last of the current revolutions is itself a trinity, closely in step with Childe's Neolithic Revolution. Indeed, archaeologist Jacques Cauvin (2000:67–72) wrote that the Neolithic Revolution was a transformation of the mind. This, Cauvin forcefully argued, was a 'revolution in symbolism' (2000:71) that he traced through the art of the period. He contrasted a mythic world of hunters with a divinity personified in Neolithic art and figurines. A new distinction, he claimed, lay at the heart of human imagination where a social order was now expressed as an 'above' and a 'below'. Most importantly Cauvin saw this psychological restructuring impacting on the economy. But questions remained:

> How can we realise the real relationship which would unite the revolution in symbolism with the production of subsistence materials which shortly followed it? May we attribute to this transformation in the structures of the imagination a dynamic sufficient to engender this series of changes? Or again . . . in what way were these changes another means of making manifest the transformation of imaginative constructs?
>
> (Cauvin 2000:71)

Prior to Cauvin's revolution, anthropologist Peter Wilson (1988) had argued that the built environment rather than the art was the touchstone to this symbolic revolution. Neolithic domestic societies, he wrote (Wilson 1988:153), live their lives by reference to a structure whereas hunters and gatherers do not. Farmers invest buildings with their metaphors for living. People are merged with places and in this way domestication anchors a person with a location (Wilson 1988:71). This process of domesticating humans by building houses had an unintended consequence on the senses, particularly vision. The basis of attention so critical to social interaction was now changed in what, to paraphrase Wilson, might be termed a sensory revolution. What resulted were novel social conditions of intimacy and privacy as houses were internally partitioned (1988:179). A poetics of architectural space (Bachelard 1964) was therefore created that transformed society not only through its means of economic production but through its sensory experience.

Wilson's message is clear. We domesticated ourselves into a different social species by living behind walls, around courtyards and in modular, cell-like villages and towns, which archaeologist Trevor Watkins (2004a) has aptly described as 'theatres of memory'. The very act of niche-construction transformed us in a revolutionary way, although Wilson does not use that terminology. Watkins (2004a:19), however, goes further, concluding that 'the world's earliest village communities were also the first to develop fully modern minds and a fully symbolic culture'. To explain why they did not appear earlier, Watkins repeats Robert Braidwood's (1960) claim that culture was just not ready.

It is this act of self-construction, making culture ready, that Colin Renfrew (2001; 2003) has termed the sedentary revolution. He spells it out with his customary clarity, combining all the revolutions involved in the trinity:

> The first great revolution or transition in the experience of our species was the sedentary revolution. It was then that humans entered into a series of new relationships with the material world. It was then that they built houses, fashioned images of deities and constructed shrines . . . The key to this process was the development of material symbols – symbols of power, symbols of rank and prestige, coveted materials that were the repositories of value.
>
> (Renfrew 2003:115)

The genesis for this sedentary revolution was people exploring the symbolic and cognitive structures of their new, more densely populated material worlds. The built environment carried all before it. Those first houses were foundation stones indeed.

But before we get swept away with the rhetoric, there are wider implications to consider. Was this sensory, symbolic and sedentary revolution really what made us human and conclusively defined our humanity? If so, then history begins with the Neolithic, whose greatest secondary product we now see was our distinctive humanity. But where does that leave the rest of prehistory, before these varied revolutions took place? Is it the case that our universal humanity is only as old as a collection of mud-brick houses by a dwindling water source with a dry wind blowing? Or is an imaginative archaeology at work here? If that is the case then the place that is described is not universal but instead one where the West and the East can, for the first time in history, be prised apart. And by prising them apart the Neolithic Revolution becomes the origin point of the modern project of European history and culture that gained definition by opposing and containing the Orient.

CHAPTER 2

The Human Revolution

HOMO nosce te ipsum

Carolus Linnaeus *Systema Naturae* 1800

One, two, three.
Hominid, hominin, human, me.
One is the lot plus the chimpanzee;
Two are the lot on the family tree;
Three is the lot, looks a lot like me.
One, two, three!

Playground rhyme c. 2000

What it was to be human

Human beings have many identities and revolution, when the prospect for change is realised, is just one of them. But where do these identities reside? Are they a result of our minds and the spectacular evolution of our brains, or are they part and parcel of our bodies, living in the world? We carry our evolutionary history in our biological makeup, while every day we go about our lives using hard-won ancestral skills that now seem second nature. When it comes to deciding what it is to be human and even more when we ask what constitutes humanity, our bodies are as important as our cultures, our minds as significant as our biology.

But interpreting evolutionary clues, whether from bodies or culture, is never easy, nor are the results definitive. Answers to any question about ourselves will always be informed by contested issues such as race, intelligence, politics, gender and age. In such company, the concept of revolution is just another arena in which differences are defined, but an important one for establishing identity. At issue is the tempo of our appearance, slow or fast, and whether we — as humans — are a recent or ancient phenomenon. And the answer matters not only because it points to our capacity for change but also to what we think we share with others, past and present.

Identity, whether of self or society, is traditionally an exercise in drawing boundaries and the identification of revolutions has provided a useful hammer to drive in the historical posts. But there are different revolutions for different jobs. The Human Revolution draws the line between ourselves and the ultimate *other*, the outgroup which defines us and gives us meaning as a species and as humans rather than animals. But unlike the Neolithic Revolution, where social strangers live among or alongside us, with the Human Revolution we only glimpse those others in the rear-view mirror of prehistory. What I question is whether these revolutions are the correct conceptual tools for understanding change, because the outcome of our evolutionary journey has left humanity equally at home in an urban metropolis and a tropical rainforest, and in societies of millions or hundreds.

Consider for a moment the position of evolutionary psychologists on this issue (Barkow et al. 1992). In their imaginary geography of long-ago, which they awkwardly call the Environment of Evolutionary Adaptedness, the time depth for humanity is very ancient indeed. They argue that our psychology was shaped by natural selection on those East African savannahs where we evolved more than three million years ago, and they demonstrate this, not by archaeological evidence, but by showing photographs of landscapes to test-subjects and asking them which they feel safest in. Results show that people like open landscapes, so long as there are no lions and it looks warm. This is sufficient evidence for many evolutionary psychologists that we carry our history in our minds and our big task is therefore to reconcile our ancient savannah psyches to the pathology of modern urban life.

Now contrast this view with the sedentary revolution that I outlined at the end of the previous chapter (Renfrew 2003). Here it is implied *the* significant change in human experience was precipitated relatively recently by our own actions as bricklayers. If village life was the true Environment of Evolutionary Adaptedness then we should get even better results in photo tests by showing subjects pictures of thatched cottages and other rural idylls. But presumably we should only show these to members of Peter Wilson's (1988) settled domestic societies and not to the peripatetic hunters and gatherers of the world.

These two contrasted standpoints nicely illustrate that human beings have many identities and that the timing of our history, ancient or recent, is a crucial aspect in determining which are significant. In this chapter I will be looking in some detail at the notion of universal humanity and discovering how the concept of an anatomically modern human, the *agent provocateur* of the Human Revolution, arose as a scientifically meaningful adjunct to the study of *Homo sapiens*, ourselves, as a diasporic species with global coverage.

Enter anatomically modern humans

Thirty years exactly separates two major archaeological discoveries in Ethiopia. The first was made in 1967 by a team led by Richard Leakey (1969) searching the Omo Valley in the south-west of the country. Here, in the Kibish geological formation, they found the fossilised remains of three adults, one represented by a nearly complete skull but without a face (Omo II) another by a skull fragment (Omo III) and the last by a partial skeleton (Omo I). No stone artefacts were found with them and their age was originally established as 130,000 years old but has recently been revised using new techniques to 195,000 (McDougall et al. 2005). The bones of all three individuals were heavily mineralised but un-distorted by the sediments and revealing no pathology (Leakey et al. 1969:1135). The real interest lay in Omo II. Its high forehead, large brain case and generally gracile features marked it out as human not hominin. Only the cranial vault survived but this was sufficient for its interpretation as a 'very early representative of *Homo sapiens*' (Leakey et al. 1969:1132). This made it the earliest human fossil anywhere and firmly pointed to Africa as our centre of origin.

Subsequently Ethiopia has continued to yield important discoveries, the most famous of which was the 3.7 million year old Australopithecine known as Lucy (Johanson and Edey 1981). However, in 1997 a joint American-Ethiopian team working in the same Afar depression where Lucy was discovered uncovered three crania in the Herto Bouri area (White et al. 2003). This time the finds represented two adults and one immature individual. Moreover, the bones were found with stone tools. Advances since 1967 in absolute dating using radio-isotopes and tephro-stratigraphy have dated all the evidence to between 160,000 and 154,000 years ago (Clark et al. 2003). The morphology of the skulls, combined with these ages, led Tim White (White et al. 2003:742), before the new dating of the Omo skulls (McDougall et al. 2005), to conclude that they 'represent the probable immediate ancestors of anatomically modern humans'. He recognised their pivotal position by naming them as a sub-species, *Homo sapiens idaltu*; Idàltu in the Afar language means elder.

The key-word that has been added to human evolution in the thirty years that separate these two important discoveries is not, however, *idaltu* but the two qualifiers to either human or *Homo sapiens*. These are 'anatomically' and 'modern'. But why were they applied? Surely *Homo sapiens* needs neither? '*Homo* know for yourself', was Linnaeus' (1800) comment to his classification of humans, and if we can't who can? Moreover, if humans need the prefix 'modern' then why not, as anthropologist Tim Ingold (1993a:388) has asked, 'anatomically modern' elephants to distinguish them from their geological ancestors?

The anatomically modern human is a hybrid concept that accommodates information from archaeological and anatomical sources that are apparently contradictory because they challenge established classifications. The Herto hominins provide a case study. The stone tools come from an old tradition, the Acheulean, that first appears in Africa one and a half million years ago associated with the species *Homo ergaster*. In Africa it has two trademark artefacts — handaxes and cleavers — both of which are large bifacial stone tools. However, the Herto bifaces and the means by which the raw material was knapped into stone flake-blanks reflect advances in stone working that are at most 300,000 years old. The Herto material is therefore regarded as final or 'transitional' Acheulean (Clark et al. 2003:750). In this case the transition is towards a Middle Stone Age when bifaces drop away and a variety of smaller tools are fashioned from blanks that were knapped from stones in a novel ordered sequence (Chapter 7).

But the Herto skulls also carry further information. They had been deliberately modified after death. The alterations took the form of cut marks consistent with the removal of the mandible followed by defleshing the skull. Then two of the crania were deliberately polished and scraped (Clark et al. 2003:751). At a much earlier date the Bodo skull, also from Ethiopia, has cut marks indicating defleshing but no further signs, as seen on the Herto skulls, of the kind of modifications that archaeologist Desmond Clark (Clark 2003:751) refers to as decoration.

So, the Herto trio bear witness to deliberate mortuary practices that could be modern, a basically archaic tradition of making stone tools and a transitional skull morphology. They are accorded sub-species status at the boundary of being anatomical modern humans. On the other side of the fence the Omo trio carry less information but shortly after their discovery

TABLE 2.1. *Recognising anatomically modern humans,* Homo sapiens *(Stringer and Andrews 1988:1263)*

1. All living humans are characterised by a gracile skeleton in comparison with that of other species of the genus *Homo*. In particular this applies to,

   - longbone shape and shaft thickness
   - the depth or extent of muscle insertions
   - the relatively thin bone of the skull and mandible

2. The cranium is voluminous, but no more so than in Neanderthals, and like the brain it contains is typically short, high and domed
3. The supraorbital torus (browridges) and external cranial buttressing are either considerably reduced or absent
4. Teeth and jaws are reduced in size
5. Probably as a result of smaller teeth, the face is tucked well under the forehead rather than sloping forward
6. A mental eminence (chin) is present on the mandible from a young age

David Brose and Milford Wolpoff (1971:1183) included them in a group they called 'anatomically modern *Homo sapiens*'.

Defining the fully modern human: bodies, brains and boats

The anatomical ideal that human palaeontologists are working towards has been summarised by Chris Stringer and Peter Andrews (1988) (Table 2.1). But having the body, and most importantly a face and head, that fits the variation shown by modern humans is not enough. There would be no need for the qualifiers 'anatomically modern' if they were also 'fully modern' in the cultural sense. With the introduction of 'fully' as a qualifier the bar is raised by archaeologists to a height that only a revolution might clear.

Richard Klein (1995:169) for one has questioned if all the anatomically modern humans in the fossil record had the same biological endowment of the fully modern brain. Without the demonstration of behavioural modernity they would remain in an outgroup to humanity, like *Homo sapiens idaltu*. Could they all talk, make images, conceive of an afterlife, remember their ancestors and plan ahead for next year? Were anatomically modern humans the ultimate hardware waiting for a software upgrade, and if so was this on a revolutionary time-scale? Language is given particular prominence and the so-called 'language gene' *FOXP2* is proposed by

Klein as that missing bit of code, although others remain unconvinced (Carroll 2003).

Although they disagree with Klein's recent Human Revolution, Sally McBrearty and Alison Brooks (2000:492–3) are nonetheless confident that fully modern human behaviour can be characterised in cognitive and cultural terms (Table 2.2).

Their scheme sets out what many archaeologists regard as a workable definition of humanity; workable in the sense that data do exist to back up the descriptions and so provide insights into the tempo as well as the geographical origin of change. But would anyone outside archaeology recognise those four cognitive skills – planning, symbolic behaviour, abstraction and innovation – as an adequate definition of what it is to be human? Even within the subject Francesco d'Errico (2003:189) regards their list as very limited and pre-judgemental of the outcome they want; namely that the Human Revolution has been overstated by judicious use of the European data and misrepresentation of the African evidence. Although they provide a check-list (Table 2.2) and a timetable it is McBrearty and Brooks' (2000:534) opinion that the unique behaviours of modern humans that would qualify them for the 'fully' prefix are to be discovered rather than prescribed. But here they become caught in the circularity common to all such archaeological exercises in origins research.

Is there an alternative? Elsewhere (Gamble 1993a; 1998) I have argued for a social explanation rather than either a cognitive re-organisation or genetic mutation to account for the differences in the archaeology. One striking feature of world prehistory after 60,000 years ago is that it is for the first time just that, a world prehistory. After this date *Homo sapiens* began their diaspora and in less than 1 per cent of the time since we last had a common ancestor with our closest primate relatives, the chimpanzees, we had migrated to the previously uninhabited islands and continents that before made up almost three-quarters of the Earth. From being a hominin long confined to a portion of the Old World we suddenly became global humans. Furthermore, for the first time in our evolutionary history we became a single species differentiated only by geographical variation. What we see in those ocean voyages, and the settlement of the seasonally cold interiors of continents, is a clear geographical signature that social life was fully released from the constraint of proximity (Rodseth et al. 1991) that explains why most primates are not world travellers. What characterises social life in humans rather than hominids is our ability to extend social relations across space and through time, a theme I return to in Chapter 8.

TABLE 2.2.   *Modern human cognitive and cultural capabilities and their tangible archaeological traces in Africa (after McBrearty and Brooks 2000:492–3)*

Cognitive skills and definitions		Cultural capabilities and archaeological evidence	
Planning depth	The ability to formulate strategies based on past experience and to act upon them in a group context	*Technological*	Evidence reveals human inventiveness and capacity for logical thinking
Symbolic behaviour	The ability to represent objects, people and abstract concepts with arbitrary symbols, vocal or visual, and to reify such symbols in cultural practice	*Symbolic*	Features of the record demonstrate a capacity to imbue aspects of experience with meaning, to communicate abstract concepts, and to manipulate symbols as a part of everyday life
Abstract thinking	The ability to act with reference to abstract concepts not limited in time and space	*Ecological*	Aspects of the record reflect human abilities to colonise new environments, which require both innovation and planning depth
Innovation	Behavioural, economic and technological	*Economic and social*	Features show human abilities to draw models from individual and group experience, to develop and apply systematic plans, to conceptualise and predict the future, and to construct formalised relationships among individuals and groups

This is in marked contrast to all our primate cousins whose social life is based on local co-presence.

I don't doubt that either the Herto or Omo trios had the capacity for global dispersal. Evidence from well travelled raw materials shows that social extension occurred (Merrick and Brown 1984). However, for some 100,000 years these people who looked like us decided to stay at home in the Old World. In this instance it is therefore by comparison with our diasporic distribution that the later, social revolution through a release from proximity emerges. To qualify human with either 'fully' or 'modern' is therefore unhelpful because it obscures in this instance the historical process of change.

The Human Revolution; ancient and modern

What had happened in the thirty years between these two Ethiopian discoveries was a fierce debate about the evolution of people like ourselves. One tradition, beginning with Franz Weidenreich (1943) and promoted by Carleton Coon (1962), argued for multi-regional evolution. Following an initial early expansion out of Africa by *Homo erectus* the various regional populations that were then established in Europe and Asia evolved into the populations that inhabit those areas today. Multi-regionalists, forcefully led by palaeoanthropologist Milford Wolpoff (1988; 1989), interpreted the scattered fossils as evidence for parallel evolution, mostly in isolation, although limited gene-flow between populations was allowed in later versions. The in-situ evolution in Europe from Neanderthal to modern human populations was a crucial test case for regional continuity due to the relative quantity of information in a subject otherwise characterised by poor samples. Wolpoff regarded both forms as *Homo sapiens*, with no need for any further sub-species qualification. But what multi-regional evolution had to demonstrate was the repeated transition from what everyone regarded as one distinctive anatomy to another.

Brose and Wolpoff (1971) tackled this issue by arguing for the appearance of a more efficient stone technology. This advance reduced the previous use of teeth for cutting as well as the application of the jaw as a vice. In addition, Loring Brace (1979) proposed a 'culinary revolution' where cooking food to make it softer now changed the selection pressures on teeth. In short, there was no longer any need for big powerful teeth or rugged musculature and bone structure. The knock-on effects for cranial mass and shape were considerable. Tools, teeth and faces co-evolved so that we unintentionally created the way we look. In technical terms:

> The loss of the distinctive Neanderthal cranial form is a direct consequence of selection relaxation for the anterior dentition and

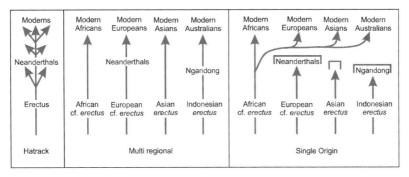

FIGURE 2.1. Candelabra, or multi-regional, hat-rack, or unilineal, and single origin models of human evolution (after Howells 1967:236; Stringer and Gamble 1993). Hat-rack models invariably matched the three fossil stages to the Lower, Middle and Upper Palaeolithic periods. The candelabra model relaxed this strict association between biology and culture.

> supporting facial architecture, and resulting change in selection acting on the static and dynamic properties of the nuchal musculature.
>
> (Brose and Wolpoff 1971:1185)

The model of regional continuity produced what William Howells (1967) described as a candelabra model of human evolution (Figure 2.1). Although preferable to the older hat-rack model, the result of some drastic pruning of the human family tree by evolutionary biologist Ernst Mayr (1950), the candelabra alternative still had problems.

Its difficulties were exacerbated by more fossil and archaeological discoveries, advances in dating and the reconstruction of population history using genetics which, when combined, provided the evidence for an alternative, single origins model. The model's foremost advocate has been human palaeontologist Chris Stringer (1996) who argues for a recent African origin for all modern peoples, citing as evidence fossils such as the Omo trio. However, the classification of fossil skulls is notoriously difficult and contentious. On occasion authors of the same article have disagreed over the fossil they are describing and each assigned it to a different species (e.g. Walker and Leakey 1978). The jury would still be out if human ancestry depended upon the fossils alone. The clinching argument came in 1987 with the publication of a genetic tree (Cann et al. 1987) based on the inheritance of mitochondrial DNA (mtDNA) that is restricted to the maternal line. Their sample of 148 women from the world's five major geographical populations demonstrated that Africans had greater diversity, and hence were older, than any other biological group. Mutation rates, the so-called molecular clock, estimates an age of between 150,000 and 300,000 years ago for the founding of the present mtDNA lineage.

The recent African origin model expects multiple dispersals rather than a single African exodus (Lahr and Foley 1994; Lahr and Foley 1998), and for whatever reason these recent dispersals of anatomically modern humans led to the replacement of older regional populations. Among those replaced were the Neanderthals of Southwest Asia and Europe (Bar-Yosef 1998; Stringer and Gamble 1993) and the dwarfed hominins, *Homo floresiensis*, from Indonesia (Brown et al. 2004; Morwood et al. 2004).

To explore the implications of a recent single origin Chris Stringer, together with archaeologist Paul Mellars, organised a conference in 1987 that brought supporters of both African and multi-regional models together. Significantly they titled the book that followed *The Human Revolution: behavioural and biological perspectives on the origins of modern humans* (1989). Of course this was not the first reference to a Human Revolution. Anthropologist Ashley Montagu, the tireless opponent of biological racism, had described the human revolution almost twenty-five years earlier (1965:15) as the moment when stone tools were first made. On present evidence this would be almost two and a half million years ago and not the 30–50,000 years ago that many of the contributors to Mellars and Stringer's volume expected. The human revolution for anthropologists Charles Hockett and Robert Ascher (1964) was similarly ancient. They examined bipedalism, language and environmental change and concluded:

> As soon as the hominids had achieved upright posture, bipedal gait, the use of hands for manipulating, for carrying, and for manufacturing generalized tools, and language, *they had become men*. The human revolution was over.
>
> (Hockett and Ascher 1964:145, my emphasis)

The point about the Human Revolution as outlined in the 1989 publication was that it was recent. To emphasise its late appearance in human evolution it is also known as the symbolic revolution, when representational art appears for the first time; a revolution best summed up by the title of John Pfeiffer's (1982) review: *The creative explosion*. This revolution was associated by William Noble and Iain Davidson (1996) with the appearance of language, by Steven Mithen (1996) with a fully modern modular brain characterised by cognitive fluidity, by Lynn Wadley (2001:210) with evidence for external symbolic storage (art, ornamentation, style in lithics and the formal use of space) and by Robin Dunbar (2003:179)

TABLE 2.3. *The major changes between the Middle and Upper Palaeolithic in south-west France (Mellars 1973; Mellars 2005:Figure 1) has more recently identified fifteen innovations that mark the Upper Palaeolithic revolution in Europe*

Material technology
A greater range and complexity of tool forms and a replacement of *stability* in Middle Palaeolithic tool forms with rapid change during the Upper Palaeolithic; a development in bone, ivory and antler working; the appearance of personal ornaments

---

Subsistence activities
A greater emphasis on a single species (often reindeer); a broadening of the subsistence base to include small game; the possible development of large scale co-operative hunting and a greater efficiency in hunting due to the invention of the bow and arrow; very possibly these changes were accompanied by improvements in food storage and preservation techniques

---

Demography and social organisation
A substantial increase in population density and the maximum size of the co-residential group as inferred from the number of sites and the dimensions of settlements; group aggregation occurs to participate in co-operative hunting of migratory herd animals such as reindeer; increase in corporate awareness

---

with the late appearance in human evolution of a theory of mind capable of the cognitive gymnastics implicated in religious beliefs.

Revolutions that were and weren't

I trace the theoretical roots of this recent Human Revolution to Paul Mellars (1973) and Richard Klein (1973) writing respectively about the Palaeolithic of south-west France (Tables 2.3 and 2.4) and the Ukraine in the period 40–50,000 years ago. What they produced, reviewed recently by Ofer Bar-Yosef (2002:365–9), were a list of traits to measure the transition between two archaeological periods, the Middle Palaeolithic of Neanderthals and the Upper Palaeolithic of modern humans. Klein (1973:122) concluded that the 'Upper Palaeolithic appears to constitute a quantum advance over the Mousterian (Middle Palaeolithic)'; a revolution in all but name.

To begin with the focus was very much on Europe but Klein in particular broadened the enquiry to include southern Africa so that twenty years later

TABLE 2.4. *Klein's updated ten-point check-list of traits of fully modern behaviour detectable in the archaeological record beginning 50–40,000 years ago (Klein 1995). The scale is worldwide*

1. Substantial growth in the diversity and standardisation of artefact types
2. Rapid increase in the rate of artefactual change through time and in the degree of artefact diversity through space
3. First shaping of bone, ivory, shell and related materials into formal artefacts, e.g. points, awls, needles, pins, etc.
4. Earliest appearance of incontrovertible art
5. Oldest undeniable evidence for spatial organisation of camp floors, including elaborate hearths and the oldest indisputable structural 'ruins'
6. Oldest evidence for the transport of large quantities of highly desirable stone raw material over scores or even hundreds of kilometres
7. Earliest secure evidence for ceremony or ritual, expressed both in art and in relatively elaborate graves
8. First evidence for human ability to live in the coldest, most continental parts of Eurasia
9. First evidence for human population densities approaching those of historic hunter-gatherers in similar environments
10. First evidence for fishing and for other significant advances in human ability to acquire energy from nature

a full ten-point list, comparable to the one Childe proposed for the Urban Revolution (Table 1.2) could be published (Table 2.4).

But why did this particular conception of a Human Revolution appear now, in the thirty years between the discoveries at Omo and Herto? One answer takes us back to the continuity backlash to the notion of the Neolithic Revolution as set out in the previous chapter. The challenge of Eric Higgs and others had a lasting, although unexpected result, on earlier research into human origins. By loosening up the cultural framework they indirectly suggested an earlier, missing revolution within the Palaeolithic. Their argument that the Neolithic was not a revolution, but instead a point in a continuous story of greater economic control over resources that ran from scavenging to factory farming, freed up the question of when we became human. Consequently, those terms 'savagery' and 'barbarism' (Chapter 1) with their economic links to hunting and farming barely made it into the 1960s (Sherratt 1997b:62). Higgs, I am sure, would find it ironic that by telling us we were wasting our time looking for the origins of agriculture he was creating the conditions for a new origins question to emerge. Doubly ironic, because the question which emerged took as its arena the replacement in Europe and the Middle East of Neanderthals and their Middle Palaeolithic tool kits by anatomically modern humans and their Upper Palaeolithic artefacts (Mellars 1996). Higgs' view that 'the economies of Palaeolithic peoples remain unstudied, largely because of the unwarranted assumption that all men were then hunter/gatherers' (Higgs and Jarman 1969:40), was extended to Neanderthals and Crô-Magnons alike. He made no distinction on the basis of tool types or skulls between these populations. Economy was the only thing that mattered and he was as content to have Neanderthals domesticating mammoths for their wool as reindeer pulling Magdalenian sleighs around the Dordogne a mere 15,000 years ago (Eric Higgs pers.comm. c. 1970).

Such an idiosyncratic critique of the Neolithic Revolution did stir-up thinking about the transition to humanity and the possibility of an additional archaeological revolution. For example, Ofer Bar-Yosef (2002: 379–81) draws parallels between the Upper Palaeolithic and Neolithic Revolutions in Southwest Asia. His approach is based on comparable geographical opportunities in the narrow Levantine corridor, increases in population size and subsequent movement to disperse the results of social and economic change (Bar-Yosef 1998; 2002). His approach decouples the arguments for change from an emphasis on the importance of biology (new species) and changes in past climate (Bar-Yosef 2002:383). The result is an evolutionary convergence in both revolutions. The outcomes were different although the starting conditions, at least in terms of geography, were similar.

But not everyone is convinced by the need for a revolution and the dissent has been greatest among those working in Africa. The attack is twofold. First, they have called into question the European-ness of the Human Revolution. The Upper Palaeolithic revolution, and the replacement of Neanderthals by modern humans is, they argue, a provincial concern and should not be extended out to the rest of the world (Henshilwood and Marean 2003; McBrearty and Brooks 2000). For example, Hilary Deacon (1995:128) claims that European criteria for cultural modernity, such as Upper Palaeolithic art and ornament, are irrelevant in the context of the African origins of modern behaviour. The African evidence he cites as critical includes, among other aspects, spatial rules of cleanliness, colour symbolism and the reciprocal exchange of artefacts (Wadley 2001:204). Second, the critics point out that Africa has consistently produced earlier examples of items in Klein's check-list than Europe or anywhere else for that matter.

Now a second front has been opened up by the Europeans themselves, questioning the inferences drawn from the archaeology of the late Neanderthals who may, just conceivably, have encountered incoming modern humans. Although notions of hybrid populations have been dropped (Darte et al. 1999), the idea that objects such as beads and bone tools were independently invented by Neanderthals rather than imitated from what they saw round the necks of incoming modern humans or even accepted as the price for a continent, like glass beads for Manhattan, has gained strength (d'Errico et al. 2003; d'Errico et al. 1998; Zilhão and d'Errico 1999).

Francesco D'Errico (2003) in particular has strongly criticised the definitions of behavioural modernity (e.g. Table 2.2) that African archaeologists use. He shows that most of the defining traits are seen among Neanderthals in Europe and the Near East. Following this demonstration he then develops a model of convergent evolution (Conway-Morris 2003). He argues that common ecological pressures, combined with permeable cultural barriers, led to the separate development of those distinctive ornaments and visual culture around which so much of the debate over behavioural modernity revolves. To account for the European creative outburst he suggests that:

> the new situation involving contact between anatomically modern people and Neanderthals and the consequent problems of cultural and biological identity . . . stimulated an explosion in the production of symbolic objects on *both* sides.

> (d'Errico 2003:196)

But while he scores a double hit, disposing of both the Human Revolution and primacy for Africa, or any other geographical area for that matter, this model still falls short as an explanation for change. What exactly are those common ecological pressures that stretched across the Old World? And if barriers were permeable to this degree then why was the response to crank out more symbolic objects to keep up with the thoroughly modern Joneses? Arguing from the European evidence, Mellars (2005) unequivocally shows that such convergence is an impossible coincidence.

A satisfactory explanation is similarly lacking in John Lindly and Geoff Clark's (1990) re-positioning of the European creative explosion from its traditional position 40,000 years ago to half that age and long after the Neanderthals had disappeared. They argue for low level symbolism in all hominins up to 20,000 years ago; a date they regard as a significant behavioural Rubicon (Clark 1992a:197) because of the quantity of visual culture that is now found, for example the cave art of France and Cantabrian Spain (Leroi-Gourhan 1968). Their argument is very reminiscent of the sedentary revolution that we encountered in Chapter 1; the moment when we became properly human because of increased and novel material output. But their explanation is disappointing since it relies on a form of cultural intensification that just seems to happen at this time. Paul Mellars' response to their paper highlights their weakness in arguing from hindsight and without an explanatory framework. He points out (1990:246) that dismissing the significance of far more radical innovations such as representational art (Table 2.4) at the beginning of the European Upper Palaeolithic is akin to dismissing the Neolithic, because things became even more complex in the Bronze Age.

With the focus on Africa rather than Europe it does indeed seem that this was, as McBrearty and Brooks (2000) argue, 'the revolution that wasn't'. What they prefer is an extended version of continuity with the slow accretion of significant traits (Figure 2.2) over a very long time-scale. Rather than a revolution they favour a gradual unfolding of modern traits and Africa, as the current evidence shows, is the place to look (Henshilwood and Marean 2003; Wadley 2001). But exactly how we will recognise modern behaviours, if we have not already specified what they are, is unclear. It seems we are to know modern humans not only by what they did but by what they chose not to do, as long as this was in Africa. McBrearty and Brooks' conclusion is that behavioural modernity is African in origin if it can be said to originate anywhere. But they are less forthcoming with an explanation other than that the pattern points to cultural intensification. But why and how is not addressed. Theirs is very much an argument based on timetables and does not deal with issues of change. The timetables are not disputed: Africa came first with many of the innovations by which modern humans are recognised. But this does not rule out, as was the case in Europe and the Near East, an explosion between 60,000 and 30,000 years ago in the frequency and ubiquity of these items (Mellars 2005), in what has been called an Upper Palaeolithic, rather than Human, revolution (Bar-Yosef 2002).

So what began as a study of archaeological transitions in 1973 (Klein 1973; Mellars 1973) had, by 1989, become a worldwide human revolution (Mellars and Stringer 1989). On the way the Upper Palaeolithic of Europe and the Middle East had passed through a major re-think (White 1982), been explained as a revolution in its own right (Gilman 1984),

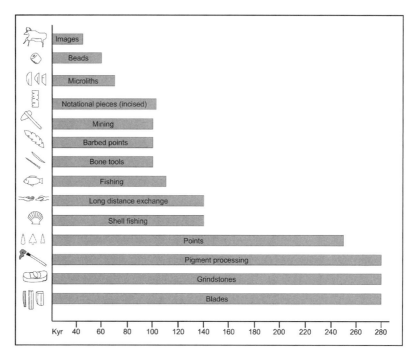

FIGURE 2.2. The appearance of modern behaviours in Africa (after McBrearty and Brooks 2000:Figure 13).

discussed in terms of the emergence of cultural complexity (Price and Brown 1985) and regarded as a 'big surprise' sandwiched between two interglacials with very different archaeological evidence for a hunter-gatherer lifestyle (Gamble 1986:370–8), dubbed as a social revolution (Stringer and Gamble 1993) and finally, at the turn of the century, described as the revolution that never was (McBrearty and Brooks 2000), but for different reasons (d'Errico 2003).

A sapient paradox to spur us on

I now have some answers to why anatomically and fully modern humans entered the archaeological story.

First, they briefly extended the life of the old hat-rack model (Figure 2.1) where fossils and behavioural capacity went together in a neat, bounded package and in a single unbroken line. Hominins once knew their respective cultural roles; you would not catch a Neanderthal making Upper Palaeolithic tools or a modern human knapping handaxes. The category of anatomically modern human accommodated the contradictory evidence by suggesting such mis-matches were present at moments of transition.

Second, once the evidence that the old associations between hominin species and discrete cultural packages were seriously flawed became overwhelming, anatomically modern humans became those not-yet-fully-modern-humans prior to the Human Revolution. They were necessary to that revolution because they were *Homo sapiens* ready for transformation and not *Homo neanderthalensis* prepared for extinction. Note how the argument parallels the Neolithic Revolution where some *Homo sapiens*-hunter are available for change to *Homo sapiens*-farmer.

Third, and most importantly, the concept of the qualified modern human substituted description for an explanation of change. Archaeologists set out the traits for recognising behavioural modernity. What became critical was the timing of their appearance. If tightly clustered and recent then the Human Revolution was supported and change was driven by biological advantage and adaptive success over the populations being replaced. If their appearance was staggered over a long time then continuity and a gradual cultural evolution explained the pattern. Digging deeper to establish the precise evolutionary mechanisms has never been particularly important although archaeologists knew which box – social, ecological, cognitive – they wanted to look in for the answers (Table 1.1).

But none of the arguments about a Human Revolution have impressed those archaeologists studying the issue from a Neolithic rather than Palaeolithic perspective. What happens before agriculture is still, it seems, irrelevant to the transformation of the species. The *other*, the outgroup to humanity, continues to include both anatomically and fully modern humans. And why? Because humanity is only made up of farmers.

This is the *sapient paradox* that Colin Renfrew (1996) has drawn attention to and that Alasdair Whittle (2003:162) attributes to the horror of the vacuum. It arises from the understanding of anatomically modern humans apparently equipped with modern minds and language, but showing none of the haste to change society, economy and material culture that is so evident after the appearance of farming. Renfrew's judgement on the Human Revolution of 40,000 years ago is revealing:

> After this momentous conjuncture (if such it was), looking at the question broadly and at a distance, there were few decisive happenings in human existence for another 30,000 years. Hunter-gatherer communities peopled

much of the earth — what the biologists term an adaptive radiation. But there were few other profound and long-lasting changes, at any rate when the picture is perceived in very general terms, until the end of the Pleistocene period.

(Renfrew 2001:127)

His argument is that sedentism and the built environment that came with agriculture allowed a much more varied relationship with the material world to develop. For Renfrew, this was the 'true human revolution' (2001:128) when new concepts of value developed and a symbolic explosion occurred that touched all aspects of social life.

Recency and a wider context for the Human Revolution

The issue that all these revolutions, and now the sapient paradox, revolve around is the notion of human recency. As the historian of science Robert Proctor (2003) has shown, this concept is a retreat from an earlier position, best summed up as we have already seen in both Montagu's (1965) and Hockett and Ascher's (1964) insistence on a very old human revolution that split us from the apes millions, rather than a few thousand years ago. The retreat from this traditional position has involved a twofold claim:

1. Early humans were not so human.
2. Humans are not so very old.

Both of these retreats are, in Proctor's (2003:227) view, embarrassments to the traditional vectors of human evolution that were once inclusive of humans and hominins, but which are now exclusive, as the extreme case of the sapient paradox shows. This is an important insight and suggests that creations such as anatomically modern humans and fully modern humans serve the cause of recency as much as revolution. The absolute time-scale is not the issue but rather who among the hominins is included in the definition of humanity.

But why is human recency an embarrassment rather than just a scientific argument about the facts? The answer requires us to historicise Palaeolithic archaeology rather than view it as a timely scientific process uncovering relevant facts with increasing precision and accuracy. The sense of embarrassment comes from the very close links that existed in the 1950s between human origins research and the refutation of racist ideologies that had led to the Holocaust in Europe during the Second World War. The intellectual link, forged by a claim of ancient human origins, was elaborated by multi-regionalists. Recency, and a single

TABLE 2.5. *A comparison of two models for human ancestry*

Biology		History
Universal humans	**Category**	Modern humans
Ancient	**Revolution**	Recent
'Big tent' encompasses biological and cultural variation	**Explanatory mechanism**	Diaspora and replacement express the historical process
Regional continuity	**Current paradigm**	Single origins model, recent African origin

African origin, present a different picture of the prehistory of race rela-tions and is seen by multi-regionalists as a retreat from the moral high ground.

The difference between the two models can be summed up as biology versus history (Table 2.5). For multi-regionalists human diversity is an expression of evolutionary principles such as convergent or parallel evolution where comparable adaptations have evolved to meet similar selection pressures from the environment. Among those who follow recent origins, biology is still important but is under selection from the many contingencies that attended the history of our diaspora from Africa. The issue in this lively and often acrimonious debate, as Proctor (2003:224) points out, is about which standpoint accords sufficient dignity to early hominins such as Herto or Neanderthal so that palaeoanthropologists can continue to escape the charge of fuelling racist agendas. To form a judgement we need to consider not just our own palaeoanthropological categories, such as anatomically and fully modern humans, but the political move to recognise humans as universal subjects because of their evolu-tionary endowment and growth.

Universal humans by decree

Why some fossil humans came to be described as 'universal' is not difficult to trace. Universal was written on the flag planted beside the corpse of racist science. It was a reaction to a world war whose politically motivated and scientifically justified atrocities needed to be combated by all nations to ensure they were never repeated.

One reaction, inspired by the principle of inclusion, was to spring--clean the human fossil record. The result lumped the metrical and morphological variation into a few species under a single genus, *Homo* (Mayr 1950). The result, according to palaeoanthropologist Ian Tattersall (1995:116), was a 'big tent' (Table 2.5) where no amount of variation was too great to be contained within a mere three species. This lumping clarified the search for a common human ancestry so that race, famously described by Ashley Montagu as 'Man's most dangerous myth' (Proctor 2003:215), could be scientifically refuted.

Central to the process of refutation was the United Nations and its agencies, of which UNESCO is the most important for my discussion. The United Nations Educational, Scientific and Cultural Organisation was established in 1945 and by 1950 it had published the *First statement on race*. According to Montagu, one of its principal authors:

> The unity of mankind while firmly based in the biological history of man rests not upon the demonstration of *biological unity*, but upon the ethical principle of humanity, which is . . . the right of every human being to the fulfilment of his potentialities as a human being.
>
> (Montagu 1972:238, my emphasis)

This statement elaborated upon the earlier *Universal declaration of human rights* (1948) where **Article 1** states:

> All human beings are born free and equal in dignity and rights. They are *endowed* with reason and conscience and should act towards one another in a spirit of brotherhood.
>
> (my emphasis)

and **Article 2** asserts our entitlement to these rights and freedoms irrespective of 'race, colour, sex, language, religion, political or other opinion, national or social origin, property, birth or other status'.

These declarations sought to sweep away ignorance and prejudice and, through scientific advances allied to education, promote universal values. And there was plenty of ground to clear. 'Biological unity', for example, sounds like a liberating principle. However, the demonstration prior to 1950 that all the races had a common origin was essentially a much older debate about the place of human diversity in the scheme of evolution (Gamble 1993a:Chapter 2). Biological unity stated nothing more than geographical races had evolved. They were neither original nor god-given. But common origin did not amount to much when it came to passing judgements on the abilities of races based on their historical achievements and their position in an imperial pecking-order (Count 1950).

The **Articles** are also strongly reminiscent of Lewis Henry Morgan's (1877:4) much earlier treatise on *Ancient society* where besides a catalogue of inventions such as fire and writing he identified the evolution of the primary human institutions; subsistence, government, language, the family, religion, house life and property. These institutions could be said to constitute an endowment that grew from his stage of savagery through barbarism before attaining civilisation. Some living peoples, in Morgan's judgement, had not yet progressed from savagery even though they were biologically the same as someone living in nineteenth-century New York. Neither were the races the only losers to biological unity. The political treatment of women rested on similar assessments of potential and the judgements of history. With hindsight the use of 'man' and 'his' in the quotation from the *Statement on race* are revealing in a collective document with such liberal intent.

Defining the universal characteristics of humanity was anthropology's great moment on the political stage (Montagu 1972). It set the agenda for the study of human evolution throughout the 1960s when the scientific treatment of earlier ancestral species was critically reviewed. Neanderthals, for example, became part of humanity, brought in from the cold by the authority of universal declarations which forced a re-think of their looks and abilities (Brace 1964; Hammond 1982; Straus and Cave 1957). Ashley Montagu (1972), author of the *Statement on race* and one of the architects of the all-inclusive big tent model for our ancestors, allowed everyone who made tools to be included in the definition of human. Multi-regionalists followed suit and signed up to the declaration by extending it to most of the other fossils in their care. Some of them did not like the alternative.

> The spread of humankind and its differentiation into distinct geographic groups that persisted through long periods of time, with evidence of long-lasting contact and cooperation, in many ways is a more satisfying interpretation of human prehistory than a scientific rendering of the story of Cain, based on one population quickly, and completely, and most likely violently, replacing all others. This rendering of modern population dispersals is a story of 'making war and not love', and if true its implications are not pleasant.
>
> (Wolpoff 1989:98)

Of course single origins supporters (Lahr and Foley 1998; Stringer and Gamble 1993; Tattersall 1995) also care equally deeply about the implications of their interpretations. And as one of them I have to question whether the imaginary archaeology of long-ago when peace not war ruled hominin affairs is in fact any older than the optimistic but troubled decade when today's senior multi-regionalists were at graduate school. A single origin standpoint also has its imaginary archaeology but with a narrative that is far less biblical in tone:

> It is pointless to seek winners or losers in the story of human evolution, for each age will place its own gloss on history. Rather, we should accept that differences exist, and use them to broaden our definitions and discussions of humanity. For although the Neanderthals were, quite simply, 'not us', they − or rather their African kin − provided the basis from which we sprang; both they and the early Moderns have a place in our prehistory, whether or not they were our actual lineal ancestors.
>
> (Stringer and Gamble 1993:219)

Difference and diversity are best seen as creative examples of evolution, rather than as the hard covers of a book within which all hominins must necessarily shelter if we are to be judged as ethical scientists and human beings.

The endowment and growth of modern humans

Palaeoanthropologists have, thanks to molecular biology, had a second bite at the issue of hominin dignity. Defining the universal rights of humanity could only take place based on the supposition, as Morgan showed, of our original endowment. In cultural terms this gift is very much the list of distinctions from **Article 2**, and where reason, conscience, language, religion, heredity, social origin and property are critical. Humanity is therefore about the moral uses of this dowry rather than the planning depth (Table 2.2) selected by archaeologists as a hallmark of humanity (e.g. Binford 1989; Kuhn 1992; Roebroeks et al. 1988). Everyone, the 1948 Universal Declaration states, has rights based on their possession of this common endowment. By implication, if a human society existed without these attributes then they would not be human.

Such a debate over the boundaries to humanity have more recently encompassed molecular data. In 1950 when the *First statement on race* was written the description of the DNA molecule by Watson and Crick was still three years away. The subsequent half-century of research has added a new dimension to our universal endowment. For instance, how significant for our identity is the 2 per cent of genes that we do not share with chimps (Marks 2002)? The changing historical circumstances within which these new tools to measure humanity emerged are summarised in UNESCO's 1997 *Universal declaration on the human genome and human rights*. The first three articles are particularly relevant to defining what an individual is in the context of the common genetic gifts which make us human.

Article 1

The human genome underlies the fundamental unity of all members of the human family, as well as the recognition of their inherent dignity and diversity. *In a symbolic sense, it is the heritage of humanity.*

Article 2

a) Everyone has the right to respect for their dignity and for their rights regardless of their genetic characteristics.
b) That dignity makes it imperative not to reduce individuals to their genetic characteristics and to respect their uniqueness and diversity.

Article 3

The human genome, *which by its nature evolves*, is subject to mutations. It contains potentialities that are expressed differently according to each individual's natural and social environment including the individual's state of health, living conditions, nutrition and education.

(my emphasis)

The 'heritage of humanity' is therefore embodied in all of us. Difference is to be expected, diversity and uniqueness to be respected. As with all endowments they can be used well or badly, which in **Article 3** is regarded as a result of the environment. Although we are all born with a common genetic heritage we cannot choose where we are born and that is what makes us different individuals. Moreover the first *Statement on race* (Montagu 1972:12) makes the point in paragraph 15 that 'equality as an ethical principle in no way depends upon the assertion that human beings are in fact equal in endowment'. We are 'all equally men' (Montagu 1972:123) since everyone possesses the elements of the basic human dowry. However, just like presents at rich and poor weddings, or indeed like genetic inheritance itself, what we get is not equal.

But even more significant is the proposition in **Article 3** that the human genome has an essential quality that precedes the environment into which we are born. It even precedes our physical conception. This essence is the quality of change, 'which by its nature evolves'. Our endowment is therefore clear. Humanity cannot stay still: growth is part of that biological endowment and is driven forward by some inherited, essential life force over which we have no control. Such a representation is reminiscent of early socio-biology where our bodies and cultures were presented as just a means, respectively, by which our genes and memes reproduced themselves (Dawkins 1976).

   This view of our endowment also needs to be set in historical context. Sadly the first *Statement on race* did not banish 'Man's most dangerous myth'. The political history of the last fifty years has had scant regard for the *Universal declaration of human rights* as genocide, ethnic cleansing and persecution have been conducted in every continent in the name of race, language, religion, social origin and property. Since 1950 geneticists have replaced anthropologists on the political stage and been given the task of defining more precisely the human endowment. But I cannot imagine the results will be much different by 2050.

Anatomically fully post-modern humans?

It is significant that geneticists supplied the clinching evidence for the recent evolution of humans in a single continent, Africa. That being the case, does the claim for human recency recognise that despite developments in transport and media technologies we live in a world that is still patently very diverse? It is tempting to see the biological metaphors of growth and development applied in this way, and at a moment when geneticists contend that our genetic diversity is declining thanks to bicycles and jumbo jets: the former widened local mate choice and the latter is creating global gene pools.

   But these genetic changes are part of a bigger project. Recency supplied a logical origin for the critical analysis of humanity's universal project of the last three hundred years that is known as modernity (Friedman 1994). Archaeology, as Julian Thomas (2004:41) shows, has played a role in this project by supplying an origin that modern societies demand to render them legitimate, as well as distracting attention away from the fact that science, with its standpoint of objectivity, is divorced from social relations. Modernity transformed the world through the forces of nationalism, industrialisation, science and capitalism. It is the process of change that Raymond Williams (1965) described in his long revolution, although he did not call it modernity. The declaration of universal human values is a fine example of the modernist project although since 1945 modernity has been increasingly critiqued as a framework of knowledge reaching a post-modernist crescendo in the 1970s.

The significance of modernity, as anthropologist Jonathan Friedman (1994:143) argues, is that it changed cultural identity by separating the symbol from what it refers to. Such a separation is regarded as another of Descartes' legacies from the seventeenth century (see Prologue). The change which modernity ushered in was that community became less to do with the rallying-call provided by local shared symbols, although these still figured, and more with participation in the structures which reproduce our global selves. This puts an interesting twist on how we understand culture. As Friedman (1994:206) points out, with a Western understanding of modernity, culture can be understood as a global product that transforms difference into essence. We belong to different cultures because we use our common endowment in varied ways. And it is the cause of that variety, summarised as culture, which is our historical essence. An explanation contained in **Article 3** of UNESCO's 1997 *Declaration on the human genome* 'according to each individual's natural and social environment'.

Friedman (1994:207) then questions this understanding, much as I would take issue with the notion in **Article 3** that the genome 'by its nature evolves'. Culture, Friedman asserts, does not depend on a prior notion that it is the way that meaning is organised. This would be a classic statement of essence where the social condition precedes the social actor. If this were the case then political and cultural determination is not possible. The system always triumphs and forces us to its will. The alternative, according to Friedman, is that culture emerges out of human agency and all its associated practices. No prior notions are needed. As Tim Ingold (2000:376) points out, we have a developmental system that evolved to underwrite our capacities but that should not be interpreted as an innate tendency to grow all aspects of humanity.

> The changing forms and capacities of creatures — whether human or otherwise — are neither given in advance as a phylogenetic endowment nor added on through a parallel process of cultural transmission but emerge through histories of development within environments that are continually being shaped by their activities.
>
> (Ingold 2003:232)

Now, human recency as conceived by palaeoanthropologists is not for a moment part of the post-modernist critique. As a concept it lies full-square in the best scientific traditions of modernity. But the timing of its appearance betrays it nonetheless as a response to a changing world view driven by globalisation on the one hand and the reaction of local communities to such forces on the other. I therefore doubt that without the academic and artistic reactions to modernity there would be any notion of a recent Human Revolution in archaeology. We can see that fully modern humans, with their global diaspora from a single geographical centre, appeared as a universal concept to match contemporary globalisation. Furthermore, those same modern humans were transformed locally as biological and cultural meanings were added to the universal product, ourselves, through those histories of development.

By now I hope I have convinced you that revolutions are not the right tools for the study of change on these vast time-scales. But neither are continuity and gradualism necessarily better descriptions since, as I argued in Chapter 1, this would only replace locomotives with the inevitability of future-creep. Instead we need to re-think those metaphors of endowment and biological growth that have emerged as central to the archaeological study of change and return to a sense of humanity that is not a universal instrument inspired by well-intentioned political action. It is time to consider our desire for origins.

CHAPTER 3

Metaphors for origins

'Perhaps it doesn't understand English' thought Alice. 'I daresay it's a French mouse, come over with William the Conqueror.' (For, with all her knowledge of history, Alice had no very clear notion how long ago anything had happened.)

Lewis Carroll *Alice's Adventures in Wonderland* 1865

Origins and desire

Revolutions bring change. But they do not necessarily bring understanding of why things changed. They are skirmishes in the larger historical battle over our origins and it is here, when the smoke clears, that justification is sought and explanations accepted. So far I have held these origins questions in reserve but now it is time to ask them. They have already been implicated in the Neolithic Revolution, through its association with the origins of agriculture and sedentism, and in the Human Revolution with the origins of language, art and symbolism. But while revolutions are a recent shock tactic, often used by archaeologists to gain rhetorical advantage, origins research is fundamental to the entire campaign, where archaeology is just one company alongside the big battalions of history, philosophy and social science.

Origins research is much older than an academic subject recognisable as archaeology. Since Classical times Western scholars have addressed religious and political issues by posing origins questions, and have answered them using a variety of sources. Modernity adapted these traditions and established as one of its central ideas that humanity, Mankind, is the subject of history (Thomas 2004) and, moreover, one that can be revealed through a systematic regard for the evidence.

But intriguingly, origins questions have not changed under the weight of data supplied by those same academic disciplines that arose to feed our curiosity. In their brief survey of accounts of human social origins, Bruno Latour and Shirley Strum (1986) analysed seven texts written over the last 350 years. The subtitle of their article, 'Oh please, tell us another story' sums up what they found: that the current wealth of facts, scientifically arrived at, were servicing the same philosophical conjectures about the origins of humanity that had been inherited from Hobbes and Rousseau, but less coherently expressed.

Why should this be? Why do the questions and frame of reference remain static while the information on ancestors, their capabilities and the timing of the evolutionary process is dynamic and kaleidoscopic? This discrepancy suggests we are faced with one of those core beliefs of Western society and science that is so deep-seated that it can accommodate almost anything that comes to light rather than face a need for change. Origins research is therefore fundamental because it is a master narrative about human ascendancy, first over our own biology and second over the forces of nature. Origins research is the way we have traditionally defined our human qualities and looked to evidence from the past for support of this belief.

In previous chapters I have shown how the Human Revolution, whether old or young, marks for many the origin point when we transcended our biology through enhanced cognitive powers. Moreover, the Neolithic Revolution apparently transformed us from slaves to nature into nature's master. Origins research takes the familiar dualisms that construct so many investigations − culture:nature, body:soul, mind:matter − and accords them historical significance and an asymmetrical authority. Hence, nature and biology once dominated human society but this position was reversed with the development of agriculture when culture and society triumphed. And like a core belief in many world cultures, this master narrative is protected by silent rituals that preserve it from change.

The entire process is driven by desire. Identifying origins in time and space creates a history of human desire and it is that force which drives our notions of change from the origin point onwards. Of course, the nature of that desire changes as part of the historical process as new interpretations of our relationship to each other and the world come into play as conditions alter. But the structure by which we understand that desire remains the same with its need for foundation. And that is what I mean by 'protecting rituals'.

So origins research, while heavily critiqued in all disciplines, including archaeology (Gamble and Gittins 2004; Landau 1986; 1991; Moore 1995), possesses a staying power that shows little sign of waning as Latour and Strum demonstrate. It is for this reason that declaring the true revolution to have been the Neolithic, or asserting the primacy of an earlier watershed over which fully modern humans spilled, is unlikely to resolve the issue because it does not need to be resolved. More importantly, it is this desire for a foundation from which universal truths and values can be distilled that calls forth an imaginative ancient geography that I will call Originsland.

Originsland

The pursuit of origins questions leads us, unhesitatingly, to Originsland: a time and space that is defined by many different interests across the arts as well as the sciences and by beliefs that are variously rational and relational, common-sense and based on faith. The many identities of Originsland differ in the weighting they give to the authority bestowed by either emotion or reason. A fundamentalist knows exactly where, when and how the Garden of Eden came into being just as a palaeoanthropologist, working within the framework of physics and evolutionary science, is confident that alternative human cradles existed, and can provide supporting dates, locations and extinct inhabitants.

The boundaries of Originsland are determined by the intellectual security that all investigation needs, whatever its basis of belief. This was Jacques Derrida's idea, and underpinned his complex notion of *logocentrism*, expressing the metaphysical desire for foundation (Hugdahl 1999). Within the discipline of archaeology, that origin point is provided by the Palaeolithic period (Gamble and Gittins 2004) from where the landscape of Originsland is mapped out in terms of difference to everything that comes afterwards.

The changing boundaries to Originsland, like those in another imaginative geography, Alice's Wonderland, are best understood by analogy. For example, the division between the Palaeolithic and the Neolithic (Old and New Stone Ages respectively), named by Sir John Lubbock in 1865, is analogous as a boundary concept to the Mason-Dixon boundary line laid out a century before to demarcate southern Pennsylvania and northern Maryland, but whose significance changed with the subsequent history of the United States. Establishing the North-South divide was not the intent of Charles Mason and Jeremiah Dixon in 1763 and only later, before the Civil War of 1861–5, did their eponymous line become the northern boundary of the slave owning states. What Mason and Dixon unintentionally did for political space in one continent, Lubbock (1865) did for archaeological time in the context of universal history. His division also came to represent a fundamental separation and sometime after 1865 his terms were widely used to characterise different and irreconcilable systems of social organisation on either side of the Palaeolithic/Neolithic divide (Chapter 1). An important internal division had been drawn within Originsland.

Just how important this division was can be judged by the peopling of this imaginative space. Within the borders of Originsland archaeologists are bound by inherited concepts that support pre-existing values and truths about human nature and identity (see also Conkey and Williams 1991; Graves 1991; Proctor 2003). From these values flows the structure of the past we are unwilling to change. For example, both the 'cavemen' prior to 'modern humans', and the economic 'hunter-gatherers' before the advent of 'farmers', are examples of logocentrism because they provide direction for the master narrative that deals with the ascendancy of contemporary human values. In particular these categories relate to the overarching concepts of Man and Mankind put forward in the nineteenth century as a universal project for history to investigate (Thomas 2004:53).

In this way the origins of modern humans and agriculture provide a secure foundation on which the core business of archaeology, the documentation of the history of later institutions and practices, can proceed. The Palaeolithic has to be different and treated as such. Originsland is indeed a foreign country where identity cards are carefully checked on departure.

The origin point and the cone of research

Archaeologists did not invent Originsland. Rather they colonised it for their own purposes. They did so because Originsland provided a ready explanation for the burgeoning discoveries, commencing in the seventeenth century that formed a material archive for the proposition of an ancient human past and later a concept of Mankind. Just as the earliest systematic archaeologists, such as C. J. Thomsen (Chapter 1), appropriated a three-age system of thinking from philosophy so too did the idea of an origins point come from wider social concerns with change.

Two images by William Blake express the contrasted interests in Originsland. The first is his celebrated vision of *God as an architect* (1794) that provides (Figure 3.1), as Erica Gittins has pointed out, a timely

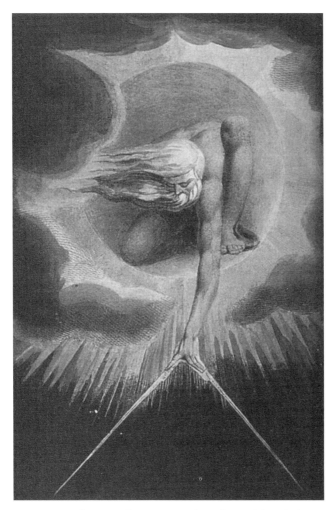

FIGURE 3.1. The cone of origins research. William Blake's *God as an architect* (1794) that appears as the first Plate in *Europe a prophecy.*

historical representation of origins thinking long before any recognisably archaeologically focused origins research had begun.

In the picture God reaches out of the circle to map the higher order of creation. But the appeal to divine authority to explain intelligible spatial order (Cosgrove 1999:19) is only one of Blake's themes. An archaeological rather than geographical reading of the image reveals the patriarch as *the* origin point formed by the compasses wielded not only by God, but also by Sir Isaac Newton in Blake's later image (Figure 3.2). Here, Newton maps

FIGURE 3.2. *Newton as a divine geometer* by William Blake (1795). Compasses were a traditional symbol of God as the architect of the Universe.

the human project from the origin point of scientific reason rather than religious belief. Blake disagreed with this standpoint; hence the descent into darkness in front of the scientist. While both images point to a mapping project, what emerges between the outstretched cone of the compasses is the archaeological time, as well as the geographical space, of Originsland.

Newton's hold on the compasses is also one of political purchase on a description of knowledge and understanding that is very familiar to archaeologists. As *Alexandra Alexandri* (1995:58; Conkey and Williams 1991; Wobst and Keene 1983) shows, such a research cone directs the production and interpretation of knowledge about human origins. Power resides with the person holding the tip of the cone, by virtue of new discoveries and the control over information they provide.

The origins cone is a dominant image. For example, the familiar and repetitive depictions of the inevitable march of male-led progress and the triumph of culture over biology (Figure 3.3).

The concept of the research cone nicely exposes what Tim Ingold (2000:Chapter 21) so dislikes about the category of modern humans. Forty years ago the category of anatomically modern humans was introduced out of laudable motives: the harnessing of evolutionary evidence to overthrow

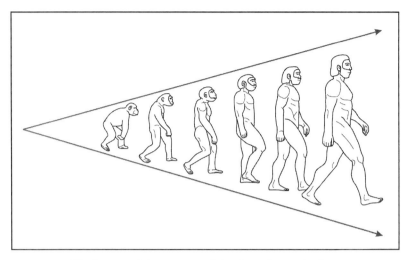

FIGURE 3.3. The human origins cone containing the male march of progress.

racist dogma (Chapter 2). But in order to make the concept of a modern human work it was necessary to take a step back to Descartes and re-assert our unique standing as a dual creature. Humans, Ingold argues (2000:389), had to be presented as both a species of nature and at the same time so emancipated from the world that it became the object of our consciousness. When we come to contemplate how this situation arose, which it apparently did not for other animals, then we are confronted by the emergence of history itself.

This position is expressed in Figure 3.4 where the origin point is that moment when we say that history, defined as the capacity to use our

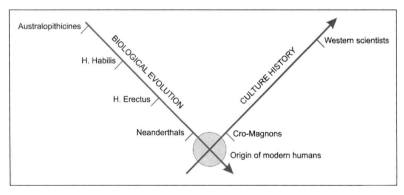

FIGURE 3.4. The origin of 'true humanity' that falls, in this example of a research cone at the intersection of evolution and history (after Ingold 2000:Figure 21).

biological endowment in cultural ways, kicks in. The concept of the anatomically modern human is just a way of isolating that moment so that very
different histories and prehistories can be traced back to a point of origin.
The idea of a modern human is essential to the marriage of biology
and culture and the unfolding of latent capacity that is history.

Archaeologists are particularly prone to accepting the structure of the
research cone. In a subject that is often seen as discovery-led the contest
revolves around who at any moment has the evidence to wrest the tip of
the cone from the hand of a rival. No wonder, as we saw in the previous
chapter, that many believe the unique behaviours of modern humans
should be unearthed rather than set out beforehand (McBrearty and Brooks
2000:534). Moreover, the notable lack of explicit theory in human origins
research (Foley 2001a:5) is only possible because the framework of the cone
is such a robust structure thanks to the Western traditions of producing
and interpreting knowledge that, like Blake's pictures, it enshrines.

Metaphors and the body

Once archaeologists had colonised Originsland we peopled it in order to
make our contribution to understanding how humans transcended the
limits of their biology. In the broadest sense, as exemplified by Gordon
Childe (Chapter 1), our task has been to signpost the way from the humble
homeland of our human identity towards the familiar conclusion; the
triumph of reason and the power of rational interpretations of the world to
transform society.

But Originsland only exists because of rhetorical devices such as
metaphor and analogy (Table 3.1) that create an imaginative geography
we can share. Although archaeologists are aware of the importance of these
conceptual devices (Bamforth 2002; Graves 1991; Knappett 2005:102; Wylie
2002) they have devoted less attention to the bodily experiences on which
they are based, preferring instead to prioritise semiotics and an understanding of experience as grounded primarily in the mind.

However, metaphors, far from simply facilitating understanding as they
are usually presented, must now be understood as governing the way we
think. In their book *Metaphors we live by*, George Lakoff and Mark Johnson
(1980:5) show how our entire use of concepts depends on metaphor, which
they define succinctly as 'understanding and experiencing one kind of thing
in terms of another'. The key word in their definition is *experiencing* since
their case rests on language referring not just to cognitive processes in

TABLE 3.1. *Two major forms of rhetorical device that are basic to speech, literature and reasoning (Harris 2005). Such rhetorical devices are rarely applied to objects but instead to the words that describe things. The distinctions in each rhetorical form are described in the text*

Metaphor (metonymy, synecdoche)	Asserts that one thing *is* another thing. It explains by making the abstract or unknown concrete and familiar and showing a relationship between things that are seemingly alien to each other
Analogy (homology)	Compares two things, which are alike in several respects, for the purpose of explaining or clarifying some unfamiliar or difficult idea or object by showing how the idea or object is similar to some familiar one. Analogy serves the more practical end of explaining a thought process or a line of reasoning or the abstract in terms of the concrete.

isolation, but rather to the experience of the world that we have because of our bodies and our senses. Embodiment plays a central role in constructing metaphors and analogies to explain a very complex material world. Our bodies therefore structure all forms of communication and meaning and are a focus for our identities.

Grounding experience in the body

This point is so central to the framework I will develop in Part II that some examples are in order. From three different disciplines they emphasise how the body is an anchor, a source of reference that structures social and cultural life. Anthropologist Maurice Bloch writes:

> The anchoring of conceptualisation in the material — the body, houses, wood, styles of speaking — and in practices — cooking, cultivating, eating together — means that the cultural process cannot be separated from the wider processes of ecological, biological, and geographical transformation of which human society is a small part...culture is not merely an interpretation superimposed on these material facts but integrated with them.
>
> (Bloch 1998:36)

Archaeologist Christopher Tilley (1999:19), in his valuable discussion of artefacts as metaphors, has remarked how even spoken language depends on an embodied basis for understanding in order to create and manipulate concepts. A truly non-metaphorical language would therefore be both dis-embodied and concept free. A spade would always be just that, a spade, and no heart could ever be broken. Speech would impart information rather than trade ideas, while language would of necessity be literal rather than abstract. Metaphor marks the difference:

> The body is the ground or anchor by means of which we locate ourselves in the world, perceive and apprehend it. The centre of our own existence is always our body, as an axis from which spatiality and temporality are orientated: the human body *inhabits* space and time. Rather than mirroring the world, speech can be conceived as an extension of the human body in the world, a kind of artefact, by means of which we extend ourselves in the world, gain knowledge of it and alter it. Metaphor is an essential part of this process. Cognition is essentially a process of seeing something *as* something and this is the core of metaphorical understandings.
>
> (Tilley 1999:34)

In an interesting parallel, many studies of artificial intelligence have now rejected Descartes' view of human cognition as a discrete 'thinking thing' and instead turned to a Heideggerian approach to being-in-the-world (Anderson 2003:91). The resultant embodied cognition of artificial life tackles the issue of how abstract symbols acquire real-world meaning. According to cognitive scientist Michael Anderson we need to recognise that:

> cognitive contents (however these are ultimately characterized, symboli-cally or otherwise) must ultimately ground out in terms of the agent's embodied experience and physical characteristics.
>
> (Anderson 2003:92)

Embodiment is therefore the mainspring for the symbolic force that resonates throughout any language structured by metaphor and more broadly applies to all aspects of materiality where, as Tilley shows, meta-phor is equally important. Through materiality we are both engaged with and constituted by, the world of objects, artefacts and ecofacts distributed across landscapes and in locales (Gamble 2004:85). To make sense of these worlds at any level of understanding requires cognition to be grounded out in our bodies; 'I feel it in my bones', rather than 'I thought it in my mind'.

Some further examples will help. Lakoff and Johnson (1980:15) describe many forms of metaphor and show how our spatial orientation – up, down, back, front, near, far — provides the experience which constitutes the metaphor:

I'm on a *high* today
He's really *low* at the moment
I am *on top* of the situation
He was *up-front* about the outcome
She has fallen *behind* in her work
Her views were *left* of *centre*
A week is a *long* time in politics
My life stretched out *before* me
It was in the *back* of my mind

The conceptual scheme arises from nothing more complicated than being in the world and surrounded rather than separated from it (Gibson 1979; Merleau-Ponty 1962). The metaphors are expressing moods, emotions, status and opinions. But they do this through the physical experience that we have of the world.

Parts for whole: metonymy and synecdoche

Metonymy (Table 3.1) differs from metaphor in the number of conceptual domains being referenced (Lakoff and Johnson 1980:265; Tilley 1999:4–6). With metaphor there are two, target and source. The latter provides the concepts used in the reasoning that is then applied to the target. For example, the 'eyes are windows to the soul', has as its source the bodily sensation of seeing and when applied to the target, the invisible soul, those principles are applied to looking into the container of the body thereby providing a routeway to the unseen. By contrast, metonymy involves only the immediate subject matter as a single domain (Lakoff and Johnson 1980:265). The source and the target reference each other rather than apply to a different concept altogether; for example, when we use the *face for the person* as in 'She's just a *pretty face*', or 'we need some *new faces* around here' (Lakoff and Johnson 1980:37). The point about metonymy, that metaphor does not share, is that it relies for its production of meaning on connections that stem from usage and that build up over time (Tilley 1999:5). As a result metonymy allows us to focus on what is being referred to (Lakoff and Johnson 1980:37) but at the price of metaphorical nuance.

Finally, there is a special case of metonymy known as synecdoche (Chapman 2000; Tilley 1999:6) that allows us to move from the part to the whole *and the reverse*. For example, 'I have a new set of wheels' takes me from a part to the whole automobile while 'the cars were bumper to bumper' takes the opposite direction to describe a traffic jam. In order to achieve this reversibility synecdoche has to be more basic than even metonymy in basing relationships on idiom and association and so avoid mixing metaphors.

Partial representation is inescapable in a study of the past. Even the best preservation produces only a fragmentary record of what once existed. Archaeologists spend a good deal of their analytical energies assessing the pathways of decay among their material evidence in order to improve their inferences about the range and complexity of the hominin behaviour that initially produced them (Lyman 1994; Patrik 1985; Schiffer 1987). As a result, archaeologists have devised a way of working that goes from part to whole, from a pottery fragment to an entire vessel or from one excavated corner of a cave or village to the complete settlement.

John Chapman (2000) has shown how such material part-whole relation-ships are comparable to metonymy (see Chapters 5 and 6). Here for instance the passport photograph of a face stands for the whole person just as their fingerprint or luggage also identifies the whole through a part. The same principle of understanding concepts in terms of something else still holds, while the part-whole relationship is particularly relevant to metaphors grounded on material culture and its distribution in time and space.

Our experience of the past as a container

Originsland is therefore my novel metaphor for a complex concept of human beginnings that has become wrapped in many interpretations. Time and geography are combined in Originsland to take us somewhere that otherwise we could neither represent nor discuss, but which we nonetheless desire.

Space and time form two common linguistic metaphors and in both instances they act as containers (Lakoff and Johnson 1980:29–32) for our actions. Everyday activities take place *in* time and are often *bounded* by a well-defined space. Neither are these times and spaces arbitrary. We understand their form through our bodies. We become hungry and tired as the day passes. We move through buildings, travel in trains and walk in the park. Our senses, sight, hearing, touch and smell set the limits and experience of these times and spaces as claustrophobic, pleasant, secure, challenging, exhausting and many other emotional states that we barely think about at all. Finally, there is our inner state to which we devote a good deal of thought. Here our bodies are not only containers that ingest and excrete substances, bear children and change as we grow and age, but are also the 'core of our being', repositories for emotions, the self and other concepts such as the soul.

Now, the object of archaeological enquiry, the past, abounds with container metaphors:

> The past is all *around* us
> She lives *in* her own past
> The past is a foreign *country*
> Knowledge *resides* in the past
> I carry my genetic heritage *within* me
> The past *in* the present
> He lives on *in* her memory
> Stuck *in* the past

As well as in explicit references to selected parts of the body:

> The dead *hand* of the past
> You felt you could *touch* the history around you
> They were in the *grip* of past events
> The *finger* of time moves on
> A *grasp* of what went before is essential
> I will *point* you to the lessons of the past
> *Struck* down by the weight of tradition
> A *walk* down memory lane

Metaphorically, the past is something we primarily conceptualise through the experience of touch rather than vision, smell or hearing. Of course, alternative metaphors can be found as in the auditory 'echoes from the past', or the visual 'a window on the past'. However, the past, or what went before, of whatever antiquity or recency is predominantly understood metaphorically through our hands, feet and bodies rather than our eyes and minds. Furthermore, the past is something that contains us and which we seek to contain, as found for example in David Lewis-Williams' (2003) recent title 'The mind *in* the cave' that conjures up a dis-embodied origin for symbolism.

The container metaphor of the domus

Archaeologist Ian Hodder (1990:41) shook up the study of Europe's earliest farmers with his use of the *domus* as a metaphor for the domestication of society. The *domus* is a concept of home and has the attributes of mothering, nurturing and caring (1990:84). His starting point is that the adoption of agriculture was a social-symbolic process where the natural was made cultural. He sets the *domus* in opposition to the *agrios*, taken from the Greek adjective for wild, and explores these two metaphors of power in Neolithic Europe. His explicit use of metaphor rather than analogy also allows him to seek new sets of relationships between different classes of material culture. Hence:

> the house, the hearth and the pot were extensively employed in the culturing process, and they became appropriate metaphors for the domestication of society.
>
> (Hodder 1990:294)

The *domus* makes use of a series of material objects as container metaphors and allows Hodder to present a novel understanding of change during the Neolithic. However, care has to be taken because in other hands the socio-symbolic metaphor of the *domus* is used to support a cultural origin of agriculture where societies 'wanted' to change (Cauvin 2000:66). I shall return to this contentious conclusion in Chapter 8 once I have explored other material metaphors in Part II.

Analogy and homology

Despite the importance of metaphor to the formation of concepts, archaeologists devote more attention to the use of analogy and homology in understanding the past. For example, Alison Wylie (2002), one of the most influential writers on the potential of analogy in archaeology, does not discuss metaphor in her major text. However, the difference is important. While metaphor is essentially understanding something in terms of something else (Table 3.1), analogy and homology are an exercise in reasoning from present conditions and we saw in Chapter 1 how Childe used the Industrial Revolution in this way. Their sources can be various — ethnographic, ethological, computing and sporting to name a few — but the form of reasoning is dominated by biology (Table 3.2). Analogies and homologies based on biology can seem stronger than other sources because the links in the chain of reasoning depend on principles such as natural

TABLE 3.2. *The biological contrast between analogy and homology*

	Analogy	Homology
Function/outcome	Similar	Dissimilar
Origin/ancestor	Different	Common
Response to selection	Convergent evolution	Parallel evolution
Biological example	*Wings of insects and birds*	*The arms of humans and bats*
Archaeological example	*Domestication of sheep and llamas*	*Knife blades and axes made from stone*

selection and reproductive success. These give the impression of an independent check on measures of similarity and shared ancestry.

Analogy is inescapable in archaeology since our interpretation of the past must feed on our experience of the present (Ascher 1961). However, archaeologists are now well aware of the dangers, particularly evident with ethnographic analogies (Binford 1972), of just re-creating the past in the form of the present, what Martin Wobst (1978) tellingly described as ethnography with a shovel. Dodging such ethnographic pitfalls has led Wylie (1985:101) to identify archaeologists' 'chronic ambivalence' to analogy in general. Dreadful errors were made in the past; for example the equation of Australian Aborigines directly with the Neanderthals of the Middle Palaeolithic in Western Europe (Sollas 1911). However, the way forward will be achieved:

> not by attempts to restrict inquiry to safe methods and the limited ends attainable by them, but by exploring more fully the potential for *raising the credibility* of those necessarily amplitative and usually analogical inferences on which archaeology must rely if it is to bring unfamiliar and otherwise inaccessible aspects of the past into view.
>
> (Wylie 1985:107 my emphasis)

Analogies of corner-shops and weeding

Two examples of raising the credibility of analogies bring into play a rational and relational approach. The first is the series of models that have been applied to the analysis of decisions among prehistoric hunters and gatherers (Marlowe 2005; Mithen 1990; Winterhalder and Smith 1981). Their strategies and adaptations can then be compared and the contribution of technology, tactical decisions concerning movement, camp size and length of occupation evaluated. Ultimately adaptive success is being measured through reproductive advantage (Bettinger 1991; Jochim 1981; Kelly 1995; Shennan 2002) and economic theory underpins the analysis.

One of these approaches explicitly uses the analogy of the small diversified business (Earle 1980:14) where economic success is governed by balancing supply and demand and where cost-benefit analysis informs strategic planning to maximise profit margins (Earle and Christenson 1980). The key currency for these corner-shop hunters is energy; how it is harvested, stored and expended. A secondary one is the acquisition, transmission and application of information about the best strategy to follow. Since reproductive success depends in large measure on the efficient and economical use of energy resources, subsistence choices, including demographic arrangements, technological innovation and settlement locations, will be driven by the selective pressure of energy as a currency for evolutionary success (Jochim 1976). Information about those energy resources increases security and, as Steven Mithen (1990) demonstrated, is an important currency in evaluating hunting decisions.

The corner-shop is one of those analogies that satisfies Alison Wylie's call to raise the credibility of this line of reasoning since its potential has been profitably explored among hunters and gatherers to demonstrate economic rationality (Kelly 1995; O'Connell et al. 1999; Smith 1991; Winterhalder and Smith 1981).

Farmers have been treated differently, most probably because economic rationality is assumed from the outset. Farmers seem particularly suited to interpretation by analogy because we instinctively understand how their economy functions. It is after all the basis of our present world. As a result analogy does not help when it comes to explaining how hunters became farmers even though both systems are thought of as rational.

Anthropologist Stephen Gudeman (1986) through his fieldwork in the village of los Boquerones in Panama provides a second example of how we might raise the credibility of analogy and an alternative to the corner-shop. He found that the peasants had the image of their land as a natural reservoir. They described to him their cultivation of maize by drawing an analogy between crops and the earth and hair and the head (Gudeman 1986:5−6). What we would call weeding they referred to as cleaning that required hoeing and combing respectively. Crops grow just like human hair and both need cutting. Both hair and crops grow under the guidance of people but not because of them or through any essential quality in the hair or seed itself. Instead the force for growing comes from what they grow in, the head and the earth. Rather than appealing to a rational set of decisions the villagers understood the practice of agriculture through a relationship to the body.

Proxies and currencies

Reasoning by present condition, the basis of analogy and homology, might give us a framework for investigating change but we still need proxies and currencies to establish that change has occurred and at what scale and rate. A proxy is a substitute for a direct observation or measurement. For example, tree rings and oxygen isotope variation are proxies of past climates and these are contained in archives, a source of information such as a tree trunk or sediment core that holds the proxy. A currency provides a measure of the proxy being studied. For example, it is not possible to directly measure the calories expended by Palaeolithic hunters as they set out daily from their camp site. One proxy would be distance since calories are burnt when walking. However, a better proxy would be the time taken to walk the same distance since that would be influenced by the topography surrounding the site. Time can be readily turned into a more widely used currency, energy, whose expenditure was the purpose of attempting a calorie count in the first place. The corner-store analogy applied to hunters and gatherers use such currencies.

Metaphors of origins

While we have all experienced the past in terms of yesterday or last year none of us can ever physically visit Originsland. It is off-limits as a means to ground out concepts through bodily experience. But spatial orientation provides only one set of linguistic metaphors. The remote prehistory of Originsland is fleshed out by a further set of embodied metaphors that deal with substance and process. Here the body is still the basis for describing a deep-time past through metaphors of endowment and growth that I have already mentioned when discussing the Neolithic and Human Revolutions (Chapters 1 and 2).

Endowment and growth

Historian of science Misia Landau (1986:46) has pointed out that palaeoanthropologists trace human destiny in human anatomy. The narrative structure of human evolution follows a predictable cycle of test

TABLE 3.3. *The structure of events in accounts of human evolution (Landau 1986:Figure 3.1)*

Evolutionary event	Endowment
Terrestriality	Shift from the trees to the ground
Bipedality	Acquisition of upright posture
Encephalisation	Development of the brain, intelligence and language
Civilisation	Emergence of technology, morals and society

and response as climate and competition pushed the humanising process through four important episodes that most authors agree upon (Table 3.3).

During the process gifts were bestowed on the hominins. These took the form of abilities and skills that arose from larger brains or more dextrous hands. Endowed with these gifts that occurred through natural selection the history and substance of Originsland is made amenable:

Survival was a basic *instinct* for early humans
The ability to make tools was *handed-down*
The *gift* of speech
Endowed with an artistic sense
A capacity for symbolic thinking was *transmitted*
The *talent* to walk upright separated humans from apes
The *marriage* of large brains and nimble hands resulted in the first tools.

Endowment, with its associated idioms of talents, legacies, marriage and transmission are common ways in which archaeologists conceptualise early hominins and lead us directly to the Human Revolution, when a full set of gifts was acquired (Chapter 2). Not all archaeologists, however, regard this as *the* defining moment (Chapter 1) preferring instead the later Neolithic Revolution when talents were finally used rather than squandered. Endowment is taken for granted and instead the metaphor switches to growth. For instance, Marc Verhoeven (2004:228) uses the metaphor of growth to describe the process of domestication in the Near East through its successive stages of germination, development, growth, retreat, dormancy and florescence.

A more nuanced example is provided by archaeologist Brian Hayden's explanation for agriculture as the result of intensification. In particular he views feasts as an opportunity for people to display their success. He regards the drive to achieve advantage through feasting as 'probably the single most important impetus behind the intensified production of surpluses beyond household needs for survival (2001:27)'. The effect is felt in the needs of child rearing (Owens and Hayden 1997:150) that generate and invest surplus wealth to make exchange and form alliances. Owens and Hayden refer to this process as growth payments (1997:Table 2), where rites of passage involving alterations to the body, such as piercing lips, septum and ears as well as head shaping and tattooing, are all a means by which the social and economic value of the child is increased. In these societies of trans-egalitarian hunters and gatherers blessed with abundant seasonal resources the return on the investment comes at marriage.

These archaeological examples of growth shadow the conceptual imagery of Originsland that draws heavily on biological development and natural events. For example, the natural processes of reproduction and growth metaphorically express:

The *birth* of civilisation
They took their *first steps* towards domestication
At that time the human race was in its *infancy*
The *birthplace* of art
Mesopotamia was the *cradle* of civilisation
Population pressure was the *mother* of invention
The *adoption* of farming
The *dawn* of humankind rose slowly.

What remains familiar is the embodied experience, as in watching daybreak, to understand changes. In this respect we also find that the concept of change is most frequently couched in metaphors of botanical growth and agricultural endeavour:

The *flowering* of culture
They sowed the *seeds* of change
The *tender shoots* of progress
It was only later that the change *bore fruit*

While also being contained in the very substance that surrounds us:

Change was *in* the air.

Primary metaphors of livelihood and change

Metaphors, as Hodder shows with the *domus* and Tilley by drawing associations between monuments and artefacts, can do more than simply describe: they can also explain why and how change occurred. They do this by establishing relations between objects, bodies and habitats. As Gudeman (1986:40) expresses it, these primary, or focal, metaphors provide a dominant idiom that constitutes and expresses events while at the same time being an organising force for a broad range of behaviour (see also Ortner 1973). These are local rather than universal models by which people make sense of things (1986:37). Significantly, 'focal metaphors of livelihood often employ one or another image drawn from the human or social body as well as linked concepts about the "self" in relation to the "other" (Gudeman 1986:142)'. In this book I use two such primary metaphors; the giving-environment and growing-the-body.

The sharing and giving environment

Nurit Bird-David (1992), in her discussion of Marshall Sahlins' (1972) influential essay on hunters and gatherers as the original affluent society, has raised the need for alternative primary metaphors in order to understand this economic category. For example, the corner-store analogy regards hunters as engaged in a game *against* their environment (Jochim 1976). By contrast her analogy, based on fieldwork accounts, is of nature as a co-operative bank (Bird-David 1992:33). This image captures for her the essence of how hunters engage with the natural environment while at the same time embodying the material basis, as well as the cultural aspect, of their economy. The bank symbolises trust and confidence and the natural environment is not providing resistance, as in the game model, but is instead a sharing partner (Bird-David 1992:31). The metaphor of the giving-environment that is my preferred form, provides a relational rather than rational insight into alternative economic realities:

> Whereas we commonly construct nature in mechanistic terms, for them [hunters and gatherers] nature seems to be a set of agencies, simultaneously natural and human-like. Furthermore, they do not inscribe into the nature of things a division between the natural agencies and themselves as we do with our 'nature:culture' dichotomy. They view their world as an integrated entity.
>
> (Bird-David 1992:29−30)

The giving-environment has its own local cosmology and structure. It will structure the manufacture and deployment of tools, and will establish relations between people and objects as well as between these categories, locales and landscapes.

Growing the body

The second primary metaphor I will employ is growing-the-body. This is not simply a description of biological growth, but rather an opportunity to bring the cultural construction of bodies into the material process of change and so address the issue of identity. Bodies are culturally created as well as biologically given. They are a material project and subject to many local models (Gudeman 1986). One example will suffice.

Anne Becker's (1995) anthropological study of feasting in Fiji abounds in images of managed growth. Individuals do not cultivate their own bodies for the reason that prestige is conferred on those with the ability to be generous with food rather than those who possess it (1995:128). Nurturing is a collective activity and indexed in the body that at a personal level is distributed within the individual's embeddedness in the social corpus. Becker makes the comparison with Western bodies where the ethic of bodily cultivation is a personal project while in Fiji the body, self and collective are intimately connected. As a result the Fijian self is located as much in the community as in a body (Becker 1995:133):

> The cultivation of bodies... represents the cumulative efforts of the collective; their care... is embodied in the members of the community. For this reason there is complacency with respect to the self-reflexive cultivation of the personal body, with a complementary motivated interest in nurturing and otherwise caring for others' bodies.
>
> (Becker 1995:129)

Feasting provides a public occasion for nurturing. Archaeologist Michael Dietler (2001) stresses the political nature of feasts where a public and ritual activity is centred on the communal consumption of food and drink. These embodied activities bring together accumulated stores of foods and the material culture necessary to transform them into political action. They are about consumption in a material sense, but also, as the Fijian instance demonstrates, in a symbolic sense by constituting broader social relations (2001:73).

Growing-the-body is not a local model for farmers alone, just as the giving-environment is not the sole territory of hunters and gatherers. I will instead use these metaphors to examine change, not as it is normally conceived in terms of rational economic difference applicable universally, but instead as a relational account with local significance. The task in Part II is to re-embody, rather than re-think, the artefacts for this purpose.

Three revolutions in Originsland

I have now examined how archaeologists use the concept of upheavals in their descriptions and accounts of change. I have placed their usage in a historical context and found that change is best understood not as a property of the archaeology being studied but rather an outcome of contemporary concerns.

The first, Neolithic Revolution was an attempt by Gordon Childe to counter the move to totalitarianism that dominated the history of western Europe and the Soviet Union in the 1930s. To be human was to acknowledge the value of self-government and Childe illustrates this through the transformation of Oriental despotism by their European counterparts. This did not result in democracy in the European Bronze Age but his point is allegorical; absolutist states do not persist and neither do they conquer all before them.

The second, an ancient timing for the Human Revolution, was championed by Ashley Montagu who fought the consequences of statutory and institutional racism with the evidence of history and science. The concept of universal humanity defined by rights and ethics and enshrined in international charters was a device to counter the genocide that had occurred in Europe in the 1940s. Montagu, and those that followed him, concentrated on human evolution because universal humans by definition need a global stage and the study of our earliest ancestry, alone among all the archaeological periods, provides it.

But the good intentions of a declaration of human rights and a statement on race have not weighed heavily on all the member states of the United Nations who signed up to them. The Dark Age that troubled Childe and the Dangerous Myth that Montagu railed against did not go away simply because diplomats agreed that they should. The parallel scientific gesture that included our ancient ancestors under humanity's big tent was by the 1970s also seen as too generous, with the result that taxonomists now excluded fossils from human ancestry. So, a third revolution, Human recency, replaced high antiquity as the time-frame for the development of moral purpose in humans. Our immediate ancestors, those fully modern humans, were truly diasporic when compared to the nearly-humans, anatomically modern but behaviourally ancient. In that diaspora we changed from a local to a global species and from a multiple to a single basic biology. This Human Revolution was not the hyper-diffusion of Grafton Elliott Smith (1929) where every innovation in human history came from one source, Egypt. Biologically we might be Africans but that morphology now varied as a result of the journey from source and culturally more has been added locally than was ever part of an original universal endowment. The paradigm of Recency backed by the framework of revolutions means that to be human is to exclude and to recognise local community and difference as valuable.

These in summary are the changes that archaeologists and palaeoanthropologists have been responding to. I believe that much of what we study is variation rather than what Williams (1965:10) would call a 'genuine revolution', change to novel conditions and interpretation. But the discovery of change, those novel social premises, is due to the process of analysis. While variation and development can be expected as the property of any system, social or biological, change according to my definition above cannot. But the study of change should not be motivated, by the assumption that it will happen sometime because that is the nature of our world. Recognising that change is often a property of the process of archaeological enquiry allows us to distance it from the object of that enquiry, past people.

Revolutions are therefore the right tools only if we continue to believe that change is an essential ingredient of the past and we only have to scrape away at the record to reveal it. But change that made us what we are, humans, as either the result of a Neolithic (aka sedentary, symbolic) Revolution or Human (aka symbolic, behavioural) Revolution is, as Proctor argues, 'the outcome of a number of evidentiary, conceptual, and ideological pressures, having to do with changing understandings of race, time, and brutality' (Proctor 2003:214).

I have now shown that Originsland, the place we construct for the purposes of Origins research, has a very clear structure (Table 3.4). I have argued in Chapter 3 how the two revolutions that divide early human prehistory are serviced by the two major metaphors of endowment and growth. The division between hunters and farmers, described by others as the difference between a passive and active view of history (Bender 1978), is supported metonymically by the way that a concept such as the group

TABLE 3.4. *A map of Originsland. The standard understanding of archaeological change based on the notion of revolutions and the metaphors that underpin origins research*

Concept of change	Human Revolution		Neolithic Revolution	
Metaphor	Endowment		Growth	
Metonymy	Group for species		Group for society	
Analogy/homology	Cognitive *Mental templates*	Biological *Memory and anticipation*	Biological *Population pressure*	Social *Status and rank*
Measurement currency	Energy and reproductive success		Energy and social competition	
Material proxies	Standardisation; Size reduction	Accumulation; Storage	Diversity; Abundance	Complexity; Elaboration
Material projects	Apprenticeship skills	Symbolic representation	Surplus production	Sedentism

refers on the one hand to a species and on the other to society. Modern humans are distinguished from their contemporaries the Neanderthals on the basis of group products that take the form of distinctive stone tools. After the Neolithic Revolution those same, but more varied, group products now lead to a culture history of changing social fortunes as a basket of traits varies across space and through time.

This metaphorical structure is underpinned by analogies drawn from three main sources. The cognitive are regarded as critical for the Human Revolution while the social inform us about those differences in the Neolithic. Added to these are biological analogies that establish a reasoned basis for origins research. They apply to both revolutions and examples would include the extent to which modern humans anticipated future needs and the push from population pressure to change the economic system to one based on domestication. The importance of biology spills over into the currencies that are used since these are dominated by energy although the descriptions alter from reproductive success to competitive advantage.

When it comes to archaeological evidence the structure of Originsland is supported by case studies that examine issues such as standardisation, accumulation, diversity and complexity and how they vary through time. These in turn form a series of material projects that reflect in direct fashion the metaphors of endowment and growth. Hence within the Human Revolution it is skills acquired through long apprenticeships to become flintknappers (Pigeot 1987), or symbolic capabilities revealed by figurative art (Lewis-Williams 2003), which confirm that new endowments had been added. In the Neolithic, growth comes to dominate as with the demonstration of economic surplus production (Gamble 1982a), or the settling down of communities of ever increasing size (Bar-Yosef and Belfer-Cohen 1989).

These are only glimpses of how the structure of Originsland impacts upon archaeological explanation. So, having invented this imaginative geographical space I now want to enhance it by considering our origins in ways that implicate our humanity with our material world.

PART II

The material basis of identity

CHAPTER 4

Bodies, instruments and containers

A bird's wing, comrades, is an organ of propulsion and not of manipulation. It should therefore be regarded as a leg. The distinguishing mark of Man is the hand, the instrument with which he does all his mischief.

Snowball the Pig in George Orwell's *Animal Farm* 1945

First things first

In the timetable of human evolution one thing is widely agreed: objects came before words. When spoken language did appear, and the date is contested, it certainly changed hominin relationships to the world and to other hominins, but did it change everything? What of the world of natural objects and human artefacts that were seen, held, kicked, touched and tasted? Compared to the deep antiquity of material culture, spoken language has a shallower time-depth as indicated by the physical limitations on phonetic speech production as well as the neural re-organisation that was necessary (Deacon 1997).

The earliest stone tools are currently 2.6 million years old (Semaw et al. 1997; Stout et al. 2005) and likely to get older. I believe artefacts will be found back to the last common ancestor six million years ago, and possibly prior to the Old World–New World monkey split another twenty four million years before that. Why? Because the capacity for tool use and even manufacture is shared by a much wider group than the hominins alone (Moura and Lee 2004; McGrew 1992;Chapter 7). *Man the toolmaker* (Oakley 1949) as a description of who we are, has not only met a long overdue gendered death but also passed away in the hands of our primate cousins.

As a result, the social lives of our earliest ancestors need to be placed in a framework where relationships were constructed from material culture, rather than spoken language, and moreover where the actions of the body had comparable weight to the accomplishments of the brain. Tools always solved problems such as how to cut up a rhino or carry water. Our cleverness in this regard is usually presented as the triumph of intelligence over an external environment whose very capriciousness is the stimulus for selection to progress our technology.

Here I am arguing for something different and definitely less Cartesian in its separation of mind from the body and people from the world. Material culture was the evolutionary channel for the construction of relationships with other hominins and, by association, with other objects. Its primary role was to provide a metaphorical understanding of those relationships. Building on the discussion of metaphor in Chapter 3, I will show how this was achieved by 'experiencing one kind of thing in terms of another' (Lakoff and Johnson 1980:5). Technological advances were an unintended consequence of these metaphorical relationships (Chapter 7), where one of the novelties was speech itself. The evolution of rhetorical devices brought us not only bows and buildings but also arrows of desire and shelter from the storm.

My central point is that devices such as metaphor, metonymy, synecdoche and analogy can be expressed materially as well as linguistically. The idea that only with language did previously mute objects and well-trodden landscapes acquire symbolic meaning and cultural significance is therefore misplaced. Language embellished and enhanced. It made possible the richly textured world of myth. But it did not break apart the social worlds of hominins into those who could and could not speak. They remained connected in webs of shared understanding and common experience by material metaphors. In the beginning was the artefact.

Our bodies as a source of metaphor

Metaphor establishes a common understanding between things that are as alien as chalk and cheese. It is the capacity of metaphor to establish conceptual connections between very different categories that makes it so creative in social life. In addition, that power to relate is based on our everyday experience, those facts of personal observation and experience, and is achieved by virtue of our body and its senses.

Take for example the symbolic expression of what goes on inside us. As Martin Hollis (1985:227) put it from a philosopher's perspective, we need metaphors to analyse this hidden, inner being that makes the whole system of human relations run and which involves concepts such as the individual, the self and the person that comprise our distinctively human identity (Chapter 5). How do we look into someone's soul except through their eyes that in turn we regard as similar to windows? Combining a metonymical citation (eyes) for the body-whole with an architectural analogy (windows) shows we understand metaphorically not only where those mysterious inner states are contained, but also how they may be accessed in others.

However, while the body is the natural starting point for the linguist and the philosopher concerned with how we think outside our bodies, why should it also be for the archaeologist studying the remote past?

I can see two compelling reasons. First, starting with the body places an emphasis on continuity rather than revolution. After all, hominins have always had a physical presence (Gamble and Porr 2005b) even if they made no tools and had no spoken language. Furthermore, these bodies produced many varied outcomes, since as Ingold has commented 'the human body is not made for anything (2000:376)'. These outcomes are translated through rhythms based on gestures, sounds, smells, taste, touch and sight, commonly described as a series of 'scapes'; bodyscapes, soundscapes, mindscapes, taskscapes, landscapes and sensescapes (Gibson 1979; Ingold 1993b), to which I will add another, the childscape, in Chapter 8. These unite, rather than separate the body from the surrounding world, so that instead of being *in* space and time, our body *inhabits* space and time (Merleau-Ponty 1962).

The second reason to emphasise the body as the basis for understanding the conventions of social life is its identification as the source of social agency (Hamilakis et al. 2002b) because it is simultaneously a biological and cultural object. Agency carries a variety of meanings for archaeologists (Dobres 2000; Dobres and Robb 2000). It has however been succinctly defined by sociologist Anthony Giddens as 'the act of doing' (1984:10), and here I use it to refer to the skills of making relationships into material and conceptual categories.

As a result, at all times and places, the present included, the body has combined biology and culture. The two elements cannot be sensibly prised apart to be analysed in isolation and then re-assembled. Instead, they must be considered together like strands in a cable, threads in an argument. By starting with the body rather than the mind, and with actions rather than thoughts, we need neither the Human and Neolithic Revolutions nor an origin point for the 'cultural' or the 'symbolic'.

Symbolic force and a social technology of the body

Anthropologist Michael Rowlands (2004:198) identifies two closely linked strategies that produce changing identities. *Materiality* attributes agency to subjects and objects and works back from a particular effect to an original cause. In such an approach, he writes, 'we start from the premise that things have some a priori existence' (Rowlands 2004), even though people and things are encountered in a mutually constitutive sense. This anthropological and phenomenological approach finds its champions in Marcel Mauss and Maurice Merleau-Ponty. The second strategy, *materialism*, is associated with Karl Marx, where the question of identity is posed in terms of formation and how the actions of making and doing constitute, as a process, both consciousness and things.

The distinctions are important when it comes to the study of change. As Rowlands (2004:197) points out, materialism sees radical breaks in history while materiality stresses continuity between different power structures in the modern world. Archaeologists, myself included, borrow from both traditions and as we saw in Part I revolution and continuity both have their supporters with regard to the major tipping points in prehistory. Where I believe a bigger division comes is between those who see semiology as the way to both chart and explain change either in the Human Revolution (Deacon 1997; Lewis-Williams 2003; Marshack 1990), the Neolithic Revolution (Cauvin 2000; Renfrew 2001; Watkins 2004a,b), or in the later power plays of state polities (Knappett 2005), and those who are less concerned with signs and symbols but instead with establishing metaphorical connections (Boivin and Owoc 2004; Jones 2002; Parker-Pearson and Ramilisonina 1998; Thomas 1996; Tilley 1999). The latter have been criticised (Knappett 2005:102) for not incorporating semiotic theory and its variable pathways through icon, index and symbol into an understanding of how material culture comes to be meaningful. Metaphor, it seems, is overprivileged as a device for creating meaning.

However, I do not necessarily see meaning as the central issue but rather the demonstration of relationships between people and things. To that extent semiotics is a later and more finely grained stage in the process of understanding change through the material basis of identity, and perhaps one better suited to archaeological periods where the possession of language, so central to semiotics, is not an issue. As archaeologists Michael Parker-Pearson and Ramilisonina (1998:310) point out in their reappraisal of Stonehenge using analogies from Madagascar, the meaning of things is arbitrary but the physical properties (e.g. hard,

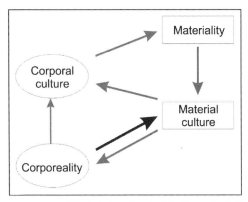

FIGURE 4.1. The hybrid network of bodies and artefacts that constitutes symbolic force. The thickness of the arrow indicates the dominant relationship in the two recursive triangles. The outcome is a social technology rather than just a set of functional techniques. (Gamble 2004:Figure 8.1.)

soft, smooth, rough) of materials, such as stone and wood, resist some interpretations and invite others. It is this materiality of the tangible world that may be a significant element in how metaphorical associations come to be made and where the non-tangible basis of semiotics obscures insight.

At issue for the metaphorical approach I favour is how the body becomes something else — in this instance a material thing? Such transformations are part of a wider process where objects become symbols with widely shared meanings that co-ordinate human action.

Elsewhere I have looked at this question using the concept of symbolic force:

> By symbolic force I mean that mainspring for action where we are both engaged with, and constituted by, the world of objects, artefacts and ecofacts distributed across landscapes and in locales.
>
> (Gamble 2004:85)

The point of reference, where the symbols are grounded-out in the experience of the real world (Anderson 2003:92), is the body. This relationship is expressed in Figure 4.1 as a network of relationships. Here I have added some complementary terms, corporeality and corporal culture, to those that are most commonly encountered, materiality and material culture.

The network expresses the transformation from corporeality to materiality and provides an answer to the question — how do objects acquire symbolic force? – through experiences and sensations that are embodied. However, although corporeality is not an origin point, in the sense discussed in the previous chapter, it is the source for the kind of comparative phenomenology an archaeologist requires in order to tackle issues of change. The outcome, as described by anthropologist Pierre Lemonnier (1993) is a social technology:

> As soon as we consider that techniques are not something to which some meaning is simply added, but a complex phenomenon in which wide symbolic considerations are involved from the start, it becomes tricky to separate the 'technical' from the 'social'.
>
> (1993:4)

Corporeality is not a traditional origin point for the reason that we never proceed directly from there to materiality in a simple act of transformation. That would imply a sort of transubstantiation, a laying-on-of-hands to imbue artefacts with the power to act on our behalf. Instead both material culture, the active world of objects, and corporal culture, orchestrate the exchange.

I start with corporeality because as anthropologist Marcel Mauss (1979:104) pointed out in 1935, 'the body is man's first and most natural instrument. Or more accurately...man's first and most natural technical object, and at the same time technical means, is his body'. The direction in the diagram is therefore *from* bodies *to* artefacts because without corporeality there can be no material culture, and without corporal culture there can be no symbolic force or materiality. Symbolic force is therefore not inherent in bodies, objects or things. Neither is it something to be found or even identified. Importantly in the context of this book, it has no point of origin. Symbolic force is instead an emergent property of the necessary relationships of human social life because that life flows in a hybrid rather than a pure network (see below).

The relationship between these four terms is also clearly understood. Corporeality is the source of the metaphorical relationships that involve how we act (corporal culture) and what we act with (material culture). In order for the relationship to create sense the path is from corporeality to material culture, then to corporal culture and lastly to materiality. The process is iterative in that materiality plays on material culture but the essential point is that materiality is the product of action, not an inherent property of action. It is in this way that any charge of essentialism is avoided.

Time for habitus

Corporal culture consists of those habitual techniques, skills and memories that are dependent on the properties of the body and its social and cultural context. This is what Mauss ((1936) 1979:101) called the *habitus*. He chose the term to emphasise the social importance of bodily techniques which might be regarded as rather mundane – swimming, digging, digesting, marching – except that they structure much of our lives.

The concept of *habitus* is better known from Pierre Bourdieu's (1977:53) description as practices laid down by repeated action and everyday routines over days, months and years in a person's lifetime, rather like the sediment in a river. These practices are made up of durable dispositions towards particular perceptions and practices; for example the sexual division of labour, morality, tastes and many others (Jones 1997:88). With the concept of *habitus* the recurrent patterns of artefacts in time and space that give a distinctive form to the past (Childe 1929:v–vi), can be re-interpreted as the actions of social agents instead of the imperatives of an innate ethnicity (Jones 1997).

Habitus, as archaeologist Chris Gosden describes it, is our 'second nature', what Bourdieu calls a 'feel for the game': 'People produce thought, perception and action without thinking about how they are doing so, but in a manner which has its own inherent logic' (Gosden 1999:125–6).

Maurice Merleau-Ponty puts the phenomenological case as follows:

> The body is our general medium for having a world. Sometimes it is restricted to the actions necessary for the conservation of life, and accordingly it posits around us a biological world; at other times, elaborating upon these primary actions and moving from their literal to a figurative meaning, it manifests through them a core of new significance; this is true of motor habits such as dancing. Sometimes, finally, the meaning aimed at cannot be achieved by the body's natural means; it must then build itself an instrument, and it projects thereby around itself a cultural world. At all levels it performs the same function which is to endow the instantaneous expressions of spontaneity with 'a little renewable action and independent existence'. Habit is merely a form of this fundamental power. We say that the body has understood, and habit acquired when it has absorbed a new meaning, and assimilated a fresh core of significance.
>
> (Merleau-Ponty 1962:146)

The routines which contribute to *habitus* are part of our practical, rather than discursive, consciousness (Giddens 1984; Leroi-Gourhan 1993);

the things we largely do without thinking, referred to by Gosden in an archaeological context as a landscape of habit (Gamble 1999:81, Chapter 3; 1994). Indeed, archaeologists have been particularly interested in the concept of the *habitus* (e.g. Dobres and Robb 2000; Hamilakis et al. 2002a) because through materiality the body becomes just another artefact.

But *habitus* is so much more than a set of muscle memories or a suite of gestures in a visual body language. As art historian Joaneath Spicer, in her study of the attitudes struck by people in Renaissance art, puts it:

> Written references [late 15th to 17th centuries] to gestures associated with the elbow are largely limited to admonitions to restrain them, and thus they fit more easily under the controversial heading of 'natural' as 'opposed to 'taught'. . . They are for that no less expressive of 'the motions of the mind'; nor no less rewarding to decode than those long identified from the canon of ritual or rhetoric.
>
> (Spicer 1991: 84)

Being 'given the elbow', or finding 'elbow room' are uses of embodied experience to express personal relationships in a familiar context. Elbows are therefore material metaphors for a range of emotions from aggression to submission that far transcends the anatomical structure that combines distal humerus and proximal radius-ulna. Elbows are cultural objects, whose use as metaphors have changed in the past and vary between cultures today. It is through such cultural comparison that the 'feel for the game' becomes apparent and where the durability and embodied character of silent action is revealed. And if the elbow is a metaphorical statement then why not artefacts such as pots that are known to embody beliefs (Sterner 1989:458) but where elbows are nowhere to be seen?

Symbolic force and culture

My network diagram (Figure 4.1) examines how objects and artefacts acquire meaning through the generation of symbolic force grounded-out in the body. To do so I have also emphasised the importance of metaphor in connecting different categories so that they become intelligible through bodily experience. However, there is a further step to take that dissolves the rational Cartesian distinction between a world of people and one of objects and things. What emerges are balanced relationships between living and inanimate categories. But why should artefacts be treated in particular ways − with respect, love, contempt, desire − as though they were people?

TABLE 4.1. *A pure relationship*

	People	Objects and things
People	*Yes*	*No*

Pure culture

At issue here is the difference between what might be termed a pure as opposed to a hybrid view of culture. In a rational approach categories such as animate:inanimate cannot be mixed when it comes to establishing relationships of meaning. Why? Because 'it stands to reason' that sheep are not people and stones cannot speak.

Consequently there is no relation to the world other than through flesh and blood people. It is only the relation of people to people that produces a social relationship, indicated by the 'Yes' in the matrix (Table 4.1). In other words you can use objects and things but you don't relate to them. Only the non-Cartesian, so-called 'primitive', mind could believe in animism and so literally talk to the trees as if they were alive (Bird-David 1999).

I have difficulty in believing that such a situation ever existed (see also Latour 1993:380; Toren 1999:4). During hominin evolution objects have played a central role in the construction and mediation of social life. The contexts might have differed but artefacts when animated, held in the hand and worn on the body, would always have acted in a relational way to the agent. While in close proximity such objects would have become extensions of the individual, changing the boundaries of their bodies, as happens for example when clothes are put on. Denying relationships between people, objects and things is not possible. The pure social relation, as described here, never existed.

Alfred Gell provides a typically robust anthropological rebuttal to the rational standpoint:

> 'Social agents' can be drawn from categories which are as different as chalk and cheese ... because 'social agency' is not defined in terms of 'basic' biological attributes (such as inanimate thing vs. incarnate person) but is *relational* – it does not matter, in ascribing 'social agent' status, what a thing (or person) 'is' in itself; what matters is where it stands in a network of social relations.
>
> (Gell 1998:123, my emphasis)

TABLE 4.2. *A hybrid relationship*

	People	Objects and things
People	*Yes*	*Yes*
Objects and things	*Yes*	*Yes*

In other words people, manufactured objects and things such as trees are not distinct categories based on biology or the possession of life. Rocks, trees and animals are all examples of material culture and as such can be part of relational networks (Strathern 1996; 1998), as well as relating to each other independently of people. For example, a hen-house is built by people. But the hens that live in it have a relation to those surroundings which conditions their actions when the chicken farmer is far away. Orwell's political satire *Animal Farm* depends, once Farmer Jones is expelled, upon the developing relationship between the pigs and the farmhouse and the other animals and their barn: a good example of how, with hybrid culture, the rational distinctions governing relationships quickly break down. What emerges in turn is a network of relationships between people, things and objects or, more simply, networks of material culture.

Hybrid culture

Dispensing with pure relationships opens the gates, or at least the hen-house door, to metaphorical understandings. The mental leap is not that great if assisted by Cristina Toren's (1999:12) characterisation of mind as 'a function of the whole person constituted over time in inter-subjective relations with others in the environing world'. A view that regards cognition as a metaphorical process of seeing something *as* something (Tilley 1999:34).

But who exactly are these 'others' that Toren talks about once the mind:body distinction has been junked? Here the concept of *hybrid culture* (Gosden 1999) is particularly useful because it combines people and objects and accords agency to both (Table 4.2). Consequently there are no 'others'. They are all implicated in our developmental process (Ingold 2000:390), growing as we grow. As a result, artefacts in hybrid culture have biographies (Chapter 5). The artefacts we make and the things we interact with such as trees, animals, rocks and hills are not, as a Cartesian perspective implies, simply passive while flesh and blood people alone are active agents. The core of hybrid culture is that relations are formed, as archaeologist Carl Knappett (2006) points out, with objects and things because we are engaged with the world in a relational rather than a detached way (see Rowlands 2004). Such a view is initially hard to accept precisely because most of us have been raised and trained to think in terms of those key oppositions such as mind and matter, subject and object. As a result we know that a carved statue is not alive so how can it have agency in the way that you and I as living beings can?

Gell (1998:96) provided an answer for one category of material culture, art. He argued that, for an anthropologist, art must be treated as person-like because it represents both sources of and targets for agency. Now, what applies to art also relates to our hand-crafted bodies, to the bespoke objects and artefacts that we make, as well as to things that we find in the world. Consequently artefacts and things draw their symbolic force from association with agents and in particular with the relationships they have with our bodies.

It is also misleading to present these relationships as lopsided. Viewed rationally, the respect:hate relationship I have with my computer should be a one-way process in a simple network of domination between subject and object. However as Knappett (2006:241) puts it,

> Neither is it the case that people have the upper hand in these networks, merely manipulating materials as they see fit; agency is distributed between humans and nonhumans such that we have to tackle them *symmetrically* rather than assume from the outset an unbalanced relationship.

Hybrid culture takes our cognitive ability to see something *as* something, the basis of metaphorical understanding, and logically concludes that in terms of materiality, something *is* somebody.

Material metaphors of the body; some examples of a social technology

The following three examples will help to clarify the power of material metaphors. They are drawn from ethnography and deal with houses, masks and kinship networks. In all cases the body, and in particular its ability to contain, is used as the source of the metaphor. In so doing connections are forged among hybrid categories and a pattern of relationships is established that has evident applications to a study of change on an archaeological time-scale.

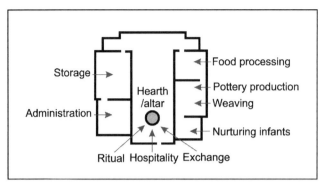

FIGURE 4.2. The tripartite house as an extended metaphor in the Late 'Ubaid of Mesopotamia 5000–4300 BC' (after Wengrow 1998:Figure 3). During this period the metaphor of the household was extended to administrative, productive and ritual actions that created, according to David Wengrow, a new work ethic and greater overall output.

Houses as bodies

The house is a material metaphor that all agree upon.

> The house is a body for the body. Houses are bodies because they are containers which, like the body, have entrances and exits. Houses are cavities filled with living contents. Houses are bodies because they have strong bones and armoured shells, because they have gaudy mesmerizing skins which beguile and terrify; and because they have organs of sense and expression – eyes which peer out through windows and spyholes, voices which reverberate through the night. To enter a house is to enter a mind, a sensibility.
>
> (Gell 1998:252–3)

The house is the ultimate container of people, livestock, tools and memories. Houses are carved, wall-papered, added-to and repaired. They are quintessential biographical objects, growing, changing and eventually dying. They are culturally relative. One person's Golden Hall is another's thatched barn. And almost coincidentally, they keep out the wind and rain.

Their construction, as is the case with a Maori communal meeting house, is a social project that in Gell's terms is not so much a symbol of the people who built it but instead an index of their collective agency, an idea that is ancestral and political in tone (Gell 1998:253). But houses are also maps of social relations (Figure 4.2) (Carsten and Hugh-Jones 1995; Denyer 1978; Morgan 1881; Wilson 1988). In societies as diverse as the Dogon of Mali (Griaule 1965) and the English aristocracy (West 1999) the layout of houses has been analysed in terms of embodiment, lifecycles, cosmology and social organisation. Houses are containers of successive human bodies and houses are people, an extension of the person and the self (West 1999:105−6).

Houses are one material metaphor that archaeologists have explored, either as a general concept of social and political change such as the *domus* (Hodder 1990), (see Chapter 3), or in Trevor Watkins' work among the earliest villages of Southwest Asia. One of Watkins' articles has the evocative title 'Building houses, framing concepts, constructing worlds' (2004b) that refers to his favoured co-evolution of human cognition and material culture into 'theatres of memory' (Watkins 2004b) during the Neolithic Revolution. Furthermore, the houses of the dead are as much explored for their ritual and metaphorical structure as those of the living (Bradley 2002; Rainbird 1999; Thomas 1996; Tilley 1996; Whittle 1996; 2003).

Masks and faces

Masks are also containers, face-houses if you like. Mauss used the example of the mask (Hollis 1985), common in all cultures, to illustrate the concept and category of self and person (Chapter 5), the material *im*personation of the identities within. Masks have attracted much attention from anthropologists precisely because of the inner structure they allude to and the social collective they represent, as in the elaborate Kwakiutl shutter masks (Isaac 1990:124−5) that contain a mask within a mask. Mauss (1979a) used these to illustrate how totems were personified by the wearer. The collective embodiment is expressed by Edward Carpenter:

> Eskimo are conventional role-players, faithful mask-wearers. Wearing a mask means to divest, not express, oneself. A mask or role is not an extension of its wearer so much as a putting on of the collective powers of the audience. The speaker assumes the collective mask of the image he presents. He manifests a corporate attitude toward life.
>
> (Carpenter 1973:198)

In archaeology masks, when they occur, are regarded as particularly valuable. In prehistory they are often used as part-for-whole interpretations, allowing us to meet head-on the person as in a portrait or a photograph of a face. During his excavations at Mycenae that began in 1874 Heinrich Schliemann believed he had found the face of Agamemnon. This golden mask justified, at least for him, the use of Homeric myths as historical facts.

However, if his famous telegram had read, 'I have gazed on Agamemnon's boot', rather than his face, his discoveries would have attracted less attention.

Masks are biographical as well as ritual objects and according to Ronald Grimes (1992:62) can be distinguished by seven phases; making, wearing, encountering, removing, exchanging, displaying and destroying. The point, however, is not that face masks are a material route to the inner self. They are not an external expression of that universal sense of self or of the wider concept of a social self. Why should face masks or animal masks be any different to, say, antique portraiture which superficially seems to flesh out the character of Roman matriarchs? The fact that masks often take on the shape of faces is immaterial. Hoods and hats can serve just as well and like masks they derive their symbolic force from the highly charged corporal culture of the head, at once both instrument and container. Moreover, many other forms of material culture, such as clothes and houses, contain the body.

Therefore masks are not a special category of material culture, a point Mauss was well aware of in his discussion of personhood as was Gell (1998) in his consideration of the agency of art. Instead much of material culture is mask-like. Not in the simple sense that it reflects our inner self in an external fashion, or that our roles are inherent in material culture so that if we don Zorro's mask we become Zorro. It is instead the hybrid networks, composed of people, things and objects, by which we constitute our social lives and fathom our inner selves which produce the masks. When worn, the mask is the person. When taken off the person is the mask. Distinguishing between the two is neither practical nor possible. Our skin is as much a container as our clothes. The pen is as much an instrument as our fingers.

Kinship networks

Kinship is the cultural categorisation of relatedness. This might be decided by biological closeness — mothers and daughters, father's brothers — or, as is often the case, it may be an entirely fictive category, such as an 'aunty' who is only a friend of the family and where no biological relationship exists. A network is a common model to describe the differences and ramifications of such elementary schemes. Both provide examples of the body as a metaphor to construct relatedness between people.

For example, anthropologist Wendy James (2003:158) reminds us that Old Anglo-Saxon kinship mapped relationships via proliferating segments of the body; head (father and mother), neck (sibs), shoulder, elbow, wrist, fingers and nails (cousins of increasing remoteness). These form a cognitive technology (Enfield 2005) and it is common to find, when people are talking about kin, that they use a range of hand gestures to emphasise social distance; for example pointing with an outstretched arm to indicate distant relatives. As a result, the categories of social distance are understood in an entirely experiential way. Such reckoning is often formalised in the equally experiential layout of settlements that might vary from the ephemeral camps of the Ju/huaonsi in the Kalahari (Johnson 1978; Whitelaw 1994; Yellen 1977) to pastoral and horticultural villages (Cribb 1991; Strathern 1998) in many parts of the world.

Network is another of those words, like revolution (Chapter 1), that changed its meaning as rational approaches gained ground following the lead of Descartes in the seventeenth century. Its original usage was to describe thread in the French silk trade (Fr. *réseau*; Eng. *net-work* was spun from the same trade term) but by the early nineteenth century it had come to describe the spatial form of a communication system. Armand Mattelart (1999) has traced the strands that over two centuries transformed its meaning. The change began with anatomists and ended with the first social scientists, while along the way military engineers played a role. The anatomists co-opted the word network to describe, for the first time, the circulation of blood in the body and the dendritic, tree-like structures of our arteries and nerves. They regarded the body as the archetype of rationality and related each part to the functioning of the whole. The social scientists, and in particular Claude Henri de Saint Simon, took this metaphor of the living body to portray the political economy. The body politic was an organic network where changes in one organ or institution would affect the health of the nation. Along the way, as Mattelart (1999:170−4) shows, the development in military engineering, particularly siege warfare, produced the network of trenches, lines of communications and ultimately border fortifications that again defined, like a protective skin, the outer limits of the body of the state.

A network is a container. Along its channels flow information, individuals and goods. It connects people and objects and establishes spatial patterns of relatedness between cultural categories that are often very different. One example is provided by that most anthropological of all concepts, a kinship network.

Kinship systems are highly technical in many societies (Fox 1967) and appear unduly complicated to Western eyes where knowing who your significant relatives are is comparatively simple. However, whatever the

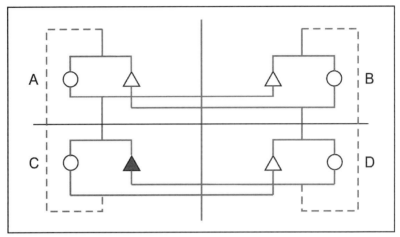

FIGURE 4.3. Tetradic kinship structure. For purposes of illustration Ego is represented by the black triangle. All Ego's sibs (*circles* sisters, female cousins; *triangles* brothers, male cousins) are also in C and they all marry in D. Their father's generation is in A (uncles and aunts) and their mother's (aunts and uncles) in B. The dotted lines show how the offspring of one generation is recruited into the next culturally recognised generation (Allen 1995; 1998). I have added the heavy lines to emphasise the compartmentalised structure. Tetradic kinship structures are commonly known as section systems and found throughout Australia and many other parts of the world.

complexity there is an underlying, container-based logic (Figure 4.3) that separates culturally significant categories and most importantly who you can and cannot marry. Anthropologist Nick Allen (1995; 1998) has described this as a tetradic model that combines the horizontal axis of the category *generation* with the vertical one of *descent*. The rules are then very simple (see also Lévi-Strauss 1969). Someone in Box C can only marry somebody in Box D and in an earlier generation their mothers and fathers followed the same rule by marrying between Boxes A and B. The children of marriages in C and D are recruited into the next cultural generation and so on as society is produced and re-produced. The names and associations that are given to these four boxes in any particular society all boil down to their function as containers of bodies and a metaphor for reproduction and relatedness.

The body-whole as an inspiration for a social technology

These three examples point to the relatedness between people and material culture. They also illustrate why I favour an embodied cognition where meanings and symbols are not just an intellectual endeavour of our minds. Our mobility, as Merleau-Ponty (1962:139) ringingly reminds us 'is not, as it were, a handmaid of consciousness, transporting the body to that point in space of which we have formed a representation beforehand'. But how often in accounts of human evolution (Table 3.3) do we find that the appearance of bipedalism advances the interests of the brain to confront new challenges (e.g. Lovejoy 1981), or that manual dexterity merely mechanically follows a mental template of what should be made (e.g. Schick and Toth 1993), like 'playing' a pianola?

The alternative is to reject such rational models and reassert the relationships that come from considering the body-whole. Brains do not tell the feet what to do. Indeed our toes are as en-minded as our brains are em-bodied. Parts of our anatomy have different functions but they do not have essential properties as implied in the Cartesian master and servant relationship of intellect and action. Our body does not impose instincts upon us from birth, but it does give our lives a common structure by developing our personal acts into 'stable dispositional tendencies' (Merleau-Ponty 1962:146) that can be termed *habitus*. What we understand by meaning cannot be just a mental activity but needs to incorporate the body-whole as well as the world it inhabits. Now, to understand this world we need those metaphors that establish the links between concepts based on the experience of the body.

We have therefore arrived at the crux of the matter. How do artefacts, and material culture generally, acquire symbolic force within a social technology? My answer does not take the semiotics route since, as we have seen, meaning is largely arbitrary. Instead the reply is made by categorising the actions of the body into two basic forms; instruments and containers. These are the proxies that move us from material to corporal culture (Figure 4.1), by resisting some interpretations and inviting others.

The distinction I draw is a simple one. It is based on the metaphorical projection of the body to understand how corporeality leads to materiality through the intermediaries of corporal and material culture as shown in Figure 4.4.

Our limbs are primarily engaged in corporal culture as *instruments* while the trunk of our body is a *container*. Instruments, in the form of hands and feet, inscribe. They make marks. Containers, the trunk, are frequently the surfaces for such inscription including tattoos, body painting and incisions. The trunk is also a literal container for embodiment as in eating and child-bearing. But the homology of the body-whole is never forgotten. The limbs also provide surfaces for inscription and of course they contain bone, blood

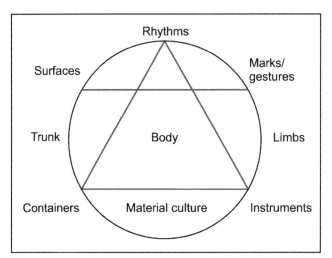

FIGURE 4.4. The metaphorical structure of corporal and material culture.

and muscle beneath the skin just as the trunk contains heart, lungs and liver. In the same way the trunk, and most importantly the head, can also be used as an instrument.

The material proxies of the body: instruments and containers

A wide range of corporal culture in the form of body techniques and routine rhythms results from agency, the act of doing. Moreover, at the same time as this variety is created material culture is also produced. Agency arises because human identity is always implicated in networks of materiality. As a result we can begin to see from this basic network (Figure 4.1) how artefacts and objects acquire symbolic force through their reference to the instruments and containers of the body-whole. For the archaeologist these artefacts are material proxies for the body and its agency in the construction of identity. From our perspective we can recover the material proxies but the rest remains hidden rather like the identity of the self, as we shall see in Chapter 5.

Material proxies and the limitations of analogy

These material proxies are arrived at by analogy. We know from ethnography and our own experience that the same generic forms of artefacts, with very similar functions, can be made from very different resources

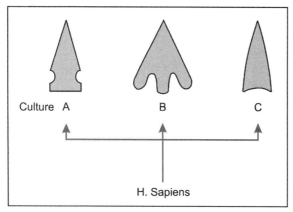

FIGURE 4.5. Analogy and homology applied to a set of different shaped arrowheads.

rather than share a common origin. For example, *bowls* are made from stone, wood, glass, cardboard, bone, plastic, fibre, metal, skin and ceramic materials; *knives* from bamboo, bone, metal, stone, glass, wood, plastic and ceramic materials. But of course, as an inspection of your cutlery drawer and crockery collection will reveal, the same raw material can provide many dissimilar homologues in artefact shape and form even though their function may be comparable.

But analogy can be confused with homology when trying to account for variation among the artefacts and cultures of the past precisely because these entities are expected to behave biologically (Table 3.2). The confusion lies in deciding on the origin, or ancestor, of the material outcome. That origin might be traced to a particular hominin species that made three distinctive types of arrowhead (Figure 4.5). But the origin of each arrowhead type might also be linked to three contemporary but separate archaeological cultures even though they were all made by the same biological species. The biological analogy would apply to the cultures (different origin) so long as the functions of the arrowheads were regarded as similar. Conversely, the biological homology would apply to the hominin species (common origin) so long as the outcome of the arrowheads, in this case their shapes, were regarded as dissimilar.

This is an important point so let me provide another artefact example to illustrate the differences. This time it will be wooden bowls and pottery bowls which, although made of different materials, have the same function, to hold soup (Figure 4.6). However, their origin from lumps of wood and clay is dissimilar. This starting point means that their method of

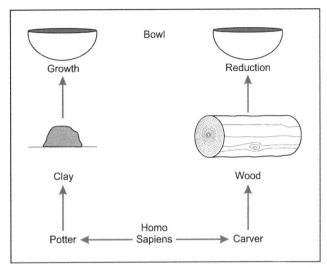

FIGURE 4.6. Similar outcomes from either dissimilar (raw material and technique) or similar (the artisan) origins.

manufacture will also differ. The wooden bowl was made by revealing a form within a piece of wood, rather like a sculptor carving a statue. In contrast to such a sequence of reduction the potter builds up the shape of the bowl from the clay.

If we take the point of origin as the raw material the artefacts were made from, then the difference between wood and clay makes any interpretation of the bowls analogous (Table 3.2). But what if the point of origin is shifted to the agent, the carver and potter who might conceivably even be the same person? Even if not they would very definitely be members of the same biological species, *Homo sapiens*. According to Table 3.2 this would make it an interpretation by homology.

But what about a situation where everything seems to be homologous with respect to origin? This would be achieved if we stuck with one origin, clay, and contrasted pottery plates and bowls. Both forms are made from clay and both are built up rather than reduced. However their functions are different. So, what accounts for such variation? Is it internal, the decision of the potter or external, driven by market forces, use and social dictates? Deciding which will never be simple or easy.

Now this is all very well but a moment's reflection reveals it to be extremely limited. What the archaeologist wants to know is not that plates and bowls are homologous or analogous but rather why there should be so many varieties of each functional category, what determined the choice

TABLE 4.3. *A metaphorical basis for the study of archaeological change*

Concept of change		Identity	
Metaphor	Chapter 3	**The body**	
	Chapter 5	Accumulation and enchainment	
Metonymy		**Limbs as corporal instruments**	**Trunk and head as corporal containers**
Analogy/homology	Chapter 3	Cognitive, Biological, Social	
Measurement 'currency'	Chapter 6	Fragmentation and consumption	
Material proxies	Chapter 7	**Instruments**	**Containers**
Material projects	Chapter 8	Sets and nets	

The highlighted terms are those discussed in this chapter. Further concepts will be developed in later chapters and the central issue of identity will be more fully explored in Chapter 5.

of wood or clay and, most importantly, will it ever be possible to decide why the choices were made (Gosselain 1999)? And it is at this stage that the biological metaphor which initiated the process of comparison starts to implode under its assumption that culture is under the same selective pressures as the structure of the hand of bats and humans. The people we need to return to are those potters and carvers and not the cultural identities we assign them on account of the materials they work with. What exactly are these bowls and knives proxies for?

Material proxies of the body

The answer is that bowls and knives are material proxies for the containers and instruments of corporal culture, the trunk and limbs of the body itself.

The relationships of the various terms are set out in Table 4.3. Deciding on which category an item of material culture belongs to takes into account the surfaces of containers (the head and trunk) and the inscription wrought by instruments (the limbs). As I showed with the examples of networks, houses and masks the metaphorical links are commonly drawn between bodies and distinctive forms of material culture. But where ethnographers rely on conversations with the makers and users of artefacts to establish their

TABLE 4.4. *Examples of the material proxies of the body*

Instruments: knives, sticks, pestles, spears, ploughs, arrows, drills, chisels, axes, shuttles, looms, needles, chop-sticks, jewellery, brushes, pens, wheels, long-bones
Containers: bowls, pits, houses, barns, caves, pots, baskets, bags, quivers, mortars, blowpipes, rifles, clothes, moulds, jewellery, graves, tombs, masks, skulls

metaphorical connections to the body (e.g. Enfield 2005; Gosselain 1999), archaeologists cannot, and hence the need for material proxies.

Bowls, knives and arrowheads are just three examples. Instruments and containers abound in material culture. Table 4.4 lists a few examples of the generic, analogous forms. Several of those listed are to be found in the check-lists of both the Human and Neolithic Revolutions (Chapters 1 and 2) and are fully discussed in Chapter 7.

This basic classification allows us to understand the difference between material and corporal culture. The former abounds with analogies because involvement with objects, as in the example of the many kinds of materials used in the manufacture of bowls and knives, can be infinitely varied as the cultures of the world, past and present, so amply demonstrate. Bodies, viewed as materials, are however less varied. Of course they can be elaborated through inscription, mutilation and adornment but the material basis remains the same, hence the homological references. But less material variety does not make understanding corporal culture any easier. As Mauss ((1936)1979:98) first pointed out, this is precisely because we expect a uniformity based on biology but are instead rewarded with diverse cultural biographies for even such obvious actions as walking, swimming and digging.

We can continue the instrument/container homology to consider how these different forms of material culture either grow or fragment the body. The body provides a surface for inscription as well as a resource that can be abridged.

- Growth through inscription: e.g. tattoos, cicatrices, body-painting.
- Fragmentation through abridgement: e.g. tooth evulsion, trephination, circumcision, shaving, clipping nails, cutting hair.

Growth can also occur through the addition of jewellery or clothes to the body. The position of ornaments also divides the body into sections, while jewellery can be broken up and distributed by taking the string away from the pearls in a necklace. At every turn in this entangled exercise we see how the concept of the body-whole is re-affirmed through hybrid networks of bodies, objects and things.

The interesting case of heads and jewellery

You will have noticed in Table 4.4 that jewellery can be both a container (necklace) and an instrument (pin). This is also the case with heads. They are containers for many of the senses and the mind but they can also head footballs and rub noses and are therefore instruments. Heads and jewellery emphasise the overlapping character of relational networks constructed from material culture and corporal culture, and consequently dispel any thoughts that containers and instruments is just another dualism.

Jewellery and body ornament points to the homology in material culture and the following outcomes.

- Those items of jewellery which enclose or encircle parts of the body: e.g. bracelets, rings, necklaces, penis sheaths. These are homologous to containers.
- Those items which pierce: e.g. earrings, labrets, nose and lip plugs which are homologous to instruments.

Piercing your navel or putting a metal stud in your tongue shows how instruments cross-cut, as I would expect, the categorisation of the body into instrument (limbs and head) and container (trunk and head). Therefore no single position on the body determines an absolute material response.

Summary: the human body as a metaphor for changing identity

Behind my discussion of metaphors, and the re-orientation they provide for many of the concepts used in human evolution and Palaeolithic archaeology, is a simple proposition: that any study of change has to acknowledge the material basis of human identity. I showed in Chapters 1 and 2 that the so-called revolutionary changes of hunter to farmer or nomad to villager are not conveniently reflected in what people made, used and left behind. There are no simple material proxies for these general, historical identities although many have been put forward; among them ground stone for farmers, tents for nomads and stone-tipped spears for hunters. Neither are there easy correlations between items of material culture and more nuanced identities subsumed by age, gender and sexuality (Meskell 1999; Sofaer Deverenski 2000).

In this chapter I have set out the case for grounding our rhetorical devices (metaphor, metonymy and analogy) in the body to produce an alternative analytical structure (Table 4.3). This scheme is relational in its standpoint and can be contrasted to the rational framework of change that I discussed in Part I (Table 3.4). The differences in the two approaches are clear. In a relational approach people construct rather than receive their identities. As discussed in the Prologue, the production of identity therefore depends on context and human agency (Dobres and Robb 2000). But agency, most readily understood as the capacity to relate, does not change. That is dependent upon interpretations by social agents of the relationships between people and things in the world of human experience. My task in the next two chapters is to explore two different metaphors for social practice, accumulation and enchainment (Chapter 5), and then assess social actions through fragmentation and consumption (Chapter 6).

Consider the alternative rational approach as enshrined in the two revolutions. For the Human Revolution a key change to our identity was language, irrespective of when it appeared. For the Neolithic Revolution it is the enriched symbolic world of sedentism when human creative potential was, after a long gestation, finally realised. Accordingly both language and sedentism broke with the past and meaning was created. The approach I have taken here to that same material evidence is already suggesting a different scenario.

Instruments and containers have great antiquity and have always been referenced to the body. Therefore, cultural meaning has no origin point among the hominins. Material metaphors that understand the world in terms of experience have always been a consequence of hominin bodies inhabiting space and time. Moreover, we know that material proxies for the containers and instruments of the body pre-date their linguistic utterance. It is therefore time to investigate those past inner identities that I believe can be accessed by archaeologists through material proxies.

The accumulation and enchainment of identity

> *One can draw an analogy between the way societies construct individuals and the way they construct things*
>
> Igor Kopytoff *The cultural biography of things* 1986

Art forms, body forms and hidden identities

Archaeologists give the impression they are ashamed of their bodies. Not, I must hasten to say, in any personal sense where, honed by the physical demands of excavation and fieldwork, they represent a golden mien among the academic profession. Rather in the curious absence of bodies in the photographic record of ancient remains. By popular convention monuments and landscapes, even artefacts, are photographed without anyone present. At best somebody appears as a scale, standing like a rigid metric pillar in a trench or next to a wall and, as Marcia-Anne Dobres (2000:Figure 1.2) has pointed out, disembodied hands holding an artefact. The effect is disconcerting, the message clear. The past is remote because it is un-peopled and definitely un-gendered. Allowing 'modern' people into the photographs changes the significance of the monuments. Stonehenge, for example, ceases to be an icon of remote time and instead becomes a contested space for many conflicting ideologies. While this convention may contribute to the continuing mystery of Neolithic Britain (Edmonds 1999) and the haunting affect of Stonehenge (Manley 1989:plate 2) it directs the archaeological gaze at external objects and the body is shamed by its invisibility.

When bodies do appear they are the product of interpretations governed by scientific accuracy and the principle of authenticity. These are the conventions that structure the work of artists who reconstruct scenes from prehistoric life: for example, a hominin family making the Laetoli footprint trail, hirsute hunters slaying rhinos and knapping handaxes or people who look like us holding flickering lamps to paint animals on cave walls. These images are informed by the details of discovery and are often produced in association with archaeologists. Particular attention and a meticulous understanding of facial anatomy is applied to the look of the hominins (Gerasimov 1971). The result is a highly technical, but ultimately sterile exercise in forensic reconstruction. The faces that are re-created as objects do not provide, as often claimed, a snap-shot of the past but instead form a poignant example of our part-for-whole appreciation of people: a case of 'your face fits' even though it may be 10,000 years old (Chapter 3).

The social contexts and historical traditions of these representations of the deep past have been well discussed (Gifford-Gonzalez 1993; Hurcombe 1995; Moser 1998; Moser and Gamble 1997). These visual images are theoretical propositions drawing on the iconography of Western art to tell the story of Originsland that I outlined in Chapter 3. The frequency with which they are re-cycled (Moser 1992) is indicative of their power in controlling origins research (Figure 3.3).

Design by numbers

But archaeologists are not alone in their shame about the body, as geographer Rob Imrie (2003) found during extensive interviews with architects. It might be supposed that architects would be concerned with notions of embodiment in our spatial relationships; in short a phenomeno-logical approach to inhabiting the world (Chapter 4). However, Imrie discovered the opposite. The dominant model of the body was just that, a set of modular metrics enshrined in the industry bible (Adler 1999) and around which buildings are designed. The notion that people's experience of space derives from their bodies was something that most practising architects had just not considered let alone been taught. Consequently, architectural drawings are 'peopled' by a de-sensitised, schematically drawn modular-man, while in a further striking parallel with archaeology, architecture journalism is full of pictures of buildings with no one in them.

Interviewer: There's a lovely quote I found from an architect that said that some architects think of bodies as impure and degenerate.

Architect   [laughs] Impure and degenerate? Well judging by the way
respondent: that architects depopulate their buildings when they
                  photograph them that probably isn't far wide of the mark.
                  Look at those photographs behind you, there's not a single
                  person in them, they must have waited ages to exclude
                  everybody (Imrie 2003:60).

'The darkness of the body'

The shame felt by both archaeologists and architects stems ultimately
from a desire to treat bodies as neutral objects, yardsticks to be dropped
into the spaces among the artefacts of the past (Gamble and Porr 2005a)
or used to determine the optimum width of a lift-shaft.

Artists do not share that rational shame. Indeed their own body is
often the source for establishing relationships to the world, as is strikingly
the case with sculptor Antony Gormley, whose working principle is: why
make a body when you already have one? It is just such an approach to the
embodied object that begins to draw together the strands of metaphor
and material culture that I have discussed at length in earlier chapters. Most
importantly, metaphors of the body are central to understanding a study
of change as an aspect of the material basis of human identity. However,
what follows is not an exploration of art and archaeology (Renfrew 2003;
Renfrew et al. 2004) but rather an examination of the metaphors of accumulation and enchainment in the construction of identity centred within
and around the body. In that sense the archaeological process of exposing
the unknown by digging through accumulated, well stratified layers,
is rather similar to artistic enquiry where, in Gormley's (2004a) phrase,
the 'darkness of the body' is revealed through 'the other side of appearances
(Gormley 2004a:134)', and where:

> I am very aware as I speak to you now that where I am is behind my face;
> my face and my body in some way belong more to you than they do to me,
> and vice versa.
>
> (Gormley 2004a:134)

Identity is more than skin deep and it cannot be uncovered by just
scratching the surface a little. It is instead made up of many layers as well as
the relationships that link together the various containers, such as masks,
kinship and houses that I discussed in Chapter 4.

Our faces, as part of corporal culture, are therefore mask-like for all
of us and in this regard are another example of the surface of a container.
This layering of mask, face and inwards into the 'darkness of the body' is

TABLE 5.1. *The ground rules of identity that emerge by collapsing familiar Cartesian dualisms in order to understand how we create ourselves and how this act is implicated with the material world of objects and things. No. 4 is of particular significance for the argument presented here about hybrid culture (after Toren 1999:4)*

1. We are individually social and socially individual
2. We are biologically cultural and culturally biological
3. Mind is embodied and the body manifests mind
4. Our understanding of what is material is always mediated by our relations with others and likewise
5. Our subjective and objective perspectives guarantee each other
6. Structure and process are aspects of one another

a characteristic experience that we can all appreciate in the construction of identity dependent on a feeling of self and personhood. The boundaries between the layers are not clear cut in terms of any precise role or meaning they might individually possess but the sense of accumulation and the enchainment, or linking, to other experiences is palpable. In that sense all material culture is mask-like in that it allows expression of that darkness so that not only can others see who we are but we can realise and experience our own identity.

Such reflexivity means we are not especially endowed to become who-we-are, but instead are self-creating and self-producing, auto-poietic in Toren's (1999:6) terms. It is from such creative negotiation that we fashion our identity.

The ground rules in this construction of identity are simple once the rational, Cartesian, approach to the same question is collapsed (Table 5.1). I will argue that a material basis of identity is common to both hominins and humans. Without a doubt, at some time in our evolutionary history language gave us fresh ways to discuss these central concerns, but material culture has always provided hominins with the means of casting a little light on the central mystery of identity contained in the darkness of the body.

Boiling eggs: or how to construct identity through agency

Archaeologists have however developed a dislike for the hidden. As a result, concepts such as intention and desire are largely written out of rational accounts of human prehistory. Choice is instead determined by the organisational properties of systems (Binford 1972) rather than people, and adherence to the rules guarantees everyday survival and reproductive success. There is little place in such social and ecological systems for the actions of the individual (Clark 1992a; Flannery 1967) and none for such rationally fuzzy concepts as motivation. The terminology in these accounts is instead about goals, budgets and strategies, nicely summarised in the analogy of hunting societies as a well run corner-shop (Chapter 3).

What is at issue here is the distinction, drawn by Gell (1998:127), between externalised and internalised conceptions of the mind and hence the inner self. His point is that sociologists, as opposed to psychologists, have to be externalists. The reason is straightforward. A theory of how the mind works which only relates actions to inner, prior intentions, is inadequate because what we intend does not always happen. Gell illustrates the distinction by asking how eggs get boiled. A scientific explanation is that they are heated in boiling water until hard. The laws of physics can be invoked to show how this is possible and the experiment repeated daily in every kitchen where eggs are served. However, the explanation he favours is that someone, an agent, *intended* that eggs be boiled. Put that person with that intention in the vicinity of an egg, a saucepan and a stove and that egg will get boiled. Physics is necessary but it is not the explanation. Without an agent with the desire for boiled eggs there will be none. The lack of boiled eggs at Olduvai Gorge two million years ago is not because Boyle's law had yet to be invented or because the fashioning of an egg cup was beyond hominin capabilities of the time. It is rather that *Zinjanthropus* didn't want boiled eggs for his breakfast.

Now the reason why the natural inclination of sociologists and archaeologists is to be externalists is straightforward. Those boiled eggs I intended to eat do not always materialise simply because sometimes the stove won't light. The prior intention by people at the hunting village of Gönnersdorf in Germany 15,000 years ago (Bosinski 1979) might have been to catch reindeer. However, excavations reveal that only horse was consumed (Poplin 1976). I can think of no way to explore their intention to eat reindeer. However, the intention to eat *something* has left a durable trace of the social agent involved. The same applies to Zinj and his boiled eggs. That he intended to eat something is as far as we can probe his inner self on this matter.

Accumulation, enchainment and identity

Those missing, shameful bodies among both the monuments of the past and modern buildings are eloquent testimony to a non-metaphorical approach to the material world. Standing stones and shopping malls

TABLE 5.2. *Two metaphors of social practice and their definitions (after Chapman 2000; Gamble 2004:Table 8.2)*

Social practice	Accumulation	Enchainment
Provides the authority for action and interaction	Relations achieved by production and reproduction	A chain of social relations achieved through exchange

are presented as independent of people, external to their existence, as revealed in the phrase 'the built environment'. If bodies are excluded then the symbolic force, the experiential basis for framing and understanding concepts, goes un-noticed, and rational design is sufficient explanation. The idea of solid, material metaphors, comparable in sensitivity and nuance to their linguistic counterparts, would not cross our field of view. The body is indeed shamed by its invisibility and with it disappear the categories of identity, self and personhood.

Accumulation and enchainment are two concepts that both correct and celebrate an alternative, visible body, through material metaphors (Table 5.2). Accumulation and enchainment are social practices that result from bodily activity as well as providing metaphors for identity (Table 4.3).

They are social practices because human beings are always implicated in networks of materiality (Gell 1998; Knappett 2006). It is through the inter-linked practices of accumulation and enchainment that relationships are enacted. Anthropologist Marilyn Strathern (1998:135), in her study of Melanesian societies, stresses that 'social relations make artefacts out of persons', although she acknowledges they are a different type of artefact. In her opinion social relationships work because people recognise the presence and intentions of others as capable of action like themselves. The way that they compute such concepts as interior and exterior to themselves is by enrolling others in their social projects.

Constructing identity is one project hominins have always been concerned with. Metaphors are needed to identify with those hidden interiors of both ourselves and others. Accumulation and enchainment, involved in all social projects, provide the conceptual access route. The two terms are not exclusive but complementary. To accumulate is also to enchain and vice versa. Moreover, these terms are not hidden in the sense that intentions and desire are. They have a visible material basis.

John Chapman's (2000) study of material culture and social change in the Neolithic of South-East Europe provides an example. His main argument is that social practice oscillates between the authority of enchainment and accumulation as individuals and communities construct their identities. These practices are always inseparable. People are always enchained (linked) through networks of variable commitment and duration. Individuals spin and are spun as social agents within such networks. While there may be social practices which fragment the sense of the individual and distribute them in time and space, there are equal and complementary practices that always accumulate and construct identities at particular locales and across larger social landscapes. The result is the construction of specific historical identities.

Accumulated identities

It is necessary to excavate the darkness of the body to explore those concepts of inner and outer that, as others are enrolled in our projects, make the system of social relations work (Damasio 2000; Hollis 1985:227; Strathern 1998). This brings us to the territory of the self and personhood, regarded as universal aspects of human identity (Sökefeld 1999); concepts that hover over the merger of interests between sociology and psychology. For example, Collins (1985:73−4) makes the philosophical point that the body is a necessary but not sufficient condition of personhood. That can only be achieved with a psychological identity that depends on social relations. However:

> If some social completion of identity is a necessary part of personhood, but no particular social identity is in itself necessary, then there will always be at least a potential gap between private consciousness and public character.
>
> (Collins 1985:74)

I would suggest that what we find in the gap between the psychological and social is corporal and material culture (Figure 4.1). These act as a metaphorical bridge using the gestures and rhythms of bodily experience to make apparent what could otherwise not be understood. Instruments and containers are the visible material proxies (Table 4.4) for embodiment and it is around and within them that identities are accumulated.

Performance and emotion

One example is provided by sociologist Erwin Goffman (1959; 1963). He used a dramaturgical metaphor for social identity when he wrote of territories of the self that are made visible through markers that include signals and objects. Individuals, Goffman argued (1967:5), present a *face*, a front and back, while acting out a *line* in social situations and gatherings. However, he was sceptical either that we possess an underlying personality or identity that we carry with us from one social setting to the next or that such concepts have common currency. Social life, for Goffman, relies upon the capacity of individuals to establish their territories of self by reading the *markers* at each gathering (Turner 1991:466). When face-to-face interaction occurs there is a rich flow of information between individuals due to the embodied character of words, frowns and gestures. But information for presenting the *face* and the *line* is also disembodied, generally being conveyed through letters, tracks and objects. The territory of the self is therefore not re-created at every gathering between people but has accumulated as a result of many previous gatherings and interactions.

A rather different standpoint is taken by neurologist Antonio Damasio (2000), although he might agree with Goffman on the richness of inter-action since in his view emotion is an obligate accompaniment of behaviour that originates from our bodies (2000:58). Damasio (2000:174 for definitions) argues for a core and autobiographical self that are components of consciousness and a proto-self we are not conscious of (Figure 5.1). These core and autobiographical selfs are carried with us but they differ between individuals because of those autobiographical memories that mediate between core and autobiographical self (Bloch 1998; Wilson 2005). This last is the archive of accumulated memories that constitute identity and help define personhood. Moreover, autobio-graphical memory enchains those experiences encountered in the territories of self during everyday life and these can be represented as layers or sedimentation in the archive of an individual's lifetime. The result is extended consciousness, defined as 'the capacity to be aware of a large compass of entities and events, i.e. the ability to generate a sense of individual perspective, ownership, and agency, over a larger compass of knowledge than that surveyed in core consciousness (Damasio 2000:198)'. Damasio (2000:198) emphasises the importance of language, reasoning and 'an even more ample endowment of memory' for humans, while at the same time believing that chimpanzees have an autobiographical self but not extended consciousness. I would emphasise other factors to explain the difference. The accumulated experiences of the autobiograph-ical self make this extension possible in humans because of our ability, using metaphor, to construct concepts from them. These experiences

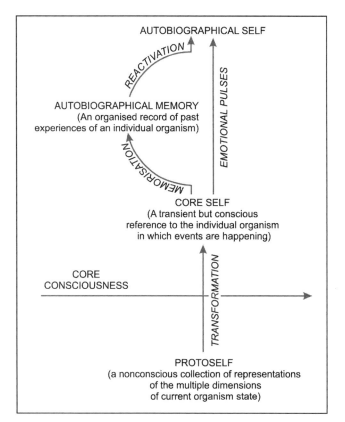

FIGURE 5.1. Three kinds of self as described by Damasio (2000:Table 7.1). The two arrows leading towards the autobiographical self signify its dual dependency on emotional pulses from the experiences of core consciousness and the continuous revisiting of autobiographical memories.

are not just linguistic in origin but related to objects and bodies that structure the performance of social life in interactions between small numbers of people.

Self-interest

But what exactly is the link between objects and notions such as that of the self? More to the point, why do archaeologists need to consider these inner workings in their study of change?

A lead comes from anthropologist Marcel Mauss (Carrithers et al. 1985; James and Allen 1998) who sought to unravel the history of the self by discussing its sociological construction and its psychological inheritance.

TABLE 5.3. *Mauss' categories of self and person (adapted from Carrithers 1985)*

Self awareness	Theory of mind	
Psychological	Moi	The self
Social	Personne	Person
	Personnage	Role, character, *mask*

To do this he separated what we call personhood, something we all possess, into layers (Hollis 1985:221; La Fontaine 1985:124). First there is a human being's self-awareness, that inner theory of mind, which is a universal property of our psychology (Table 5.3). Mauss saw this awareness as a fusion of body and spirit and thus argued for a united rather than divided personhood.

Second, there is the independent psychological category of self. And finally, there is the social concept of the person that broadly equates with individuality, everybody's own interpretation of the universal condition of personhood that stems from self-awareness, located within the structures of social life and informed by roles and categories.

Mauss also proposed a historical trajectory that started with pure role without self and ended, in the modern world, with pure self without role. Therefore:

> the *category* of self emerges to replace the mere *concept* of self which went before and each person now has his own self-ego, in keeping with the various Declarations of Rights.
>
> (Hollis 1985:220, my emphasis)

But what Mauss never told us was how the *concept* became the *category* of self in the stark contrast he drew between personhood in the non-Western and Western world. In fact, as philosopher Martin Hollis elegantly showed (ibid. 1985:230), the category of self is found in Classical Greece, much earlier than Mauss anticipated. Nor can such historical divisions be replicated in the contemporary world. Janet Hoskins (1998:197) found that Kodi villagers of Eastern Indonesia were largely separated from those forces — literacy, popularised psychology and the privacy necessary for introspection — that form the modernist idea of self. However, she did find a comparable interest in reflections about the self such that a Western category and a non-Western concept of self could not be easily distinguished.

Hollis' demonstration that people were never, as Mauss suggested, natural first and social afterwards (ibid. 1985:232), led him to conclude that the journeys from concept to category are different expressions by different cultures of what, in all times and places, has underlain a universal sense of self. This was the task which Kant set the self, that of 'securing a world of persisting, causally related objects amid a mass of experienced phenomena (ibid. 1985:229)'. Making sense of who we are by judging what we experience in the roles we play. Others, such as Hobbes and Hume, saw the issue differently, with the inner sense of self separate from any role we might have, echoing the distinction discussed in Chapter 4 between the materialism of Marx and the anthropological materiality of Mauss (Rowlands 2004:198).

The boldness of Mauss' scheme was his fusion of sociology and psychology. He may not have been entirely successful but went some way to merging two disciplines and thereby dissolving the unhelpful distinction between cultural construction and biological endowment that I have been criticising in earlier chapters. However, it is not always necessary to attack such dualisms but rather recognise, as Gell (1998:127) did, that disciplines are dedicated to external (sociology) and internal (psychology) analysis of our inner states for good reasons. And both Gell and before him Mauss, recognised the importance of material culture in this synthesis.

An answer to the question I asked concerning the link between objects and notions such as the self is provided by Mauss' example of the mask (Hollis 1985), common in all cultures, to illustrate the concept and category of self and person. Masks in his terms are *personnage* the roles and characters which someone takes on (Table 5.3): Goffman's (1959) face presented to the world, the material *im*personation of the identities within. But there is still a sense of separation, a division between the concept of self and the materiality of the mask. Furthermore, it is because objects mediate between the social and the psychological, the gap Collins (1985:74) speaks of, that archaeologists need to consider these concepts in their study of change as the material basis of identity.

Layering and the biography of objects

Thinking through the body and objects gives us some purchase on those inner identities in the darkness of the body. Our access route mimics the process of archaeological excavation where layers of soil are removed to uncover spatial relationships between the things we find: an analogy that psychologists ever since Freud have used to dig into the unconscious.

Accumulation as a social practice (Table 5.2) can best be described as a layering process (Knappett 2005; 2006), the laying down of layers like second skins and where the containers of material culture we live in and move between (clothes, rooms, buses, churches and cities) extend the boundaries of our bodies in space and time. Those sedimented practices, the durable dispositions of Bourdieu's *habitus* (Chapter 4), are also layerings that accumulate memory at places and in regard to people and objects. Accumulation is also, in Chapman's sense above, the physical gathering of objects such as bricks in a wall, bodies in a cemetery or bronze swords for a metal hoard. The magnetic-like effect of the practice of accumulation is only possible through enchainment and the distribution of action across space as well as time. People and artefacts circulate, change hands and come to rest. To talk of enchainment necessarily leads us to accumulation and vice versa. But ultimately the force of these practices relates to the experience of the body that created them as metaphors to understand its hidden internal landscape.

For these reasons it is now common, following the lead of Igor Kopytoff (1986), to study the biography of objects (Hoskins 1998; Jones 2002:Chapter 5). Such biographical concerns dispense with the people: object dichotomy and recognise the importance of artefacts in both mediating and constituting our relationships and identities. From an archaeologist's viewpoint Chris Gosden and Yvonne Marshall (1999: 169–70) draw the following distinctions for material culture:

- *Use-life*, where artefacts are treated as passive things that through use become smaller, worn, repaired and discarded. A use-life approach that is common among studies of stone tools (Keeley 1980) under-stands a one-way relationship with the user as master, tool as servant.
- *Biography*, extends the term life-history by considering artefacts as active in the construction of meaning because social life is mediated through them. Biographical objects are exemplars of a hybrid culture (Chapter 4).

For Kopytoff (1986:67) 'biographies of things can make salient what might otherwise remain obscure', while Hoskins (1998:2) discovered in her conversations with Kodi villagers that the biographies of people and objects could not be separated. People recounted their lives by talking about objects. If asked about themselves they just listed their children, but when asked about the betel bag a man carried she learned a wealth of social information and heard a complex life history. She describes these objects as memory boxes.

> A coherent [autobiographical] narrative constructs a unified image of the self out of the disparate, messy fragments of daily experience. It is perhaps significant that the 'biographical objects' my informants selected were often containers (the betel pouch, the hollow drum, the funeral shroud).
>
> (Hoskins 1998:5)

It is the emotional significance invested in such personal memory boxes that gives them a 'charge of psychic energy' (Hoskins 1998:22).

Objects are not only invested with significance but can be direct expressions of the emotions contained within the body. Starting with an explicit use of pots as a metaphor for the human body (body as container), potter Jonathan Keep (2005) worked with hospital patients to give physical form to the emotions that arose from their illnesses. Rather than a course of art-therapy, the ceramics the three patients produced were material metaphors for depression, an altered body image through the intervention of a colostomy bag and breathing exercises to relieve asthma and respiratory difficulties. In all three pots the biographical charge is evident.

Enchained identities and extended minds

If the body, and for that matter the mind, is a container then it is more like a sieve than a saucepan. Not for the reason that it ingests and excretes substances through a variety of orifices but rather because our personhood does not stop at the skin. It is instead distributed in the world of people and objects (Busby 1997; Lambek and Strathern 1998; Strathern 1988), encapsulated in hybrid culture. Moreover, as Knappett asks, 'mind extends through the interface of the body into matter; mind also draws matter into the bodily scheme. How does this happen?' (Knappett 2006:243). Knappett answers his question by examining layering and networking, what I refer to as the complementary concepts of accumulation and enchainment that I have used to examine the biographical facets of self and personhood. Now it is the turn of enchainment/networking, but I must stress that their separation from accumulation is only a convenience to assist exposition. I do not imply that the way we extend in the world is solely through networking.

Different categories of individuals

I will start by returning to the contributions from sociologists and psychologists in Mauss' categories (Table 5.3). From this external perspective, material culture, of which masks are an example, conveniently focuses attention on the construction of our internal state, my own individual, psychological understanding of the world. But that internal state is influenced by my relationship with and contribution to a wider social world. As Collins (1985:73) puts it 'in logical terminology persons are physical particulars but psychological *relata*'. What ties it all together are those hybrid networks (Gell 1998; Knappett 2006) that we create through negotiation and interaction as we enrol others in our projects.

At this point it is the sociologists, in the guise of anthropologists, who gain the upper hand as we move from an internal to external standpoint. Two models, reminiscent of the concept and category of personhood, describe the individual as the product of social relationships. These are the Melanesian and Western individual (Gosden 1999:132–6), summarised by anthropologist Edward LiPuma in Table 5.4.

The Western individual

Let me start with what we think we know about ourselves. The Western view of the individual acknowledges the impact of Cartesian thinking upon our notion of a person (Hollis 1985). It allows us to recognise individuals and individuality for the simple reason that according to this view bodies contain minds and the individual quite literally stops at the skin. Raised as a Cartesian this makes sense to me, but then it would, wouldn't it? I have no direct access to another person's mind except through a theory of mind. I cannot read your thoughts because rationally I know that minds are separate and unique to the individual. I can build representations of those thoughts in other people's heads based on how I conceptualise the world, and in particular the social world, as working. For example, I expect the bus conductor to sell me a ticket and he expects me to pay him. I anticipate that my students will sit quietly in my lecture, taking notes. They hope it won't be too boring. I don't question these routine arrangements because I believe we are all sharing in the same representations of acceptable behaviour in well defined social situations. Therefore, one outcome of the Cartesian separation of minds and bodies is to produce norms of behaviour. Such norms can then be studied and compared.

When it comes to material culture this view of the separate individual structured by norms requires that artefacts — masks would be a good example — *reflect* these norms. Hence for many years archaeologists expected the distribution of wealth such as gold or palaces to reflect the pyramid structure of the social order, with kings and chiefs at the apex supported by successive ranks of lower social grades until the commoners and peasants were reached at the base. Put another way, a hierarchy of bigger and better masks. These views, while now strongly challenged within

TABLE 5.4. *The contrast between Western and Melanesian personhood (LiPuma 1998:58—9). I have selected those aspects from LiPuma's full list that relate to my discussion and emphasised some of the key concepts in italics*

Western	Melanesian
Persons are conceptually distinct from the relations that unite them and bring them together	Persons are the compound and plural site of the relations that define them
Singular person is an individual	Singular person is composite
The person is the subject of an explicit and visible ideology — *individualism*	There is *no explicit ideology of persons*, only contextually situated images
An individual's behaviour and intentions are interpreted as the public expression of inner qualities (honesty, greed, etc.)	An individual's behaviour and intentions are interpreted in terms of his/her actions in context
Persons *mature biogenetically* as a consequence of their own inner potential	Persons *grow transactionally* as the beneficiary of other people's actions
Persons *depend on themselves for knowledge* about their internal selves, i.e. self-knowledge	Persons *depend on others for knowledge* about themselves, and they are not the authors of this knowledge
A person's power lies in his/her control over others; *power is a possession*	A person's power lies in his/her ability to do and act; *power is a relation*
Society stands over and against the individual as an external force that imposes norms, rules, and constraining conventions	*Society runs parallel to the individual*; it is embodied as dispositions to think, believe, and feel in a certain way
Its *commodity logic* leads people to search for knowledge about things and to make an explicit practice out of knowing the nature of objects	Its *gift logic* leads people to search for knowledge about persons and to make a practice out of knowing the person-making powers of objects

archaeology (Gamble 2001), still hold sway outside it, and like the singular Western individual show little sign of decline.

The Melanesian dividual

Godfrey Lienhardt (1985) has strongly criticised the value of the Western individual as a universal model. From his ethnographic experience in East Africa he concludes that the mind:body dualism:

> Is achieved at the price of severing all the traditional bonds by which man has been joined to other men and the world around them, but also of

splitting in two the personal union of mind and body and expelling the instincts of the latter.

(ibid.:152)

The price paid is also the loss of hybrid culture. Our material culture not only exists outside the body but outside social relations. We use it to act on the world, for example when digging the garden, but not to inhabit the world in a mutual manner with instruments such as spades and forks.

Anthropologists, Marilyn Strathern (1988) and Nurit Bird-David (1995; 1999) have re-thought the concept of the Western individual. Based on their anthropological fieldwork in Melanesia and India respectively they propose a distributed person or partible individual, also known as a *dividual*, and by Roy Wagner as a fractal person (1991). The dividual does not stop at the skin but is instead dispersed through networks of exchange and relationships of all kinds. It is for example through such networks that the androgyny of the body becomes gendered (Strathern 1988). People are therefore composites and created through sets of relationships to one another as well as to material culture (Gosden 1999:124). Wagner (1991:34) sums it up well when he points out that a model such as the Melanesian dividual emphasises the centrality of relationships and that all modes of 'relating' are basically analogous. The alternative, natural systems of kinship that Morgan saw arising from the facts of genealogy and biology, starts from the institution not the individual and the relationships through which they exist. The flow of analogy to create these relationships may consist of protocols governing how people relate, incest taboos for example, but the major symbols that articulate the sequences between relationships are normally those of body substances and the spirit world (Wagner 1991:34−5).

As a consequence the biological reality of individual separateness breaks down and in its place a collectivity emerges that also removes, as advocated above by Lienhardt (1985), the distinction between mind and body. Most importantly these analytical elements are re-united in the concepts of the body-whole and into their landscapes of habit (Gamble 1999; Gosden 1994).

Strathern (1988:13) describes the distributed person as a homologue because in one sense the singular (individual) and the plural (social collective) are 'the same' (Table 5.4). She describes the relationship, based on her fieldwork in Papua New Guinea, as follows:

The bringing together of many persons is just like the bringing together of one. The unity of a number of persons conceptualized as a group or set is achieved through eliminating what differentiates them, and this is also exactly what happens when a person is individualized...Social life consists in a constant movement from one state to another, from one type of sociality to another, from a unity (manifested collectively or singly) to that unity split or paired with respect to another.

(ibid. 1988:14)

The body is central to such distinctions. In her ethnographic study, Anne Becker (1995) distinguishes between the cultivation of the personal body in Western societies and the cultivation of the bodies of others in Fiji. For Fijians the body is a way of integrating the self into the community rather than a vehicle for expressing personal identity (Becker 1995:128).

The neutral individual

But as LiPuma (1998:63) points out, the dividual:individual, if applied as a rigid distinction between a Western and a Melanesian personhood, emerges as yet another dualism. He believes the way forward is not to see such starkly contrasted systems but rather to use Strathern's insight and recognise that persons emerge from that tension between dividual and individual aspects and relations (ibid. 1998:57). Moreover, LiPuma argues that the terms and conditions of this tension will vary historically. As a result so will the range of persons, that local expression of common personhood. Caroline Busby agrees in her wider comparative study:

> In Hagen (Papua New Guinea) it is relationships which make persons. In India (Kerala) it is emphatically persons who make relationships.
>
> (Busby 1997:273)

Her study in South India shows how individuals are connected to each other through exchange, but that these substances are a manifestation of the person and not the relationship as Strathern found in Melanesia.

The outcome is important. Enchainment can be both rational and relational. Moreover, as we saw earlier with the demise of Mauss' scheme for a move from a concept to a category of self, no historical develop-ment existed between Melanesian and Western personhood. As Bird-David (1999:87; Ingold 1999:81) points out the issue is one of authority. Currently the modernist project of Western science, as bemoaned by Lienhardt, has eroded much of the authority of relational ways of understanding. An individual in Medieval Europe was indivisible from the world while today we are an indivisible part of a divisible world (Bird-David 1999:88). But both systems of authority still exist in the predictions of the astrologer and the science of the astronomer. And even though they draw on a different social authority both the individual and dividual can vote in a democracy or dance to the beat of the collective drum.

But even this simple characterisation of changing authority is too black and white. The unfamiliar hominin past is not to be portrayed as history against modernity, a re-discovery of what we have lost. There have been changes in the practice of authority as shown by social actions involving material culture. This balance, however, is always shifting. What emerges are historically specific constructions of identity rather than universally applicable revolutions.

Networking and autobiographical resources

Networking/enchainment needs resources to create relations and three such can be readily identified: emotional, material and symbolic (Gamble 1998; Turner and Maryanski 1991). As Toren describes it:

> Any act, remembering, for instance, implicates the embodied cognitive processes that constitute it. In other words, it implicates the whole person; so any act is at once affective, symbolic and material — i.e. intentional.
>
> (1999:111)

But at the same time the quality and number of relationships derives from the differential investment of these three resources into the craft and business of creating networks. Through the act of constructing networks individuals author their identity and create an autobiographical self (Damasio 2000). At the same time they are authored by all the other people with whom they interact and who are also building their own networks.

The model I propose has three ego-centred networks with modular demographic outcomes. These networks are differentiated by the use of emotional, material and symbolic resources (Table 5.5).

Networks will vary in density and complexity as the skills and capacities of individuals to construct and maintain them also varies (Gamble 1999:Chapter 2). As Marilyn Strathern puts it:

> The concept of network summons the tracery of heterogeneous elements that constitute such an object or event, or string of circumstances, held together by social interactions; it is in short, a hybrid imagined in a socially extended state. The concept of network gives analytical purchase on those interactions.
>
> (Strathern 1996:521)

TABLE 5.5. *The use of resources to build ego-centred networks of differing size and function (after Gamble 1999:Table 2.8)*

	Resources		
Networks	*Emotional*	*Material*	*Symbolic*
Intimate (~5)	Affective self and others		
Effective (~20)		Practical self and others	
Extended (100—400)			Distributed self and others

Approximate modular sizes are indicated. These are expected to vary greatly between individuals but are constrained by the psychological and cognitive loads incumbent upon interaction. For further discussion see Chapter 8.

As a result networks are much more than channels between nodes and down which goods and information flow. Instead a social network, like culture, is a hybrid. In other words it is made up of both persons and objects, layers and links in opportunities for accumulation and enchainment.

Bottom-up or top-down societies

This may seem to put too much emphasis on the individual as the starting point for any social project, and to ignore pre-existing institutions and structures. Here, network models can also contribute to the argument over which is most appropriate, a top-down or bottom-up approach to the study of society (Gamble 1999; Hinde 1976), and whether the group (Clark 1992b; Flannery 1967) or individual (Gamble and Porr 2005b; Mithen 1993) is the archaeologist's primary unit of analysis. From a network perspective both approaches start with an assumption of original forces best described as agency. An individual is never inchoate precisely because we are all born into society. We are social agents by both birth and upbringing. In the same way the system, that aggregate of individuals, needs to derive its force, its identity and legitimacy, from somewhere. It is not enough to assert that because cultural systems persist for millennia — like the Magdalenian or the Pre-pottery Neolithic — they therefore exist as a greater reality than the individuals they subsume. However, to shout loudly that the individual is primary simply because of the property of agency would be to commit the same error. That is why I prefer to start with the body-whole and trace the varied networks within which it is caught up, and where different contexts present identities that are sometimes singular and at other times fractal.

Cutting the network, growing-the-body

As a final illustration of the embodied character of networks let us consider how hair, a commonplace bodily resource, can be used in the act of building these different networks en route to constructing personal identity.

When part of the body, and growing, hair is a resource for a person's intimate network (Table 5.5). It is something to be groomed, shaped, coloured, ruffled and pulled for all sorts of reasons that support the close affective bonds in this immediate, small network. When cut by someone outside this network it becomes a material resource. Lying on the hair-dresser's floor it represents a practical relationship based on a transaction as would be expected in an effective network. But if acquired surreptitiously it ceases to be a transaction and changes its meaning. While still material culture, whose power stems from the close association with a person's body, it is also a symbol, like the strand in the locket of an inamorata or the snippet in the witches' cauldron. Through either desire or magic it impersonates the extended network of the person casting and directing the spell. Hair also serves (Chapter 3) as an analogy for weeding and cultivation when it is used as a root metaphor (Ortner 1973:1341) to make sense of a social project such as agriculture.

Summary: lifting the lid on social archaeology

One of the most notorious put-downs in archaeology was delivered by the anthropologist Sir Edmund Leach. The occasion was a conference that heralded the arrival in the UK of the New Archaeology (Renfrew 1973) that set out to examine past societies as functioning systems rather than historically specific entities. The notion of archaeology as anthropology, forcefully championed by Lewis Binford (1962) opened the way for a social archaeology to replace the archaeologist's major activity of cataloguing stone tools and other artefacts. Leach, who summed up the conference, was un-impressed. Abandon 'what questions' at your peril, he warned the audience (Leach 1973:764), because 'you are moving away from verifiable fact into the realm of pure speculation'. According to Leach the past is a black box where too much is hidden or conjectural for any meaningful things to be said about the intricacies of social life.

Thirty years later the New Archaeology has become a Processual archaeology dedicated to the scientific study of variation and change. As a way to study society it is still criticised but by archaeologists interested, as I am, in relational rather than rational accounts of the past. Processual archaeologists would now probably agree with Leach that we will never be able to identify concepts such as the individual/dividual because they are hidden in the black box that a scientific approach cannot open.

However, Leach was wrong in characterising the pursuit of the hidden as 'pure speculation'. The quest may be guesswork to the rational method that he followed in his kinship studies but when a relational perspective is employed then a different standpoint emerges. I have now shown how an internal and external identity, familiar for example to the different per-spectives of psychologists and sociologists, is amenable to archaeological enquiry through the proxies of material culture. However, I still have to demonstrate how this identity extends to both our human and hominin subjects and that I will do in Part III. For the moment I have developed the metaphors of accumulation and enchainment and the material proxies of instruments and containers to develop a route to such understanding. The body remains the reference point, the symbolic force (Chapter 4) and ultimately the source of agency that establishes the relationships that define us. I have also suggested that if we understand change as a study of the material basis of human identity then we need to appreciate the shifting authority between rational and relational ways of interpreting the world. Now, however, it is time to develop methods to track such variable influ-ence and introduce a currency for these metaphors of accumulation and enchainment. The relationship between cutting hair and harvesting crops can now take us to the social actions of fragmentation and consumption that complete my model for identity based on material metaphors.

CHAPTER 6

Consuming and fragmenting people and things

> *Fragmentation*: *Refers to the condition of a disk in which files are divided into pieces scattered around the disk. Fragmentation occurs naturally when you use a disk frequently, creating, deleting, and modifying files. At some point, the operating system needs to store parts of a file in noncontiguous clusters. This is entirely invisible to users, but it can slow down the speed at which data are accessed because the disk drive must search through different parts of the disk to put together a single file.*
>
> Webopedia 2005

> *'I did not have three thousand pairs of shoes,*
> *I had one thousand and sixty.'*
>
> Imelda Marcos 1987

Musical chairs

The singing began at sunset, the dancing a little later. The women, some with their children, gathered in the large open space surrounded by the small, round huts of the village. A fire was lit and the dogs shooed away. They sang in high rhythmical voices, the clicks of their language now drowned by the clapping of their hands. Four men danced around the women and their fire. They wore rattles on their legs and as they stamped out their dance they struck percussion sticks together and answered the women's song. After a while the oldest dancer grew tired, his rheumatism hobbling his steps. There would be no shaman's trance tonight. He moved towards the fire, broke the circle, and the performance was over.

Sometimes being an ethnographic tourist, as I was that night in August 2001 at Makuri village in the Nyae/Nyae Conservancy, northern Namibia (http://www.namibian.org/travel/community/nyae.htm), offers unexpected souvenirs. On reflection I could have gone to any tropical beach to hear singing and see dancing around fires. But I had come to Makuri with a TV crew to meet hunter-gatherers, and film them doing what they do best; being what we want them to be. The hunter-gatherer is a dubious concept at the best of times (Bird-David 1994; Schrire 1984; Wilmsen 1989) and has often been downright dangerous in the hands of archaeologists investigating origins and revolutions (e.g. Johnson and Earle 1987; Sollas 1911). We use them to provide a starting point for the project of how we became civilised, and a cautionary reminder of what we would lose — laws, literacy, architecture and hierarchy — if our social fabric was unpicked. As a much re-worked category they currently appeal to our desire for re-wilding, a return to original human values, and so provide some much-needed colour in Originsland (Chapter 3).

But there in remote Namibia the question had to be turned around. The category under scrutiny was not the hunter-gatherer but me. Why travel such a distance to consume a paid performance? Was I still following, like many before me, in the footsteps of the French philosopher Joseph-Marie Degérando, who in 1800 made explicit the link between distance and history?

> The philosophical traveller, sailing to the ends of the earth, is in fact travelling in time; he is exploring the past; every step he makes is the passage of an age. Those unknown islands that he reaches are for him the cradle of human society.
>
> (translation Moore 1969:63)

The answer to both questions was no, and for the reason that travel fragments us as much as it consumes others. As historical geographer Felix Driver (2004) has shown, the scientifically fuelled voyages of exploration produced knowledge not so much by a process of accurate observation that tamed the variety of the world, but through exploiting the disturbance that arose as the bodies of Western explorers experienced distance. In many cases their bodies were fragmented and consumed by disease, failing eyesight, hunger and emotional scarring as recorded time and again in the literature of travel. However, the accumulation of such bodily sacrifices either for science or Empire were always conducted in an enchained world of objects and fellow travellers. For example, for five years starting in 1810 the naturalist William Burchell 'sailed' across southern

Africa in a Cape ox-wagon that calibrated global functions, since it made scientific measurements possible, to the local conditions of difficult terrain (Driver 2004:83). His container was kept afloat by the labours of many servants and a constant process of enchainment with African and Boer farmers where the coloured beads he handed out were the material proxy for the relationship.

I had reached Makuri village in the comfort of a Land Cruiser pulling a trailer-full of objects including tea mugs, tents and tobacco. We carried our disturbance with us like a bow-wave. Every time I used those familiar objects I was reminded of the stretched character of the journey that was only possible because we can fragment our social selves in time as well as across space. The efficiency of the transport was secondary. And unlike William Burchell, we left with the added luggage of bracelets and necklaces made from ostrich egg-shell beads that I had bought in the village.

Architecture without walls

Time travel was not on my mind as I watched the dancing at Makuri but I was definitely up for an experience that I could take away as an individual souvenir.

The next morning I returned to the deserted dance floor with an archaeologist's eye and I was rewarded with a bargain. The night's activity had left a clearly marked performance space, an oval track of about eight metres diameter with a central hearth (Figure 6.1). These solid mementos were all that the vivid performance had created, about as significant, you might think, as a stick of Brighton rock to remember a fine day out. How could I ever infer from this faint trace in the sand that the most human of cultural traits, the skills of music applied to language and ritual movement had taken place? Would I though be willing as an archaeologist to interpret the invisible actions other than as mundane evidence for sitting and walking?

The answer would always be no, so long as I approached the interpretation of such spaces with linguistic rather than material metaphors. Linguistically I would have to say that nothing survived to suggest what went on beyond the mundane although the oval track might be ritual, whatever that means, rather than functional behaviour. But if I switched to material metaphors the picture changed. Immediately I was presented with a container in the form of the oval within which the women had sat. This space was nested within the larger container of the village while at the

FIGURE 6.1. Makuri village performance space. The night before twelve women and children sat around the fire while four men danced around them.

micro-scale the hearth was encircled by the women and contained branches, embers, smoke and flame. What I learned from my ethnographic day out was that architecture does not need walls to be a container, that material proxy for the body. Containers are indicated by the singing coming from the body, by an embrace, being seated in a circle or tracing one around other people and objects. In addition, the act of inscription, or marking, that made the oval visible is only possible because of the other material proxy for corporal culture, the instrument. Feet stamped out the track while hands clapped or struck percussion sticks together. The rattles on the dancer's legs encircled the instruments that marked the ground.

Machines for the suppression of time

Let me be clear about what the Makuri dance was not. It is not a model to infer that music and language structured an activity in the past. It validates no universal metric of the human body that can unlock the meaning of spatial patterns on camp sites past and present (e.g. Binford 1983). We will get no closer to the archaeological inaudibles of music, language and their involvement in ritual by analysing such occurrences as the Makuri dance with the optic of the ethno-archaeologist.

Instead my souvenir relates more to anthropologist Claude Lévi-Strauss' (1966a:26) enigmatic claim that music and myth are 'machines for the suppression of time'. What he means is that the last note of the symphony is implied in the first so that the linear character of time is inhibited. Instead of a narrative of action there emerges instead the opportunity for metaphorical understanding, that in the case of music is 'at once intelligible and untranslatable'. Now Lévi-Strauss is above all else, as Tilley (1999:272) has reminded us, a master at teasing out metaphorical under-standings. He does this by tracing relationships rather than relying on rational associations and uses both myth and music to extract meanings from the most intractable materials (see Knight 1983; 1991).

The reason archaeologists find such musical chairs mysterious is that we are little practised in exploring metaphorical associations. Many would rather follow the austere dismissal by neuroscientist Steven Pinker (1997:534) that music is nothing but 'auditory cheesecake'; itself a tasty metaphor employed to sideline music rather than give it status on the high-table of evolutionary explanation (for an alternative view see Mithen 2005). Pinker, however, is a dedicated Cartesian. The brains he studies are largely disembodied machines driven by evolutionary processes to solve problems and represent the world. The historical purpose of such brains is to produce language and so unlock cognition. It is not surprising in such a rational view that music is the dessert rather than the main course.

Consumption and fragmentation as social actions

If the metaphors of accumulation and enchainment mean anything for the study of change at archaeological time-scales then I need actions to back them up. These are provided by fragmentation and consumption (Table 6.1).

The terms are reciprocal. To fragment is also to consume and vice-versa. Neither does one term refer only to accumulation and the other to enchainment. These are actions and practices which suppose the other, but whereas the latter are to be interpreted in terms of authorising identity (Chapter 5) the terms fragmentation and consumption provide connec-tions between people and objects in networks of relationships.

The notion of fragmentation has been brought to prominence in archae-ology by John Chapman (2000; Jones 2002:99–102). Breaking things on

TABLE 6.1. *A model of social practice and social action and its definitions (after Chapman 2000; Gamble 2004:Table 8.2; Miller 1995)*

Social practice	Accumulation	Enchainment
Provides the authority for action and interaction	Relations achieved by production and reproduction	A chain of social relations achieved through exchange
Social action	**Consumption**	**Fragmentation**
Connects the elements in the hybrid network	To embody, for the purposes of creating relationships either through accumulation or enchainment	To divide, for the purposes of distributing relations either through enchainment or accumulation

purpose, he argues, is the social action by which the practices of enchainment and accumulation can be studied. As Chapman points out:

> The two principles of fragmentation and accumulation have been fundamental to human behaviour ever since food sharing and lithic production. Sharing the portions of meat produced by butchering a carcase and distributing the ever-smaller flint flakes knapped from a natural nodule both entail part-whole relationships which can act as metaphors for social relations.... The sharing of an object produced for the group by a single individual and the combination of elements produced by several persons for consumption by a single individual — these are fundamental forms of social relations based upon human-object interactions. It is anticipated that these forms of social relations pre-dated other aspects of enchainment and accumulation, acting as analogies for such later developments.
>
> (2000:222)

By locating such practices deep in hominin ancestry Chapman has done a great service in removing the social barriers between Neolithic and Palaeolithic, farmer and hunter (Chapters 1 and 2). But the gain is compromised because he developed his methodology to investigate an origins question, the appearance of metallurgy (see below). Moreover, as the passage above shows, he uses the terms enchainment and fragmentation interchangeably. On the contrary, I think a stronger case can be made for Chapman's relational perspective to material culture by giving the terms significance as practice and action respectively. Andy Jones and Colin Richards (Jones 2002:Chapter 6; 2003:49) provide an example drawn from their work on Neolithic Orkney. By fragmenting and then recombining discrete categories such as animals, humans, pots and buildings they show how these elements can be brought into metaphorical relation through accumulation and enchainment. The heterogeneous and the hybrid are given a cultural significance beyond the usual rational accounts of subsistence and shelter.

Bricoleurs rather than builders

These actions that combine and associate can be described as the work of *bricoleurs* rather than builders. The bricoleur is anthropologist Claude Lévi-Strauss' (1966b) untranslatable term to describe 'handy-men' solving technological problems by using the things to hand. The result is *bricolage* where often unlikely things are brought into relation with each other and meaning constructed from action rather than from a predetermined mental plan (ibid.:20). We recognise the latter as the solution of the engineer, rationally conceived and applied. Bricoleurs make 'unlikely' associations because they adopt relational rather than rational approaches to gain knowledge about the world; building metaphorical understandings rather than building houses.

Bricoleurs accumulate and enchain and they also fragment and consume as they order the material world. Fragmentation applies to objects, bodies included, and the result can be to enchain or accumulate them in webs of identity. But fragmentation is not the only action that relates such practices. Consumption, conceived of here as a facet of embodiment (Table 6.1), is an equal partner in hominin involvement with the world of people and things. In a contemporary context consumption is now one of the main ways in which people forge a relationship with the world (Appadurai 1986; Douglas and Isherwood 1978; Miller 1995a) and so create an identity by establishing self-hood (Friedman 1994:104). This use of consumption owes much to Hegel's notion of objectification where people create a physical world of their internal desire by buying and using things (Gosden 1999:165). In anthropologist Danny Miller's opinion this is achieved by the consumption practices of the household, so that 'moral, cosmological and ideological objectifications are constructed to create the images by which we understand who we have been, who we are, and who we might or should be in the future' (1995:35). He then makes a crucial point that today it is the 'sheer scale of the object world (Miller 1995a:35)' that fragments the objectification of such inner desire and belief. Partial connections abound in the face of such a volume of material things

TABLE 6.2. *An archaeological model of social practice and social action (adapted from Chapman 2000)*

Social practice	Accumulation	Enchainment
Material projects	Sets (place)	Nets (landscape)
Examples	Caches, stores, flocks, cemeteries and housing 'offspring and family'	Stone, bone, shell and pot transfers 'friends and relations'
Material proxies	Containers	Instruments
Social action	Consumption	Fragmentation

and results in their often contradictory significance at different times and places of their consumption. There are no single meanings for these images since context is all important, a point that is brought home to us by the disturbance of travel.

Material projects: sets and nets

However, the equation of breaking things and passing them around, or hoarding them at some places and not others is too simple a linkage with the contrasted notions of personhood such as the Western (individual) and Melanesian (dividual) (Chapter 5). Neither was there ever a simpler social existence. Even in the Palaeolithic hominins had to cope with Miller's 'sheer scale of the object world' although it differed both quantitatively and qualitatively from our own.

Rather than simply fragmenting and consuming things, hominins have at all times been engaged in material projects (Table 6.2), a necessary consequence of inhabiting the world and being social. They enrolled others in these projects (Strathern 1998:135) and by doing so they created distinctive identities based on an understanding of those hidden cognitive processes (Chapter 5) supplied by solid and linguistic metaphors referenced to the body. Western and Melanesian personhood are just two glimpses of those hidden social categories but with no particular historical position to each other.

Material projects vary in scale and commitment, for example cooking a meal, raising children or building a boat. These on-going projects involve maturation, as Bloch (1998:33–5) found in his study of Zafimaniry houses on Madagascar, and where house building and the development of a marriage were intimately tied together. The dance I paid to see at Makuri village was, from my perspective, an ephemeral project but one rich in material and corporal culture as well as emotional and social significance for the dancers. The question for all these projects is, how has the reality of that particular social situation been defined (Turner 1991)? Sociologist Erving Goffman (1959; 1963; 1967; Turner 1991:467) would no doubt have dwelt on the performance of the self, stressing everyday rituals of interaction such as how we attach and detach ourselves from social gatherings and how we present ourselves in terms of a front. Language plays a role as part of those rituals but would not necessarily be accorded prime position in defining the social reality.

Archaeologists, however, usually miss the end of the show, often by several millennia. Rather than studying the performance, our concern is with the social actions of fragmentation and consumption and how they were informed by concepts based on metaphor. Our assumption is that there was an understanding among participants.

This understanding, I maintain, explains why the evidence from the past is so strongly patterned that we can slice it by time and space, carving history at its joints. These patterns take the form of *sets* and *nets* of material culture, the proxies for material projects. I have given some examples in Table 6.2 and these will be amplified below and in Part III. In general terms sets are most closely associated with the creation of place while nets carry us out into landscapes. Sets and nets are a further instance of a mutual rather than binary distinction since it is difficult to say where one ends and the other begins.

Archaeologists are expert carvers of historical turkeys, well aware that their evidence consists of patterned sets and nets of material located in time and space. These are our building blocks, that we describe as assemblages, hoards, pit groups, caches, structured deposits, chains of connection, redistribution networks, trade systems, interaction spheres and cultures (Gamble 2001). We arrange them by phase and tradition using measures of frequency and resemblance while independent age estimates verify the historical order. Such sets and nets consist of complete and incomplete, whole and fragmented, objects.

Technologies of the person

The utility of differentiating practice and action (Table 6.1) can be shown by considering further those categories of personhood, Melanesian and Western or the dividual and individual (Table 5.4), and how material culture provides solid metaphors for such social relations. To recall,

TABLE 6.3. *Fragmentation and two technologies (after Chapman 2000:39)*

Fragmentation		
Reductive technologies		Additive technologies
Flint knapping	*Combination tools*	Ceramics Textiles Metallurgy
Woodworking		
Butchering animals		

Knappett (2006) reminds us that cognition is embodied, distributed and situated both in a body and an environment (see also Anderson 2003; Barrett and Henzi 2005; Wilson 2005). The boundaries of the body are not immutable but change through contact and association with objects, much as the psychologist James Gibson (1979) argued in his ecological approach to understanding perception. Finally, as LiPuma (1998) pointed out, the distinction Melanesian:Western may have rhetorical value in challenging some rational views of categories such as personhood but that fundamentally both forms of openness and closure can be found in all societies. What matters is the authority accorded to each of them.

Therefore, the hunt is not on for the material correlates of the dividual. Neither are we in search of a chaîne opératoire (Leroi-Gourhan 1993; Schlanger 1994; 2005) that would create an individual through an ordered sequence of techniques that brought together, and then shaped, the resources needed to undertake the task. Rather, as Knappett (2006) argues, we are examining those instances of layering/accumulation and networking/enchainment in the construction of personhood. I would go about this by considering those social actions of consumption and fragmentation that use material culture in metaphorical ways to accumulate and enchain through the proxies of sets and nets to material projects.

Once again Chapman (2000) provides a valuable lead and a pointer to a possible methodology. He argues that the distributed person can be tracked archaeologically through the deliberate fragmentation of material. To do this he recognises two major forms of technology, reductive and additive (Table 6.3), which either produce or are subject to intentional breakage followed by the distribution of the parts as representative of the whole; a material expression of that variety of metonymy (Chapter 3) known as synecdoche (Chapman 2000:67).

In both technologies fragmentation begins with a complete object. The difference is that in the additive case the object was made-up, like a pot from a lump of clay, while in the reductive example it was made-down, like an arrowhead from a nodule of flint (see Figure 4.6). Chapman's thesis is that with additive technologies people were making things in order to intentionally break them and so have materials for enchainment. He points out, moreover, that the simple distinction between these two technologies of growth and reduction is blurred by combination tools. For example, the microliths inserted into the shaft of an arrow or the blades in a sickle are clearly part of an additive technology. In the same way the beads in a necklace or the accumulation of long bones in a tomb are also additive. The actions of consumption and fragmentation therefore provide a basis, when applied to material culture, for the metaphorical expression of such concepts as embodied cognition and distributed personhood.

How material projects accumulate and enchain

Chapman defines sets as '*integrally related* groups of individual elements, as in the examples of flints forming a composite lithic tool or beads comprising a necklace' (2000:46, my emphasis).

Recognising sets depends on assessing integral relationships. For example, links are confirmed through the choice of raw material establishing similarity and difference. Elements in a set such as a tool-kit can be very different, as with chisels and saws, but they nonetheless have a formal-functional relationship as 'wood-working tools'. Chapman (2000:46) also recognises a set as composed of disparate-looking elements linked in a symbolic chain of contrasts and opposites. For example, the 263 heterogeneous items, including bowls, spoons, and a purse, sword and shield, found in the Anglo Saxon ship burial at Sutton Hoo (Carver 1998) form a disparate set gathered over some time from across Europe and deposited in eastern England 1,400 years ago. It is a set recognised by association, in this instance through the contiguity of items within the burial container formed by the ship.

Sets enchain and can take the form of reductive, additive and composite technologies which have been present from the Palaeolithic onwards. Sets can also be broken up without breaking the items in the set. The beads in a necklace can be distributed and new relationships are therefore created. The enchainment relationship would be expressed metaphorically as follows:

Part	← →	Whole
Element	← →	Set

Furthermore, to create a set is to accumulate and consume.

The concept of sets leads seamlessly between enchainment and accumulation (Table 6.2). Sets, like nets, depend on the concept of expansion. According to Chapman whole objects are fixed, i.e. completed, but sets of them can be expanded indefinitely as Imelda Marcos showed with her shoe collection.

Sets, of course, are well represented by hoards of metalwork, a key category of archaeological data in Later European prehistory. These are the real focus of Chapman's enquiry and his methodology has to be judged accordingly. He argues (2000:47) that sets, complex sets and collections are three types of hoard that take on a special significance with metallurgy because it is apparently uncommon to find items deliberately fragmented, a factor which Chapman puts down to the choice of raw material.

This is where accumulation comes in to play. Chapman's argument (2000:48) is that fragmentation creates people through objects because the relationships are inalienable (Gregory 1982; Mauss 1967; Thomas 1991). By contrast, accumulation opens up the possibility of alienable relationships underscored by abstract values such as wealth. Chapman regards this development as a by-product of the Whole←→Set relationship. Moreover, the possibility of accumulation through manufactured sets of similar objects was, he argues, first realised with metal artefacts (Chapman 2000:43ff.). The technique of manufacture using moulds led to replication and the generation of sets on a massive scale.

Hoards of metalwork are, however, only one example of a material project. Rather than seek the origins of such technologies I prefer to use Chapman's insights to consider the broader implications of hominin involvement with material culture. Archaeologists will always find nets of material culture because hominids have always been peripatetic. Fission and fusion is a fact of social life for primates as well as hominins. But at the same time we will always find sets. The rhythms of material life which take place in the context of practice and action lead to association and accumulation. Even the simplest stone tools in the archaeological record reveal these spatial-temporal characteristics. For instance, what is a family group if it is not a set of embodied, accumulated and enchained relationships built in varying ways from emotional, material and symbolic resources (Table 5.5)? To that extent a set is nothing more than a congealed net, a knot in the string. The difference I would draw is that such congealing defines *places* while nets articulate the use of *landscapes* which people cross by paths while enchained by objects into wider social structures (Table 6.4).

TABLE 6.4. *A scalar framework for studying hominin society (after Gamble 1999:Table 3.1)*

Locales	Rhythms of material and corporal life	Regions
Encounters and gatherings	Enchainment & accumulation *Chaîne opératoire* *Taskscape*	Landscape of habit
Social occasions and place	*Paths & tracks* Consumption & fragmentation	Social landscape
Individuals	← Sets & nets →	Networks

Table 6.4 also points to the important issue of scale, particularly between locales and regions, and their connecting rhythms of material and corporal life and that is discussed further in Chapter 8.

The creation of nets, and indeed sets, of material culture, what Chapman sees as the primary directive of fragmentation, is therefore to be expected in all hominin societies, and their creation will lead to variety among their proxies. There will be times when sets are ubiquitous as relationships are accumulated either through fragmentation or consumption. At other times nets will dominate the record as social practices enchain through those same actions. What determines the outcome of this tension between sets and nets, then, is the structure between the practices of accumulation and enchainment and the actions of fragmentation and consumption that are mediated by material and corporal life (Table 6.4). Instruments and containers and their constellation into nets and sets are therefore my chosen proxies for the study of the variety of social life over nearly three million years of hominin use of material culture (Part III).

When the music stopped: the burial at Saint-Germain-la-Rivière

But before the broad sweep can be attempted a practical example is in order to clarify some of the terms and methods advocated in this chapter.

I have chosen the rockshelters at Saint-Germain-la-Rivière, 30 kms east of Bordeaux. Like many in the region these have produced rich collections of Palaeolithic stone and bone implements. In 1934 excavators uncovered the burial of a young adult female, more recently dated directly by radiocarbon to some 19,000 years ago (Drucker and

FIGURE 6.2. The burial container at Saint-Germain-la-Rivière. The body was found within the small tomb. A bison skull, horn core fragments and reindeer antler were found close by (after Vanhaeren and d'Errico 2003:Figure 2 with permission).

Henry-Gambier 2005; Vanhaeren and d'Errico 2003; 2005). This was a time when much of northern Europe had been abandoned due to the spread of ice sheets from Scandinavia onto the northern plains, including the British Isles. Bordeaux would have been at the leading edge of the southern refuge for human populations and further from the ocean due to the lower sea levels. Most of the people in the southern refuge were clustered in Cantabrian Spain and Portugal (Gamble et al. 2005).

The young woman lay on her left side with her legs tucked up, her right hand shielding her face. She lay, covered in ochre pigment, within a container formed of four stone blocks covered by two slabs (Figure 6.2). Seventy years later the excavator's records are not all that we could wish for, but in a recent re-examination Marian Vanhaeren and Francesco d'Errico (2005) are certain that at least eighty-six objects, that they regard as grave

TABLE 6.5. *Four sets of grave goods with the young woman at Saint-Germain-la-Rivière, France (Vanhaeren and d'Errico 2005:Table 1). The rodents almost certainly have no cultural significance*

Sets/Nets	Proxy	Number of categories	Elements
Ornaments	Containers	4	Shells (2 species), steatite bead, red deer canines
Bone tools	Instruments	2	Deer rib and antler 'dagger'
Animal parts	Instruments	4	Taxa: Reindeer, Saiga, Fox and Rodent
		3	Elements: Foot bones (2), jaw
Stone tools	Instruments	8	Blade, notched blade, bladelet, burin, endscraper, burin/endscraper, bec and core

goods, were originally found with the body. These form four related sets (Table 6.5).

Three of the sets are dominated by instruments while the ornaments form the largest set with seventy-five items. These in turn are dominated by seventy-one red deer canines that were commonly used in the Lateglacial to make either necklaces or sewn onto clothing (d'Errico and Vanhaeren 2002). Each has a hole drilled through the root (Figure 6.3). Twelve can be paired with the other from the same animal.

This set, as Vanhaeren and d'Errico (2003; 2005) show, came from fifty-eight male and eight female red deer. The latter represented animals of all ages while among the males equal proportions of 2–4, 4–6 and 6–12-year-olds were present. Two-thirds of the stag canines were decorated with small incisions, but only a third of the hinds.

However, the set of canines is also a net. It demonstrates the principles of extension and expansion since red deer were not present in the Bordeaux area at this severe glacial time. The most likely source for the canines is 300 km to the south-west in Cantabrian Spain where the red deer was a notable refuge species (Altuna 1979). The fauna in the rockshelter is instead dominated by the bones of arid- and arctic-adapted species, saiga antelope and reindeer respectively (Delpech 1983). But stable isotope analysis by Dorothée Drucker and Dominique Henry-Gambier (2005) has shown that at most saiga contributed only 25 per cent of the woman's diet. Instead 70 per cent must have come from either bison or aurochs. These are poorly

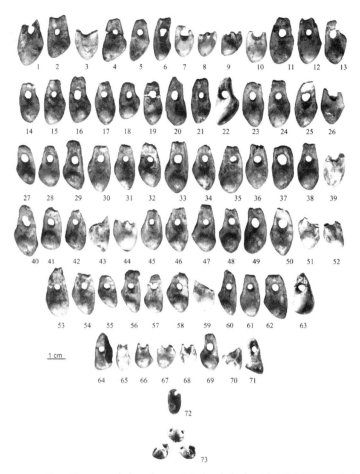

FIGURE 6.3. Grave goods directly associated with the burial at Saint-Germain-la-Rivière. 1–71 are red deer canines, 72 is a steatite bead and 73 three perforated shells (after Vanhaeren and d'Errico 2003:Figure 6 with permission).

represented by bones in the faunal assemblage of the locale but their significance in terms of meat weight must not be underestimated (Drucker and Henry-Gambier 2005:Figure 7 and Table 4). The isotope study raises the possibility of further sets of joints of flesh, bones and portions of fat as well as hides and horns being brought into association. As Jones (2002:101) puts it:

> Breaking and sharing material culture establishes affiliation between people. Similarly the act of accumulating objects and the act of creating composites out of distinct fragments harnesses the relations established in

sharing through cementing and articulating together shared social bonds, and thereby re-articulates a new set of social relations.

Several material projects are therefore on view at Saint-Germain-la-Rivière. The rockshelter was a container for social space that has its own distinctive sets of ornaments, stone tools and animal parts (Vanhaeren and d'Errico 2005:Figure 12) that varied through time but that have a mostly local signature as determined by the raw materials used.

These artefacts are distinct from the burial of the young woman. Her project took the form of a detaching ritual (Gamble 1999:404ff.) from the social gatherings of that place. The actions involved consumption, as shown by the embodied focus of the project, with a strong emphasis on containers as shown by the slabs, the necklace and almost certainly the clothes she was dressed in. The choice of material culture, including a rockshelter, in the act of consumption enfolded this person. However, the accumulation of contiguous sets – the woman, the grave goods, the grave architecture – also continued to enchain her as though alive.

For example, the seventy-one drilled deer canines are a material proxy that expresses in metaphorical form the practices of accumulation and enchainment. They acquired symbolic force by being referenced to her body, although sadly their precise associations with head, neck and clothing are now lost. But what we can say is that they stand in metaphorical relation to the distributed character of the woman's personhood. They were collected as the result of transactions elsewhere and over many seasons. Rather than material memories they can be understood as a metaphor for a distributed mind (Malafouris 2004).

The eight stone tools are acts of fragmentation irrespective of exactly when and where they were made, as are the body parts of animals and the two bone tools. Unlike the composite technology of the ornaments these instruments were made by reduction (Table 6.5). Among both the instruments and containers it is possible to see how this person was extended beyond the boundaries of her own body or the narrow confines of a rockshelter. Just as the single stone tool or the individual deer canine refers metonymically either to complete animals or blocks of stones so the woman is a part of a distributed social network. Around both her and the objects found with her there must have been a wealth of associations: a net cast over large distances and lengthy time periods.

Therefore the burial at Saint-Germain-la-Rivière was not an event given character either by who she was or how she died. She was not singled out for special treatment because of her parents or the charismatic force of her personality. In a hybrid network of people and objects she was the project by which the construction of identity, that hidden mask-like experience, was metaphorically understood.

But we need to lift our eyes from the grave. This project 19,000 years ago was not primarily the burial of a body but the performance of identities inspired by those primary metaphors of the-giving-environment and growing-the-body. The social practices of accumulation and enchainment and the actions of fragmentation and consumption resulted in her body forming a set with its associated materials (Table 6.5). Moreover, her identity was simultaneously a part of a whole with the mourners and their material networks.

Neither did this project finish with her death but continued after the stone slab had been placed over her corpse. What we find at Saint-Germain-la-Rivière and those other rare 'rich' late Palaeolithic burials in France, such as the infant burial at the rockshelter of La Madeleine (Vanhaeren and D'Errico 2001), is that moment when the music stopped and the circle was broken. The networks were cut not necessarily because she died and had to be buried but because by burying her with these extended sets such fragmentation was turned into an act of consumption, the circle restored and the 'dance' continued. Relations were confirmed.

The rational view sees it differently. According to this, the woman belongs to the category of complex hunter-gatherer (Owens and Hayden 1997; Price and Brown 1985; Vanhaeren and d'Errico 2003; Woodburn 1991). What she wore is interpreted as reflecting her special status within society. She was symbolically charged because of who she was, her position and status. Moreover, since these burials are rare, the find points, in the authors' opinion (Vanhaeren and d'Errico 2005), to hereditary ranking systems in a society based on inequality. But this assessment ignores the dominant burial rite in Lateglacial France (23−11,000 years ago) that was not internment in a container, as at Saint-Germain-la-Rivière, but instead the fragmentation of bodies and their distribution through time and space (Table 6.6). The evidence comes from sixty-four rockshelters and only one open site (Le Mort and Gambier 1992). The bones of adults dominate (Table 6.7).

At present it is not possible to say if these human bones also came from far afield, analogous to the deer canines from Saint-Germain-la-Rivière. However, I would not be surprised at such a result once stable isotope analysis is applied so that geographical sourcing can be established. The human material may also have been in circulation for some time, further evidence for the temporally as well as spatially distributed character of

TABLE 6.6. *The fragmentary character of human bodies in the French*
Lateglacial (Gambier 1992; Le Mort and Gambier 1992)

	Number	%
Inhumations	13	6
Dismembered often with traces of cut marks	94	40
Bits and pieces	125	54

TABLE 6.7. *The population structure of human remains in Lateglacial France*
(Gambier 1992; Le Mort and Gambier 1992)

	Number	%
Adults	166	72
Children	66	28

personhood that invariably is counterbalanced by accumulation at particular places. It is in this way that sets and nets stand as the proxies for relationships that are more subtle, personal and provocative than the search for a complex society of hunter-gatherers.

Discussion: running with the social sets

Chapman's methodology is immensely helpful for a relational approach to archaeological evidence. However, his definition of a set as integrally related elements does raise some problems. The fact that elements in a set can be similar or heterogeneous, functionally or symbolically related, seems to cover too many possibilities. It suggests that whenever two or more objects are gathered together they naturally form a set. Neither does quantity seem very important. Emphasis is placed on the context to determine if we are dealing with a set or not. But since the set is integral to our understanding of the context how can it then be used to classify itself? Therefore, all we are presented with is a statement about the nature of archaeological contexts and their contents. Contexts contain sets because sets relate contexts to people, seems to be the conclusion. Simple associations are all that is needed to make a set, but what analytical value does that have? Chapman's definition is therefore too broad to be useful precisely because it is too focused on the origins of metallurgy.

Chapman's methodology is valuable but needs revision in two regards. In the first place, we should forget origins because they bring too many conceptual problems (Chapter 3) and recognise instead that the value of his methodology lies in the links between material culture and a relational, rather than essential, identity. However, as discussed above, Chapman uses enchainment and fragmentation interchangeably, which leads to confusion, while in accepting accumulation and metallurgy as his end point he seems to suggest that those rounded dividual/individual persons (Busby 1997; LiPuma 1998) did not exist until the Bronze Age. The implication is that human identity was for much of prehistory, and certainly the Palaeolithic, distributed and enchained. Alienation of the symbol from its source was an event, post-agriculture, and foreshadowed the origins of modernity (Friedman 1994:143; Thomas 2004). If this was the case then our understanding of change is very similar to earlier notions such as the rise of barbarism, the Neolithic Revolution and the sapient paradox.

And second, Chapman's fragmentation theory misses an obvious target of archaeological enquiry: the notion of the complete object. We have been trained to identify complete objects and our archaeological classifications, not to mention museum displays, reflect this education. However, this is another example of what Iain Davidson and William Noble (1993:365) have rightly termed the 'fallacy of the finished artefact'. We cannot assume that the shape we have in front of us was intended. In Chapter 4 I mentioned Alfred Gell's (1998:257) description of the Maori meeting house as a material project which brings together a rich array of material culture and what he calls *indexes* of agency (1998:253).

These indexes are inferences about cultural meaning achieved not by induction or deduction but by abduction, that leap of faith from the data to its explanation (Levinson 1995), an intellectual short-cut to understanding and often the first strand in the cable of interpretation. Neither are the meeting houses simply symbols of either the community or the craftsmen who built them. They are in Gell's analysis vehicles of that collectivity's power. And because the collective has to socially re-produce itself, so these meeting houses are never finished. The house being built or used now is a project, that index of agency, for houses in the future (Gell 1998:253). It is an example of personhood distributed in space and time and, at his suggestion, could be applied to tombs, shrines and, I would add, the accumulation of elements into sets. All of these examples 'have to do with the extension of personhood beyond the confines of biological life via the indexes distributed in the milieu (Gell 1998:223)'. Projects as foci for individual and collective action are never finished. Sets, like houses, are always available for expansion. Even the simplest tools such as handaxes or wooden digging sticks are unfinished when we assess them as relational rather than rationally constructed artefacts. The handaxe is the vehicle for an individual's power, that symbolic force constituted through materiality.

Therefore the handaxe left behind, apparently carelessly, while still to our eyes serviceable, is part of the project of the next handaxe that will commence in minutes, days or years. In the same way the biological death of an individual is never the finishing point. Not only is that individual's index of agency part of the fabric of material culture but the distribution of artefacts including body parts ensures that relations extend beyond the grave. There can never be a complete artefact set since the concept of expansion always allows for growth. So too there can never be a complete artefact since it only exists in relation to other elements in the network of material culture and those relations are subject to growth and decay, reduction and addition. The young woman buried at Saint-Germain-la-Rivière was not the finished article either in terms of her personhood or her special status. Social life is never finished. It is a continual dance around others, around a flickering fire with tourists looking on.

Raising the bar

Throughout the past three chapters I have drawn down concepts and developed methods to examine my basic proposition; that a study of change must address the material basis of hominin identity. Change is not about revolutions and origins but rather the shifting patterns of authority in our understanding of the reality of the vast array of social projects: an authority that I have shown is based on the experiences of the body as a source for interpretation.

To this end I have provided a framework that builds on earlier models of a social technology (Gamble 1999) and charts in more detail the link between social practices and actions and the material proxies that allow us to investigate such concepts. In Chapter 3 I discussed analogy and homology and remarked on Alison Wylie's (1985:107) call to raise their credibility as inferences within archaeology. In this section I have put the case for a much larger group of rhetorical devices that can be grouped under metaphor. As several archaeologists (Gosden and Marshall 1999; Meskell 2004; Tilley 1999) are now pointing out, such metaphors should not be conceived as simply linguistic. Instead the ability to understand something in terms of something else depends on all the senses of the body and most importantly relates to material culture rather than the spoken word.

But if we are to raise the bar for material metaphors, and so elevate their discussion in archaeology, I am well aware that we meet head-on a major obstacle. This takes the form of another authority tussle, this time between the competing claims of reason and emotion as satisfactory explanations. Archaeologists have predominantly favoured the former, casting their subject as a science. Emotion and bodily experience are accorded a lowly place, if any. But while the advances of such an approach have been considerable in the last forty years there is a real sense that the bar needs re-setting if archaeologists are to make any contribution to the study of material culture (Hamilakis et al. 2002b; Tarlow 2000). As Carl Knappett (2005:167) has pointed out, the crux of the matter is that we work with nothing but objects but currently set ourselves the goal of investigating past attitudes and ideas that are conceived of as non-material. 'Aspiring to mentalism but condemned to materialism, it is hardly surprising that many archaeologists have given up the former altogether (Knappett 2005:168)', and among those who accord a place for phenomenology what remains undeveloped are the methodologies to give the senses and emotion authority in the place of reason.

Hence the long discussion in this section about terms and methods. I have concentrated on metaphor (Tilley 1999) rather than semiotics (Knappett 2005) because of the broad narratives that I want to examine in Part III. The terms I have discussed are intended to stimulate the discussion of the material past as a set of metaphors concerning identity. It is the ways in which those metaphorical relations are connected that is of interest and I have addressed this through a framework that proposes accumulation and enchainment as metaphors for social practice (Tables 6.1 and 6.2), and traced them through material proxies (Table 4.4) that are in turn dependent on actions such as consumption and fragmentation that implicate the body in the material world. Examples have been given of how such concepts as the distributed person can be understood through material culture and each chapter in Part II has been illustrated by those most metaphorical, and usually to archaeologists most mysterious, of hominin qualities: language, art and music. Certainly there are many further meanings here that a semiotics approach could tease out. But my concern is with a structure that pulls the history of the hominins together rather than shatters it along the lines of prior expectation. Let us now start the narrative.

PART III

Interpreting change

CHAPTER 7

A prehistory of human technology: 3 million to 5,000 years ago

> *Sadly, we are about to witness the premature death of Concorde, an*
> *aircraft whose structure still has no finite life. . . . For the first time in*
> *evolution, humankind is about to go slower.*
>
> Brian Christley, Ex-chief Concorde instructor,
> *Guardian letters* 20 October 2003

Highways to the future

I have often thought that the Age of Enlightenment would be better
described as an Era of Entanglement. In their search for a tipping point
for the origins of the modern world, historians motor up and down between
the fifteenth and eighteenth centuries, identifying changes in attitudes
to society, politics and knowledge (Hampson 1968:15). Such a broad
carriageway is strewn with the crashes that resulted from speeding
revolutions, and although the road is initially bumpy the surface improves
as the journey progresses. Technology is an inescapable element in the
narrative. Indeed, the Scottish engineer John Loudon MacAdam, after
whom tarmacadam, or tarmac is named, was born in 1756 at the heart
of the Enlightenment with the Industrial Revolution getting into full
swing. It was his idea to use broken stone 'which shall unite by its own
angles so as to form a hard surface (http://www.hotmix.org/history.php)',
while later hot tar was employed as a bond to keep the surface together
and reduce dust.

Where would the modern world be without tarmacadam pavements?
Caught in the ruts of history no doubt, but more to the point entangled in
other different strands of change. The oldest asphalt street, from the
Greek *asphaltos* meaning secure, is currently a processional way built

in Babylon in the seventh century BC. This was hardly a motor-way system but the Romans, for example, never used asphalt to surface the impressive roads that served their empire.

A technological advance such as road building does not so much slip the ties of history, as revolution implies (Chapters 1 and 2), as entangle the process of change even further. The greatest entanglement of that long Enlightenment carriageway was the discovery and annexation of the New World. When European countries went global they were as much agents of change as changed by their imperial and colonial experiences. They were entangled, if not enlightened, in the process by their experiences of the customs and societies of diverse peoples as well as by vast natural resources, such as the asphalt lakes of Trinidad and Venezuela that one day would pave the United States with MacAdam's idea.

The history of technology, those bright ideas which light our lives and heat our homes, is pre-eminently a narrative about human identity. These identities involve complex interactions between people and objects, cultures and landscapes that are aptly described by anthropologist Nicholas Thomas (1991) through Darwin's metaphor of the tangled vegetation on a bank, that famously appears on the last page of *The origin of species*. The result, as we have seen in earlier chapters, is the hybrid character of human culture where objects as well as people have biographies.

This might suggest that an overview of prehistoric artefacts would be better phrased in terms of material culture, described earlier (Chapter 3), and where I drew a parallel with corporal culture as one of the axes by which symbolic force can be generated (Figure 4.1). However, I have chosen technology not because it is a synonym for material culture, which it certainly isn't, but because from its derivation (Greek *tekhne*) it addresses concepts of skill and knowledge as well as tools and equipment. Technology provides the long view and has been the subject of many studies that chart its development from throwing sticks to supersonic aircraft, drawing conclusions about the pace of progress and, as the Chief Instructor of Concorde implies in my opening quote, noting the need to keep moving ever faster, higher, deeper; the desire of modernity.

But there is another reason to use technology as the framework for a study of change. While philosophers have for a long time examined science as one of their primary concerns there has, by contrast, been little interest in technology other than as applied knowledge (Tiles 2001:483).

However, that view needs to change. As philosopher Steven Woolgar points out:

> Discussions about technology – its capacity, what it can and cannot do, what it should and should not do – are the reverse side of the coin to debates on the capacity, ability and moral entitlements of humans.
>
> (Woolgar 1987:312)

MacAdam used broken stones, but so did hominins 500,000 years ago. The former, by re-arranging them, constructed an identity that is the epitome of the Enlightenment. He fragmented in order to accumulate and through such actions spun a network of technology along which people walked, drove and later cycled, motored and skateboarded. As a result armies could move faster while cities could be provisioned from further afield. The blacktop became a road to freedom, a human right, and as this material metaphor shrank time and distance for individuals and communities, so a space for the performance of identity was created structured by age, gender and technology.

Hominins 500,000 years ago also used their skills and knowledge to construct identities. They fragmented and accumulated stone at specific places and performed identities that danced to comparable tunes. However, *Homo erectus* or the Neanderthals have never been considered as living in an Enlightenment like John MacAdam because their skill in breaking stone is considered inferior.

It is because I want to address these issues of skills and identities that technology rather than material culture is the proper theme. As archaeologist Andy Jones (2002:90) puts it, 'technologies weave together the material, social and symbolic dimensions of human life'. Since the beginning of the discipline archaeologists have been entangled in the history of technology and how it came to calibrate human identity, past and present. But rather than recount again the Three Age System of stone – bronze – iron (Chapter 1) as though it were an archaeologist's tarmacadam pavement, let us dive right into the tangled bank of historical relationships from which it came.

The value of materials

Here we find that the roots reach down to the development of a comparative ethnology that arose from the Spaniards' encounter with indigenous Americans. As expertly laid out by historian Anthony Pagden (1986), the response of sixteenth-century Spanish theologians tasked to explain New World societies was to start with Aristotle's notion of natural slavery that had served the Ancient world well. Francisco di Vitoria, author of the influential *De indis* published in 1539, set out to understand the indigenous Americans using Aristotle's body/soul dichotomy which underpinned the principle that the rich govern and the poor labour. However, when applied to the Americans there was a problem since Aristotle also adhered to a hierarchy of occupations valorised by materials. The harder you worked the more splendid would be the material culture that surrounded you. In this hierarchy stone was more noble than wood which in turn had greater value than mud brick (Pagden 1986:72–3). The pyramids of Central America and the stone-built cities of Peru indicated an unexpectedly advanced level of achievement and therefore a dilemma for an imperial power looking for a clear mandate for rule by right as well as force.

The solution was to devise an explanation for the paradox of material value and social insignificance. Vitoria, and the Salamanca School of sixteenth-century Spain, proposed that the indigenous American was socially a peasant and psychologically a child. They were therefore outside the web of affiliation of civilised men, being only half-reasoning, passion-dominated beings (Pagden 1986:104–5). As a result they were not a different species but rather some form of fully grown child, useful as slaves and labourers to mine the asphalt in Lake Trinidad and pave the way for the Enlightenment.

The fate of the indigenous Americans was therefore entangled with Classical philosophy, technological metaphors and real-politick (Pagden 1986:106). There is an irony that the Classical sequence of change, mud – wood – stone, based on the relative skills of the artisan and the inherent value of materials should, when translated by archaeologists in the nineteenth century, be reversed. The value of skilled stone working was nothing compared to metallurgy, while a single mud-brick village with agriculture was worth all the chipped stone of the Palaeolithic.

And the same technological values persist. The entanglement rather than enlightenment continues with archaeologist Colin Renfrew's (1996) sapient paradox, where he claims that for 30,000 years people possessed the modern mental capacity to use symbols, but either could or did not want to, until a sedentary, farming life allowed them to realise their full potential and assume a modern identity (Chapter 1).

TABLE 7.1. *Two readings of Marxism applicable to changes in technology (after Rowlands 2004; Tiles 2001:489)*

Historically determinist	
Changes in technology and society occur in a historically determined sequence and are largely independent of the actions of individuals	Devices (instrumental)
Dialectical materialism	
Each generation is formed by social and economic structures but at the same time modifying and adapting to changing circumstances	Techniques (substantive)

Why technology changes

Karl Marx has undoubtedly had the greatest influence when it comes to asking why technology changes for the reason that he set out two pathways (Table 7.1). Either route produced the same result: by the application of scientific knowledge through technology, humans were freed from the enslavement of Nature (Tiles 2001:487).

Accordingly, the longest running historical project of humankind, first set out by Plato and Aristotle, has been the pursuit of leisure in order to *cultivate* the rational faculties. The agricultural metaphor is well placed since for these Classical philosophers reason distinguished humans from beasts and knowledge acquired through leisure distinguished the citizen from the peasant.

When the order of change is fixed, as it is for a historical determinist (Table 7.1), then so too is human nature with its wants and needs (for full critique see Pfaffenberger 1992:496). Consequently, the history of technology will be about *devices* that met those unchanging purposes and so established direction. Such fixity can be found, for example, in the universal mechanism of evolutionary descent with modification and the demands this places on the acquisition of subsistence.

Stephen Shennan (2000:811) goes further, arguing that if archaeologists are to explain change then they must view their data from the perspective of a cultural 'descent with modification'. Seen in these terms, selection produces better artefacts and groups of artefacts, archaeological cultures, for the task in hand; reproductive success (Dunnell 1978:199). The objects that serve such purposes remain value-free and need no other reward for a job well done than a historical nod of recognition. Stone tools, fire and the wheel all stand simply as markers on the evolutionary journey.

The process works through incremental change long favoured by pioneering archaeologists such as General Pitt-Rivers who saw a progressive development in technology from crude to fine and simple to complex. His Darwinian faith supported his political convictions since 'the law that Nature makes no jumps can be taught . . . in such a way as at least to make men cautious how they listen to scatter-brained revolutionary suggestions (Pitt-Rivers 1891)'. Thankfully in other circles these laws of progress have long been laid to rest (Sauer 1952:3), and although the tempo of change is also incremental in studies of cultural descent no historical goal is attributed to technological advances (Shennan 2002).

Indeed, studies of cultural transmission foreshadow the dialectical approach to technological change (Table 7.1) with its emphasis on response and adaptation. But the difference is that with a dialectical standpoint human nature is not fixed in the ways described above but dependent on context. Here the emphasis moves away from devices and towards *techniques* that comprise technological systems and technical practices (Tiles 2001). With an emphasis on context, technical knowledge is no longer something that is transmitted between generations. Rather it is produced through social action that involves the relationships between people and things as first laid out by Mauss (1936), and discussed in Chapter 4. Social reproduction rather than reproductive success drives the process. The common-sense, or instrumental, view of historical goals for technology is replaced by a consideration of how it changed both humanity and Nature.

Social technology

I would go much further. Histories of technology (e.g. Basalla 1988) rarely draw attention to the link between technology and human identity. When they do (e.g. Tiles 2001) the accounts are curiously free of either a theory of material culture or an anthropological perspective on body techniques and performance: in short, that thing called agency. Instead of objects having inherent values they are, as we have seen (Chapter 5), implicated as agents in networks of materiality (Gell 1998; Knappett 2005). It is necessary to extricate ourselves from the tangled bank of rational explanations that involve technology and turn instead, as I have done throughout this book, to a relational understanding of those same objects.

In my view any account of the prehistory of technology depends for its form on an understanding of human identity, which is why I refer to a social technology, that 'universality of the process of simultaneous embodiment and production of meaning by a technique (Lemonnier 1993:4)'. Techniques, as anthropologist Pierre Lemonnier points out, are not something to which meaning is added. Instead they involve from the start the incorporation of wider symbolic considerations precisely because technologies are always social constructs (Tiles 2001:486).

Throughout Part II, I presented arguments and evidence to illustrate how technology is actively involved in the construction of identity. This involved a simple division of artefacts into containers and instruments in order to bring out the metaphorical use of material culture to express hidden processes that are understood through bodily experience, processes that are doubly hidden because they are in the past and internal to the person. These material metaphors were structured through the social practices of accumulation and enchainment and the actions of fragmentation and consumption (Table 6.2). The identities that emerge are not the social labels of plant gatherer or ploughman, priestess or king, but rather the negotiation through material relations of a once-inhabited space. Moreover, this approach was taken to support my general proposition that any study of change has to acknowledge the material basis of human identity.

What follows is an account that develops my proposition about change and identity. It will be familiar in places and yet unfamiliar as archaeologists have generally adopted an instrumental approach because, like Gordon Childe (Chapter 1), they follow Marx, changing hats as it suits them to be either a historical determinist or a dialectical materialist (Table 7.1). What I am suggesting needs neither revolutions nor origins to make the subject of change explicable, only an assumption of relatedness and the confidence that bodily experience is habitually expressed metaphorically in a material world.

The technology of eats, roots and leaves

Hominins are not alone in defining their identity with technology either as devices or as techniques that encompass skill and knowledge. Most recently wild-living capuchin monkeys in Northeastern Brazil (Moura and Lee 2004) have joined the technology club. They have been seen on an almost daily basis using stones to crack open seeds and innovatively even for primates, dig for roots and tubers. In evolutionary terms this discovery is equivalent to a virus jumping between species. The New World-Old World monkey split is a foundation event in the course of primate evolution and occurred some 30 million years ago. Until capuchins were observed in the Caatinga dry forest the selection, manufacture and use of a range of artefacts was thought to be exclusive to Old World primates and in particular chimpanzees. The South American evidence from a relatively small brained primate strongly suggests that tool-making and tool-using is an ancestral hominid trait of some antiquity. While these skills could have arisen at different times and places through convergent evolution, they nonetheless dramatically point to material engagements by hominids, not just hominins, in the construction of their worlds.

None of this is of course surprising. Instances of nest building, storing food, amassing residues and selecting shiny objects is commonly found among animals as diverse as birds, reptiles, mammals and insects and comprise what John Odling-Smee (1993) describes as niche construction. Animals fragment and consume on a daily basis while at the same time they also accumulate and enchain themselves to others, often as a requirement of rearing young.

But primate technology is treated differently because of their ancestral relationship to ourselves. The iconic photo by Hugo van Lawick of a wild chimpanzee using a termite probe caused a stir among archaeologists when published in the 1960s. Although captive chimps had long been applauded for their intelligence here was a wild animal showing unsuspected capacities for problem solving. With one image the development in parallel of tools and large brains that archaeologists had long championed was called into question.

Forty years after Jane Goodall's pioneering observations at Gombe, and van Lawick's photograph, no one doubts the technological capacity of chimps that is now spoken of as material culture (McGrew 1992) and compared to human culture (Boesch and Tomasello 1998). In addition, despite the current lack of an archaeological record for chimpanzee material culture, these contemporary observations provide many archaeologists with a starting point for the prehistory of human technology (Davidson and McGrew 2005; Gowlett 2000; Schick and Toth 1993).

The standard view of technology

The first account of capuchin tool use by primatologists Antonio Moura and Phyllis Lee (2004) also provides a characteristic explanation for their presence. They suggest that the stone tools and termite probes were developed by capuchins as a result of the dry forest environment they live in. This environment is a hard one for a small monkey and time and energy are at a premium. Any device that reduces the time spent in getting food therefore stands a strong chance of being selected for and digging for tubers with stones fits the bill. In short, tools provide a more secure subsistence that has a direct benefit in terms of reproductive success for both the capuchin individual and group.

This explanation nicely summarises what anthropologist Bryan Pfaffenberger (1992:493–5) has described as the standard view of technology. What drives such a perspective is the principle that necessity is the mother of invention. Pfaffenberger (1992:496) shows how this derives from the modernist view that there are universal human needs – and how better to demonstrate these than through the technological skills of a wild primate who in the case of the chimpanzee also happens to be a close genetic cousin (Marks 2002)? Primate technology, as Moura and Lee show, is treated as comprising devices to satisfy needs, and for hominids as different as capuchins and chimpanzees these are food and sex. Hominins fare little better in most archaeological accounts. As expressed by archaeologist Steven Kuhn (1995:16) the imperative is that 'in order to bring technological data to bear on major changes in human adaptation, it is essential to explore how toolmaking was related to hominid subsistence behaviour'. Kuhn is writing about the Neanderthals who were present when 'modern' humans arrived in Europe. The controversy about the status of Neanderthals as artists, linguists and morticians (d'Errico et al. 1998; 2003; Gargett 1989; Noble and Davidson 1996) addresses our perception of their nature and needs. Obviously, modern humans had symbolic and spiritual needs in addition to food and sex. Allow these same needs to Neanderthals through possession of ornaments, art and burials and the force of Woolgar's (1987:312) comparison of technological capacity and human entitlement strikes home.

Pfaffenberger, however, is not much concerned with Neanderthals. His target is the notion of universal needs and human nature that technology serves. But if, as he argues, this is a false characterisation then neither does technology meet universal needs nor is it a response to necessity (Pfaffenberger 1992). We remain human even if we have not yet purchased an MP3 player. Our technological identity is not determined by our fixed, inherited needs. Our nature is no more hitched to the hunter's moon as it is to the farmer's wagon or the metropolitan's star.

TABLE 7.2. *A range of behaviours found across six populations of chimpanzees and classified in terms of instruments (I) and containers (C)*

Foraging behaviour with tool use		Groups present	Communicative behaviour		Groups present	Body-oriented behaviour		Groups present
Ant dip	I	4	Missile throw	I	4	Fly whisk	I	3
Honey dip	I	2	Branch haul	I	2	Index hit	I	1
Bee probe	I	1	Stick club	I	3	Ground nest	C	1
Leaf sponge	C ?	4	Hand clasp	I/C	3	Leaf napkin	C	2
Marrow pick	I	1	Leaf clip	I	3	Self-tickle	I/C	1
Nut crack	I	2	Play start	I	3			
Pestle pound	I	1	Knuckle knock	I	1			
Hook stick	I	1	Leaf groom	I	3			
Gum gouge	I	1						
Termite fish	I	3						
Algae fish	I	1						

Data from Boesch and Tomasello 1998:Table 1; McGrew 1992:Table 8.2.

Chimpanzee culture

Even chimpanzees do not have a universal technological nature. The patchy distribution of widely recognised technological and cultural behaviours among six groups of wild chimpanzees spread across tropical Africa (Table 7.2) appears to ape the archaeological definition of culture as a polythetic set in time and space (Gamble 2001:Chapter 3). For example, nut cracking is found in only two of the six groups because of the availability of nuts, while ant dips are present in four (Boesch and Tomasello 1998:Table 1) even though ants are there to eat in the other two areas.

What is very apparent from Table 7.2 is the predominance of instruments among the foraging and communicative behaviours. This point has previously been made by primatologist Bill McGrew (1992) who has commented on the lack of containers in chimpanzee technology. As a result they cannot carry water at all and remain restricted in the amount of food, fruits for instance, that can be transported. The closest they get to a container is the use of leaves as sponges to soak up water from small puddles that they otherwise could not drink from. Leaf napkins are used to wipe parts of their bodies, often after sex (Goodall 1986;

McGrew 1992:187—8), so they form at best a very ephemeral wrapping for the body. But when placed in another environment:

> Chimpanzees spontaneously use containers in captivity, so their absence in nature is not due to lack of intellectual appreciation of the principles involved. Nor is the absence of the container due to lack of raw materials; wild chimpanzees have access to leaves and suitable skins of animals.
>
> McGrew 1992:115 and Figure 10.2

But how does such 'spontaneous use' by chimpanzees differ from the family cat appropriating a cardboard box to sleep in, or a swallow building its nest inside a barn? Chimpanzees might not fashion themselves containers such as grass skirts or skin waterbags but like all animals they inhabit their worlds and its varied affordances. We have no evidence to suppose that they make any distinction between categories such as natural and man made. Their individual identities are therefore contextual rather than given by a roster of universal chimpanzee needs. What makes a chimpanzee a chimpanzee is socially generated at the local level rather than dependent upon some fixed universal nature.

Other animals, such as bees, might seem to lead to a different conclusion. How for example could you be a bee without a honeycomb? But the significant comparison is not that bees make honeycombs while chimpanzees vary in their use of leaf sponges (four out of six groups in Table 7.2), but that both cannot be separated from the environment in which they live as bees and chimpanzees (Barrett and Henzi 2005). The problem with studies of chimpanzee technology that regard it as cultural because it involves social learning (Boesch and Tomasello 1998:592) lies in their markedly determinist approach to the chimpanzees' needs and hence the emphasis on technological 'solutions' to environmental 'problems' (Table 7.2).

The standard view of those needs and the necessity of technological evolution are well illustrated by McGrew (1992) who conceives of containers solely in terms of transporting food and water. In his opinion containers are essential for a fully human society based on reciprocal sharing and the division of labour. His study identifies the external function of technology for a species but not the relations that are created through materiality that I outlined in Part II. Consequently, my definition of containers is much broader than McGrew's. It would include those 'nests', or rather sleeping pallets, that all great apes construct on a daily basis (McGrew 1992:210) as well as the concave mortars which hold the nuts for chimps to crack with hammers of wood and stone (ibid. 1992:Figure 7.7).

These examples of containers could be increased to include gestures and movements that encircle and embrace but which involve no artefacts other than the body and its corporal culture.

Ratchets and ships' anchors

The chimpanzee evidence strongly suggests that a social technology of instruments and containers, based on metaphors derived from the body, is simply part of being a hominid. It is not something unique to hominins or humans although our propensity to elaboration, what Danny Miller refers to as the 'sheer scale of the material world' (Chapter 6), and its continual re-interpretation most certainly is. How we got to this complexity is explained by primatologists Christophe Boesch and Michael Tomasello (1998:602) as the *ratchet effect* of cumulative cultural evolution. They give the following example:

> The way in which human beings have sheltered themselves has evolved significantly over human history as individuals in particular cultures have adapted their existing shelters to shield them from various aspects of the weather (e.g. rain, cold, sun) and various types of predators and pests, to provide themselves with privacy and protection from groupmates, and so on.

The ratchet analogy is chosen since it is a device that keeps things in place while the user prepares to advance them further. Shelter is never abandoned as an idea but weather-proofing provides a spur to technological advance. Their argument is therefore determinist (Table 7.1), based on a common-sense view of how technology satisfies needs (Tiles 2001). Furthermore, it derives its rhetorical force from the baseline it adopts and where chimpanzee technology is set by the supposedly fixed nature of their limited needs. But a ship's anchor provides a better analogy than a ratchet for the process they describe, and where a taut cable leads in a direct, upward line from the deep of primate ancestry to the deck-side complexity of human cultural life. The progressive nature of technology is indeed, as Jones (2002:89) comments, one of the prime structuring principles of Western capitalism.

Stone Age innovation

The standard view, that the history of technology satisfied universal needs, has to be re-assessed by archaeologists. A decade ago Marcia-Anne Dobres and Christopher Hoffman (1994:215–16) set out how the study of past technology requires a simultaneous concern with social interaction, the practical knowledge of techniques and the environment as well as belief systems. They acknowledged the considerable difficulties facing archaeologists interested in these aspects of technology that have since been addressed in more detail (Dobres 2000; Dobres and Robb 2000a). Technology could be used, they argued (Dobres and Hoffman 1994:216), to understand both worldviews and systems of representation as well as the dynamic nature of social production and reproduction. Sensibly at the time they confined their agency-centred approach to the last 20,000 years, leaving evolutionary issues to one side.

Re-assessing the standard view over a longer timespan needs to start by according agency and the associated concept of hybrid culture (Chapter 4) to all hominins as well as hominids such as chimps and capuchins. This inclusivity acknowledges that technology is about more than problem-solving and involves skills and identity. What this means in practice is abandoning a strictly linear analysis of technology in favour of understanding change in terms of the social activities, relationships and tensions involved in hominid and hominin involvement with the material world (Dobres and Hoffman 1994:215).

John Troeng (1993) provides a valuable account of the standard view. He has identified 53 technological innovations that occurred in worldwide pre-literate societies. Writing is therefore absent from his scheme. Any such list is necessarily selective and more recently Brian Fagan's (2004:14) survey covers seventy inventions over a slightly longer time-frame. The technological groupings of the two schemes are comparable but organised differently (Table 7.3).

When presented as a timeline both studies show a compound increase in terms of innovations and in Fagan's case an exponential rise after 7,000 years ago. This ratchet effect would have an even greater impact if the phenomenal diversity of artefact types made possible by the later inventions — pottery or glass for example — were added to the charts. Either way the result appears as an overwhelming endorsement for ratcheted change and could, if wished, be used to explain the Human and Neolithic Revolutions (Chapters 1 and 2).

Three movements in the history of technology

But what if we reject such a teleological approach to the history of technology and analyse these same lists in terms of material metaphors? I have done this in Table 7.4 for Troeng's list, classifying the same

TABLE 7.3. *The history of technological innovations by major categories (Fagan 2004; Troeng 1993)*

Technologies (Troeng 1993)	Number of innovations	Technologies (Fagan 2004)	Number of inventions
Crushing	2	Hand-held artefacts	12
Stone	11	Shelter and subsistence	18
Bone	3	Transportation	11
Structures	2	Hunting, warfare and sport	10
Composite artefact	5	Art and science	14
Axe and adze	3	Adorning the person	5
Skin and fibre	4		
Mineral	4		
Aquatic resources	4		
Plant resources	3		
Animal keeping	3		
Symbolic	4		
Fire and containers	5		
Totals	53		70

inventions as either containers or instruments, those material proxies for the metaphors of bodily experience (Chapter 4). When the two proxies are sorted on a timeline (Table 7.4) we see that a drift occurred from instruments to containers as the dominant mode of innovation. For clarity and yes, I admit, tradition's sake, I have divided this huge timespan into three, from the oldest stone tools in Ethiopia (Semaw et al. 1997) to the appearance of writing in Mesopotamia (Fagan 2004) (Table 7.4; Figure 7.1). For narrative purposes, and because I am describing a social technology, I will call these divisions, starting with the oldest, the long introduction, the common ground and the short answer. I think of them as temporal movements in a musical sense since they are of different duration yet contain repeated themes and phrases.

The take-home message from these charts (Figure 7.1) is not that there was a container revolution some 20,000 years ago but that throughout the evolution of human technology both material proxies have existed. The exact ratio will always be difficult to gauge because, as every archaeological study of technology observes, containers are often made with organic materials and so have a poorer chance of preservation, matched only by instruments such as wooden spears. Finally, it is important to point

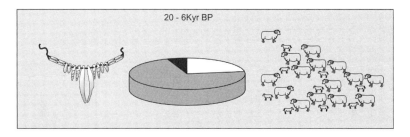

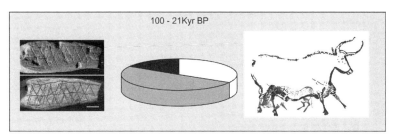

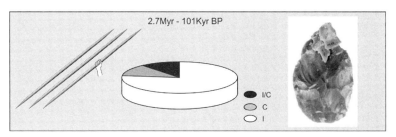

FIGURE 7.1. The changing proportions of technological innovations from instruments to containers (instruments = I, containers = C, and hybrids = I/C) see Table 7.4. The time periods refer to the three technological movements, Table 7.5. See Figures 7.7 and 8.6.

out that Figure 7.1 only addresses the issue of devices and not the wider techniques where the body itself acts as a container and instrument in the day-to-day activities of living and nurturing (see Chapter 6).

I have also assessed the fifty-three innovations in terms of reductive, additive and composite technologies (Table 6.3). As proposed by Chapman (2000) these provide an assessment of technical knowledge and skill. The proportions for the three movements are shown in Table 7.5.

Once again there are obvious changes in the frequency of techniques. Additive technologies are more important in the short answer while reductive technologies dominate during the long introduction. However, the point to note is that all three technologies are found in all movements. What now follows is a brief discussion of the archaeological evidence

TABLE 7.4. *The timing and classification of 53 innovations as material proxies during hominin evolution (after Chapman 2000; Fagan 2004; Troeng 1993)*

Innovation	Instrument container	Minimum horizon Ka BP	Technology Reductive	Additive	Composite
L Stone flaking	I	2600	×		
O Stone pounding	I	1800	×		
N Stone tools	I	1700	×		
G Pointed stone tools	C	1700	×		
Control of fire	C	1600		×	
I Stone bifaces	I	1400	×		
N Stone cleavers	I	1400	×		
T Cave occupation	C	1400		×	
R Stone ball weapons	I	500	×		×
O Wooden spears/javelins	I	400	×		
D Stone points	I	390	×		×
U Ochre use	I/C	380	×		
C Stone flaking – prepared core technology	I/C	240	×		
T Stone blades	I	220	×		
I Stone points – leaf-shaped	I	220	×		×
O Stone end scrapers	I	160	×		
N Human burials	C	130		×	
Bevelled bones	I	130	×		
Beads or pierced pendants	C	95	×		×
Barbed bone points	I	90	×		×
Hearths suitable for cooking	C	80		×	
Bone awls	I	70	×		
Water containers – ostrich eggshell	C	70	×		

172

	Activity	Type	BP				
C	Stone grinding	I/C	58	×			
O	Mining	C	44	×			
M	Shellfish collection	C	41			×	
M	Fishing	I/C	41			×	×
O	Stone microblades	I	40	×		×	×
N	Stone axes/adzes	I	40	×		×	×
	Stone adzes	I	35	×		×	×
G	Rock Art	C	32			×	
R	Geometric microliths	I	31	×		×	×
O	Stone boring	I/C	30	×		×	×
U	Figurines	I	30	×		×	
N	Textiles	C	30			×	
D	Ceramics	C	30			×	
	Twining and plaiting	C	27			×	
	Sewing	C	26				×
	Keeping dogs	C	21			×	
S	Storage	C	20			×	
	Pottery	C	16			×	
H	Stone points – transverse	I	14	×		×	×
O	Water craft	C	13	×		×	×
R	Fish-hooks	I	12	×			
T	Rectangular dwellings	C	11			×	×
	Legume use	C	11			×	
A	Edge grinding of stone axes/adzes	I	10	×			
N	Propagation of plants	C	10			×	
S	Keeping of ruminants	C	9			×	
W	Cultivated cereals	C	8			×	
E	Keeping of non-ruminants for food	C	8			×	
R	Cultivation of fibre plants	C	7			×	
	Metal use	I/C	6				×

BP = Before Present, instruments = I, containers = C, and hybrids = I/C. See Table 6.3 and Figure 7.1.

TABLE 7.5. *The changing proportions of social techniques applied to Troeng's 53 innovations*

Social technology movements	Ka BP	Reductive (%)	Additive (%)	Composite (%)	No.	Ka BP	Europe & Asia Palaeolithic	Africa Stone Age
The short answer	20–6	20	55	25	20	50–10	Upper	Later
The common ground	100–21	40	33	27	30	300–50	Middle	Middle
The long introduction	2600–101	72	14	14	21	2600–300	Lower	Earlier

The total of 72 is accounted for by some innovations being represented by more than one technique (see Table 7.4). The traditional divisions for the Eurasian and African Palaeolithic are also shown (see also Table 7.7).

for the three categories, instrument, container/instrument and container that appear in Table 7.4.

Instruments (N = 27 Table 7.4)

We have become accustomed to stone tools alone providing the long introduction to human technology. The earliest are currently 2.6 million years old (Semaw et al. 1997) from Gona, Ethiopia, and certain to get older. Stone cobbles, preferentially selected for their fracturing properties (Stout et al. 2005), were knapped to produce at least two components; sharp edged flakes and the core from which they were struck that may or may not have had a further function. That depended on the context. The struck artefacts were hand-held instruments used for fragmenting the world of plants and animals. Wielded as knives, hammers or scrapers they pounded open bones to reveal the marrow within, split nuts and large fruits and cut branches and grasses. They could even have been thrown. They are not heavy, weighing much less than a nursing infant, but were never carried very far, a few hours walk at most (Féblot-Augustins 1990; Jones 1994; Stiles 1998). On occasion the cobbles were piled up into small caches and parts of animal carcasses brought to them where they were broken open (Potts 1993; 1988).

From the outset we have evidence for techniques that fragment and consume, while accumulation and enchainment were common social practices. The distances may be small in spatial and social terms and the stone piles and animal carcasses unimpressive by later standards. Even so, the material basis for the construction of identity was not something that had to evolve since it was always present as a condition of material life.

Instruments in stone dominate the long introduction to technology (Table 7.4). New forms appear such as hand-held bifaces, also known as handaxes, and a plethora of smaller tools with reduced edges that include endscrapers, triangular points and other forms suitable for projectile tips. During much of the Palaeolithic stone is not worked into containers such as bowls, cylinders and pipes or used to build houses, the trademark container. Neither is there much evidence for the use of other materials to build shelters, clothe bodies or wrap food.

The picture of the long introduction provided by stone instruments is, however, illusory. Forty years of observations of tool use among wild chimpanzees (McGrew 1992) has emphasised the importance of organic instruments (Table 7.2) and the vagaries of preservation among organic materials at Palaeolithic time-scales. Hence the justified excitement when wooden spears are recovered from locales such as Schöningen (Thieme 1999; 2005) and planks from Gesher-Benot-Ya'aqov (Goren-Inbar et al. 2002b). The identification of plant residues on Acheulean bifaces, as at Peninj in Tanzania (Dominguez-Rodrigo et al. 2001), indicates their regular use on organic materials, especially wood. However, in the absence of material evidence the prevailing view is that for much of human cultural evolution technology was reductive rather than additive (Chapman 2000) and as a result instrument-based. Furthermore, the expectation that composite technologies may have existed is generally low (Schick and Toth 1993).

Organic instruments finally make an impact after 100,000 years ago

Wood may preserve poorly but bone, antler and ivory present an organic medium that survives in a variety of circumstances, although they too are rarely found prior to the common ground 100,000 years ago. Many examples of points have been suggested, in particular from the Spanish locales of Torralba and Ambrona. However, a detailed analysis by Paola Villa and Francesco d'Errico (2001) did not authenticate them as artefacts although elsewhere bone was used to make bifaces as at Castel Guido, Italy (Villa 1991).

During technology's common ground the evidence increases. At Salzgitter-Lebenstedt, Germany, 23 instruments, among them a triangular bone point (Gaudzinski 1998; 1999:Figure 13), were made from mammoth ribs and fibulae. In Africa the picture is richer. At Katanda, Democratic Republic of Congo, Alison Brooks and colleagues (1995) have found a well crafted set of barbed and unbarbed harpoons that date to c. 90,000 years ago. They come from three contexts beside the Semliki River and were probably hafted to fish spears. At the coastal cave of Blombos, South Africa, and in Middle Stone Age levels in excess of 70,000 years old 28 shaped and polished bone tools have been excavated (Henshilwood et al. 2001). These include awls and points, one of which has indentations which probably assisted binding to a haft (Henshilwood and Sealy 1997:Figure 6). The organic points from both Blombos and Katanda are very different in terms of the shaping skills employed than the sharpened mammoth ribs and fibula of Salzgitter-Lebenstedt. If a comparison of technical skill is to be made it is with the much older wooden javelins from Schöningen.

The important point to take away from this short review is that all of these organic artefacts are instruments. Moreover, they are the product of reductive rather than additive technologies. Only in rare instances do we glimpse composite technologies as with the 75,000 year old lump of pitch resin from Königsaue (Mania and Toepfer 1973) and the bitumen still adhering to a stone tool from Umm el Tiel, Syria 40,000 years ago (Boëda et al. 1996). Both finds indicate that stone tools were hafted.

Questioning reason and need

The standard view is well stated by Villa and d'Errico (2001:106) who suggest that the lack of organic points during technology's long introduction was the result of technological necessity. Hunting involved shooting heavy, stone tipped projectiles into large and medium sized-game from close quarters: a strategy confirmed by the African evidence. Longer range hunting with, or without the assistance of a bow or spear thrower requires, among other things, weight-reduction, which would be achieved by the use of bone. Further subsistence change led to the hunting of alternative prey such as birds and a dependence on fishing, underscoring the necessity of weight reduction for spears, arrows and hooks.

Studies of technological change have therefore been directed towards the description and then interpretation of differences, through time, in artefact technology and typology. Linking stone tools to subsistence was the imperative (Kuhn 1995), resulting in rational explanations for any change or variation; tools met subsistence and social needs and both their manufacture and shape were under selection. In this way changes in tools, whether of bone or stone, must confer adaptive advantage otherwise there would be no clear direction to change over time. However, Pfaffenberger (1988:242) reminds us of Marx's insight that 'the Western ideology of objects renders invisible the social relations from which technology arises and in which any technology is vitally embedded', and most archaeological studies of stone tools provide a good example of exactly how hidden they are.

The standard view is undoubtedly encouraged by the common perception of stone and wood as inanimate, summed up by idioms such as 'turned to stone' and 'flinty-hearted', not to mention 'a wooden performance' by 'bumps on a log'. But isn't there also the 'living rock' and the 'tree of life'? Many other cultures regard stone as animate and as a result display a relational attitude towards minerals (Boivin 2004; Parker-Pearson 2004). Archaeologist Adam Brumm (2004:147) points

TABLE 7.6.   *Defining blades and bladelets (after Bar-Yosef and Kuhn 1999:323)*

Typological: any flake that is more than twice as long as it is wide is a blade. However, ratios of 2.5−4:1 are often preferred.

The maximum length of blades is conditional on the raw material. At Étiolles, France, blades of between 30 and 40 cm in length have been found and refitted to their parent core (Pigeot 1987). Smaller raw material in Upper Palaeolithic locales in southern Germany produced blades up to 12 cm in length with a mean of 3 cm (Owen 1988).

Technical: elongated blanks with parallel or slightly converging edges.

Normally blades possess one or more ridges running parallel to their long axes that gives them a triangular or trapezoidal cross-section.

Bladelets: these are distinguished from blades by an arbitrary maximum width of between 10 and 15 mm (Owen 1988; Tixier 1963).

The width sets limits on the maximum length that bladelets can achieve rarely exceeds 45 mm with most being under 35 mm (Goring-Morris 1987:375).

Microblades: are even smaller than bladelets and are normally produced by pressure flaking.

Microlith: a boundary of 9 mm in width is used to distinguish unretouched from retouched bladelets (Tixier 1963). Retouched pieces falling below this threshold are normally called microliths.

to the correlation among indigenous Australians between the power of place and the power of stone. The Ngilipitji quartzite quarry in eastern Arnhem Land (Jones 1985; Jones and White 1988) has a special significance for the Yolngu who are its traditional owners. For them quartzite grows in the ground where it is 'pregnant' with 'baby stones' or 'eggs'. The sparkling quality of quartzite is likened to blood which has a brilliant quality, *bir'yun*, and anthropologist Howard Morphy (1989) has argued that this brilliance confers aesthetic value. Such resources are therefore valued over and above their properties to make efficient spear points. They enchain people materially and through memory, as shown in Kim Mackenzie's classic film of a visit to Ngilipitji, *The spear in the stone*, and detailed for many other parts of Australia through the stone axe trade by Isabel McBryde (1978; 1988; 1997). Then, as always with stone, the action of fragmentation and the practice of accumulation are strongly represented, and with them a relational approach to material culture is possible. Rather than stone tools these are mineral veins, lithic networks of people.

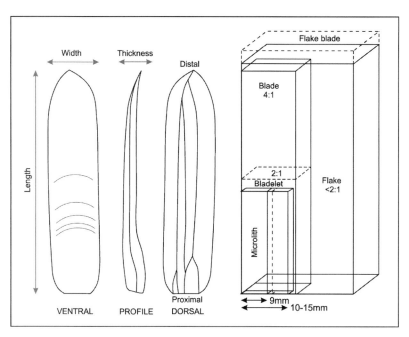

FIGURE 7.2. The family of blades, bladelets, microliths and flakes. Each member of the family is distinguished by measurements and ratios. These refer to length and width and less commonly to thickness.

The fuss about blades: a study in rational and relational change

Both views of technology, rational and relational, can be illustrated by a stone artefact with about as much charisma as an iron nail but with an equal measure of indispensability for holding the world together. Stone blades are a versatile element of material culture found in all three movements of the social technology (Table 7.4). Few other stone items in the innovations list enjoy such popularity. For instance, bifaces and cleavers that are widespread in the Old World (Gamble and Marshall 2001; McNabb et al. 2004) do not make it into technology's short answer, while polished stone axes that you can see your face in, and chop down a tree with, are no older than this last technological movement (Fagan 2004). In addition blades figure large in discussions of the Human Revolution as both a device and a technique (Chapter 2). They provide me with the opportunity to contrast the standard view with my preferred social technology (Table 7.6; Figure 7.2).

To understand what the 'big deal is about blades' (Bar-Yosef and Kuhn 1999), Steven Mithen (in Fagan 2004) has used the analogy of the

Swiss Army Knife to underscore their utility and versatility. Not only can they act as tools in their own right with long, straight cutting edges but they serve as blanks that can be snapped, ground and retouched in a number of ways to form lightweight components ideal for combining into composite tools and weapons. They can do everything that those cores and flakes did at Gona 2.6 million years previously, but they can do it better and they can do more. As pointed out fifty years ago by archaeologist André Leroi-Gorhan (1957; Tactikos 2003), they do it more efficiently so long as the accepted measure of efficiency is cutting edge per kilo of raw material and an overall weight reduction of blade blanks (Figure 7.3).

Blades, cores and the human revolution

Where would the Human Revolution be without stone blades? They certainly dominate the Upper Palaeolithic lithic technologies of Europe as well as the Later Stone Age of Africa but they failed to impress during technology's common ground in either Australia or the Western Pacific (Allen and Gosden 1991; Holdaway and Stern 2004). Now this could be comparable to some chimpanzee groups using stones to crack nuts and others choosing not to (Table 7.2). But more importantly the production of blades is only one variant in a larger family of prepared core technologies, abbreviated to PCTs, that are found in all three technological movements.

The important technological concept in PCT is the *core* since it brings together skills, knowledge and technique (Schlanger 1996). Cores, however, are often difficult to define in precise terms (Holdaway and Stern 2004:37−8). This is because their visual and tactile characteristics are not discrete but shared with other categories of stone tools, notably those flakes and tools that are struck from them. Furthermore, since the whole process starts with a lump of raw material when exactly does the knapper stop fragmenting a nodule and commence on working a core? It is like asking at what moment does eating produce the core of an apple, and stone cores therefore provide a good example of an on-going project rather than a finished artefact ready for classification (Chapter 6).

Exactly how archaeologists classify a chipped stone as a core is not, however, my main concern. It is enough to appreciate that cores are the result of both fragmentation, knapping a nodule of raw material, and the consumption of those fragments that is structured in a social technology by accumulation and enchainment. Cores are also a good example of a material metaphor where the body provides an understanding of the skills

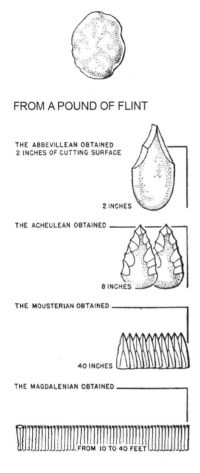

FROM A POUND OF FLINT

THE ABBEVILLEAN OBTAINED
2 INCHES OF CUTTING SURFACE

2 INCHES

THE ACHEULEAN OBTAINED

8 INCHES

THE MOUSTERIAN OBTAINED

40 INCHES

THE MAGDALENIAN OBTAINED

FROM 10 TO 40 FEET

FIGURE 7.3. A progressive view of stone technology. Efficiency is measured by an increase in the amount of cutting edge that different knapping techniques produce (after Leroi-Gourhan 1957).

and technique involved. The outer covering of a stone nodule is called the *cortex*, from the Latin for bark, and has a skin-like appearance. As flakes and blades are detached from the nucleus, or core, they are described in terms of two different *faces* (Figure 7.2), ventral (front) and dorsal (back). The terms proximal and distal are applied to the *head* and the *foot* of both cores and flakes as determined by the origin of the force applied, a geographical proxy for the knapper herself (Figure 7.4). The act of fragmenting is spoken of as leaving *scars* on the core's surface. These are

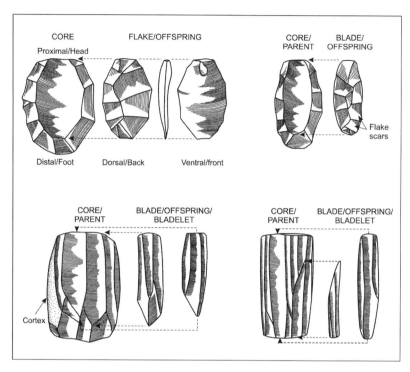

FIGURE 7.4. Lithic parents and offspring in Prepared Core (flake/blade) Technology. Top left PCT1 = Levallois with a flake, and descriptions that refer to the body. The arrows show the direction from which the offspring were detached by a blow from either a hard or soft hammer, with or without a punch placed on the striking platform to direct the blow; PCT2 = Levallois with a blade; Bottom left PCT3 = Prismatic core with blades struck from one direction; PCT4 = Prismatic core with blades and bladelets struck from two directions (bipolar) thereby increasing the number of recognisable offspring. Note how the concave surface of the cores after the flake/blade instruments have been struck-off forms a shallow container.

ridges and hollows that can on occasion be re-fitted to the struck fragments. It is the convex and concave shapes of the surfaces that makes the cores in a PCT both instrument and container (Table 7.4).

The description of actions involving cores and their products abound in bodily references. The skill of the knapper resides in 're-juvenating' the core to extract more material and a spent core is often referred to as 'exhausted'. A flake with two ventral faces is a Janus flake, after the Roman guardian of doorways, while there are also waisted blades, shouldered points and pieces with curved backs and noses.

Cores are regarded as parent material although the 'useful' fragments, the flakes and blades, are never called offspring but are given names as various types of tools; endscraper, point, awl. Set besides these useful elements are the by-products of knapping, the chips, chunks and rejects, that are often called waste; ejecta rather than excreta.

Fragmenting cores is described by Nathan Schlanger (1996:248) as thinking through the hand, a sequence of bodily techniques that interplay with the material and are described by Leroi-Gourhan's term *chaîne opératoire* (Boëda et al. 1990; Gamble 1999:214–23; Julien 1992). PCTs have been used to indicate forward thinking and the ability to conceptualise the desired object in the stone and realise it through knapping. Schlanger argues differently. Instead of a prior concept, or mental image, the product emerges as a suite of gestures that have been learned and assimilated as body techniques. The evidence of preparation in a PCT is not therefore in thought but in action. Cores are material metaphors rather than cognitive templates and refer to the bodies that created them. We understand them as material culture because they are embodied.

The best known PCT is the Levallois technique (Boëda 1994; Brantingham and Kuhn 2001; Dibble and Bar-Yosef 1995; Holdaway and Stern 2004; Schlanger 1996) that is widespread throughout the Old World and Australia. This PCT is at least 300,000 years old and probably much older still. The essence of Levallois PCT is the preparation of a nodule as a core prior to detaching flake-blanks of desired shape and size (Bordes 1980). Large flake-blades are often produced using the Levallois PCT, but these differ in size and shape (Figure 7.4) from the blades described in Table 7.6. Levallois flakes can also be likened to a Swiss Army Knife (see above) but they would be larger and heavier and there would be fewer 'gadgets' than the top-of-the-range blade model.

'True' blades require a prismatic rather than a Levallois core. To produce one involves bifacial flaking to prepare ridges on the face of the core. The technique can be recognised by its characteristic by-product the ridge straightening flake (Fr. *lame à crête*). The long parallel scars on the surface of the core look like fingers drawn through sand or wet clay.

With two versions of a Swiss Army Knife on offer it comes as little surprise to find that the Levallois PCT has also been proposed as the archaeological marker of the Human Revolution sometime towards the end of technology's long introduction. Using Grahame Clark's technological modes (Table 7.7), bioanthropologists Robert Foley and Marta Lahr (Foley and Lahr 1997; Lahr and Foley 1998) have proposed that his Mode 3 represents the emergence and subsequent diaspora of anatomically modern humans.

For Clark, Foley and Lahr the Australian sequence indicates little beyond a Mode 3 technology even though the continent was first colonised

TABLE 7.7. *Technological modes in the Palaeolithic (after Clark 1969:31). Clark offered the modes as a homotaxial sequence which at least in Africa and Eurasia, at the time he was writing, followed the progression from Mode 1 to Mode 5. However, although he was writing a world prehistory Clark never claimed his modes were universal stages (1969:30). Instead they were his attempt to escape from the historical thorn bushes of what to call prehistoric hunters and gatherers in different continents. For example, they certainly were not Palaeolithic in Australia or the Americas. The main problem with these modes is that they unduly privilege stone tools and all other aspects of technology and material culture are forgotten*

Mode	Dominant lithic technologies	Conventional divisions in Europe	Examples of PCTs
5	Microlithic components of composite artefacts	Mesolithic	Bladelet, Naviform
4	Punch-struck blades with steep retouch	Upper Palaeolithic	Prismatic
3	Flake tools from prepared cores	Middle Palaeolithic	Levallois
2	Bifacially flaked handaxes	Lower Palaeolithic	Victoria West
1	Chopper tools and flakes		

when Mode 4 was widespread in the Old World. Their argument is that Mode 3 is a more reliable archaeological signature of Modern humans than Mode 4 since it can be found with them in Africa at 300,000 or Australia 60,000 years ago. Furthermore, Mode 3 was available to other species such as the Eurasian Neanderthals during this quarter of a million years which implies that the cognitive and evolutionary changes which began around 300,000 years ago in Africa and Eurasia had significant consequences for the social technologies of more than one hominin.

In Foley and Lahr's (1997:26) opinion 'blades are regionally not globally important'. For them the later development of blades has more to do with the subsequent differentiation of groups through material culture and is not indicative of the first appearance of modern human behaviour (Foley 2001b:192). Consequently both prismatic and Levallois PCTs are widely cited as evidence for planning and anticipation (Table 7.8) that would be expected with modern human behaviour (Bar-Yosef 2002).

The case that these two forms of PCT should be treated equally is reinforced by their long chronological overlap and their patchy presence in

TABLE 7.8.   *Binford's definitions of forward thinking associated with Modern humans rather than Neanderthals, blade rather than flake PCTs (1989:19–20)*

Planning depth
'The potentially variable length of time between anticipatory actions and the actions they facilitate, amount of investment in anticipatory actions, and proportion of activities so facilitated'

Tactical depth
'The variable capacity, based on stored knowledge of mechanical principles, environmental characteristics, and hence opportunities, to find more than one way to skin a cat'

Curation
'The degree to which technology is maintained . . . While planning depth may be present without curation, it is difficult to imagine curation without planning depth'

many regions. Advances in dating are repeatedly pushing back the anti- quity of prismatic blades and Levallois flakes. But there are also much older PCTs such as Kombewa (Tixier and Turq 1999) and Victoria West (Mitchell 2002) that produces a single large flake from a big cobble. This serves as a blank for bifaces and cleavers and is common in Africa (Gamble and Marshall 2001).

For a long time blades simply came and went rather than carried all before them as a significant technological advance might be expected to do. Ofer Bar-Yosef and Steven Kuhn (1999) have pointed out there are many examples of blades which pre-date by a considerable time the European Upper Palaeolithic (Conard 1992; Révillion and Tuffreau 1994; Tuffreau 1993). For example, the Amudian assemblages of the Near East contain blades and at Tabun, one of the Mt Carmel caves in Israel, these are now dated to between 270,000 and 300,000 years old (Bar-Yosef and Kuhn 1999:325; Jelinek 1990). Furthermore, blades are found in large numbers at early dates in Africa, most noticeably at Kapthurin in Kenya (McBrearty and Brooks 2000) dated to 240,000 years ago, and in the later Howieson's Poort assemblages across southern Africa, 60,000 to 80,000 years ago (Deacon 1995; Mitchell 2002; Parkington 1990). Here, Klasies River Mouth (Singer and Wymer 1982) is the most important locale on account of its long stratigraphy that shows the fluctuating fortunes of blades and flake-blades in the technological repertoire. Furthermore, flake-based assemblages continue long after blades are widespread; for example the Badegoulian of western Europe (Hemingway 1980), the Ahmarian of Israel (Bar-Yosef and Kuhn 1999:329) and the many regional traditions in Australia (Lourandos 1997).

As a result, Bar-Yosef and Kuhn believe there is no justification for linking the appearance of blades to changes either in hominin anatomy or behavioural capacity. Rather the question is 'why so many blades, in so many places?' (ibid.:331) throughout the Old World after 250,000 years ago. The question they pose is what problem blades solved that other PCTs such as Levallois could not? Were they, for example, convergent responses to recurrent environmental problems?

But their question could equally be applied to Levallois flakes after 300,000 years ago. As Nicolas Rolland (1995:351) has shown, Levallois PCT emerged independently in several regions of Africa and Europe. Moreover, this PCT involved different knapping routines to produce the flake blanks that were secondarily retouched into tools. Neither is it the case that once found such PCTs then became ubiquitous. The frequency of Levallois technique can, as François Bordes (1953; 1968) famously showed, vary from assemblage to assemblage within a single locale and between locales within small regions such as south-west France.

The standard view of blades: preparation, planning and anticipation

The most common answer to Bar-Yosef and Kuhn's question about the problems which PCTs and especially blades solved is presented in terms of organisational planning. Levallois PCT shows some preparation, while the production of blades points to increased planning and anticipation of future needs.

Traditionally the appearance of blades has been explained as a consequence of adaptation. They are lighter than flakes (hence the description *leptolithic* which was once applied) and therefore suitable for hafting (Churchill 1993). It is argued that composite tools such as arrows for bows and spears propelled by spear-throwers (atlatls) represent greater energy investment so that anticipation and foresight are indicated. This reasoning is underpinned by the currency of energy and the proxies of time and distance. It is best shown in archaeologist Lewis Binford's classic discussion of technological responses to the geographical distribution of resources in terms of curated and expedient solutions (Table 7.8).

Binford (1973; 1979; 1989) analysed the organisational differences between the two forms of PCT. His focus was on the European Middle and Upper Palaeolithic and what he brought to their analysis was a model

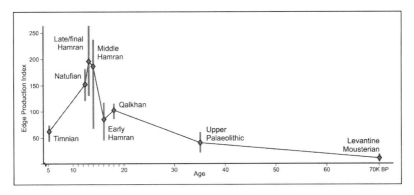

FIGURE 7.5. Changing measures of edge efficiency in the Southern Levant (after Henry 1995:Figure 21.4).

of land use (Binford 1980) and technological organisation (Binford 1977) inspired by his ethnoarchaeological work in northern Alaska. The first stage in his argument was to propose distinctive biographies for tools. These range from expedient (pick it up, use it, throw it away) to curated (recycle, repair, re-use it). Expedient tools provide the archaeologist with a fine-grained signature of what went on at a locale. Curated assemblages are sampling other places in the region and other times of the organisational cycle.

At the heart of his distinction lies the currency of energy (Chapter 3). The time spent in obtaining raw materials, the skill evident in turning them into tools and the care they received all pointed to curated tools as having higher energy inputs. The selective pressure behind such investment is directed towards more secure returns and the route to this goal lies (Binford 1989:19) in planning depth, tactical depth and curation (Table 7.8).

However, the efficiency of blades over flakes has been questioned by Joanne Tactikos (2003) in a study combining archaeological and experimental assemblages. Her goal was to test Leroi-Gourhan's (1957) claim that changes in technological efficiency could be measured by the increase in the ratio of the amount of cutting edge to the mass of the original stone nodule (Figure 7.3). In her study Tactikos found little difference in values between flake and blade PCTs until the Mesolithic 10,000 years ago when microblades dominated. Donald Henry's (1995) study of edge production values in the southern Levant (Figure 7.5) comes to similar conclusions with the only significant increase in values occurring after 20,000 years ago when microblades were also common (Goring-Morris 1987).

Since a currency such as energy provides a measure of the artefact proxy being studied (Chapter 3) then it is not casting much light on the evolution of prepared core technologies even though they are embedded in the archaeological literature as the best thing before sliced bread.

Why blades? A frozen accident or the need to relate?

I have dwelt at length on stone blades for two reasons. Not only are they present in all three technological movements but archaeologists have also attached particular significance to them for the study of change. At one time the possession of blades in a Palaeolithic tool-kit was a passport to modern human status, equivalent to other symbolic markers such as a chin, art and the habit of burying the dead. By adopting blades a hominin could challenge their anatomical identity of being a Neanderthal, like St Césaire (Lévêque et al. 1993), and stake a claim to be a fully modern human like ourselves (Chapter 2).

Bar-Yosef and Kuhn (1999:332) answer their own question about what problems blades solved by identifying a dual shift in the allocation of technological effort and a change in social networks. With blades technological effort was 'frontloaded' by putting time into planning and making composite tools well before any return from the use of tools in hunting or trapping. The co-ordination and co-operation this required led to the re-casting of social networks in order to support such a significant delayed return on labour. However, they are quick to point out that complex composite tools are neither a necessary nor sufficient condition for the proliferation of blades, and they conclude by suggesting that the preference for blades in western Eurasia was a 'frozen accident' in the evolution of technology; a trait fixed by historical circumstances rather than a measure of adaptive success (1999:333).

So what is my solution to the question of blades — particularly as the studies by Tactikos and Henry dispel any idea that the Human Revolution saw a significant increase in technological efficiency that gave an adaptive advantage to people who wielded blades?

I would start by challenging the assertion that there was a problem to be solved in such a rational fashion. Of course people needed to eat, keep warm, identify with friends and oppose enemies. And of course technology assisted them and some tools did it more efficiently than others, just as rifles increase hunting success over bows and arrows. The rational arguments of the standard view are therefore entirely logical and I commend them to you. However, my point is that there was no *problem* because the inspiration for a corporal life of instruments and containers, the body, was never itself a problem that needed a solution. Instead, the body was a source of symbolic force (Chapter 4) when associated with instruments and containers. There was never a problem to be solved by an external technology because it was always integral to that creative, social power. What we understand by changes in lithic technology are not simply extra-somatic solutions to a capricious environment. Rather they are intra-somatic expressions of our social agency that because of enchainment are simultaneously inter-somatic as well.

The Western understanding of the individual who stops at the skin was examined earlier (Table 5.4) where I showed that concepts of person-hood range from distributed, where inter-somatic linkages are constituted through relationships, to the socially separate individual. Neither are these identities in any evolutionary order. Just as instruments and containers have always been proxies for corporal and material culture so too have hominins constructed their identities along this spectrum from distributed to separate. Since this is the case we must expect variation and change in the material proxies of the body that express such identities metaphorically. The differences in technology, for example the changing emphasis in instruments and containers (Figure 7.1), has to be viewed in relation to the creative use of the body as a suite of corporal metaphors for material outcomes, one aspect of which is identity.

I propose therefore that blades do not come and go to meet needs where weight and versatility, the Swiss Army Knife effect, and a con-cept of efficiency or risk minimisation provide an explanation. Instead explanation is to be sought in the production of many more recognisable progeny from the parent core. These offspring are what marks the difference and we acknowledge them through attributes of size, symmetry and standardisation (Elefanti 2003; Knecht 1997; Marks et al. 2001; White 1989). These technologies were therefore local models (Gudeman 1986:37) that made sense of things and hence the variation in blade or flake numbers as identities were constructed by enchaining and accumulating across landscapes and at locales. Hominins never followed a universal scheme whereby individuals exercised choice in the face of multiple goals while constrained by scarce means. They never operated as a corner shop (Chapter 3) whose business plan was determined by the laws of neo-classical economics.

For these reasons the significance of blades over flake PCTs lies in the output with the former of many more standardised blanks. They out-reproduce in a material sense. Unfortunately, information is difficult

TABLE 7.9. *Some major forms of PCT (Bradley 1977; Quintero and Wilke 1995) and an indication of the number of standardised blanks they produce. Knapping, of course, produces many other products, usually termed débitage or waste, and these less standard forms were often used. What I am interested in here is the replication of blanks of specific dimensions*

	Numbers of blanks/offspring		Numbers of blanks/offspring
Flake PCT		**Blade PCT**	
Levallois	3–8	Prismatic	125–150
Victoria West	1	Naviform	20–40
Middle Palaeolithic/Earlier and Middle Stone Age		**Upper Palaeolithic/Later Stone Age/Neolithic**	

to gather on this matter (Table 7.9) and necessarily hedged around with caveats such as the size of raw material and whether unstandardised knapping products should also be counted. More information is clearly needed. However, in answer to Bar-Yosef and Kuhn's question, whatever problem was being solved by these Levallois and prismatic PCTs it required, as shown by Table 7.9, significantly more standardised blanks, or offspring, in the case of the latter.

The prismatic PCT was not chosen because it guaranteed more successful eland or gazelle hunts than the Levallois PCT, but because it produced material elements for enchainment and accumulation that arose from fragmenting the stone nodule and consuming, in a social sense, its creative potential. These were social technologies rather than functional answers to the spatial distribution of resources and the seasonal vagaries of the food supply. The exponential jumps in blank production (Table 7.9) now take on a different significance than that of the production of lightweight, interchangeable components for a hand-crafted compound technology.

Blades in transition in a social technology

Let me give one final example of how to re-interpret blades using a relational rather than rational approach. This time it is a classic study using Palaeolithic data from a survey of the Negev desert undertaken by archaeologists Anthony Marks and David Freidel (1977). Here the distinctions between PCTs, flakes and blades are elided at locales such as Boker Tachtit (Marks 1983) dated to 45,000 years ago where identical blanks were, on occasion, produced by different knapping strategies from the same nodule of raw material. They literally began knapping with a Middle Palaeolithic technique and finished the job with an Upper Palaeolithic strategy.

From a detailed technological study of the refitted pieces Marks and Freidel concluded that, 'Blade technology is ... more efficient relative to the objectives of the tool makers, the objectives being tool curation rather than core curation' (ibid.:153). In other words, Upper Palaeolithic knappers were indeed extracting more edge per nodule (see Figure 7.5). Marks and Freidel noted many instances where Upper Palaeolithic cores were abandoned prior to their exhaustion as potential blade and bladelet producers. Furthermore, they describe the later Upper- to Epipalaeolithic trend, where bladelet production was maximised at the expense of other blank forms, as a slow one. What marks the difference between the Middle and the Upper Palaeolithic in the Negev is the selection of particular lithic products in the *chaîne opératoire* (Schlanger 2005) to make distinctive tool types. Four major products were selected from Upper Palaeolithic *chaînes*. In order of their sequential removal from the nodule, these were,

1. large flakes from core shaping
2. large blades
3. core tablets
4. small light blades

In other words, blanks were being extracted from the *chaîne opératoire* at set stages in the sequence, and turned directly, through retouch, into consistently repeated types. The contrast with the Middle Palaeolithic is dramatic. Here Marks and Freidel (ibid.:152) found that all classes of tools in their typology were made on any of the products from the *chaîne opératoire*. Therefore, the selection of blank type by either size or weight for any given tool class approached randomness. A sidescraper could be made on *any* flake and hence be of *any* size or weight. The only exceptions were the Levallois flakes which were curated and transferred across greater distances, a feature noted in the Middle Palaeolithic of Europe for the same technology (Geneste 1988).

When it came to raw materials Marks and Freidel found a greater use of non-local materials in the Upper Palaeolithic of the Negev, although their region is small in size. From this they developed a land use model of radiating (sedentary) and circulating (nomadic) patterns, summarised in Table 7.10.

TABLE 7.10. *Patterns of land use in the Middle East (after Marks and Freidel 1977)*

Settlement pattern	Circulating (Upper Palaeolithic)	Radiating (Middle Palaeolithic & Natufian)
Mobility	Nomadic	Sedentary
Curation focus	Tools	Cores
Blank selection	Precise	Random

Hence their explanation for repeated shifts from a flake PCT to a blade PCT, which is also found at locales such as Klasies River Mouth with the Howieson's Poort (Singer and Wymer 1982) and at the Haua Fteah in Libya with the pre-Aurignacian (McBurney 1967), is that 'a general shift in adaptive strategies from radiating to circulating settlement system(s) can explain in systemic fashion the transition from flake technology to blade technology which characterised the Middle Palaeolithic/Upper Palaeolithic demarcation' (Marks and Freidel 1977:153). Economic patterns linked to environmental changes selected for change in lithic technology combined with the additional pressure for more efficient flaking strategies.

But is this elegantly constructed example of the standard view a convincing explanation? If circulating and radiating patterns of land use were a way of coping with climate change and the re-distribution of resources then why do blades, after a stuttering start, sweep the board at some point during the common ground of technological evolution? The arguments given above that question planning depth as an explanation for the transition between the Middle and Upper Palaeolithic would also apply to Marks and Freidel's account. By contrast, a relational view starts from the premise that there are always a variety of ways of solving the basics of subsistence through the use of resources, and where, with whom and for how long to inhabit a locale and a landscape. If, as discussed in Chapter 4, the primary metaphor of the environment is changed from a resisting to a giving relationship (Bird-David 1992) then the cores and tools take on a different interpretation as the proxies for bodily metaphors. A parent–offspring (core–flake/blade) relationship is defined not only through the actions of fragmentation but also through the consumption of those actions in different locales. When settlement is circulating, the enchainment of blanks and people occurs, and identity is distributed. When radiating (Table 7.10) accumulation has greater authority. There is no general shift reflecting more efficient use of resources. Instead there is the active construction of identity that shows only a single trend throughout the evolution of technology: to experience social life through the metaphor of containment.

Containers/Instruments (N = 6 Table 7.4)

Six items on the list have a split classification. Most of these are reductive technologies which produce a container as a result of use; for example the concave grinding slab, the mortar to the pestle and the dished surface of the PCT that once held the flake or blade. Ochre was reduced like a crayon through use while it also covered bodies and walls. Fishing as an activity can be by net and trap, both containers, as well as hook, line and sinker, that are all instruments. Stone boring is a composite technology because many of these artefacts were hafted, such as digging stick weights and stone maceheads. Metal use is additive and composite since it needs clay moulds into which gold, silver, copper, bronze and iron are poured. These moulds produce both instruments such as pins and swords and containers like buckets and breastplates.

Two further dual items do not appear in Troeng's list (Table 7.4) but should. The first is the wheel, which is an instrument that first appears on burial carts in Slovenia 5,500 years ago (Fagan 2004:136). At the same time the potter's wheel appears in Mesopotamia. Instruments making containers are nothing new: for example, adzes that hollowed out tree-trunks to make log-boats.

The second omission is the plough. This has an even worse record of preservation than wooden spears, being best known from marks in the soil and pictograms. The ard, or scratch plough, is an instrument present in Mesopotamia at least 5,000 years ago (Fagan 2004:96). Both ards and wheels are instruments/containers because to work they must be composite. Wheels propel a container such as a chariot or a paddle steamer while the plough needs a container in the form of humans, oxen or horses to pull them. Ploughs and wheels are extended material metaphors since like the domino effect in politics and economics (Gudeman 1986) they have many implications beyond their initial meaning.

Containers (N = 21 Table 7.4)

Enough of instruments. They have dominated this account for too long, as they dominated technology's long introduction. Besides, the view that instruments were original and containers a later technological break-through needs to be challenged. The lack of recognisable containers for several million years is not necessarily evidence of their absence. Two observations suggest this is the case. First, there is the growing body of data that complements those early finds of wooden instruments with the repeated use of fire. The hearths at Gesher-Benot-Ya'aqov (Goren-Inbar, et al. 2004), Schöningen (Thieme 2005) and Beeches Pit (Gowlett 2005) are by virtue of their contents and construction examples of containers. Second, earlier hominins regularly sought out containers in their land-scapes of habit as sleeping sites. For example, the limestone caves and fissures of the Sterkfontein valley in South Africa (Brain 1981) where evidence for fire is also present (Brain and Sillen 1988). Caves and rock shelters are places to accumulate social relationships (Moser 1999; Parkington and Mills 1991). The caves and rock shelters of the Old World abundantly testify that in the Palaeolithic such accumulation involved material culture (Bonsall and Tolan-Smith 1997; Bordes 1972; Galanidou 1997).

The increase in evidence for containers is the hallmark of technology's common ground. For instance, one natural container, ostrich eggshells, were used for bead manufacture in the Later Stone Age of East and Southern Africa from at least 40,000 years ago (McBrearty and Brooks 2000−4), and the choice of a container as a source for beads is significant. But the use of eggshell as a container, long before beads were made, is known from much older Middle Stone Age locales such as Blombos (Henshilwood et al. 2001:435). Here two pieces from a small collection had been thinned by grinding, which is a feature found on contemporary ostrich egg shell water flasks. Similar finds have been reported from the Middle Stone Age of Namibia (Vogelsgang 1998).

Textiles; wrapping the body

Additive technologies are also a feature of the common ground. Olga Soffer et al. (1998) have made a detailed examination of 90 impressions of cordage and textiles/basketry in the fired clay material from Dolní Vestonice and Pavlov in the Czech Republic, dated to 30,000 years ago. The cordage is both unmodified and knotted while the fibre based weaving technology is particularly fine-gauge. The exact items cannot be specified but nets are almost a certainty, as are clothing and baskets. The presence of clothing as a container for the body is confirmed by the contemporary well-dressed female figurines (Soffer et al. 2000) which are found at Dolní Vestonice, Willendorf in Austria and in Russia at Kostenki and Avdeevo as well as in France at Lespugue and Brassempouy.

In particular heads are covered in a variety of caps while bodies are bound by a variety of belts and armbands. Mariana Gvozdover (1989:Figure 8) has shown how the same textile motifs on the figurines are applied to other bone and ivory objects from the two Russian locales (Figure 7.6), leading Soffer et al. 2000:522 to conclude that:

> What was important and 'talked about' some 29,000 to 20,000 (uncali-brated) years ago across Europe was woven and plaited clothing and headgear made of plant materials which were associated with one category of Upper Palaeolithic women.

The textile motifs on ivory objects that serve as a synecdoche for the figurines (Figure 7.6) raise interesting possibilities for other material containers which have not survived. For example, at Blombos Cave and older than 77,000 years there are purposefully engraved ochre pieces (Henshilwood et al. 2002). These commonly take the form of hatched net-like motifs set within a rectangular frame (Figure 7.7). At a much older date the deliberate incisions by earlier hominids on an elephant foot bone from Bilzingsleben (Mania 1990:Abb.232) also describe a rectangular frame, raising the possibility that containers existed which have since perished.

Burying the body

The material metaphor of containment strikes a particular chord that begins during social technology's long introduction. Burials within caves are widespread among several hominin species and include the ossuary at La Sima de los Huesos at Atapuerca in northern Spain some 350,000 years ago where at least 32 bodies were placed (Bermúdez de Castro and Nicolás 1997). Towards the end of the long introduction there are burials in caves in Israel at Tabun (Neanderthals), Skhul and Qafzeh (anatomically modern humans) (Grün et al. 2005) while Neanderthal burials after 100,000 years ago during technology's common ground, such as Kebara, are well known (Bar-Yosef et al. 1992; Stringer and Gamble 1993:Appendix). These are often double containments, both within a cave and within a pit as at La Chapelle aux Saints where an arthritically riddled, nearly

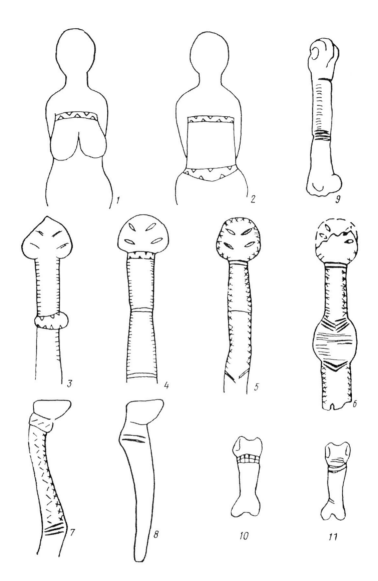

FIGURE 7.6. Textile motifs and their arrangement on figurines and other bone and ivory objects from Kostenki and Avdeevo that indicate containers (Soffer 1987:Figure 2). Reproduced with the permission of the author.

toothless man barely 40 years old was interred (Stringer and Gamble 1993:94–5).

Double containment takes a different form in Europe with the appearance of burials after 40,000 years ago for the first time in open rather

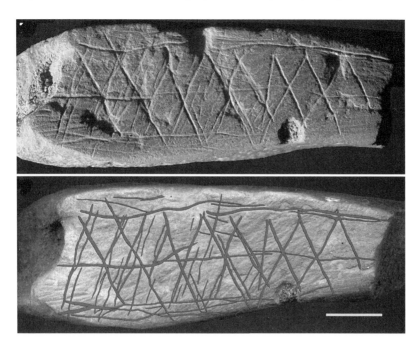

FIGURE 7.7. Engraved ochre from Blombos Cave, South Africa (Henshilwood, et al. 2002). Ochre when applied to the face and built up in layers on the body must also be regarded as a container. Reproduced with the permission of the author.

than just cave locales. The double container is indicated by the grave pit and the clothes the corpse was dressed in. The evidence for clothing comes from the position of beads and ornaments sewn onto caps and tunics as at the triple burial of Dolní Vestonice (Klima 1995), the graves of two children and an adult man at Sunghir (Bader 1978) and the Grimaldi burials, Italy, studied by Daniela Zampetti and Margherita Mussi (Mussi 2001; 1991). In all three cases ivory arm and ankle bands also encircled the limbs. The corpses were contained within shallow graves at Sunghir and Markina Gora (Kostenki 14) (Praslov and Rogachev 1982:Figure 53), pits at Kostenki sites 14 and 15 (Praslov and Rogachev 1982:Figure 55) and huts, as with burial XVI on the western slope of Dolní Vestonice 2 (Svoboda 1991). The corpses were often bound in a crouched position; the use of bonds invoking comparison with the contemporary figurines that had also been 'buried' in pits (Gvozdover 1989). An extended burial of a man in the lunettes at Lake Mungo in the Willandra Lakes of Western New South Wales, Australia, dispels any idea that this use of a container was purely an Old World circumstance. Mungo 3 was placed on his back in a pit and red ochre had been scattered over the body. The clay lunettes around these former lakes also contain abundant evidence for hearths as well as the cremation of a young woman, Mungo 1, dated to the common ground. Her body had been burnt, the bones collected, broken and then buried in a small pit (Flood 1990:250; Webb 1989).

Why pottery?

Once regarded as a material marker of how the Neolithic Revolution changed human identities, the historical significance of pottery has now altered. It remains, with the house, the archaeologist's premier container since it is abundant, ubiquitous and has a prehistoric pedigree. It also very obviously contains, whether functionally when holding beverages, perfumes, foods and poisons, or as a memory box full of ashes and souls.

But our view of pottery has altered in two ways. First, its early history, as I will show, is decidedly non-functional in the carrying, cooking and storage sense. Second, even when these tasks are being performed by clay vessels they are, due to their form and decoration as well as the techniques of manufacture, widely recognised as symbolically charged. The ceramicists' slogan 'Pots are people', has led to them being accorded agency, as discussed in Chapter 4, and their properties discussed and related directly to the body (Knappett 2005; Thomas 1996; Tilley 1996). Even their construction embodies in material ways. For example, the inclusion of grog, ground-up sherds of pottery, in the clay to act as a temper during firing can be interpreted as the inclusion of the ancestors in the next generation of pots (Morris 1994) rather than simply as a functional trait. The association between women potters, the pots they make, cooking, storage, pregnancy and childbirth intermingles the corporal and the material in very intimate ways that are metaphorically available for reproducing identity (Sterner 1989). When a potter dies, the person-pot is fragmented through grinding and then consumed in the process of re-production as a new pot-person.

David Wengrow (1998) has reminded us of the changing face of clay in the momentous transitions from the villages to the cities of Mesopotamia. Clay, he argues, did not just meet functional needs but rather, as J. L. Myers put it in 1923, prehistoric pots were eloquent 'fictions' of the potters' memory and imagination, 'figments' of their will (in Wengrow 1998:783). In Wengrow's opinion, the advent of pottery should not be used to mark a Neolithic Revolution. Instead it illuminates a continuous story through its changing applications, and these in turn provide access to the interplay between 'symbol and practice, meaning and means' (1998:783).

Such strong support for a metaphorical approach to technology contrasts markedly with my earlier discussion of stone blades where we saw that archaeologists only allow functional interpretations. Without doubt an additive technology such as pottery lends itself more readily to such an approach since to the archaeologist the act of making is intimately linked to a model of cultural learning where knowledge is built up, stored and passed on. Reductive technologies such as stone-working only have the same resonance to our local models of how things work when they contribute to a container. Hence stones cut for a house are understood differently from stone flaked into a handaxe.

And so to the question why pottery? Karen Vittelli (1999:188) has studied some of the earliest pots in Greece, from Francthi Cave. When she reconstructed the capacities that these pots held she found that it was insufficient to store the volume of seed needed to plant even one hectare. The annual production at Francthi was only some three or four small pots (Vitelli 1995:60). Neither was there any evidence that these pots had been used on the fire. So at a stroke storage and cooking can be ruled out. Her conclusion is that the potters were more interested in the process of making than the product itself, the recipe rather than the meal. This is shown by the use of inappropriate temper that made their manufacture a performance. Vitelli's conclusion is that functional pots were a by-product of such significant performances. Moreover, it is only at the end of the Greek Neolithic that pots and food preparation can be closely associated (Vitelli 1995).

A comparable situation has been shown by Olga Soffer and Pam Vandiver (Soffer et al. 1993) studying the clay animal figurines from Dolní-Vestonice and Pavlov in the Czech Republic. At 30,000 years old these are currently the oldest ceramic objects (Table 7.4), and two small kilns are also known from the locales. The local clays were perfectly sufficient for making clay figurines but the artisans added temper that resulted in thermal shock. As a result the pieces exploded during firing. Such deliberate fragmentation in an additive process produced a memorable performance for the consumption of all those watching and listening (Gamble 1999:402–4).

The history of pottery, as opposed to fired ceramics, is relatively straightforward. The oldest known pots from Jomon, in Japan (Aikens 1995), and the southern Sahara of Libya-Niger-Chad-Sudan (Barich 1987; Close 1995:Figure 3.1) have nothing to do with farmers but are predominantly found among the house structures and in the caves of hunters. In her survey of the evidence, Angela Close (1995) regards these pots as symbolic since there are simply not enough sherds to support a functional origin. Significantly, both Jomon and early North African pottery is decorated with cord impressions, making them look like baskets and suggesting some continuity with earlier perishable containers. In Africa pottery is at least a thousand years older than the first pottery in the Near East (Moore 1995) while Jomon pottery extends back to 16,000 years ago (Fagan 2004).

But is this also a misrepresentation of the technological process? Why should a symbolic, experimental phase precede a functional one? Was the Pre-pottery Neolithic of the Near East more symbolic than the later ceramic Neolithic because of its lack of a functional set of clay vessels? Such a two-stage process is an example of the standard view at work. If pottery cannot run closely with the invention of agriculture then it must, it seems, be explained as non-rational and hence the insistence on symbolism and ritual. However, pottery is a container irrespective of how many or few were made. What is more, most regions in the world experienced at some time in either their prehistory or written history an aceramic phase, just as we saw with those older 'true' blades that they came and went. For example, after rich traditions of Neolithic and Bronze Age pottery, many areas of Wales abandoned pottery altogether in the Iron Age. At a much smaller scale anthropologist Napoleon Chagnon (1977:100) asked Yananamö villagers in the Amazon region of Venezuela why they did not make pottery when their neighbours did. They replied they had never made pottery and did not have either the raw materials or the skills, relying instead on exchange to obtain pots. Chagnon records his surprise when hostilities broke out between these villages and that the 'aceramic' village suddenly 'remembered' how to make sophisticated pottery again.

Pots as material metaphors

The way to understand containers such as pottery and how they relate to change is therefore as material metaphors. An example is provided by archaeologist Paul Rainbird (1999) who has analysed changing practices towards those universal but culturally highly varied activities, disposing of the dead and incorporating the ancestors with the living. His case study from the Pacific presents archaeologists with a typical example of change through time. On the island of Pohnpei, Micronesia, people arrived with pottery and then stopped making and using it. At the same time as they became aceramic they started building megalithic tombs in the landscape. Traditionally, archaeologists would have seen such culture change as diffusion and population replacement. Today, a cognitive approach might well associate tombs with more settled life, the demarcation of territories, possibly as a response to population increase on a small island, that led to an expected, and hence explained, expansion in symbolic diversity.

Rainbird proposes an alternative using a relational analogy between bodies and material culture. He suggests continuity rather than a change in function for the different types of material evidence, pots and tombs. The highly decorated Lapita pots have 'tattooed' surfaces (Figure 7.8) similar to the surface treatment of bark cloth and the human body. They are more than just pots to hold liquids, they are embodied containers. They may not have held the cremated remains of the dead but they did hold the symbolic force of the deceased individual (see also Sterner 1989) since at this time burial was at sea. Tombs were also embodied containers which later held the physical remains of the deceased. Therefore, in Rainbird's (1999:222) opinion, pots basically became tombs. They had analogous roles as containers and homes for the ancestors. How to embody the ancestors remained the social question irrespective of what happened to their corpses. This question was resolved because people were engaged in hybrid networks that gave symbolic force to the different material solutions. Consequently, the decision to put the dead in tombs should be regarded on an archaeological time-scale as continuity rather than an innovative change in social practices with a shift from pots to stone tombs. What has changed is the use of material culture to construct identity.

Domestic containers

It now seems that the first domesticates were not sheep and wheat, maize and turkeys but the hominins themselves, and that containers were central to the process. But among all the containers that could have been discussed one in particular, the house, has been given special attention. As anthropologist Peter Wilson explains (1988:4), 'I want to show that domesticated society relies to a great extent on the house as both a dominant cultural symbol and a central rallying point and context for social organisation and activity'. Wilson draws a distinction between hunters and gatherers who have a focus and farmers who have a boundary (ibid. 1988:5). In other words sedentism, with its walls and rooms, provided the means by which we domesticated ourselves first and the plants and animals later. More recently Helen Leach (2003:359) has explicitly linked the criteria of domestication to biological changes brought about through living in a culturally modified, artificial environment of settlements with houses. Hence changes such as reductions in body and skull size, sexual

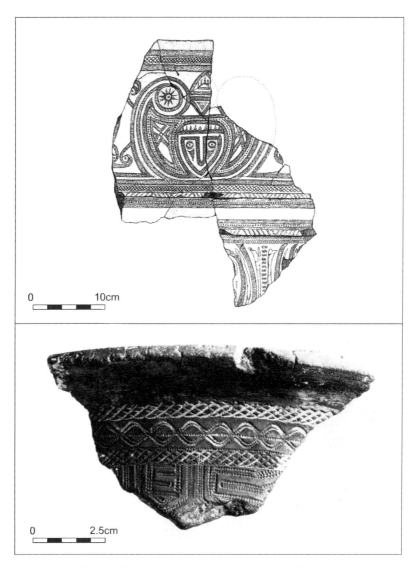

FIGURE 7.8. Tattooed Lapita pots from the Pacific (after Kirch 1997:Figure 5.5), Reproduced with the permission of the author. Photo courtesy of C. Gosden.

dimorphism and greater phenotypic diversity that are well known for the domestic animals also apply to humans. She reminds us that this was pointed out some time ago by Franz Boas (1938) who drew parallels between animal breeds and human races based on the effects of shelter, changes in diet and reduced activity levels.

Sedentism is therefore the process and the house the material proxy for change. Rather than humans driving the process as masters and creators of animals and crops, it is an unintended consequence of acclimatisation to the built environment (Leach 2003:359). Others see external climate at the end of the Pleistocene as playing a part. Ian Hodder (1990:294) favours this view and articulates the process as one where more and more resources were brought from the wild into the house, the *domus* (Chapter 4). The discourse of power in these societies during the last 20,000 years was conducted in terms of the house and the activities associated with it (Hodder 1990:38). As we saw in Chapter 3, Hodder regards domestication as a culturing process that involved the house, hearth and pot. These artefacts came to stand as appropriate material metaphors for the domestication of society (Hodder 1990:294).

This metaphor of the power-house whereby society was transformed ideologically and materially from hunting to farming makes containers of us all. A domestic species, whether it is a yak or a dog, wheat or potatoes, is domestic because it is contained. But archaeologically these and many other resources are more readily understood through the social practice of accumulation rather than the discourse of power. Fields of planted crops, herds and flocks of animals, rows of storage bins in granaries and streets of houses are sets of containers that express metaphorically the principle of accumulation. The domestic identity depends on containers to relate people to the world by engaging them in material projects and as a result of such social re-production what is contained is also changed.

But just a moment — why do we privilege some containers the house, pot and hearth as well as the sheep, cow and corn cob over others such as the cave, clothing and boat? What in particular is so special about the house, apart from its obvious significance to us, that this one container changed humans forever as Wilson and Hodder claim? Is this another instance of origins research rearing its head like a well-pitched roof (Chapter 3)? Chronologically the house is pre-pottery, pre-crops, pre-domestic animals (Table 7.4). It therefore fits origins research like a glove. But as I have pointed out repeatedly in this chapter, containers can be found much earlier during technology's long introduction and we should be aware of this before we concentrate, as usual, on the technological excitement generated in the last 10,000 years. A social technology based on accumulation and enchainment does indeed allow us to follow up Woolgar's (1987) perceptive observation that the history of tech-nology is the reverse side of a coin that debates the capabilities and rights of humans.

Summary

It is almost twenty years since Bryan Pfaffenberger (1988:242) dismissed the way archaeologists approach the history of technology with a rational view and set out the task of an anthropology of technology as bringing hidden social relations to light. I have attempted to do this here by focusing on technology, the concept of change and using the proxies of instruments and containers to explore three temporal movements in the history of technology. I conclude that whereas the evidence for much of human evolution is strongly weighted towards instruments, this basis for material culture was never exclusive. The situation is similar to the apparently overwhelming archaeological evidence for meat eating in hominid diets and the assumption of male led hunting (Nitecki and D. V. Nitecki 1987), a view that has been successfully challenged by Nancy Tanner (Dahlberg 1981) and Linda Owen (1996) and now supported by the discovery of organic and artefactual evidence for nut cracking at Gesher-Benot-Ya'aqov in Israel 780,000 years ago (Goren-Inbar et al. 2002a). Comparable discoveries of containers are a distinct probability if further ancient wet-lands can be found, and such discoveries would confirm Glynn Isaac's (1989:383) characteristic insight that the oldest technology was probably the bucket, bag and sling. His suggestion was based on the strong selective pressure that daily foraging from a home base would exert for a technical solution to carry water, food and children. I would add a relational perspective to his standard view whereby, for several million years, hominins have used containers and instruments as a social technology to narrate their lives to others. Either way we should not make the mistake of looking for a 'Container Revolution' at any time in human evolution.

But while there was neither an origin for containers for example at the chimp-hominin split, nor a revolution in their use during the Palaeolithic, the material record does show a changing authority between the two material proxies. Containers commonly survive in many mediums after 100,000 years ago during technology's common ground (Table 7.4) when evidence for graves, houses, cylinders, clothes and basketry are found and boats as containers can be reliably inferred from the initial peopling of the Western Pacific and Australia (Gamble 1993a). At best, then, the history of technology is as John Gowlett (2000) has described it, a gradient rather than a revolution. However, I have still not accounted for this pattern, and that is now my task.

CHAPTER 8

Did agriculture change the world?

> *These procedures which we apply to animals men voluntarily apply to themselves and to their children. The latter are probably the first beings to have been trained in this way, before all the animals, which first had to be tamed*
>
> Marcel Mauss *Body techniques* 1936

A nod in the right direction

Have you noticed how news reporters always start their on-air answers to questions from the studio anchor with, 'Yes', 'Well', 'Absolutely', 'Umm' and 'Uh'? These are the linguistic prefaces, or pre's, that prepare the viewer for what is to come, just as the pre in pre-history alerts the reader to what many regard as the main course. Pre's can also be gestures, like nodding, or fidgeting with a pen, so inconsequential that we barely register them. Yet in these tiny details, argues linguist Jürgen Streeck (1995:87), lies the very heart of social collaboration that arises from people interacting with each other. What is more, these little acts that present us to others belong to a social intelligence that is much older than spoken language and is shared by many other animals.

My task in this chapter is to identify the changing face of human identity during the course of hominin evolution. To achieve this end I have already shown (Chapter 7) that the history of technology is a complex landscape where the emphasis shifted through time from instruments to containers and from reductive to additive and composite techniques. These gradients were not, however, long, slow ascents to the present. Neither were they cliff edges over which our ancestors tumbled and that might be described mathematically as catastrophes (Renfrew and Cooke 1979) or historically as revolutions (Childe 1942). Moreover, the temptation is always to explain such long-term changes by concentrating on particular innovations that act as artefactual pre's, items that indicate new forms of social collaboration based on our human talent for language, music and reckoning kinship. As a result the question that has inspired origins research is whether these symbolically based behaviours so changed the character of the gradient that they fundamentally altered the nature of hominin identity, personal and public, and created the human character we know today. If so, then the archaeologist's main task seems to be finding pre's, such as the oldest symbolic artefacts (e.g. Marshack 1990), that indicate by their rarity and unique forms the imminence of language and associated ritual endeavours.

However, technological innovations (Table 7.3) are not to be read as a series of pre's indicating the development of symbolic expression. Technology is more than simply an indication of some greater and more transforming human attribute such as language or art. A social technology is always indicative of the production of identity irrespective of its form. Handaxes are as significant as projections of personhood as jaguars, either animal or automobile. What we see during the history of technology are countless expressions of that hidden identity, the self and the engagement of others with that representation. What we have to decide is whether, during the same history, the enlargement of our brains (Dunbar 2003) or the development of institutions with agriculture (Maryanski and Turner 1992) changed the rules of engagement.

But this is a lot to bite-off, hence my chapter title is a question to provide a much needed focus for these slippery issues. So, did agriculture change the world? The answer, I will argue, is *no* in the expected sense of villages, crops and gods and goddesses, but *yes* in the novel sense of a changed primary metaphor for constructing identity: *growing the body*. I use it to signal change in the timeless project of renewing social life and where previously the *giving environment* (Chapter 3) served as a major, but not the only rhetorical device. The body, that source of symbolic force (Chapter 4) is integral to both primary metaphors. Growing and giving, as I will show, can be differentiated by tracing those practices of accumulation and enchainment and the actions of consumption and fragmentation as applied to material projects. I will show that the change in primary metaphor is revealed through a material project as hidden, archaeologically, as the self. Children are that project.

The changes that brought us children were neither Neolithic in date nor Anatomically Modern in biology. As a result they were hardly revolutionary. Accordingly, an origin point for change will remain as elusive as a satisfactory conclusion to the legal, theological and scientific argument over when, exactly, a human life begins.

If archaeologists are to investigate the technology of children they need to re-direct their primary metaphor to acknowledge the relational as well as the rational and also accommodate the emotional. 'I change you as you unfold and you change me as I unfold' is how psychotherapist Sue Gerhardt (2004:31), reporting infant researcher Beatrice Beebe, has described the journey of development that we have all been through by growing the body that we are. Those changes we call agriculture, I will argue, were not so very different.

The social cage

Writing about the sociology of the Stone Age, the social and political scientist Garry Runciman (2005:137) asks when 'society as we know it' came into existence. Society from his perspective involves social roles and their accompanying formal institutional inducements and sanctions. This is the social world of assemblies, markets, law courts, temples, armies and permanent public positions of power that were achieved through ability but also ascribed to individuals by virtue of who they were by accident of birth (Runciman 2005:129). His answer is that such a society is no older than the Neolithic where these institutions can be inferred from the architecture of villages and towns, and where their functions as economic centres provided the apparatus for state power to emerge.

This accords with the sedentary revolution proposed by archaeologist Colin Renfrew (1996; 2001) when humans were fundamentally changed by the opportunity architectural spaces provided for the symbolic construction of society. A similar viewpoint is provided by anthropologist Peter Wilson (1988) who regards architecture as domesticating social life by its ability to interrupt attention and interaction that depended primarily on sight and hearing, and so led eventually to the creation of private worlds.

The conclusion to be drawn from these three different disciplinary perspectives is that we built our way out of older social arrangements. It does not matter much if these earlier societies are classified as egalitarian, hunting and gathering economies or biologically non-modern people. What is important is that the potential for such a fundamental change had existed for at least 30,000 years before the first villages, and probably much longer (Table 7.4), when anatomically modern humans painted cave walls, carved ivory and limestone into figurines and buried their dead with ornaments. What, asks Renfrew (2001:127), was so novel about this new hominin species, the modern human, if so few decisive happenings in human experience accompanied its appearance?

To Renfrew's mind the long wait for agriculture is a sapient paradox: why have advanced cognitive powers if they were not used as we know they can be? His answer is that architecture and settled communities were a form of pressure cooker that released the full potential (Chapter 2). Not only did the institutions of 'society as we know it' make their appearance in the Neolithic but so too did people as we know them. His view is widely supported by other archaeologists working in the Neolithic (e.g. Bar-Yosef 2001; Sherratt 1997a; Hodder 1990). For example, in his review of the Near Eastern evidence, Trevor Watkins (2004b:19) concludes that 'the world's earliest village communities were also the first to develop fully modern minds and a fully symbolic culture'. These villages were in his phrase 'theatres of memory' (ibid.), while for Renfrew (2001:127) the close association of people and material culture led to objects taking on symbolic power. It was this process of 'forced' engagement with objects by virtue of living in settled communities that led to new concepts for organising social life. One result, Renfrew suggests, was the ascription of social value to particular raw materials such as gold and classes of manufactured objects that included the paraphernalia of rank and religion.

Complicated social bonds

I would group all these models under a single heading and describe them as a social cage. The description is used by Alexandra Maryanski and Jonathan Turner (1992) in their synthesis of sociology and primatology to understand the evolution of society. The consequence of elaborating social structure beyond that of the egalitarian hunter and gatherer was to put humans in a social cage of their own construction (Maryanski and Turner 1992). This they claim violated our genetic tendencies and led to two further cages; a cage of kinship created by horticulturalists and the cage of power that agrarian societies built. It is only with industrial societies, they believe, that we have broken out of these cages, thanks to scientific analysis, and so been able to see them for what they are.

The image of the cage also appeals to primatologist Shirley Strum and historian of science Bruno Latour (1987). They begin by proposing that primate and human societies differ because the former are complex and the latter complicated (Gamble 1999:41–2). When social life is complicated it is made up of a succession of operations that are literally folded in to create more permanent social bonds. These operations simplify social negotiation by calling on resources other than the social actor's body to structure action and perform society. Without such external symbols it would not, they suggest, be possible to organise others on ever larger scales and where many different societies, differentiated by customs and cultures interact.

The complex societies of the great apes never achieve these scales because they lack the all important symbols that state and re-state a particular view of 'what society is'. However, while humans build cages to live in from symbolic materials, not all cages are equal. That depends where you find yourself in the trajectory of social evolution. Hunters and gatherers may, according to Strum and Latour, have complicated societies but these compare poorly to agriculturalists and recent industrial nation states that have an increasing level of material and symbolic resources at their disposal. The prime characteristic of 'society as we know it' is therefore the ability to organise others on ever vaster scales. In a statement that foreshadows the sedentary revolution of Watkins and Renfrew, they conclude that 'once individuals are aggregated and choose not to avoid each other, there must be a secondary adaptation to a new competitive environment of conspecifics (Strum and Latour 1987:796)'. Humans achieve this by engaging with their material and symbolic worlds while different types of human societies are created depending on the extent to which new resources are used (ibid.:796).

The social cage model is therefore clear about one thing; agriculture, or more precisely sedentary communal living, really did change the world. The pre's in this case will not, as Renfrew points out, be the earliest art or rich burial but rather the constellation of structures that indicate settled life. The social cage may be spun like a web from changes to the networks that linked individuals and communities (Maryanski and Turner 1992). A process driven, as archaeologist Brian Hayden (1990) has described it, by persons who exploited the symbols of their worlds, especially those of food, through aggression and the inherent drive for aggrandisement. This would not have been possible without settling down.

The social brain

Cages are a most interesting container. An example of composite technology involving a set of instruments, the bars, and a small amount of bindings, glue or solder. A cage defines a space that is both inside and outside and is permeable depending on the concepts and bodies it encompasses. Like a rabbit-proof-fence it is a net thrown over an elusive quarry that does not always result in capture.

However, there is not much point in my citing examples of symbolic pre's, for example the engraved pieces of ochre (Figure 7.7) at Blombos Cave, South Africa 80,000 years ago (Henshilwood et al. 2002), to refute the sedentary revolution because its supporters have already declared that it is the scale of the new systems that is important not their meagre antecedents. Similarly, a much used hunting camp at Dolní Vestonice, Czech Republic 30,000 years ago (Gamble 1999:387–414; Svoboda et al. 1996), does not allow us to recognise the first assemblies and institutions, those decisive happenings that Renfrew locates in the Neolithic. Society, so defined, will always start with agriculture.

But we can always choose to look between the bars of the cage rather than at them. If institutions make society, and we derive our identity from them, then we are forever within the cage. However, as Strum and Latour (1987) contend, if society is performed by social actors as they negotiate their society then we also have an existence outside the cage.

This may sound contradictory given that I have just criticised Strum and Latour for characterising hunters and gatherers as rich in material and symbolic means to create society, when compared to baboons, but 'impoverished' when judged against farmers and modern industrial societies (Strum and Latour 1987:791). The hardship experienced by hunters and gatherers would seem to be their lack of material goods that is, according to Strum and Latour, responsible for their tiny populations. The stricture, 'Go forth and multiply' applies to technology and material culture first, and population numbers second. To be modern, it seems, is to be numerous and so in need of organisation. It is this notion of impoverishment that I take issue with, not their demonstration of how hominid society is performed and created through interaction in a bottom-up rather than top-down manner (Gamble 1999:33–8; Hinde 1976).

However, what exactly are the implications of larger symbolic universes constructed from more objects and people? In terms of human demography should we conclude that at the time of the Domesday survey in AD 1086 the 2 million people recorded would have had 100 per cent larger symbolic universes than the 20,000 hunters and gatherers who lived in England at the end of the Ice Age (Gamble 2004)? And by the same calculation the 50 million people living in England today would have symbolic worlds 25 times greater than their Anglo-Norman ancestors. In terms of material culture the number and diversity of styles and types of objects far exceeds these simple ratios and defies measurement. A supermarket alone contains over 30,000 separate items. Standing in front of the long shelves of toothpaste I often think that as our material inventories have increased so our symbolic universes have shrunk.

The release from proximity

The way to unlock the cage and its imprisonment of everything but the present is to visualise it as a web or network that, as we saw in Chapter 4, takes us back to the body. From this perspective the appearance of a society we might recognise is not a matter of institutions and assemblies but instead of solutions to problems of absence and the maintenance of social life. Once again the primatologists provide a lead and in particular Lars Rodseth and colleagues' (Rodseth 1991:240) discussion of the *release from proximity* that is the hallmark of human societies. Apes and monkeys depend on face-to-face contact to forge and affirm the social bonds that structure their networks of allies. What a primate cannot see, hear or smell does not concern them (Robin Dunbar pers. comm.). Dispersal, driven by the fission and fusion of primate groups as they look for food, often diminishes rather than enhances social networks (Rodseth 1991:232). By contrast, humans regularly create alliances between people who have never met or who encounter each other infrequently. Hence the importance of proximity for social life is released. Social relationships are uncoupled from spatial proximity through the mediation of culture and language (ibid.:240).

All human societies recognise a release from proximity, irrespective of whether an individual's identity is based on a distributed or singular personhood (Chapter 5). As a result, the issue of how we influence social outcomes when we are not present is regarded as a central problem for the social sciences. How, as sociologist Anthony Giddens (1984:35) asks, are social relations 'stretched' so that the limitations of creating society through face-to-face interactions are overcome?

Such extension of social ties beyond the immediate is what we all do well (Gamble 1993a, 1998, 1999) and have been doing well for at least the last 60,000 years when open sea crossings took people to Australia for the first time (Roberts et al. 1990). This was a dramatic development (Gamble 1993b) that measures in a stark geographical absence/presence the appearance of the ability to extend social relationships. Nick Allen (2005) in discussing the appearance of tetradic kinship (Chapter 4) also uses the founding population of Australia to indicate the likely antiquity of this ability to categorise relationships.

The earliest Australian evidence provides a minimum age for the intentional separation of people and emphasises that the ability to construct social life over distance is at least as old as the common ground of the social technology I discussed in Chapter 7. Human dispersal at this time was significant. In 60,000 years we changed our status from a suite of genera and species confined to a part of the Old World to become a global *and* singular species for the first time in our evolutionary history. Some 75 per cent of the surface of the Earth was first settled in 1 per cent of the time that has elapsed since the chimp-hominin split five million years ago (Gamble 2004). Although dismissed by some as merely an adaptive radiation rather than a decisive happening (Renfrew 2001:127) these dispersals, conducted for the most part by people who fished, hunted and gathered, indicate that a solution to the problem of maintaining social bonds over time and at distance had been developed by this time.

The evidence for extension

The social technology involved in such extension was varied. Among examples of containers the most important were boats. At present these can only be inferred; for example by the arrival of people in the Pleistocene continent of Sahul, when low sea levels linked Tasmania, Australia and Papua New Guinea. An open sea crossing to Sahul was always obligatory and involved a voyage of at least some 65 km (Gamble 1993a:216). These are small distances compared to the voyages into the deep Pacific that began 3,500 years ago (Evans 1998; Irwin 1992) in double hulled canoes capable of carrying 400 people (Davis 1999), their plants and on occasion domestic animals.

Containers in the form of sledges and domestic dogs to pull them may have been important in the dispersal of people into another Pleistocene low sea-level continent, Beringia, and from there into North America (Anderson and Gillam 2000; Fagan 1987; Martin 1973; Meltzer 1993). Alternatively containers in the form of boats supported a coastal colonisation (Fladmark 1979). However, neither type of container has yet been found and only more accurately dated sites either on the coast or in the interior will help decide which route was taken.

A second and more tangible line of evidence comes from the transfer around the landscape of stone materials. The pattern during much of technology's long introduction was for hominins to use local raw materials. Very little of it is transported more than a few hours walking away from its geological source.

Gesher Benot Ya'aqov (Goren-Inbar et al. 2000) at 780,000 years old provides a good example of the local rule. The raw material for the manufacture of Acheulean bifaces is basalt found at, or within, 4 km of the locale in the Jordan rift valley (Madsen and Goren-Inbar 2004:47–8). The quantities of artefacts, manuports and boulders which were accumulated at the locale were harvested from within only a few km². The artefacts have often been described as 'African'; first on account of the raw material, which is decidedly un-European, and second for the large and sometimes giant cores (Madsen and Goren-Inbar 2004) from which flakes were struck to make bifaces (see Chapter 7).

But the local rule is broken during the later part of technology's long introduction. The evidence comes from a number of obsidian (highly distinctive volcanic glass) artefacts from later hominin locales in the Kenyan Rift Valley and in Tanzania that have been identified to source using x-ray fluorescence (XRF) and electron microprobe (EMP). Analyses revealed that seven pieces of obsidian from the Mumba Rock Shelter in Northern Tanzania came from 320 km away (Merrick and Brown 1884). The Bed VI levels where they were found contain stone tools dated to 100–130,000 years ago (McBrearty and Brooks 2000:515). At Gadeb, Ethiopia, and Kilombe, Kenya, Acheulean bifaces also made of obsidian have been transferred from up to 100 km away (Féblot-Augustins 1990). As archaeologists Sally McBrearty and Alison Brooks document (2000:514–17) there are many examples in both technology's long introduction and common ground of stones moving between 100 and 200 km. Numbers are, however, never large and in their African examples applies to less than 1 per cent, a few pieces, of any stone tool assemblage.

This stone data demonstrates that small numbers of instruments were commonly transferred over distances that far exceeded any daily foraging range. What is not known is whether these rare items were passed from hand to hand, thus enchaining people, or carried by individuals in their travels and simply thrown away when no longer of any use. Given the distances involved I favour the former hypothesis (Gamble 1999), which is also supported by the demonstration that these instruments conform to a simple rule first established by Jean-Michel Geneste and Alain Turq (Geneste 1988; 1989; Turq 1990; 1993), and documented more widely by Jehanne Féblot-Augustins (1997). These archaeologists found that as distance increased so the type of instrument changed. Those from furthest away were invariably retouched flakes and blades that could be classified as shaped tools, often manufactured using the Levallois PCT (Chapter 7; Geneste 1988). Below a threshold of 20 km from the source of the stone the proportions were reversed and unmodified flakes and blades as well as cores and evidence for working nodules dominated (Gamble 1993b).

The obsidian bifaces from Gadeb and Kilombe would be a good example of how only selected, and on occasion, highly modified instruments were travelling down these tracks, creating chains of connection as they went (Mulvaney 1976).

Group size and networks

Extending our social presence is an important aspect of being able to construct societies of a kind that we would recognise. The social brain hypothesis put forward by evolutionary biologist Robin Dunbar (1992a; 1996; 2003) and bio-anthropologist Leslie Aiello (and Dunbar 1993) addresses the cognitive implications of this ability and in particular the impact on group size. The core hypothesis is that our social lives drove the enlargement of our brains to a size where they are almost three times larger than expected in a primate of our size (McHenry 1988). Three million years ago a probable ancestor such as *Australopithecus afarensis* had a brain of 450 cc (Johanson and Edgar 1996) and today the brain size of *Homo sapiens* is nearer 1,500 cc.

The history of brain evolution suggests that it was a mosaic process (Jerison 1982). The extraordinary encephalisation of humans saw the size of the brain's neo-cortex increase significantly faster than other areas. The neo-cortex is the 'grey matter' and as its popular name suggests it is the thinking part of the brain that stores memories and organises social relationships. Primates also have large neo-cortices relative to the rest of their brains and when this ratio is plotted against the mean group size they live in (Figure 8.1) a strong positive relationship can be seen. As the neo-cortex ratio increases so too does group size with humans out in front as might be expected. The correlation between brain size and the size of groups it can organise lies at the heart of the social brain hypothesis (Dunbar 2003:169).

But such a massive increase comes at a price. The brain is a very costly organ using 20 per cent of all our energy intake but only accounting for 2 per cent of our body weight (Aiello and Wheeler 1995). Therefore, as Dunbar (1998:93) points out, selection for an increase in such an expensive tissue must have been very strong. Better foraging efficiency might have provided a strong impetus in spatially and seasonally complex environments where remembering where food is to be found would be an advantage (Gibson 1986). But such ecological explanations do not adequately account for the subsequent exponential rise in brain size. A more parsimonious hypothesis is that social life drove such dramatic

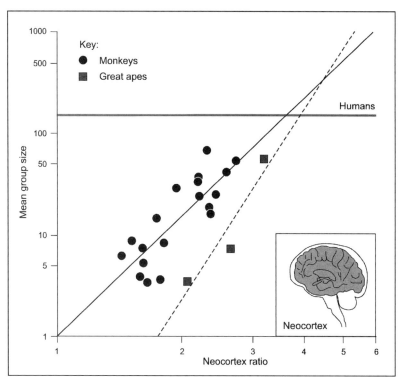

FIGURE 8.1. The relationship between the size of the neo-cortex and group size in extant primates (after Dunbar 1996; 1998). The neo-cortex consists of the frontal, temporal, parietal and occipital lobes of the brain all of which have expanded dramatically during hominin evolution.

encephalisation and that the larger group sizes that resulted satisfied a number of concerns, including increased reproductive choice, security against predators and psychological well-being.

Among apes and monkeys group size depends on interaction established through finger-tip grooming and face-to-face contact. For example, Strum and Latour (1987) describe baboons as competent social actors limited by their bodies in terms of what they can do. Grooming is the means by which key social partners are recruited and defined. Moreover, as the overall group size increases so too does the time spent by any individual grooming his or her core of intimates. The pay-off for this time consuming activity, apart from the emotional pleasure grooming produces, comes at moments of conflict when this support clique will come to your aid.

TABLE 8.1. *Resources and networks (after Gamble 1999:Table 2.8 with references). Sample descriptors for small-world societies are taken from primate, anthropological (hunter-gatherers) and sociological literature (for an update and confirmation of network sizes see Zhou et al. 2005)*

Ego based network	Principal resource	Size	Sample descriptors of modal size
Intimate	Emotional affect	3–7	Support clique Significant others Nuclear family
Effective	Material exchange	10–23	Sympathy group Colleagues and friends Minimum band Local group, Clan
Extended	Symbolic 'positive style'	100–400	Friends of friends Dialect tribe, Connubium Maximum band
Global	Symbolic 'negative style'	2,500	Non-significant 'Others' Linguistic family

Human groups are rather different and you might be surprised from Figure 8.1 that they are only 150 persons in size. To understand why groups are this size and not measured in terms of thousands or even millions, I return to the discussion of Ego based networks (Gamble 1999) that I introduced in Chapter 5 (see Table 5.5). Four network sizes exist (Table 8.1) differentiated by the variable use of the three negotiating resources – emotional, material and symbolic (Turner 1991) – that define them.

As sociologist Robert Milardo (1992:455) comments, the intimate network with a cross-cultural average size of five has a disproportionate impact on an individual's decisions, psychological security and network building in comparison to 'the sheer number of people contacted in the routine business of daily living and the breadth of opportunities they present or deny in terms of opportunities for social comparison, companionship and access to scarce resources'. The size of networks varies between individuals, as might be expected, and also changes with age. But as Milardo says it is through these relatively small webs, with their social bonds of variable strength and commitment, that we navigate the limitless demographic universes of London and New York.

TABLE 8.2. *Community size predictions and language outcomes (adapted from Dunbar 1993)*

Age, millions of years	Representative taxon	Group size	Communication
<0.1	Modern humans	150	Metaphor and technical
0.3	Neanderthals	120	Socially focused 'gossip'
<2	*Homo ergaster*	100	Vocal chorusing
5	Australopithecines	70	Primate grooming

Group size and language

There are cognitive limits to the sizes of networks we can negotiate and maintain, but what needs organising is the time available for social life. Time, as Dunbar (1992) shows, is a crucial limiting factor when the performance of social bonds depends on physical grooming and the re-playing of roles on a daily basis. Among primates none have been observed to spend more than 20 per cent of the waking day grooming. The rest of the time is devoted to finding food, caring for infants and eating. This places a limit on social group size of about 50 (Figure 8.1), clearly well below humans and predictions from the social brain hypothesis for hominin community sizes (Table 8.2). Moreover, although several social monkeys do live in much larger aggregations, they interact on a regular basis only with the smaller numbers in their sympathy groups.

It is here that the social brain model comes into play. It is concerned with the limits to group size rather than average group sizes (Dunbar 2003:171). If these thresholds can be accurately documented then they have evolutionary significance and need explaining. Although the model does not deal with the varied forms of social organisation (see Foley 1996; 2001a; Foley and Lee 1989; Rodseth et al. 1991) it does address the consequences for the time management of relationships as numbers increase. The predictions of group size for some hominin species are shown in Table 8.2 and Figure 8.2.

One inescapable consequence of increasing group size is that the primate mechanism of regulating relationships by grooming is no longer possible due to time constraints. With such strong selection for increasingly dense and complex social communities the development of language from vocal chorusing is, as Dunbar argues, a strong possibility (Table 8.2). Words now supplemented fingers as the means to create socially negotiated

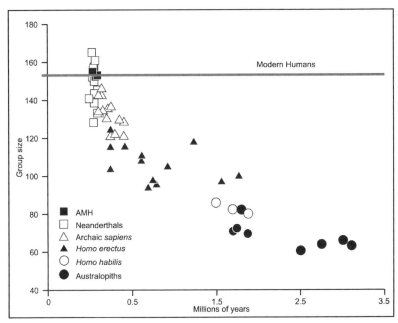

FIGURE 8.2. Predictions for group size in fossil hominins (after Dunbar 1993; 1998 and Aiello and Dunbar 1993). The estimates are based on the neo-cortex/group size ratios shown in Figure 8.1.

bonds. Language changed the rules by which social bonds were performed. It provided a vocal means to 'groom' a larger number of partners than could be achieved in the same time by touch. The emphasis in social interaction shifted from the tactile to the aural in face-to-face gatherings.

When the brain size of fossil hominins is plotted (Figure 8.3) we see that the primate threshold for performing the social bond by touch grooming was crossed at least 600,000 years ago indicating a long ancestry for vocal grooming if not language as we know it with its habitual use of rhetoric (Table 8.2). At this time the graph predicts group sizes of 120 which rise eventually to 150. The language that was needed previously depended on factual gossip — who is doing what with whom — to monitor relationships, rather than rhetorical devices to account for why they should be in a ménage à trois, and that absence does not always make the heart grow fonder.

While these groups are stable human social units they should not be thought of as societies. Rather they are networks that we all negotiate and build in our daily activities and interactions with others. The numbers correspond to the lower limit of our extended networks (Table 8.1) where we use symbols such as Christmas cards to sustain a weak social bond when

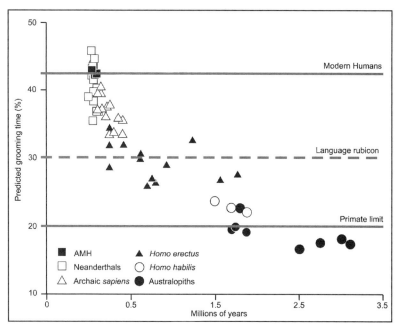

FIGURE 8.3. The threshold for the appearance of language among fossil hominins as predicted by the social brain hypothesis (after Dunbar 2003). Increased group size (Figure 8.2) exacerbated time constraints on physical grooming as the mechanism of social bonding. When these reached 30 per cent of the day's activities language, it is proposed, emerged to meet the selective pressure for novel forms of communication.

compared to the smaller but more intense networks. These figures also bring a perspective to the question of how we can live in cities of many millions or villages of several hundreds. The answer is through modularity, amalgamating networks of similar size and integrating them into ever larger units. The hierarchical devices that integrate such sets have been an object of much archaeological enquiry (e.g. Feinman and Marcus 1998; Flannery 1972a; Johnson 1982; Meskell 2004; Renfrew 1972). In contrast to these top-down approaches, beginning with the emergence of institutions as the question, the cognitive and psychological building blocks identified through the social brain model provide a much needed bottom-up perspective on the same issues.

Language, metaphor and mimesis

At the heart of all these debates is the issue of how society is performed. How exactly do the social actors enrol others in their internal view of social life and as a result attribute actions to others that are understood by reference to themselves? In particular, how important are language and metaphor in these exchanges and the ability to both create and share representations? In his multi-faceted approach to this question, Dan Sperber (1996:1) has asked why some ideas are contagious, a process he describes as an epidemiology of representations that links the micro-scale of the individual to the macro-scale of society, whatever its numbers and complexity of institutions. Belonging in such social situations is established metaphorically. As Sperber explains, 'a representation involves a relation-ship between three terms; an object is a representation of something, for some information-processing device' (ibid.:61). That device can be a human individual engaged in creating networks for action and pursuing material projects.

Anthropologist Chris Knight (1991; 1998) has studied these questions with reference to the ways in which collective rituals based on trust emerge between a speaker and listener and enable both to share in these internal fictions. What supports these inventions is a false statement, a metaphor, because who has ever seen, for example, a dreaming spire or a shadow crossing the mind? Our existence as a ceremonial animal (James 2003) nicely encapsulates our immersion in these fictions and their resolution through rituals and performances – exactly the distinction that Strum and Latour (1987) draw between the complex societies of the primates and complicated human social constructions. Apes engage in tactical deception (Byrne and Whiten 1988) but not in metaphorical expressions of that aspect of social intelligence.

I should, however, qualify this last statement. The majority of research on metaphor, social intelligence and how society is represented among hominids is treated as a question about language. This is hardly surprising. Language is so clearly important either as a technique of vocal grooming or providing a flight of fancy through wonderland. As we saw in earlier chapters the experiences of the body have their place but even here, as philosopher Peter Carruthers (2002) has shown, there is still a lively debate concerning the necessity of language for thought, those internal conversa-tions we have with ourselves. He is also sceptical of the assertion that language is needed to make conscious propositions – what others would call discursive consciousness, as opposed to practical consciousness where habit accounts for action (Gamble 1999:81; Giddens 1984; Leroi-Gourhan 1993:231−2). Although spoken language is important in this regard Carruthers does not see this function as its main cognitive role. Instead he favours the importance of language in integrating the outputs from a wide variety of embodied conceptual faculties; vision, hearing, touch and smell. Such co-ordination is not regarded as unique to humans but was shared with other hominins. For example, using a segmented model of the mind archaeologist Steven Mithen (1996:67) has argued that language allowed multiple connections not only between these familiar sensory domains but also with the integration of dedicated intelligence domains that deal with such concerns as technology, natural history, social life and language. To these four intelligences he adds a fifth, general intelligence, that preceded them. The evolution of the mind as opposed to the brain has, in Mithen's opinion, involved forging strong relationships between the general and specialised intelligences in ever more creative ways. Mithen (ibid.:70) refers to this as cognitive fluidity while Jerry Fodor (1985:4), the architect of the theory of modular mind, regards it as the mind's passion for analogy. While such approaches may be overly modular in dividing up areas of cognition and experience it serves as a powerful heuristic device to understand what the brain achieves in relating inputs to unexpected outputs, and that is the essence of metaphor.

A social brain, as opposed to a social intelligence that is common to many animals, is therefore about making connections, establishing bonds. Psychologist Merlin Donald (1991; 1998), who prefers a domain-general to modular model of how the brain works, has proposed that prior to language as defined above there existed a mimetic style of thought and communication. Significantly, he regards this, and not the much later development of spoken language, as our key skill. Mimesis is the 'ability to model the whole body, including all its voluntary action-systems, in three dimensional space (Donald 1998:49)'. A mimetic style of thought was, in Donald's view, a necessary platform for language and preceded it by some distance. What it boils down to is the principle of similarity (ibid.:61) measured through the full range of the senses. This principle links actions to their referents that are stored within the body-whole. And when it comes to communicating this information to others the social actor can call on what Donald terms an 'implementable action metaphor (1998:61)', that is familiar to us (Chapter 4) from body techniques and the rhythms and gestures that structure everyday life. Mimesis produces conformity that in terms of action metaphors is often described as routinisation or habituation. Studies of technology have recognised the immensely stable production of particular artefact forms, for example the Acheulean biface that lasts, essentially unchanged, for over a million years. It is the classic example of *tendance* (Lemonnier 1993:26; Leroi-Gourhan 1993), the canalisation of techniques and forms that would be expected to vary considerably over such time periods and across the grain of ecological variation, if functional adaptation alone was determining design.

Learning to think through emotions

What I take away from this brief discussion of language evolution is the proposal that there are other ways of thinking that involve the body and technology in constructing metaphors of what society is. This proposal is of course provisional, as is everything written about language and in particular its origins (see for example the commentaries on Carruthers 2002), but arising from it are issues regarding the ways in which these metaphors are not only communicated but learned. I have already addressed the first of these by looking at performance spaces (Chapter 6), the body (Chapter 5) and in particular the symbolic force (Chapter 4) that underpins my argument for treating much of material culture as proxies for corporal culture in terms of containers and instruments. The second, learning, can be addressed by studying the development of babies' brains and the demonstration that they think before they speak (Bloom 2004).

But we need to know what it is that has to be learned so I will start with the theory of mind that describes different orders of intentionality. Humans are capable of four levels and on occasion even five. A belief in the supernatural provides an example of these mental gymnastics where 'I have to *believe* that you *suppose* that there are supernatural beings who can be made to *understand* that you and I *desire* that things should happen in a particular way' (Dunbar 2003:177). The four levels are shown by the italicised words. This level of co-ordination exceeds normal social interaction where three levels of intentionality are involved, 'I *intend* that you *believe* that you must behave in the way that the rest of us *want*' (ibid.). This everyday aspect of social life is however beyond the great apes who at best can achieve Level 2 intentionality in gathering allies to their social cause. Provocatively, Dunbar (2003:Figure 4) has applied these levels to the brain sizes (Figure 8.4) of all primates and by extrapolation to the fossil hominin record. According to this graph Level 4 intentionality came very late in human evolution, returning us to the notion of extension as our basic social skill along with mimesis as the core ability upon which much later and more advanced symbolic structures are based. Belief in the supernatural, not just as a presence but as a controlling force, is another example of going beyond, of the extended mind stretching those social relationships to extraordinary degrees.

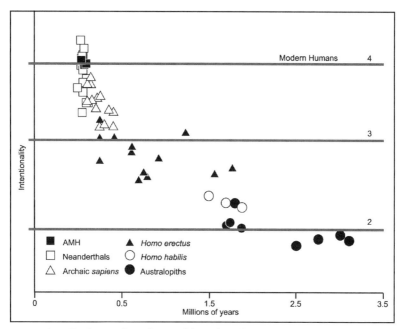

FIGURE 8.4. Predictions from the social brain hypothesis for the levels of intentionality in a theory of mind among fossil hominins (after Dunbar 2003). These can be compared with group size (Figure 8.2) and language (Figure 8.3).

And this is where children enter the story. Babies, we know, will later achieve Level 4 intentionality, that ability to project outside themselves. But they have to grow into it. A crucial threshold in their journey is provided by accepting false belief, recognising that someone has a different under-standing of a situation than you do. For example, you see someone put a book on a shelf before leaving the library. Then you see someone else move that book to another location. The first person returns: where do they look for the book? If you have the capacity for false belief, as children older than three and four do, you know that it will be where they left it. If not, then you will expect them to look on the shelf where you saw it was moved to.

In this regard, as psychotherapist Sue Gerhardt (2004:18) has put it 'babies are like the raw material for the self'. They are an interactive project and not a self-powered, automatic process. To achieve their potential of Level 4 intentionality their brains not only have to grow to full adult size but they have to become, through interaction, the kind of social brain that can achieve this. Gerhardt (2004:37) discusses the extensive literature that shows how the orbitofrontal cortex acts to control emotions by linking cortex and sub-cortex. It is this area of the brain that fine-tunes our behaviour by managing feelings. Most importantly this area of the brain develops almost entirely after birth and is structured by the interactive experiences that the baby has with its carers and the world it inhabits, and not just by genes alone. Gerhardt's thesis is that as well as being social our brain is predominantly emotional. Those feelings that alert us to danger, love, fear and happiness are guides to action and enable us to adapt more precisely to the unique circumstances that we find ourselves in as growing babies (ibid. 2004:85). Our minds emerge through interaction with others and not in isolation. It is the emotional landscape of that development that is all-important.

Human social intelligence is therefore particularly sensitive to experiences occurring between the ages of six and eighteen months in a baby's life and so well before language skills and false belief are apparent. In a study by child psychologists Susan Hespos and Elizabeth Spelke (2004) the conceptual ability of five month old infants was tested by watching them observe objects in space. There are two points of interest here. First, the researchers studied English and Korean children to see if learning very different languages shape, as many believe, their subsequent mental life. Second, their study deals with objects. These involve either a cylinder and a container or a ring placed around a post to examine spatial concepts of loose and tight fit and such experiential prepositions as 'on' and 'in'. Think of a mortar and pestle or an arrow in a quiver and you have the idea. Hespos and Spelke's study provides us with an opportunity to observe growing minds in relation to instruments and containers, an example of how Donald's 'implementable action metaphors' might be learned.

On the first count the results showed that languages as different as Korean and English are not what is important in the learning process. Hespos and Spelke use the cylinders and containers to ascertain if the babies from these two linguistic backgrounds are sensitive to categorical difference. Here the 'category' is the visual relationship between two objects. The baby is shown a cylinder that is a 'loose fit' in a container. Eventually they get bored, or rather habituated to this category and so stop looking. Then they are shown a new category with the same objects, this time a 'tight fit', to see if their attention returns. Both Korean and English babies respond in the same way to new categories and look longer, their interest aroused. From this the researchers conclude that thought, in the form of representations of how the world works, precedes language. Here the babies are thinking in material categories and judging the relationships between forms in an experiential, metaphorical manner. Put another way, the study suggests that they understand the 'in', 'on' and 'around' as material prepositions *before* they articulate them as speech acts. Their body is already providing those spatial positions and experiences of the world (Chapter 3) that only later are glossed by words and organised syntactically. As the preorbital cortex is growing and being shaped by emotion through daily interaction, so too is the conceptual basis of an object-world being developed in mimetic form, and that form is metaphorical. Paul Bloom has commented that these contrasts of loose and tight fit, a relationship between container and instrument, are meaningful because they make sense of the world. He concludes:

> Language learning might really be the act of learning to express ideas that already exist, either because they are unlearned or because they have been learned through experience with the physical and social world.
>
> (Bloom 2004:411)

Bringing up baby

The relevance of this recent child psychology study to the origins of agriculture is, therefore, as follows. Babies have the pre-language, pre-theory of mind ability to differentiate categories in the material worlds that surround them. This being the case the structure and organisation of that world will establish, in the process described by Donald as mimesis, what the metaphors will be that structure their relations to others and to the world they inhabit. Primary metaphors, such as growing the body and the giving environment, will depend upon the array of objects that are associated from the outset with growing a social brain, as the orbitofrontal cortex enlarges during the first eighteen months of life, and then an extended mind that is well underway by the age of four. It is during this period that the autobiographical self is established building on the skills of the core self and where, as Damasio (2000) has shown (Chapter 5), memories and references are stored as a result of experience rather than language.

The period of infancy where the self is laid down and the skills of being human are grown is therefore critical for the creation of identity. Moreover, the importance of the material and corporal culture (Figure 4.1) that surrounds the infant will have direct bearing on the concepts and categories which are significant for the establishment of the relationships that will structure future projects. Therefore, the visual and tactile array of material proxies for the body that are presented to babies by their hominin carers will be important both for the construction of identity and the shape of society. When, as indicated by the innovations list (Table 7.4), a gradient occurred during technology's three movements from a dominance of instruments to an ascendancy of containers I propose this had a profound *affect* for the psychological and cognitive identity of the child and, moreover, an *effect* that resulted in what, with hindsight, we see as change. The project of making the child was, and remains, rational and emotional, relational as well as material.

The importance of children: sets and nets

Children do not figure much in archaeology. They were buried and on occasion their weaning foods, a sticky mash, have been recovered (Mason et al. 1994). In the innovations list (Table 7.4) there is no children's technology and no description of cradle, pacifier or carrying sling (Fagan 2004; Troeng 1993). Their toys can be confused with ritual objects because small size is a poor guide to identification. Their tiny footprints and shoes indicate they were present (Roveland 2000), but they would be, wouldn't they? Children are like pre's: inconsequential so un-noticed.

This state of affairs, as archaeologist Joanna Sofaer (2000) points out, has the outcome of making children a biological rather than a cultural category. A child is a child because of age and size. It is a preface to an adult who is able to reproduce both socially and sexually. As Sofaer points out this makes it important to do for children what has already been done for women in the remote past by engendering them (Gero and Conkey 1991). Women and children are categories that are culturally constructed rather than biologically determined. They need to be gendered and aged because of the discrepancy in interpretation towards androcentric, adult categories. In addition, concepts of motherhood and childhood are not universal in their attributes of devotion, care and dependence but rather local constructions, if they exist at all.

A rational approach to archaeological evidence has been frustrated by the lack of children's things. This is unlikely to change by deliberately searching for children among the artefactual evidence although the demonstration of apprenticeship has held out some hope (Grimm 2000; Janik 2000; Pigeot 1990; Roux 1999). Instead the change that is needed requires a primary metaphor to make them visible. This will not necessarily allow the correct identification of their toys or a schoolroom for stone knapping. Instead it will combine the symbolic force of the body's biological development with the material metaphors that give it cultural significance.

Raising children

Growing is the metaphor that expresses the category of children and is accessible to archaeologists through the practice of accumulation and enchainment and the actions of fragmentation and consumption. Children can also be conceived as material projects (Chapter 6, Table 6.2) and as a result we can trace their importance through the proliferation of sets and nets of those proxies for the body, instruments and containers. Growing replaces the metaphor of the giving environment and as a result the emphasis shifts from instruments to containers and from reductive to additive techniques (Figure 7.1).

But what has this to do with agriculture or even questioning the significance of a Human Revolution? Anthropologist Tim Ingold points the way when he observes that 'growing plants and raising animals are not so different, in principle, from bringing up children' (2000:86). His point is that activities such as weeding fields and tending livestock do not make domestic plants and animals but rather establish the environmental conditions for their growth and development. Through their labours farmers and shepherds set the environmental conditions within which the crops and livestock will grow, just as parents establish the elements in the emotional and material arrays that surround the development of the baby and child. Furthermore, in Ingold's opinion the distinction between gathering and cultivation, hunting and husbandry is no more than 'the relative scope of human involvement in establishing the conditions of growth' (Ingold 2000:86).

Children, crops and herds are projects for our agency and as such form sets and nets of material culture. For instance, a herd of cattle is a set that also casts a wide net of relations as illustrated so graphically in the classic social anthropology of East Africa. The accumulation of the herd is possible by growing it as well as by exchange through marriage. Likewise, crops are grown in order to accumulate and enchain through their consumption and transformation into food. The herd is never finished just as its owner 'lives on' materially, distributed in time and space so that the actions of the living combine with the authority of the ancestors. Families and communities are similarly sets of relationships that arise through accumulation and enchainment. The material culture of villages that includes pottery, querns, sickles, cemeteries,

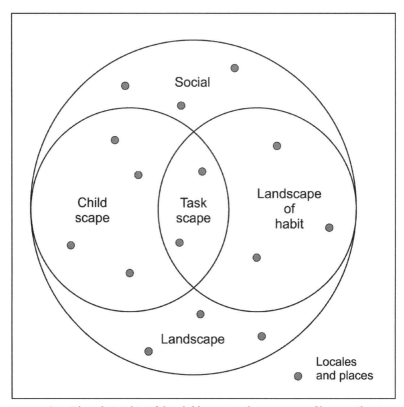

FIGURE 8.5. The relationship of the childscape to other concepts of human identity.

grain stores and stables are therefore responsive to the metaphor of growing the body because they are also sets that can be added to and dispersed.

Childscapes

The material project of growing children needs to be investigated at two interlocking scales, the locale and the landscape that together I refer to as the childscape: the environment for growth (Figure 8.5). At locales there is always the possibility for the accumulation of sets of material and corporal culture in the form of dances, fires, huts and all the accoutrements of a social technology. Through these activities these locales become *places*, sites of memory and woven into the autobiographical self, narrated with words, objects and sensations.

For the child these locales are often places of safety, an environment to grow with as well as in. Childscapes are therefore composed of emotionally charged arrays, including material culture. These arrays are learned as related categories and used as an individual authors their own emerging networks and identity. Fragmentation and consumption are always occurring at locales, acting out through bodily rhythms the metaphorical expression of a giving-environment and growing-a-body. The childscape is where our identity is created and its metaphorical basis established through references to emotional, material and symbolic resources (Tables 5.5 and 8.1). The childscape, like the self, is hidden. Memories of those early years are for all of us piecemeal, erratic and do not compare with those that form the later and larger chapters in our autobiographical selves.

Locales articulate to wider networks in what I have previously called a social landscape (Gamble 1999:90–1) and where I drew a distinction between these and the landscape of habit and the taskscape that were common to all hominins. The landscape of habit is an area of habitual action while the taskscape, as used by Ingold (1993), focuses on the act of attention where we hear, see and smell life through its varied activities. By contrast I introduced the social landscape to deal with the extension of social life that occurred comparatively late in human evolution as discussed earlier in this chapter.

These terms still have value, although there are perhaps too many of them. They can be simplified using the childscape, as defined above, that has its own interlocking locales, landscape of habit, taskscape and social landscape (Figure 8.5). By virtue of growth and development, the spatial and social scales will be different from the adult conception that dominates my earlier use of these terms (Gamble 1999) and which on reflection dealt more with the giving-environment for mature actors rather than growing-a-body, and an identity, for the young.

Childscapes and material projects

Insisting on a change in the ways through which the world was understood is all very well but what is needed is a definition of those material metaphors that formed the conceptual universe of these hominins. Rather than write an account from the cradle — what baby saw — I will tackle this task by describing the archaeological evidence from the three technological movements I identified in Chapter 7. What follows is necessarily selective and points the way to more exhaustive future studies. I will concentrate on material projects focused on the body, and employ a social technology in order to explore the changing metaphors that underpin agriculture and institutions that we can recognise in our search for origin points.

The material project enacted through the childscape is growing the body. This involves a range of attitudes that result in caring and altering as well as reproducing the body both biologically and materially. The material arrays that faced Palaeolithic babies will be examined here through the sets and nets of material culture and those proxies of container and instrument (Chapter 7) that reference us back to the body itself.

Sets and nets around hearth and home

Material projects are created through fragmentation and consumption and they appear as distinctive patterns to the archaeologist through the practice, common to all hominins, of accumulating and enchaining. What is of interest is how these simple principles have themselves grown during hominin evolution. Sets and nets provide a means to assess this growth and the arrays of material culture that formed the childscape. I will concentrate here on the sets and nets that define two elements of the environment of growth; hearth and home.

I will approach these elements in two ways. First, I will take the hearth and examine it not only as a container that can be formed into sets but also as a focus for the instruments and containers that are made and accumulated around them. Of particular interest are locales with no hearths, even though preservation is good, and the nets that are found across landscapes.

Second, I will investigate another container, the house, and examine how material projects relate to them. This will be done by looking at changing densities of material and the emphasis will be on the evidence for fragmentation and the creation of materials for nets.

My framework is chronological to lend clarity to an otherwise cluttered narrative. Each technological movement is summarised and then followed by some of the evidence on which it is based. Selected locales are presented as case studies to indicate the wealth of evidence that awaits future analysis.

Fire, hearths and homes

At issue is not the existence of fire. Archaeologists can find evidence for its presence during much of the long introduction through burnt bones, flecks of charcoal and fire cracked rocks (e.g. Bellomo 1994; Brain and

Sillen 1988; Callow et al. 1986; James 1989; Perlès 1976), but rather the control of fire so that it forms a container. Demonstrating that hominins controlled fire is not straightforward, as John Gowlett (1981) has shown in his study of one of the earliest occurrences at Chesowanja, Kenya, dated to a million years ago. Small fires, lit once, not only preserve badly, but the archaeological evidence is also open to alternative suggestions such as lightning strikes and bush fires. What is of interest for the childscape is the creation of fire in a container so that we have not only fire but hearths. Hearths can be elaborated in many ways by digging fire pits, adding stone settings and creating clay ovens. The fires they contain have to be cared for. Ash and cinders need to be raked out and dumped elsewhere while activities that fragment things in order to enchain and accumulate feed them with leaves, wood, bone and peat. Fires consume and alter whatever is placed within them. Here they are analogous to eating because fires also embody and transform resources. Hearths attract bodies and care for them by providing warmth and keeping predators beyond the circle. The relationship is reciprocal. Hearths need those social agents if they are to grow, while people need the social technology of hearths, not just for practical reasons, but to involve others in projects. Hearths are an emotional resource for a diurnal animal. They have always formed a focus for the childscape because they act as nodes in the net gathering people into those intimate and effective networks. Fire and people form a ring of agency, a hybrid project.

Houses are also hybrid material projects, a point that has been made earlier (see Chapter 3) and does not need to be rehearsed again. My concern here is not with the *domus* (Hodder 1990), privacy (Wilson 1988) or theatres of memory (Watkins 2004a), but instead with the contribution of the house to the childscape and so to my theme of the material basis for identity and change.

Houses and shelters are made from sets of materials — stone, clay, leaves, mud, wood, reeds, turf, bone, ice — some of which are intentionally transformed by fire as is the case with bricks. They are a purpose-built container for accumulation and enchainment and they have contents: sets of material, including hearths, that are both similar and dissimilar and which, by being intentionally contained, acquire an integral relationship that defines them as a category (Chapman 2000). Houses grow and change. They have biographies shaped by the practices of accumulating and enchaining. They are a focus for fragmentation and an arena for consumption of those emotional, material and symbolic resources (Table 8.1) with which an individual creates the networks of their social life.

The long introduction, 2.6 million to 100,000 years ago: an appreciation

The social technology of the childscape during this long introduction is dominated by instruments. The control of fire is well documented but hearths, when they occur, are simple and at any locale only a few are found. The sets of material that surround them are often diffuse, showing little spatial patterning or internal organisation so that it is often difficult to 'read' the sets as material metaphors. Logical puzzles abound; for example the piles of mammoth and rhino bones stacked beneath a granite cliff at La Cotte de St Brelade, Jersey (Scott 1986), and landscapes densely strewn with what seem to be perfectly serviceable but apparently discarded stone bifaces (Pope 2002). These puzzles are compounded by the hegemony of knapped stone and broken animal carcasses, materials with which we are unfamiliar and where contemporary analogies can be hard to come by to order experience (Chapter 3). As a result, the claims for shelters and huts are always controversial, while convincing evidence for items that wrapped the body, such as jewellery or clothes, is hard to find.

But even without an interior, house-bound life the childscape was hidden and separate. Many significant actions took place elsewhere in the landscapes of habit patrolled by adults, unseen and unheard. Those dwelling in the childscape were related to this wider landscape of habit by what was introduced, the kill brought back to the hearth or the stones collected from the next river. As a result the childscape was continually created and reproduced by these gifts from an unseen environment experienced vicariously through material culture rather than immediately through the sensations of the body. The inhabitants of the childscape knew the landscape of habit through the immediate actions of fragmentation and consumption. These created the form of the childscape and the material identity of those growing within it.

As an example, consider what happened at death. The evidence consists of body parts rather than skeletons. Carnivores played their part along with other agents such as soil erosion and weathering. Rather than using containers in the form of either pits or protective slabs (Chapter 6) to arrest the process of disintegration, the process was in fact hurried along by using stone tools to fragment the corpse.

Those in the childscape learned the landscape of habit into which they would grow through the instruments and the activities of fragmentation. For example, they experienced instruments in relation to other instruments, sharp edged stone working softer wood to make spears. Short chains of connection established a metaphorical basis for immediate consumption of the gifts from the environment.

The major association of instruments and containers was the fragmentation of animals and the cracking open of nuts and seeds. Fires were fed but they were not unduly cared for. Childscapes were created constantly throughout the environment, interlocking at each new locale with the adult landscapes of habit and fused through the range of activities that comprised the taskscape and which related child and adult, male and female in a variety of gendered and aged material projects.

The social technology of the long introduction was a material project of the open-air rather than the enclosed space. It was a world of landscapes rather than places. The bulk of the archaeological evidence comes from landscapes where fires were never lit, although if they had been they would have been preserved. But even in such 'featureless' environments there were rules that created sets of stone within a landscape, the patches among the scatters as Glynn Isaac (1989) dubbed this distinctive signature, while the nets so created were spatially short. Some interpretations of piles of stones as huts are best regarded as accumulations that also follow the rules by which place was created and memory inscribed. These same locales are normally described in terms of hunting opportunities for single large animals as well as herds. These animal 'containers' were an essential element of the giving environment. They were fragmented, like the stone tools, and distributed around the landscape. They were embodied through consumption but this was not always in association with the hearths that were elsewhere in the landscape.

Evidence from the long introduction

Fire

Some of the best evidence for the control of fire in technology's long introduction comes from Gesher Benot Ya'aqov, Israel (Goren-Inbar et al. 2004), where burning consists of wood fragments, tiny flint chips, nuts and seeds. Here, 780,000 years ago, the paucity of burned items in the excavated area and their clustered distribution led the archaeologists to infer small, repeatedly used hearths. They conclude, 'the domestication of fire by hominins surely led to dramatic changes in behaviour connected with diet, defense, and social interaction' (Goren-Inbar et al. 2004:727). This was undoubtedly the case but there is more to be inferred. Hearths as containers create place through accumulation and at Gesher Benot Ya'aqov this is indicated by the repeated use of particular settings in the locale to build fires.

The repeated use of hearths 400,000 years ago is also found at the lakeside locales of Schöningen in eastern Germany (Thieme 2005) and among the fire features at Beeches Pit, eastern England (Gowlett 2005). The evidence at Beeches Pit consists of small but distinctively coloured patches of burnt sediment that are sometimes associated with fire-cracked stones. Gowlett has drawn attention to a striking similarity at both these open locales in the way hominins positioned the small hearths along the edge of water bodies, away from the main scatters of lithic materials. At one Schöningen locale, site 13 II-4, the accumulation of lithic materials away from the lake shore forms a continuous spread 800 m in length with local densities of up to 150 stone fragments per m^2 (Thieme 2005:Figure 8.3). The four hearths (Thieme 2005:Figure 8.8) lie towards the lake, on the edge of this dry open area across which lie the parts of at least twenty horse skeletons as well as a number of wooden artefacts, including spears. The stone material is interesting since there is no evidence for the initial stages of knapping (Thieme 2005:121) implying that every piece was carried in from somewhere else in the Schöningen landscape.

Hearths in caves are also known from the long introduction but tend to be isolated. At the Grotte du Lazaret, Nice (de Lumley et al. 2004), the excavated surface UA 25 dated to 160,000 years ago contains a single well-made hearth (ibid. 2004:Figure 56), while nearby in two discrete locations is a high density of broken flakes and a small, circular pile of broken animal bones (ibid. 2004:Figure 51).

Splitting the container

Food resources, as discussed in Chapter 7, are a form of container. Plants are poorly preserved but when waterlogged conditions allow, as at Gesher Benot Ya'aqov, it is possible to see how important they were (Goren-Inbar et al. 2002a). Animals provide the bulk of the data, their importance partly explained by the value of meat and fat as high energy foods that the expensive tissue of the growing brain fed on (Aiello and Wheeler 1995). The importance for reproductive success of minimising the risk of dietary failure and maximising food returns has also led to a lively debate over the role of scavenging and hunting in the Old World (Binford 1981; Bunn 1981; Marean 1998; Marean and Assefa 1999; Stiner 1994; 2002).

Two of the key locales in this fluctuating debate are Ambrona and Torralba in central Spain, where a conjuncture of Acheulean handaxes and elephants gave rise to a big-game hunting scenario (Howell 1965), only to be later re-interpreted as scavenging and river transport of the same bones (Binford 1985; Shipman and Rose 1983).

The debate now seems to be resolved for this and other locales. Recent excavations at Ambrona by Manuel Santonja and Alfredo Pérez-González (Santonja and Peréz-González 2001) provide decisive evidence. In particular, the discovery of the remains of an elephant skeleton in layer AS3, has allowed a detailed biographical study (Villa et al. 2005) under modern conditions of recovery. The precise stratigraphic observations of how the remaining parts of the elephant skeleton had been moved and buried, combined with a microscopic examination of the bones themselves was revealing. No traces of either carnivore tooth marks or cut-marks made by stone tools were discovered. A few stone tools were found at the perimeter of the scatter of elephant bones and several of them had abraded edges showing they had been transported some distance by the river. Combining the Ambrona evidence with the re-examination of claims for scavenging in the common ground (Stiner 1994) has led Paola Villa (Villa et al. 2005) to conclude that there are no sites in Europe which show that earlier hominins, including Neanderthals, scavenged on a regular basis.

The Schöningen spears and the evidence for single large animal kills of horse, as at Boxgrove (Roberts et al. 1997), puts hunting skills back in the hands of hominins during much of the long introduction. Other examples of a single butchered carcass found with stone tools include the elephant carcasses at Aridos in the Jarama valley, Spain (Arqueológica 2002; Raposo and Santonja 1995; Santonja et al. 1980; Santonja and Villa 1990); Notarchirico (Piperno 1999) and other elephant localities in Italy (Mussi 1995).

For consumption to take place these containers had to be fragmented; so much is obvious, but they were also accumulated, most dramatically at the headland site of La Cotte de St Brelade, Jersey (Scott 1980; 1986). Here two large bone piles are preserved and they represent the actions of Neanderthals 150,000 years ago who stampeded two small herds of mammoth and woolly rhino over the cliff. Their project did not end there but involved dragging and stacking skulls and selected limb bones under the protective overhang. The rational puzzle is why go to this effort and then not use the resources?

However, was hunting a material project that contributed directly to the experiences of the childscape? It is unlikely that children would be allowed at the base of the La Cotte headland when so many tons of mammoth and rhino came tumbling over! The longer the period of child development the more parents will protect their investment for sound evolutionary reasons (Pianka 1978). But that is not quite the point. Once split open these fragments were not placed in another container, such as a house or pit or stored under a pile of rocks to keep other predators like bears and hyenas away. Neither were they always brought to a hearth. Chains of connection were short as measured by the degree to which they extended relationships across an individual's social landscape.

Where are the huts?

The dominance of instruments in the long introduction is well illustrated by the problem of finding huts and shelters. No one disputes that caves were used throughout the Old World. They acted as containers and within them are found hearths. These are rarely superimposed on top of each other and mostly single as at Grotte du Lazaret (de Lumley et al. 2004). Fragments of stone and animal bone dominate as they do at the open locales. Hominin remains from caves are nearly always fragmentary either because of post-mortem disturbance or possibly because of intentional fragmentation by the hominins themselves.

Central places have been proposed to counter the lack of huts and shelters. These are defined in terms of the density and diversity of material and form patches within the background scatters of archaeological material across large areas. When Isaac (1978; 1989:Figure 4.14) proposed this model he did not, however, see it as needing a hut or house as a central focus for returning hominins but rather a shady tree or a rock overhang with a watersource nearby. This, for example, may be the case at the Eastern German locale of Bilzingsleben where the excavator Dieter Mania (1990; Mania and Mania 2005) interpreted the evidence to represent three oval huts by the lakeshore. The evidence, however, is open to other interpretations (Gamble 1999:153–72), and while sets of stones, animal parts and hearths and at least six rhythmically marked bones (Mania and Mania 2005:110–13) were accumulated at the lakeshore locale, this might have been around a burnt tree stump rather than in the confines of a container. As Lewis Binford (1987) perceptively points out, by searching for camp-sites as though we were doing an ethnographic study, archaeologists are in danger of missing the significance of the evidence they have. Instead of places marked by huts there was an episodic use of the landscape that produced Isaac's scatters and patches of stone and bone material.

Case study: Boxgrove, southern England 500,000 years ago

An example of this unfamiliar use of landscape can be found at the Acheulean locale of Boxgrove (Pitts and Roberts 1997; Roberts and Parfitt 1999). This ancient landscape has exceptional preservation not only of animal bones and a few skeletal elements of *Homo heidelbergensis* (Roberts et al. 1994), but also of their spatial arrangement. When visited by hominins 500,000 years ago a grassy coastal plain existed in front of a collapsing sea cliff. Following successful hunts of single animals, flint was collected from the cliff, carried out onto the plain and knapped into bifaces. One element that might be expected is, however, lacking from this pristine archaeological site. There are no hearths. Instead there are many clusters of stone working, in particular around what might have been a waterhole where a spring emerged from the base of the cliff. Neither are there any traces in the fine-grained sediments of post-holes from which archaeologists can reconstruct simple shelters and tents.

Matt Pope (2002; Pope and Roberts 2005) has studied the numerous artefact scatters and patches in front of the cliff. In particular his work focuses on explaining why some of these patches were rich in well-finished stone bifaces (handaxes) knapped from flint taken from the cliff, while others were very poor. The distances across the Boxgrove landscape are short with flint artefacts found up to 250 metres south of the cliff line. The decline in bifaces away from this topographic feature, the source of the raw material, is very consistent even though the distances are so short.

Pope uses this fine detail to reconstruct a half million year old landscape structured by intentional actions. Within the Boxgrove landscape there were places visited once, such as the single horse butchery locale, site GTP17, and others such as the 'waterhole' in Quarry 1/B where he is able to show that visits were repeated over several years. At the short-lived gatherings such as the horse butchery locale few or no bifaces were found. Eight blocks of flint were brought in to this locale, presumably by eight individuals. Symmetrical, ovate handaxes were knapped as revealed by the refitted flakes. But all eight handaxes were carried away from this locale and deposited elsewhere. As Pope (2002:171) concludes, where artefacts were released from the hand, and not used again, depended on those places being visited more than once, implying the association of memories with place.

FIGURE 8.6. Excavations at Quarry 1/B at Boxgrove. A set of over 300 ovate handaxes (inset) have so far been recovered from this part of the locale that may have been a waterhole. The evidence from the stone tools and knapping activities reveals a dense, but local net of connections.

One such site of memory is the 'waterhole' in Quarry 1/B (Figure 8.6) about a kilometre west of GTP 17. Here in the Middle Units of these freshwater deposits the excavators found not only the richest density of cores and struck flakes but also a set of 321 bifaces, not all of them showing traces of being used. Boxgrove bifaces (Marshall et al. 2002) are distinctive, ovate forms of similar size and many bear a distinctive signature in the form of a specialised re-sharpening flake struck from their tips. It is this similarity that makes them a set. The Boxgrove hominins had repeatedly brought in these bifaces to the waterhole no doubt alongside other items of material culture such as horseflesh and the occasional antler and bone that was used as a soft hammer to knap flint.

Are there any nets at Boxgrove? Here the evidence is plain. The raw materials are local and the artefacts are dominated by instruments. The distances travelled are small, of the order of 250 m, but the criss-crossing of people between the cliff and the plain and the different elements they carried in their hands and accumulated at agreed locales makes an intricate web of invisible tracks. At the horse butchery locale the flint blocks and the refitted tools form a net across the carcass when the conjoining pieces are linked together.

Biface rich assemblages as sets with rules

Pope (2002:286) argues that the structured pattern of landscape use he was able to reconstruct at Boxgrove was one of the mechanisms by which more complicated systems of land use evolved. Bifaces stood as proxies for individuals (2002:28), assisting group cohesion through the daily routines of fission-fusion. Bifaces provided cues to behaviour and responses as hominins returned, indicating that 500,000 years ago culture was a hybrid network involving relations between people and objects. At this time, as predicted by the social brain graph (Figure 8.3), hominins were probably using a form of language. But they also had a tradition of material metaphors, encapsulated in the biface, that was already a million years old by the time Boxgrove was visited.

Furthermore, this structured pattern of biface rich assemblages was widespread in the Old World (Pope and Roberts 2005). Pope's (2002) study shows that as soon as the distinctive Acheulean bifaces appear about 1.5 million years ago in Africa (Leakey 1971) they were left at locales and on landscapes according to the rule that re-visiting a locale entailed bringing and leaving a biface. There was, if you like, a habit for getting rid of a biface – or as I would put it, accumulating them at places. Moreover, using the Boxgrove data from southern England, and comparing it to older locales in Africa, Pope (2002) shows that the size of individual bifaces results in their being treated differently. They accumulate in different parts of these open landscapes.

At Aridos, Spain (Arqueológica 2002; Santonja et al. 1980) hominins took the finished tools with them when they moved away from the elephant carcass and deposited them elsewhere, a situation very similar to that known from Boxgrove. At Aridos 1, the fact that at least two bifaces were made on site but not left behind is shown by the discovery of distinctive flakes, known as *coup de trenchant* (Manuel Santonja pers. comm.). Elsewhere in Europe further examples have also been found where the landscape is partitioned according to these rules of butchering the carcass and accumulating sets of handaxes in other places (Gaudzinski and Turner 1999).

Much older patterns of biface accumulation in Africa have been commented upon by John Gowlett (1991) for the Kenyan locales of Kilombe (Gowlett 1996) between 800,000 and 1 million years old, various localities at Olorgesailie (Isaac 1977; Potts et al. 1999) of comparable age, and Olduvai Gorge, Tanzania (Potts 1988). Where the effects of deflation or the hydraulic action of rivers and flash floods can be factored out, as they can at

Kilombe and Olorgesailie, then we are left with impressive accumulations of bifaces. These comprised sets, based on raw material, size, morphology, symmetry and parameters of knapping skill, that have been much discussed (e.g. Gowlett 1996; 1998; Marshall et al. 2002; Potts 1991; 1993:331; Roe 1968; 1994; Wynn 1993; 1995). However, the similarity that produces patterned sets for the archaeologist also results in a paradox in that the diversity of tool forms is low but the variability within sets at a locale and regional level can be considerable because of the range of attributes taken into account (Gowlett 1998). On closer inspection many of the sets emerge as rather fuzzy, and this may be another instance of archaeologists searching for crisply defined sets and missing the fact that most of them are not. It therefore comes as a relief to note a strong pattern that, in the vast majority of cases, the raw materials for these bifaces is local, coming from no more than 20 km away and normally much less (Féblot-Augustins 1990). The exceptions to this finding have already been discussed (page 213).

The common ground, 100,000 to 20,000 years ago: an appreciation

The social technology of the childscape during the common ground is marked by an increase in the use of containers as material proxies for the body. And with these containers comes a sharper focus among the sets of material culture. For example, hearths now appear regularly as sets in time and space. In rock-shelters they were rebuilt and relit in the same place, often over millennia, while in open locales they are found in neatly spaced rows. Hearths were regularly made from sets of materials such as river pebbles and slabs of stone and bone. Their presence was respected in settlements where they were tended and altered during their life. The small spatial patterns of everyday life were created around them.

The material project of creating a childscape had changed, confirmed by the growing association between hearths and shelters. Sets of animal bones and antlers, and later pits and semi-subterranean dwellings, were accumulated at chosen locales. These were often closely associated with graves and human bodies. These bodies were also contained, their boundaries altered, as shown by widespread finds of ornaments, jewellery and by inference clothing. The application of iron oxide pigments changed the body's colour just as wearing a fox-tooth necklace re-modelled the shape of the neck or a dentalium shell cap modified the forehead of its wearer.

The childscape, the environment of growth, was replete with relation-ships based on material proxies of the body. What changed during the common ground was the authority, from the standpoint of the childscape, for making sense of the world: in particular the connections that containers and instruments established between the childscape and the landscape of habit.

In technology's long introduction the landscape of habit was learned and grown into through material metaphors of the body based primarily on instruments. With the use of both containers and instruments the childscape and landscapes of the common ground were revealed in more familiar metaphorical detail, not only by building sets but also extending the networks of relationships. In metaphorical terms the childscape was 'fitted into' the landscape of habit, rather than 'gifted' by it. As well as giving, growth now established relationships, as illustrated by a new interest in small animals that were rapid breeders.

The material project which points to these subtle changes concerns the reproduction and growth of the body. Taskscapes now resounded with the sights, smells and noises of the fragmentation and consumption of stone, wood, resins and bones, as well as animals and plants, for the purposes of enchaining locales to landscapes. For example, the manufacture of blades rather than flakes (Chapter 7) was a social technology involved in extending relationships in space and time. Not only could the body be reproduced through material proxies but identity could also be distributed across time and space.

The process was reflexive. Into the childscape came 'exotic' materials and new categories of relationship that fitted things together and built them up, as was the case with textiles and baskets (Chapter 7). Learning about the larger social landscape was therefore supported, for those dwelling in the childscape, by material metaphors that expressed relationships in terms of how the body experiences being in the world of people and objects.

None of this happened instantaneously. During the common ground the evidence for containers varied in time and space across the Old World. There was no tipping point to suggest that spoken language guided that change in authority. The social brain model predicts increases in group sizes from 120 to only 150 in this technological movement (Table 8.2). The role of language was significant during the earlier long introduction and its appearance was not associated with the move to material metaphors that during the common ground after 100,000 years ago came to emphasise containment.

What is important, as discussed earlier in this chapter, is the varied evidence from land and sea of extension to the social landscapes of these hominins. An extension based upon the understanding of the world beyond the childscape/landscape of habit and the relationships that sustained it.

It was here during technology's common ground that the ways in which hominins constructed their identities changed. The rules of landscape and locale that we saw with bifaces were now supplemented by rules of place. Sets were grown and exported. Landscapes were harvested and tended. The primary metaphor remained one of relationships based on a giving environment, its authority now supplemented by the opportunity to engage with another powerful metaphor, that of growing the body. But the identities so created are still unfamiliar to us because the accumulation and enchainment of sets and nets is closer to the work of *bricoleurs* (Chapter 6).

Evidence from the common ground

Fire

Hearths varied a good deal. Shallow scoops and concentrated patches of burning are found in many caves in the Middle East (Bar-Yosef 1989), such as Kebara (Bar-Yosef et al. 1992), and Europe (Rigaud et al. 1995) and among piles of animal bones at Molodova in the Ukraine (Chernysh 1961; Goretsky and Ivanova 1982; Ivanova and Tseitlin 1987). However, their construction becomes more elaborate some time before 50,000 years ago with the stone-built hearths at Vilas Ruivas, Portugal (Vega Toscano et al. 1999:23−4). Later such stone-lined and cobble-filled constructions are common, as at the Abri Pataud in southern France (Movius 1966; Perlès 1976). In both examples the accumulation of stones defined hearths that were repeatedly raked out and re-used.

Hearth building is also matched by alignments and arrangements. The Abri Pataud hearths are regularly spaced in a line beneath the large rock overhang. They form a set not only through re-use and re-modelling but also in their relation to each other. The long stratigraphic sequence at Shelter 1B at Klasies River Mouth, South Africa (Henderson 1992:23) shows, in levels dated to between 70,000 and 80,000 years old a clear preference in unit PCP for lighting, on at least five separate occasions, small fires, 50 cm in diameter, in the same spot. Moreover, each occasion was stratigraphically distinct with each visit to the rock shelter possibly separated by a few years.

Contrast this with large open air hearths, fed with mammoth bone, at Kostenki, site I-1 and site IV-2 on the Don river in southern Russia

(Hoffecker 2002; Klein 1969; Praslov and Rogachev 1982). These were regularly spaced 3 m apart in the central area of the locale and surrounded by pits and subterranean dwellings.

However, hearths are not always a focus for sets or spatial patterns as commented on by Henderson (1992) at Klasies River Mouth, and by Lyn Wadley (2001) at Rose Cottage Cave, South Africa (see also Kolen 1999). At Rose Cottage the oldest hearths are 31,000 years old in the Middle Stone Age, layer Dc, and twenty ash-hearths in an area of 26 m² have been excavated. The ash-hearths are of variable size but on average only 40 cm apart. People kept returning to that part of the cave and thirteen of the ash-hearths are covered by 23,500 lithic pieces of which only 273 are retouched tools (ibid.:Figure 2). This very high density (903 per m² or 9,791 per m³) masks any small-scale spatial patterning either by size or type of artefact. Wadley sums up the result as:

> un-structured camp organization with a clutter of artefacts and food waste usually in close association with hearths. Some evidence for refuse dumping is present but, apart from food processing or cooking, no special purpose activity areas can be recognised.
>
> (Wadley 2001:212)

Precisely the same conclusion was arrived at by Jan Simek (1987) at the earlier 130,000 year old level VIII of Grotte Vaufrey in southern France where a concentration of charcoals identified the hearth. Even when artefacts were refitted little spatial patterning could be found (Binford 1988; Rigaud and Geneste 1988). In addition, artefact densities were much lower than at Rose Cottage, a mere 85 per m², so that patterns were not being swamped by too many lithics.

This fuzzy picture gains greater clarity once hearths are defined by stone settings, arranged in rows and regularly cleaned out, as was the case at Abri Pataud (Movius 1966). It was Binford (1978a) who drew attention to the creation of circular and horseshoe patterns in the materials that accumulate around such hearths where people sit to talk and eat. Moreover, the materials within these rings are sorted by size; small objects trampled by feet close to the fire, larger items in a ring up to 3 m away (Gamble 1986:256–63).

Huts and shelters

There are many containers which are interpreted as huts (Desbrosse and Kozlowski 1994; Djindjian et al. 1999; Sklenár 1976); intentionally built to house people. The deliberate behaviour that results in circular and oval shapes with footings and weights has, however, been questioned by Jan Kolen (1999). He sees much of the patterning as mimicking the intention to build, arising instead from living among materials and moving them around a limited lifespace in a centrifugal manner, as at Molodova site I/4 (Goretsky and Ivanova 1982:Figure 8). Even at locales such as Kostenki (Figure 8.7) (Efimenko 1958; Praslov and Rogachev 1982) and Pavlov (Svoboda 1994), where there is general agreement that a range of shelters have been correctly identified (Roebroeks et al. 2000), most of them are unique projects as judged by setting, materials, shape and contents. This has led Alexander Verpoorte (2001:131) to question if they are indeed what we think they are and to wonder why architecture has such a low visibility in this technological movement.

What is lacking throughout the common ground is a repeated set of modular structures to match, for example, the frequently found hearths spaced 3 m apart. I have puzzled over this lack of modularity (Gamble 1986), as eager as the next archaeologist to identify huts and villages to support a Palaeolithic social revolution (Gamble 1993a). But if I am honest these huts from technology's common ground are unfamiliar forms, especially when compared with the serviceable houses and villages from the last few thousand years of the Arctic, let alone the archaeology of farmers, and where instantly I can recognise familiar material *and* metaphorical forms (Binford 1993; Chang 1962; Damas 1984; Grønnow et al. 1983; Morgan 1881).

Instead each of these huts or locales is a material project put together by a *bricoleur* rather than a builder, assembled by repeatedly accumulating sets of materials at a place rather than having a design (Chapter 6). The sets these bricoleurs, Neanderthals as well as Modern humans, used in their material palimpsests included hearths, pits, post-holes, ivory, food, ornaments, furs, ochre, stone and human bodies. They dug, cut, skinned, carved, knapped, whittled, twined, wove and pounded and by these and many other rhythmic gestures attached themselves to the locale and created a place to live (Gamble 1999:412–14).

Case study: Kostenki-Avdeevo-Pavlov-Willendorf 28,000 years ago (Figure 8.7)

The open air locales of Kostenki-Avdeevo-Pavlov-Willendorf, located in Russia, the Czech Republic and Austria are some of the richest Upper Palaeolithic locales in Russia and Europe (Soffer and Praslov 1993;

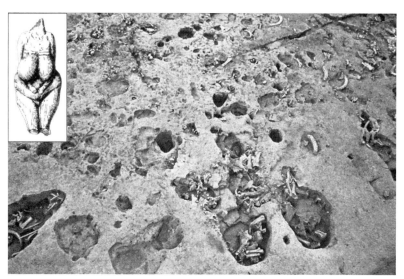

FIGURE 8.7. Kostenki site 1 level 1 excavations by Nikolai Praslov (reproduced with permission). Many pits were dug at this locale and contained a wide range of materials. Some of these, such as shells and amber, came from well beyond the local vicinity. Figurines, some of them intentionally fragmented (inset) were found in pits across the locale and form a distinctive set. The pits are not entirely convincing as subterranean houses suggesting the work of bricoleurs rather than engineers (see text).

Svoboda et al. 1996). They have produced multiple sets of instruments and containers that link them across 1,800 km some 28,000 years ago.

These sets include the much described 'Venus' figurines (Abramova 1967; Delporte 1979; Gamble 1982a); made of limestone, marl, ivory, and at Dolní Vestonice in the Czech Republic, fired clay. Among the lithic artefacts they share in common are the Kostenki shouldered knives. Furthermore, all the locales are linked by their use of mammoth for food, fuel, raw material for tools and building materials and an enthusiasm for digging pits that is especially marked in the Russian locales (Efimenko 1958; Gvozdover 1989). A recent study by Alexander Verpoorte (2001:Figure 3.22) of the structured settlement at Dolní Vestonice-Pavlov reveals the complexity in the structured deposition of figurines that complements the pyrotechnic displays (Soffer et al. 1993) and the textile containers (Soffer et al. 2000) I have already described (Chapter 7). Bound human burials, e.g. Dolní Vestonice XVI an adult male, were found near hearths inside a shallow scrape interpreted as the base of a hut (Svoboda 1991:Figure 6) and e.g. Dolní Vestonice III, a gracile female, under a protective covering of mammoth scapulae (Klima 1963).

The Kostenki-Avdeevo locales were used many times. The people dug repeatedly into the active zone above the permanently frozen ground to make fire hollows, hundreds of shallow scoops, and pits, graves, as well as larger 'pit-houses' dug to a depth of between 60 cm and 1 m (Grigor'ev 1993; Rogachev 1957) depending on the depth of the permafrost. Objects were then planted in them. These included the following sets:

- Mammoth tusks and selected bones, often in anatomical order. For example Pithouse A at Kostenki I/1 contains 12 closely associated tusks, ten of which have their points towards the centre of the pit (Efimenko 1958:Figure 11). At Avdeevo (Rogachev 1957:Figures 9 and 12) sets of tusks are also arranged in pits.
- Wolves and arctic foxes. Grigori'ev (1993:60) describes a pit at Avdeevo with 12 wolves in complete anatomical order.
- The deliberate placing of artefacts in pits. Gvozdover (1995:23−5) describes the three mammoth ivory female figurines placed on purpose with other objects of bone and flint (Gvozdover 1989:Table 4) on the bottom of one of the Avdeevo pits. They were placed back-to-back, touching. In two other pits at Kostenki and Avdeevo two figurines were found together.
- Human burials. These are usually found in pits in a crouched posture, as at Kostenki sites 14 and 15 (Praslov and Rogachev 1982:Figures 52 and 55). Sets of jewellery and instruments in ivory and mammoth bone accompany them.
- Eleven complete and eleven fragmented female figurines in either ivory or chalk/marl are known from Kostenki and Avdeevo (Gvozdover 1989:Table 4). They were deliberately fragmented and then spatially arranged to make sets. At Kostenki I/1 there is a wide scatter of marl figurine fragments while the more complete, ivory examples are clustered in pits at the eastern end of the locale. One of the marl figures, excavated in 1988, came from a small pit. Both the head and feet are missing and Nickolai Praslov (1993:166) believes it was broken elsewhere and then intentionally placed in the pit. Figurine 10, made of mammoth ivory, from Avdeevo (Gvozdover 1995:25−6) was found in two pieces; one at the bottom of a pithouse and the other 14 cm away in the fill. The figurine was broken by a strong vertical blow. It still lacks its head and both legs and is reminiscent of the marl figurine from Kostenki.
- Several sets of both containers and instruments exist (Gvozdover 1995:Table II). Among the containers are decorated needle cases

made from bird bones; necklaces of pierced fox teeth and beads made from the long bones of small animals; bracelets and stone pendants (Abramova 1967). Instrument based sets from Avdeevo include adzes or mattocks made of ivory, engraved wands and spoons, as well as a wide range of points and awls made of ivory and bone (Gvozdover 1995). Comparable sets come from the Kostenki archaeological sites (Abramova 1967; Efimenko 1958; Praslov and Rogachev 1982).

Case study: Blombos Cave 80,000 years ago

Blombos Cave, South Africa, is a showcase for the diversity of material life at the start of the common ground as hominin bricoleurs constructed metaphors for living. It is a small cave with well dated deposits. At ages in excess of 77,000 years ago Christopher Henshilwood and his team have recovered several sets from 13 m³ of excavated deposits (Figure 8.8).

The consumption of material culture at this locale is impressive. The density of stone artefacts in two of the levels is even greater than those at Rose Cottage Cave. Organic preservation is also good. The sets include:

- Stone tools. 99 and 67 Still Bay bifacial points from levels BBC1a and BBC1b respectively. These were made on silcrete and knapped using a soft hammer. There was a distinct preference for this fine grained raw material both at Blombos and other Still Bay locales (Henshilwood et al. 2001:446).
- 7,914 pieces of mineral pigments of which 1,448 were >10 mm and 283 bore traces of utilisation (Table 8.3).
- Two geometrically engraved ochre pieces from BBC M1.
- 28 bone tools, awls and points mostly from level BBC2 (Henshilwood et al. 2001). Fifteen of the points came from 4 m³ and the rest from 8.4 m³ of the excavation.
- 41 perforated tick shells (*Nassarius kraussianus*). These carried traces of red ochre and were found in clusters of 2 to 17 beads. In the opinion of the archaeologists they are evidence for a necklace (Henshilwood et al. 2004).
- Containers in fragile and perishable materials. Ostrich egg shell was worked to form water containers. Henshilwood (et al. 2001:446) suggests that the bone awls were used to pierce leather to make bags and clothing.

FIGURE 8.8. Sets at Blombos Cave, South Africa. From the small cave a number of artefact sets have come. The shells (upper inset) formed part of a necklace and are therefore a container (reproduced with permission from C. Henshilwood). They relate to nets within the landscape of habit. The Still Bay stone points (lower inset) were widely distributed instruments and are recognised from several locales across southern Africa by their similarity (reproduced with permission from T. Minichillo).

These sets also acted as nets across the landscape. The tick shells came from the coast, then some 20 km away, while the source for the pigments is some 15–32 kilometres inland (Henshilwood et al. 2001:433), within the scale of a landscape of habit.

Case study: Salzgitter-Lebenstedt, Germany c. 80,000 years ago

The Neanderthal bricoleurs who came on several occasions to the open locale of Salzgitter-Lebenstedt had, by comparison to both Blombos

TABLE 8.3. *The ochre sets consisting of utilised and un-utilised pieces compared with the density of lithic material at Blombos Cave. Four stratigraphic levels, older than 77,000 years, are shown (Henshilwood et al. 2001)*

Level	m³ density of stone artefacts	Number of ochre pieces >10 mm	Number of utilised ochre pieces	% of utilised ochre pieces
BBC1a	30,208	} 246	78	32
BBC1b	13,443			
BBC2	2,935	85	18	21
BBC3	29,284	1,117	187	17

and the much later Kostenki site I-1, a limited number of sets. These included:

- 156 antlers from 82 individual reindeer, dominated by adult males (Gaudzinski and Roebroeks 2000:502).
- Proximal metatarsals from 44 individual reindeer, and smaller sets of other skeletal elements (Gaudzinski and Roebroeks 2000:Table 2).
- Selection of body parts with a higher food value as judged by food quality and quantity (Gamble and Gaudzinski 2005; Gaudzinski and Roebroeks 2003).
- 5 Neanderthal body parts (two femurs, three skull fragments) (Gaudzinski and Roebroeks 2000; Hublin 1984).
- 11 bone tools made of mammoth ribs and fibula (Gaudzinski 1998; Gaudzinski 1999:Table 1).
- Plano-convex bifaces made with Levallois PCT (Bosinski 1967; Pastoors 2001), following the rule of letting artefacts go at places which are re-visited (Pope 2002).

There were no hearths, pits, scoops or accumulations of animal remains that suggested a hut or shelter (Tode 1953; 1982) for the autumn hunting that took place there (Gaudzinski and Roebroeks 2000).

Does the limited evidence for bricolage by the Neanderthals of Salzgitter-Lebenstedt point to their only making rational decisions about what to hunt in order to meet their dietary requirements in as efficient a manner as possible? The answer is no, and for the following reasons.

From a relational perspective a comparison can be drawn with Lewis Binford's (1978b) classic study of reindeer processing by the Nunamiut people of northern Alaska. Binford provides a wealth of detail about the 'maze of pathways' (ibid. 1978b:248) that initiates the movement and distribution of food. He also provides a method to measure the degree of dismemberment of the carcasses to position a locale within those pathways by the proportions of marrow yielding bones (Binford 1978b:64). On all scores the Salzgitter-Lebenstedt reindeer assemblage shows relatively complete carcasses, as would be expected for a locale that stands at the start of those chains of relationships (Gamble and Gaudzinski 2005).

However, a major difference emerges between the ethnographic and the Neanderthal examples. The Nunamiut have a network of highly differentiated locales in their social landscape. These are widely scattered over a large territory and revolve around a hub, Anaktuvak Village, situated on a caribou migration route. Such a well-differentiated settlement pattern is lacking among the Neanderthals of Central Europe (Conard and Prindiville 2000:304; Gamble 1999). The significance of the regional settlement pattern impacts directly upon the creation of place at locales such as Salzgitter-Lebenstedt where the emphasis was on accumulation. Enchainment did not extend much beyond the limits of the locale. The Neanderthal bricoleurs brought together sets of people and animals, stone and bone tools in a project we call hunting but which is better understood as 'gifting' these categories to each other. The instruments they used to create such associations were themselves material proxies for relationships. Ultimately the Neanderthals understood these connections metaphorically through the experiences of their bodies.

The contrast with Blombos or Kostenki is that the sets these bricoleurs accumulated were 'fitted-into' each other, closely enchaining childscapes with landscapes of habit and growing identity alongside the body. The array of containers and instruments and the creation of sets and nets through fragmentation and consumption give each of the three locales a distinct feel, irrespective of whether Neanderthals and Modern humans were involved or their languages revelled in a passion for either gossip or analogy.

Feeding the body

A similar appreciation of earlier and later hominid place/landscape relationships is emerging from a larger sample. The competence of Neanderthal hunters is now well attested (Burke 2000; Gaudzinski and Turner 1996; 1999) through the multiple hunts of prime aged animals recorded at locales such as La Borde (Jaubert et al. 1990) and Mauran, France (David and Farizy 1994); Wallertheim, Germany

(Gaudzinski 1992; 1995); Gabasa, Spain (Blasco Sancho 1995); and Ortvale Klde, Georgia (Adler et al. 2006). Curtis Marean (Marean and Assefa 1999:34) has widened this sample to include Kobeh Cave in the Near East and the Middle Stone Age levels at GvJm46 at Lukenya Hill, Kenya where a single species focus is evident. Richard Cosgrove (Pike-Tay and Cosgrove 2002) has similar results from Tasmania where in several caves with deposits more than 30,000 years old (Cosgrove 1999) specialised hunting of Bennett's wallaby produces comparable sets in terms of age, body parts and seasons to those of the reindeer, horse and bison hunters during the common ground in Europe (for details see Gamble 1999:Tables 5.12 and 6.27).

Katie Boyle (1990:269–70 and Table 2.7), in a comprehensive study of the use of animals in the French Upper Palaeolithic, has noted a recurrent pattern where the high food value anatomical parts, described by Binford (1978b:Table 2.7) as 'gourmet' assemblages, are invariably associated with the dominant animal in the fauna. By contrast, the background fauna in such collections form 'bulk' assemblages made up of low value body parts.

Large mammal hunting does not, as once thought, distinguish between hominins (Adler et al. 2006). But at the same time attention has been drawn (Stiner et al. 2000) to increases in diet breadth during technology's common ground, reminiscent of Flannery's (1969) broad spectrum revolution that was applied to the earliest agriculture. Here the emphasis is on the strategies prey possess to avoid predators. Mary Stiner and her colleagues (2000) argue that fleet-footed prey such as hares, rabbits and birds, were increasingly used from 30,000 years ago while even slow-moving small prey, such as tortoises, show heavier predation as evidenced by their declining size. This trend is put down to larger hominin populations and an increase in child survivorship (Stiner et al. 2000:58). They conclude, 'we do not know who in Palaeolithic societies did the inventing, but innovations in trap, snare and net technology for hunting small prey could have been the province of women, children, and the elderly (Stiner et al. 2000:58)', since these would be the individuals who benefited most from these small food packages. These innovations are of course containers and, if this suggestion is correct, we see with these material metaphors how the childscape might have fitted into the landscape of habit. The project of growing the body creates an understanding of other worlds before they are directly experienced. As a result identity was changing by being extended through social networks.

TABLE 8.4. *Changing raw materials and some of the major artefact categories in the sequence at Klasies River Mouth, South Africa (Singer and Wymer 1982:Table 7.1)*

	Total stone tools	% Nonlocal rocks	% of total stone inventory		
			Cores	Flake-blades	Crescents
MSA IV	2,101	0.7	2.7	20.5	0
MSA III	6,577	3.7	1.4	18.7	0.1
Howieson's Poort	119,336	25	1.0	10.6	1.2
MSA II	95,418	1.2	2.0	26.6	0.01
MSA I	31,812	0.4	1.3	31.7	0

The majority of all artefacts in all levels consist of unmodified flakes (MSA = Middle Stone Age which lasts from 130,000 (MSA I) to 50,000 (MSA IV) years ago (Mitchell 2002:80ff.)).

Reproducing the body

But what evidence exists for the metaphorical reproduction of the body and its distribution over longer chains of connection?

Case study: Klasies River Mouth

An example comes from the long sequence at Klasies River Mouth on the southern coast of South Africa with its impressive numbers of stone tools (Singer and Wymer 1982:Table 8.4).

Were these numbers produced solely with rational solutions to survival in mind? Their excavator John Wymer (Singer and Wymer 1982:64) regarded the overwhelming evidence for overproduction as intentional, functional behaviour. The abundant quartzite at the cave encouraged overproduction so that blanks of preferred shape and size could be readily selected from a pile and hafted in composite artefacts such as fish spears.

Alternatively, did they fragment stone in order to consume, accumulate in order to enchain and so reproduce the body in extended form? Here the relational argument returns to the notion of parent-offspring outlined in Chapter 7.

Table 8.4 shows that local rocks, picked-up in front of the cave, dominate in all phases of the Middle Stone Age (MSA) except one, the Howieson's Poort where 25 per cent are silcretes from the Cape Folded Mountains

TABLE 8.5. *Fragmentation and breakage among the flake-blades at Klasies River Mouth (Singer and Wymer 1982:Table 7.1)*

	Number of stone artefacts per core	Total flake blades	% Unbroken	Pointed	Broken
MSA IV	37	431	39.4	21.1	39.4
MSA III	72	1,233	46.8	2.3	50.9
Howieson's Poort	99	12,600	39.6	0.4	60.1
MSA II	48	25,374	65.3	9.5	25.3
MSA I	77	10,072	72.3	5.3	22.4

around 15 km away inland (Deacon 1989:560; McBrearty and Brooks 2000:516). The Howieson's Poort interest in non-local rocks coincides with the smallest proportion of flake-blades (Table 8.4) and the largest number of large crescents (N = 1,374) many of which have deliberately blunted backs, indicating to the archaeologists they were hafted as composite tools (Singer and Wymer 1982:112). In Shelter 1A, 35 per cent of the crescents were made from non-local rocks. These raw materials point to an expanded form of enchainment away from Klasies River Mouth during the Howieson's Poort 80–60,000 years ago (Mitchell 2002:Table 4.2). But this scale does not persist into Middle Stone Age III and IV as shown by the return to local rocks.

But the distinctive crescents in the Howieson's Poort levels come at the expense of flake-blades (Table 8.4), and when we examine further the evidence for breakage of these same flake-blades (Table 8.5) another interesting contrast emerges.

Sixty per cent of the Howieson's Poort flake-blades are broken segments. In the Middle Stone Age levels the proportions vary. The two earliest phases that Wymer recognised, MSA I and II, are dominated by unbroken flake-blades. Phases III and IV, after the Howieson's Poort with its non-local rocks, shows much higher proportions of broken and pointed pieces.

The large sample of Howieson's Poort flake-blades from Shelter 1A (N = 11,370) shows that breakage is much higher among the local quartzites at almost 70 per cent (Table 8.6), and Wymer (Singer and Wymer 1982:64) addresses the issue of whether these flake-blades were broken accidentally or intentionally. The local quartzite is brittle so many pieces broke, apparently accidentally, during knapping. Trampling and breakage in the

TABLE 8.6. *Raw material and breakage in flake-blades at Shelter 1A Klasies River Mouth, South Africa (Singer and Wymer 1982:Tables 6.3 and 6.4)*

	Number	%
Non local-rocks		
Unbroken flake-blades	1,246	54.3
Broken flake-blades	1,049	45.7
Local rocks		
Unbroken flake-blades	3,195	35.2
Broken flake-blades	5,880	64.8

ground was probably slight. However, Wymer concludes that many of the middle sections of these thick flake blades were probably intentionally broken and would have served, in his opinion, as useful knives or scrapers if mounted in wooden handles.

Quartzite is rarely knapped today as flint is considered more tractable. But an expert stone worker, Farina Sternke, has achieved a high level of proficiency in order to study the use of quartzite in the German Middle Palaeolithic. She has shown (pers. comm.) that if flake-blade segments are required then knapping such blades in quartzite will automatically produce them. The choice of raw material may therefore be intentional. The difference between fine-grained silcretes and flints and coarse rocks such as quartzite is that the latter lose their edge more quickly when used.

Applying Sternke's observations to the Klasies River Mouth assemblage leads to a different interpretation to Wymer's suggestion of functionally appropriate blanks. The interest of the stone knappers was instead in the balance of fragmented and complete pieces. Their knapping was a form of consumption that established an identity for Klasies River Mouth as a place, through the accumulation of very large stone sets. This identity varied between the MSA and Howieson's Poort occupations through varying degrees of enchainment to wider social landscapes. It also varied in the flake/blade:core ratio (offspring:parent, Chapter 7) where fragmentation reproduced the body in a distributed form. At Klasies River Mouth and Rose Cottage Cave (Wadley 2001), the proportion of retouched tools (scrapers, borers, notches, etc.) is never more than 1.6 per cent of the total stone assemblage and as low as 0.5 per cent in the Howieson's Poort (Singer and Wymer 1982:Table 7.1). However, the ratio of flakes to cores ranges from almost 100 for the Howieson's Poort to between 37 and 77 for the Middle Stone Age. Social extension resulted in changing patterns of fragmentation and consumption, and blades were appropriate to this social technology.

I conclude that hominins at Klasies River Mouth, Rose Cottage Cave and Blombos engaged in fragmentation to produce products for accumulation rather than simply elements for an additive or composite technology. If the latter was the case then there would be more evidence for utilised segments and much lower core ratios for these flake and flake-blade sets. Instead they were more interested in reproducing the body through material metaphors than making fancy fish spears. They were bricoleurs, not engineers when it came to putting things together.

Social extension and the childscape

Distances of 15 km are, however, small. In technology's long introduction there are examples from Africa of a very few tools being found several hundred kilometres away from their geological source (McBrearty and Brooks 2000). What we see during the common ground is a spatial increase in social extension (Gamble 1999:Chapter 7). In Europe, all stages of the chaîne opératoire are now found more than 20 km away from the source of the stone material whereas previously it was only the final stage, the so-called finished tool (Gamble 1999:Table 7.3). In addition, the distances over which lithics were regularly transferred increased markedly between the Middle to Upper Palaeolithic (Gamble 1999:Figure 6.13) when blades gained the upper hand over flakes in lithic assemblages These greater distances were further augmented by the traffic in marine and fossil shells that on occasion came from up to 800 km away (Floss 1994; Soffer 1985; Taborin 1993). The childscape now contained sets and nets from worlds that might never be visited but which were nonetheless understood. The bricolage of material that framed these environments of growth had made the essential metaphorical relation for agriculture by on the one hand accumulating at the locale and on the other through chains of connection harvesting relationships from a social landscape as imaginary as it was material. The project of growing the body was soon to be realised.

The short answer, 20,000 to 5,000 years ago: an appreciation

What happened in this technological movement to divide the world economically and socially into hunters and farmers? At one level nothing.

The giving environment still structured the childscape in different regions of the Old World such as the Near East and Europe. Children remained a material project, their identities grown through the association of hybrid sets and nets of objects and people. But the childscape now had latent potential for growing bodies and identities in more varied ways because of the authority that containers had brought, during technology's common ground, to material representations of the world. Without containers, composed of additive and composite techniques, there would be no growing the body to make the social world meaningful, intelligible and potentially different.

At first the story is more of the same but more so. Fragmentation among stone tools increased to near manic proportions as a process of miniaturisation, known as microlithisation, swept large parts of the Old World (Elston and Kuhn 2002). Tools measured in millimetres took on standard, sometimes geometric forms with triangles, trapezes and rectangles enjoying regional popularity. Composite, multi-component artefacts such as arrows, harpoons and knives were now commonplace.

But there is much that continues to form a rational puzzle. Overproduction was still common at many locales, and fragmentation of both animals and stone resulted in impressive accumulations that fuel claims by some (see Hodder 2001) for a symbolic revolution in the Near East that ushered in the modern mind, domestication and society as we know it. The preface to something new was dramatically declared by fragmenting vast quantities of stone and animal bone, none of them domestic, to create places without domestic architecture. At Göbekli Tepe in southeast Turkey (Watkins 2004a), a hill of fragments covered a circle of large standing stones with bas-relief animal carvings. At other less spectacular locales in the Levant, some houses were regularly filled-up while others were swept clean.

What remains familiar is the tradition of bricolage, bringing sets together to create understandings of place and landscape. This is evident in the lack of modularisation among the earliest houses of the sedentary revolution. What was novel is that these social technologies became more predictable in terms of which sets were repeatedly associated. It took some time for standard house forms, as regular in their own way as geometric microliths, to be assembled into compounds and villages. What we then see is the growth of these structures *and* their related sets. The latter included furniture, for example hearths, platforms and storage bins as well as ground stone tools, such as mortars, pestles and bowls built into the house fabric, as were skulls and skeletons.

Growing the body now drew on the authority of containers as a proxy for the symbolic force of bodily experience. Baskets, clothes and stone bowls grew into houses, villages, fields, flocks and pots. And just as the sets that formed composite instruments had become more standardised through microlithisation so too did the containers that now acted as material proxies for the body, and the construction of identity for individual and group.

In Europe there was of course no indigenous move to agriculture and domestic animals, although there could have been as the independent experience of Asia, the Americas and Africa shows (Bar-Yosef 1998). But there was still, as in the Near East, the materiality of bodily experience using the joint authority of instruments and containers. The tradition of bricolage continued, most notably with the painted cave and rock art that witnessed journeys from the light to the dark, hidden interior of the landscape. On the surface huts are more convincing: some have hearths within them, but they remain uncommon, idiosyncratic structures. Well-cared-for hearths are usually outside and defined the locale, as at Rekem, in Belgium (de Bie and Caspar 2000). Burials are also rare and not until much later at Lepenski Vir in Serbia (Chapman 2000:136; Radovanovic 1996) was there a regular association between huts and bodies. Elsewhere skeletons were usually fragmented (Chapter 6) and the body parts probably widely distributed. Large sets of engraved slabs and carved bone and antler artefacts were accumulated at chosen locations (Davidson 1989), for example La Madeleine in southwest France (Capitan and Peyrony 1928) where a child burial with a rich set of shells and deer canines was also found (Vanhaeren and d'Errico 2001). The social landscape commands our attention as the volume of exotic materials increased to feed an appetite for extension apparent in both the glacial refugia such as the Dordogne (Straus 2000) as well as through the re-settlement of formerly glaciated landscapes (Gamble et al. 2005).

Variety was the hallmark of technology's short answer. Excavation continues to uncover surprises and new material associations at locales adjacent in time and space. Well-defined chronological patterns are rare because the material metaphors are often mixed, as with burial practices during the Natufian and earliest Neolithic of the Levant (Belfer-Cohen 1995; Byrd and Monahan 1995; Kuijt 1996).

But rather than using this variety to concentrate, as is normally the case, on the economic and social divergence between Europe and the Near East I would stress the different childscapes that emerged around the hearth and home.

In the Near East the childscape is difficult to identify. What dominates is the landscape of habit, an adult world where bodies, crops, animals and settlements are grown, and which now encapsulated the childscape. The child grew as the crops ripened, the herds reproduced and the households in the village expanded and contracted. The networks of material culture within which they were implicated affirmed the process. The childscape was no longer a project to be fitted-in to the landscape of habit. It was instead constructed-inside, just like the hearths within houses, so that the array of material metaphors was controlled and selected, just as the animals and crops were respected for their growth as much as their gifts.

Buildings, as Peter Wilson (1988) has pointed out, are important for their imposition of boundaries to interaction. By the end of technology's short answer the world of containers formed a material representation of a theory of mind that we feel at home with: by which I mean the understanding that another person's inner state is similar to your own and that we know the ancestors are watching and the gods understand everything. Access to hidden intentions and representations of the self could be understood by people who may never physically have entered another house other than their own. The internal map of hearth, storage bin and sleeping platform was reassuringly similar although not directly experienced. However, this was not, as some argue, the origin of the modern mind, only a material representation of a mind that had, since at least technology's common ground, been accessible through the same material proxies by bricoleurs who learned and experimented with metaphorical connections in the social space of the childscape.

Evidence from the short answer

Containers dominate and the multifarious sets they form have been extensively studied by archaeologists. The material arrays in the short answer are exponentially greater than for the previous two technological movements. Therefore I will concentrate exclusively on hearth and home, concluding with a case study not of a locale but rather the process of how we recognise a changed primary metaphor that structured social life through material proxies. Table 8.7 charts the chronology that includes two important pre's; the pre-agriculture of the Natufian that is within touching distance of crops and domestic animals, and the Early Neolithic that is pre-pottery or PPN.

TABLE 8.7.   *The chronology of the transition to agriculture in the Levant (after Wright and Garrard 2003:Table 1). PPN = Pre-Pottery Neolithic. Although pottery forms an important chronological marker in the Early Neolithic, containers in the form of baskets were present throughout*

	Years ago	
Late Epi-Palaeolithic		
Natufian	14,700−12,000	Villages
Early Neolithic (aceramic)		
PPNA	12,000−10,950	Cereals
PPNB	10,950−8,900	Flocks
PPNC	8,900−8,350	
Late Neolithic (ceramic)		
Pottery Neolithic	8,350−7,400	

Huts, houses and hearths

The house became a major project for the childscape, the environment of growth. At the start of the short answer there are circular mammoth bone structures in the Ukraine and southern Russia at Mezhirich, Iudinovo and Kostenki site 11 (Abramova 1993; Praslov and Rogachev 1982; Soffer 1985). Sets abound with stacked mandibles, tusks and ribs. At Gönnersdorf, Germany, a winter house was built with wooden poles making the frame across which skins were stretched (Bosinski 1979). The floor of the Gönnersdorf hut was paved with slate slabs many of which carry the superimposed traces of animals and human figures finely etched with stone tools (Bosinski and Fischer 1974). Changing the surface of containers such as houses, clothes and rock shelters was now well established.

All of these houses are more convincing than the palimpsests of sets from technology's common ground (Figure 8.9). They even form small clusters as at Mezin (Klein 1973) and Mezhirich (Soffer 1985) that has led to their description as villages. This is also the case at the much later, c. 8,000 years ago, locale of Lepenski Vir (Chapman 2000:194−203; Radovanovic 1996). Here the 137 trapezoidal houses have complex sets of hearths, boulders and sculpture, eighty-five burials, similar in concept if not in detail to the Natufian and earliest Neolithic of the Levant.

A strong feeling of bricolage still pervades these Near Eastern locales as shown by Nigel Goring-Morris' (1988) survey of the varied settlement evidence in the Negev and Sinai deserts over the initial 10,000 years of technology's short answer. This is also the impression from Ohalo II,

FIGURE 8.9. Making connections at Iudinovo (inset top left) and Kostenki site 11 level Ia (inset right). Collections and sets of mammoth bones, in particular stacks of mandibles at Kostenki (inset bottom left), defined circular containers. While it is tempting to interpret them as collapsed huts they may have had more significance as bricolage used to construct places through material metaphors.

by the Sea of Galilee, Israel (Nadel 2002; 2003) dated to 21,000 years ago (Nadel et al. 1995). At this well-preserved, waterlogged locale six brush huts, six hearth complexes, a pit, a human grave, middens and a stone installation have been excavated (Nadel 1994). The floors of the huts varied in size and shape; the largest being 13 m^2 and the smallest 5 m^2. The floors were dug to form a shallow bowl and were unpaved but covered in large quantities of flint artefacts, animal bones and plant remains in what the excavator considers to be their original position, the result of continuous accumulation (Nadel 2003:39). No cleaning took place. Small sets of implements were found in the huts and a number of small stones had been deliberately buried upright beneath the floor, while larger erect stones where found in situ on the floors. Hearths were between the huts in public areas.

Several of these observations hold for the Natufian, regarded as the key archaeological culture in the appearance of sedentism and the transition to

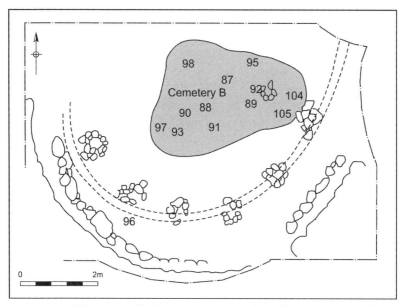

FIGURE 8.10. The evidence for Natufian architecture from Shelter 131 at Ain Mallaha. The semicircular ring of stone-packed postholes define the structure that contains a small cemetery (after Valla 1988:Figure 1).

agriculture (Bar-Yosef 1998; Bar-Yosef and Valla 1991; Belfer-Cohen 1991; Byrd 1989; Goring-Morris and Belfer-Cohen 1997) and dated to between 12,750 and 10,050 years ago. The evidence forms sets of structures, circular or oval, dug into the slope and defined by perimeter stones and post-holes (Cauvin 1978). At Wadi Hammeh 27 in Jordan three deeply incised limestone slabs formed part of a wall (Edwards 1991:133) while caches of ground stone mortars and pestles, chert picks and a heterogeneous set consisting of a bone sickle, gazelle foot bones and a stone tool-kit have also been found (Edwards 1991:Figure 5).

Houses for the living and the dead

The most cited Natufian settlement is that of Ain Mallaha (Eynan), Israel (Perrot 1966; Perrot and Ladiray 1988a; Valla 1991) and in particular shelter 131 (Figure 8.10) where stone-packed post-holes have been reconstructed as a semi-circular, timber framed structure partially dug into the slope (Valla 1988:Figure 1). Within the 20 m^2 plus this structure covered were found hearths as well as thirteen burials, twelve of them grouped together in cemetery B (Byrd and Monahan 1995; Perrot and Ladiray 1988). As with the forty-eight burials from Hayonim Cave (Belfer-Cohen 1988) there is a great mixture of ages and internment patterns leading Byrd and Monahan (1995:265) to conclude that no standardised regional burial tradition existed. But Watkins (2004b) makes the point that locales such as Ain Mallaha were houses for both the living and the dead irrespective of the varied funerary rituals that fragmented some bodies, or placed sets of objects, including art, with others. One adult female was even buried with a puppy (Valla 1975). At Hayonim cave perforated fox teeth and variable amounts of dentalium shells, probably from decorated caps and garments, were found in the graves. Burial 25 had a bracelet of twenty-five beads made from the leg bones of partridges (Belfer-Cohen 1988; Pichon 1983). Other containers in the form of groundstone pestles and a goblet shaped mortar broken into five pieces were found not in the graves, but in the earth used to fill them (Belfer-Cohen 1988:305). This association of bodies and containers carries on into the Early Neolithic where the Natufian tradition of bringing skulls into the houses continues, although grave goods are rare (Byrd and Monahan 1995). Plastering the faces of these Neolithic skulls is a distinctive feature (Kuijt 1996:319–21; Watkins 2004a:102).

Ian Kuijt (1996:331–2) interprets this Early Neolithic evidence as the continuing influence of Natufian, hunter-gatherer, egalitarianism. It was, he believes, a deliberate choice by communities to prevent the fragmenta-tion of their existing corporate life that social complexity, now based on food surplus, might jeopardise. I would argue differently. Rather than egalitarianism acting as a social principle by which people made their decisions, I would return to the shifting authority which accumulation and enchainment and their supportive social actions make during social reproduction. The construction of authority is enacted and embodied, rather than consciously stated, as a belief in egalitarianism implies. The outcome is constrained by materiality, of which the childscape is an exam-ple, because of the way such environments of development are negotiated by associating people and objects. I am not saying that people never think about change because their 'thinking' is done for them by objects and artefacts but rather that we are autopoietic, self-creating and dealing with the world as presented. Moreover, we are not socially free-agents always ready to take the plunge and create fresh identities. Cultural anarchy is never an option, even among bricoleurs.

For example, burial within the house was not a universal practice but a local tradition. At Netiv Hagdud, an Early Neolithic locale without pottery in the lower Jordan Valley, there is abundant evidence for 'furniture' within the oval houses including hearths, grinding slabs, stone storage bins and boulders with cup-holes (Bar-Yosef and Gopher 1997:Figures 3.6, 3.9, 3.15, 3.21). However, here the association of bodies and houses was often close rather than integral. At Netiv Hagdud (Bar-Yosef and Gopher 1997:201–8) adults were buried either in yards or in abandoned houses rather than in the floors of lived-in dwellings as was the case at Jericho (Cauvin 1978; Kuijt 1996). Furthermore, throughout the Early Neolithic burials are only rarely associated with grave goods. This is in marked contrast to the sometimes richly adorned early Natufian burials. This has led Anna Belfer-Cohen (1995:15) to question the importance of symbolism as permanent settlements appeared and then grew in size and complexity. If rich graves indicate social differentiation during the Natufian then what, she asks, was happening when such evidence disappears? It is a good question and points to the idiosyncratic use of material metaphors by people who were interested in constructing identity locally rather than following a universal agenda of cultural evolution. Agriculture was the product of bricoleurs placing unfamiliar categories into new conceptual arrangements.

Domestic resources

This pattern is also illustrated by the transition to domestic crops and animals (Bar-Yosef and Meadow 1995; Garrard 1999). At Abu Hureyra, a tell locale on the Euphrates river in Syria (Moore et al. 2000), the second village in the sequence lasted for over two and a half millennia between 10,600 and 7,800 years ago. During this time the transition occurred from hunting gazelle during their summer migration to year-round herding of goats and sheep (Moore et al. 2000:Figure 14.2). At the same time wild-plant gathering was attenuated as cereal and pulse cultivation came to dominate. As archaeo-botanist Gordon Hillman (Moore et al. 2000:422) has shown, what began as foraging from a large number of small micro-habitats in the vicinity of the locale came, by the end of the 2,500 year life of Village 2, to represent a significant narrowing of dietary diversity. Rather than harvesting the gifts of the environment, the settlement itself, like the rye, wheat, barley and legumes, had to be grown as a container in its own right. Such growth directly impacted on the body. The seeds, threshed from the ears of wheat that held them, were ground for several hours each day by the women until their bodies changed through the pain of their labour (Moore et al. 2000:503). And as their bodies changed under the arduous nature of processing wild and then domestic cereals, so the material proxies of these identities also changed (Wright 1994). Additional labour followed the

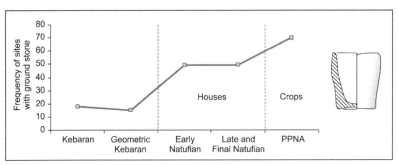

FIGURE 8.11. The changing frequencies of ground stone tool containers in Natufian and Early Neolithic locales in the Levant (after Wright 1994:Figure 8). The inset is a stone bowl/mortar.

introduction of querns and grinding slabs that replaced existing mortars and bedrock mortars (Figure 8.11). Bodies were grown and identity established, through the authority of the container.

Containers altered the body in many ways. At Abu Hureyra, bio-anthropologist Theya Molleson found distinctive grooves on some of the skeletons' front teeth that can be interpreted as the result of holding canes while weaving baskets (Moore et al. 2000:503). Traces of mats and baskets, but no pottery, were found during excavation.

Responding to the environment

The impact of a widespread cooling event, the Younger Dryas 12,650–11,500 years ago (Björck et al. 1998), is presented persuasively by Ofer Bar-Yosef (Bar-Yosef 1998; 2001; Bar-Yosef and Meadow 1995) as the environmental trigger on this path to ecological simplification and fundamental economic change. Lewis Binford (2001) has identified a density threshold among hunters and gatherers that is critical to subsistence change and that might arise from an event such as the Younger Dryas (Moore and Hillman 1992). Binford refers to this as packing: defined as the patterned reduction in subsistence range arising from a regional increase in population. In particular, at packing densities greater than 9.1 per 100 km^2 Binford has established there can no longer be a primary dependence on land animals and that mobility, the key tactic available to hunters and gatherers to solve resource fluctuations, is not an option. Faced with this situation their first move will be to use aquatic resources, followed later by harvesting plants. The resources at locales such as Ohalo II

(Nadel 2002) and Abu Hureyra (Moore et al. 2000) suggest that this was indeed the route followed. Sedentism results from packing – the number of social units – and not from pressure of population numbers alone (Binford 2001:438).

However, what was significant was the interpretation by the people living at Abu Hureyra of this changing environment. To do this they brought into association material forms that encompassed both the biological and material worlds so that growing new bodies and identities commenced. What they brought to this task were their own bodies and the material proxies of containers and instruments that had always been the means to construct identity in the face of change. As philosopher Andy Clark (1997) has put it, what matters is identifying the 'proper context' within which such an embodied, social intelligence exists and how it relates to change. That context is not an external environment against which hominins struggle either as hunters or farmers to make a living and maximise returns. Instead it is integral to material projects such as the childscape and the environment of growth.

Case study: growing the body with material metaphors

Since sedentism is regarded as a turning point in human cognitive, symbolic and social life it forms the basis of my last case study. Here I draw on the last Palaeolithic and earliest Neolithic in the Levant (Table 8.7) between 12,000 and 6,000 years ago (Bar-Yosef and Belfer-Cohen 1989; Byrd 1994; Byrd and Monahan 1995; Flannery 2002; Gamble 2004; Goring-Morris 1987; Hayden 2000; Henry 1985; Kaufman 1992; Kuijt 2000; Rocek and Bar-Yosef 1998; Valla 1991).

Kuijt (2000) sets out the sequence to sedentism (Table 8.8) and points to a significant rise in settlement size from the Natufian through the Early Neolithic. The estimated population on these settlements increases by some 5,000 per cent over a period of 3,000 years. For example, Village 2 at Abu Hureyra grew from an estimated 2,500 people to a possible 6,000 in two and a half millennia (Moore et al. 2000:494). At its height Village 2 had doubled in size, covering 16 ha with densely packed mud-brick rectangular houses. Such population growth is not, however, matched by a proportional increase in burials, as Table 8.8 reveals, with the Late Neolithic being particularly poorly represented. Moreover, the number of sites with skeletons declines from twelve in the Natufian to six in the PPNA, rising to nineteen in PPNB (Nadel 1994:Table 1).

TABLE 8.8. *Trends in sedentism in the Mediterranean zone of the Levant during the Late Epi-Palaeolithic, Pre-Pottery Neolithic (PPN) and Ceramic Neolithic (compiled from Kuijt 2000:Tables 1 and 2 and Figures 4 and 6, Nadel 1994)*

	Site area ha	% increase from Epi-Palaeolithic	Population estimate	Compartments per 100 m²	Number of burials
Pottery Neolithic	~0.2	0	400?	No data	>10
LPPNB	7–14	5,000	3,293	14.5	}>350
MPPNB	0.5–4.5	1,500	764	6.4	
PPNA	0.2–2.5	500	332	2.4	>320
Late Natufian	0.2	–	59	1.6	>420

But while we do not find evidence for more burials to match much larger population sizes what we do find are more containers. It is with the Early Neolithic that we can believe in the archaeological evidence for houses, as Verpoorte (2001:131) points out with some relief after the problems we saw during the common ground. Modular architecture has finally arrived with the Early Neolithic. Not only do we feel, like Verpoorte, at home with the evidence but we can also see in this modularisation the changed primary metaphor of growing the body.

> Abu Hureyra represented an extreme form of nucleated settlement. Its multi-roomed houses, with floors often made of coloured gypsum plaster, were set close together with only narrow passages and courts between them. The construction of large numbers of such dwellings constituted an architectural revolution. The houses were of the same kind from one end of the settlement to the other, and seem to have filled up much of the inhabited area of the site . . . We found no large open spaces between the houses, no substantial storage buildings, and no workshops in the areas we excavated.
>
> (Moore et al. 2000:494)

In his analysis of the history of the Early Neolithic (PPNB) village at Beidha in southern Jordan, Brian Byrd (1994:658) has drawn attention to the modular sizes of the mud-brick houses (Table 8.9) and to the changes in social relationships which these architectural forms imposed.

As the village grew (Figure 8.12) so restrictions occurred on access and visibility into buildings, thereby limiting the opportunities for sharing and

TABLE 8.9. *The mean size in m² of the interior sizes of three architectural categories at the Early Neolithic locale of Beidha (Byrd 1994:Table 3). Phase A is the oldest*

Phase	Small building	Medium building	Large building
C	3.9	10.6	32.6
B	6.9		34.9
A	4.1	12.8	71.4
Number	17	22	6

promoting household autonomy. Architectural decisions now led to the partitioning of social space by using these modules to create sets.

This trend is well shown in Kuijt's (2000) study of compartmentalisation of village space during the same process of sedentarisation (Table 8.8, Figure 8.13). The division of architectural space rises from 1.6 compartments per 100 m² in the Natufian to 14.5 by the end of the Early Neolithic. In the PPNB there was what many regard as an excessive division of house space, best known from Basta, also in southern Jordan. Here the small claustrophobic compartments, often no more than 1.5 m², are interpreted as storage rooms. Kuijt (ibid.:89) sees them as a response to the stress of social crowding as the community grew in size so that privacy and ownership of personal goods now acquired a premium.

Sedentism is therefore about the use of containers in the social practices of enchainment and accumulation that grew bodies. Both practices can be seen in Byrd and Kuijt's analyses of these early villages. The accumulation of houses in the three phases at Early Neolithic Beidha (Table 8.9) (Byrd 1994:Figures 3, 5 and 7) is also matched by the increasing enchainment of the units. The latter can be seen in their physical linkage as the settlement became more compact (ibid.:658) as well as the increase in the internal divisions of the houses as identified through topological analysis (ibid.:Figure 4).

These related practices can in turn be associated with the social actions of fragmentation and consumption. The fragmentation of space, so clearly seen at Basta, was also prevalent in phase C at Beidha. But space was also being consumed, and it should perhaps come as no surprise that the context provided by these social actions and practices led, as Byrd (1994:658) argues, for new forms of production, storage and the circulation of goods and resources.

FIGURE 8.12. Growth through the accumulation of sets. The Early Neolithic locale of Beidha grew through the addition of modules and the partitioning or fragmentation of containers (after Byrd 1994).

Here is an example of the potential of both fragmentation and consumption to create material outcomes for a hybrid network at locales in the wider social landscape (Jones and Richards 2003:45). The body is grown by creating new containers in the form of mud-brick houses and

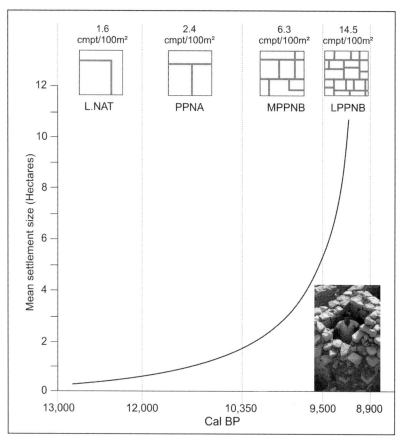

FIGURE 8.13. The fragmentation of social space in the Early Neolithic of the Near East (after Kuijt 2000). As settlement size increased so did the compartmentalisation (cmpt) of living space. These resulted in the tiny containers at the locale of Basta (inset).

multiplying them in the easiest possible way by making them smaller through fragmentation. The architecture is not so much an exercise in modularisation as one of micro-lisation comparable to the overproduction of lithic components for the reproduction of the body that I discussed earlier.

Linking properties

The Early Neolithic houses and villages were also enchained across social landscapes through items such as marine shells (Bar-Yosef Mayer 1991; 1997; 2000), and stone beads (Wright and Garrard 2003). The latter have been studied by Andrew Garrard and Katherine Wright at the sixteen

FIGURE 8.14. Jilat site 26 in the Azraq basin. These Early Neolithic locales produced abundant stone beads (inset, courtesy of A. Garrard) that enchained people across the Near East.

excavated locales in the Jilat-Azraq basin, Jordan (Figure 8.14). Evidence for bead-making abounds and was found inside buildings (Wright and Garrard 2003:270). But unlike Abu Hurerya or Ain Mallaha the Jilat-Azraq locales were short-lived settlements on the edge of the desert. What is striking is the amount of unfinished materials, drawing comparisons with the much earlier overproduction of microliths. The majority of unfinished elements are a green Dabba marble while the finished elements come from a much wider range of colours, all but a few found within 20 km of the Neolithic locales. Wright and Garrard conclude that 'the beadmakers were making a much narrower range of bead materials than they were actually using (consuming) at these sites' (Wright and Garrard 2003:279). But were they producing stockpiles for export as the authors suggest and if so why leave them behind at these seasonal camps? Beads are widespread across the Levant although the numbers of exotics are always small. They are unremarkable but they undoubtedly enchained. Wright and Garrard see the significance of the beads in terms of new identities based on larger trade networks that came from domesticating sheep and goat (Wright and Garrard 2003:282). I prefer to see them as elements in growing a body. Their suspension indicates that they are a container changing the body's boundaries by association; harvested in the desert, selected by colour, ground like grain to produce their shape and planted as sets in other locales within the social landscape of the Levant to grow relationships.

The well-swept home

The move from circular (Natufian) to rectangular (Early Neolithic) structures has long been interpreted as a reflection of fundamental changes in household organisation during the process of domestication and surplus food production (Flannery 1972b; 2002). But I have shown that it is no longer possible to regard material culture as a simple reflection of systemic developments. Such a position is well demonstrated by the Late Epi-Palaeolithic, Harifian locale of Abu Salem (Marks and Scott 1976) in the Negev desert. The locale has a surface concentration of artefacts covering 2500 m² and an excavation of 10 per cent of this area found a series of oval and circular architectural features ranging in size from 1 m to 4 m in diameter. But what is more interesting than this evidence of an early village is the treatment of these containers as places to accumulate material culture. 'House-cleaning' was not one of their routines (Goring-Morris 1988:240). The fragmentation of chipped stone inside these structures and their intervening spaces produced impressive lithic densities, even when deflation and other taphonomic processes are considered. Structure 1, for example, produced 16,901 lithics per m³ and a nearby trash pit some 9,864 pieces per m³. Such accumulation overshadows any figures from locales in Palaeolithic Europe (Gamble 1986:Appendix 1) but is not uncommon in the Levant (Garrard 1991; Goring-Morris 1987; Muheisin 1985). As Chapman (2000) pointed out the fragmentation of stone can be to produce instruments for the purpose of enchaining people between locales. However, at Abu Salem fragmentation produced materials for accumulation within containers at that locale.

What occurs elsewhere during the Early Neolithic is a cessation of such accumulation in architectural containers. For example, Watkins' (1992; 2004a; 2004b) excavation at Qermez Dere, a PPNA locale in northern Iraq, found no artefacts on the various floors within the architectural structures or burials beneath them. At Qermez Dere burial took place near the house with the skulls, once removed, then coming back to the house. The house was also remodelled on several occasions, regularly re-plastered, and through such accumulation a place, re-used over almost three centuries, was defined.

But are the 'house-proud' owners of Qermez Dere that much different from the earlier Harifian 'slobs' at Abu Salem? Was increasing sedentism in the Early Neolithic leading to more varied engagements with the material world and a symbolic explosion? Both were using containers in their material and social networks. Both accumulated traditions at specific locales in the landscape. Both were involved in fragmentation and consumption although using very different materials. What differentiates them is the authority constructed from accumulation and enchainment and the social actions upon which they were based.

Houses become pots

These differences are best expressed as the intersection of material and corporal culture (Figure 4.1) and the question of why you fragment and how you consume the results. During technology's short answer the *why* part of the question shifts further towards the practice of accumulation and the *how* continues the move from instruments to containers. This transfer of authority was neither a home-grown revolution nor an outside replacement but instead a different expression through materiality that social life was now to be container rather than instrument focused, and that growing the body was the primary metaphor for the elaboration of those material proxies.

The implications were considerable. For instance, the dramatic downsizing in settlement area, numbers and known burials which occurred in the Levant with the appearance of pottery (Table 8.8) can now be understood in terms of this move to a material culture that favoured containers. I would suggest that we have an analogous history of change to Rainbird's (1999) analysis of the pots and tombs of Pohnpei described in Chapter 7. The excessive compartmentalisation of the later PPN settlements such as Basta was replaced by another form of container, pottery, to embody people's social networks that included the living and the ancestors. This form of container had in turn the almost infinite potential for further divisibility and reproduction, just by making more pots. Little wonder that the settlement patterns and sizes changed dramatically (Kuijt 2000:Figure 4). The materiality of social reproduction had changed but the social practices remained similar.

Summary

I have suggested in this chapter that agriculture did not change the world, or rather not in the ways that we usually credit its impact. In particular it did not give rise to society-as-we-know-it (Runciman 2005) or the modern mind

(Watkins 2004a) simply because there are too many antecedents in the use of material culture to provide meaning to place and landscape and to create social relationships. But by the same token, neither did modern minds appear 30,000 years ago with evidence for external storage systems such as art (Wadley 2001:210). The institutions and the architecture that flow from agriculture had obviously never been seen before but I hope I have demonstrated that these novelties do not lie at the heart of human identity and the construction of the self.

What I have shown is that rational puzzles such as the hill of fragments at Göbekli Tepe, or the piles of mammoth bone at La Cotte de St Brelade are not clues to points of origin, the start of revolutions and the path to modern minds. I have suggested instead that much of the archaeological evidence points to people creating and reproducing identities by bringing sets and nets of materials into association through the habitual practices of accumulation and enchainment and the actions of fragmentation and consumption. This constrained experimentation is best described by Lévi-Strauss' term of bricolage and coming from the master of metaphorical readings is well suited to the task of understanding how the experience of the world is mediated through material objects. To further that analysis, I introduced here the project of the child and the concept of the childscape, the environment of growth. It is apparent even from the few data I have been able to present that the childscape, so crucial for the development of a social brain and a distributed personhood, varied enormously in terms of the sensory arrays that it contained. The material proxies for the body, those containers and instruments, and through which experience is understood and enacted, had a fundamental role in the self-creation of identity and an understanding of others' intentions and desires. These emotions were shaped, just as the bodies of the women at Abu Hureyra were bent into new forms, by the objects themselves. Through the three long technological movements described in outline here, I have shown how the authority of containers came to eclipse that of instruments, and with that came the possibility of agriculture. I agree with Donald (1998) that a mimetic style of thought that models the body, and the objects that are like the body, is our key skill rather than language, important as that was for elaboration and undoubtedly social extension. Mimesis has been with hominins ever since they had a social technology 2.6 million years ago and is probably much older still. Language as predicted convincingly by the social brain model is at least half a million years old.

Where I do think my approach points to change is in the primary metaphors that generated the sets and nets and selected containers and instruments as proxies for the body, that source of symbolic force. Growing the body can be demonstrated by the sheer consumption of the material world and where eventually rules had to be followed and as a result we became engineers as well as bricoleurs. An alternative metaphor, the giving environment, while never extinguished, does lead to different identities and uses of the material world. If there is a pre in human prehistory, that trigger movement of the batsmen before the ball is released, then it is to be found in that most hidden category, the childhood of the self.

The good upheaval

The Stone Age did not end for lack of stone,
and the Oil Age will end
long before the world runs out of oil

Sheikh Zaki Yamani
Former Saudi Arabian Oil Minister to OPEC
The Economist 23 October 2003

I began this book with a digested read that boiled the contribution of prehistory down to the inevitability of well-directed change. This of course was an unfair caricature. Although prehistoric evidence has often provided an illustrated guide to the idea of progress, archaeologists left much of this baggage behind in the last century. But not everyone has caught up. The caricature still defines the broader landscapes of that imaginary geographical place I call Originsland where the history of human desire is the force that drives change onward. But in Originsland archaeologists are only one small tribe with a quiet voice. They are outnumbered and drowned-out by bigger battalions investigating our conventional history and technological achievements in order to inform a public past. In this company human prehistory provides little more than a convenient starting point for familiar descriptions of change.

Change driven by human desire is classical in origin. Aristotle, for example, asserted that only agriculture can civilise humans (Pagden 1986:91). Civil society, he argued, required a change in the way the Earth was roamed and its resources taken. The benefits of civilisation were good government, strong laws, moral codes and a world ordered by the written word.

Human identity has been built on these ancient principles: the legacy of an early literate society with fine stone architecture and some compelling metaphors, such as the prisoners in Plato's cave, for the nature of reality. These principles, and their supporting rhetoric, have shaped the landscapes of Originsland for every subsequent age. At the core is the sense of the *good upheaval*, a revolution in human affairs that became its own point of origin for the subsequent development of humanity and society. It seems that we are basically content with the contribution the past makes, in the form of several good upheavals along the way, to how we understand ourselves. And while archaeologists may have left the baggage of progress behind, they still carry the guiding principle of the good upheaval in their hand luggage. This is the principle they return to when interpreting prehistoric data as instances of fundamental change.

And change happened. Hominin material culture saw many innovations during two and a half million years. The end product was a social and technical world of enhanced potential, peopled by very different creatures from those that started the process. Moreover, there was a marked quickening of pace that over the long run of human evolution occurred relatively recently.

That things and people changed is inescapable. But I evaluate the facts differently. I dispute that change proceeded by a number of upheavals to create a set of universal identities applicable to early hominins and finally to ourselves. Changes to our universal identity, those familiar components of self and personhood, may need a rational explanation of how the world of people and things have evolved together, but that does not mean we have adequately described the object of change: the material basis of human identity.

As a result, the Human and Neolithic Revolutions are obstacles to understanding what changed as we evolved. The good upheaval that gave us Modern humans falls back on evolutionary science and a single geographical origin point for a universal identity. The alternative, convergent evolution to the same end result but in geographically separate locations, just stretches the notion of a universal identity too far. But this convergence is, of course, exactly the case for the worldwide Neolithic Revolution that took place independently in unconnected regions; Near East, China, Africa, the Americas and many smaller ones besides. The result, although based on very different local resources, was a new but essentially similar human identity, the farmer-citizen. These worldwide changes during the last 20,000 years have taxed archaeologists set on finding common reasons — climate, population numbers, food crisis, social packing, environmental windfalls to name a few — for such obviously beneficial upheavals that led to a shared identity.

I argue differently. Alter the standpoint on change from a rational to a relational one and the face of Originsland is transformed. Instead of our burgeoning endowment marked by revolutionary step changes we have a gradient (Figure 9.1) with an uneven surface, as indicated by the relative fortunes of instruments and containers, those material proxies for the body. These were always used as solid metaphors for hominin identity, their forms sourced to the experiences of the body. The gradient has a logarithmic time-scale during which the authority for understanding the world shifted imperceptibly from instruments to containers. It was through that change, neither gradual nor abrupt, that some very different understandings of identity were produced. A gradient from instrument to container could just as well, as Sheikh Yamani observed, be from stone to oil since neither runs out nor had to be 'invented'. Instead we fashion identities out of such engagements with the material world. We do not use such resources to construct a pre-conceived identity however much we rationalise the outcome to that effect.

I can be sure of my conclusion because a supposedly universal category, such as *Homo sapiens* or the Modern human, only exists in contra-distinction to equally universal categories with different identities, such as Neanderthals or archaic humans. These widespread identities may have been sufficient even fifty years ago when the distinctions drawn between farmers and hunters, citizens and barbarians would have made Aristotle feel very much at home. This is the rational model of the past founded on the master narrative of Western society that re-counts human ascendancy over nature.

In contrast to this account is my relational perspective where hominin identities have always been woven out of local conditions. Alasdair Whittle (2003:166), writing about Neolithic Europe, has pointed out that there are alternative prehistories to a grand narrative of directed change. His emphasis is on local diversity, rather than universal processes. In Figure 9.1 this interplay is indicated by the wavy line that traces the changes in my geographical metaphor, Originsland. The line is irregular to indicate that at any one time we can never be quite sure what we will find. A situation brought home for example in Chapter 5 when I discussed the Western and Melanesian concepts of personhood and in Chapter 8 with the work of bricoleurs and engineers among the earliest huts and villages.

When the material basis of identity is examined anywhere on these time-scales it is local diversity that emerges. And why? Because the body was always a source for the basic metaphorical forms of material culture, while the actions of fragmentation and consumption led to their elaboration

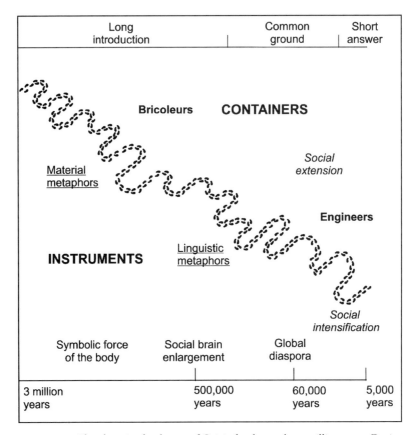

FIGURE 9.1. The changing landscape of Originsland over three million years. During this time there has been a movement from instruments to containers as the material proxies for framing concepts about identity. The bumpiness of the gradient is indicated by the wavy line. Some of the consequences are also indicated such as the development of linguistic metaphors and the social extension associated with the late global diaspora. The position of the descriptive labels is to clarify the components of changing human identity and do not represent origin points. The gradient was first suggested to me by John Gowlett.

through accumulation and enchainment into sets and nets. So, what I now realise is that my starting definition of *change* as 'organisation based on novel social premises' needs to be re-phrased as 'experience articulated through novel material metaphors'. It is the importance of material metaphors, as simple as a stone tool, rather than just the forms of social relationship, that have to be appreciated as the basis of a relational identity. Once the conceptual shift from mind to body-whole is accomplished it can be seen as liberating for the study of two and a half million years of hominin prehistory. One example is the potential such acts of liberation open up for the study of a neglected category such as hominin children. This will not be done by finding the Palaeolithic equivalent of a stuffed toy but through a childscape, the environment of development, where the interplay of experiences on our growing social brains are first understood by senses and sensations involving objects and things, rather than language. Concepts such as the childscape depend upon relational rather than rational approaches to the same data.

But not everything in the past is attributable to local diversity. I have stressed how the primary metaphors of the-giving-environment and growing-the-body take on wider geographical significance. The former characterises much of European prehistory that I have discussed here, while the latter came to organise social technologies in the Near East. Consequently, there is no single root metaphor to explain agricultural origins worldwide. Instead during the last 60,000 years the conditions for change were intensified through the scale of sets and nets, resulting in social extension and a global diaspora.

I have concentrated in this book on only two root metaphors to show how they are supported by material proxies. Originsland should have many more and in the future these can be explored. For example, in our own society, as geographer Tim Cresswell (2006) has discussed, there are very different, and often conflicting notions of mobility. In a distinction that takes us back again to Aristotle, the hunter, the nomad, the migrant or the tramp are regarded as a social pathology. They present a threat to the social order and need to be controlled. By contrast sedentary life is the foundation of culture through tradition and sending down roots. In an illuminating passage, that lacks the irony you might expect from an American living in London, the poet T. S. Eliot (1948:52) wrote that: 'On the whole, it would appear to be for the best that the great majority of human beings should go on living in the place in which they were born'; and in a passage clearly influenced by his contemporary Gordon Childe: 'When people migrated across Asia and Europe in pre-historic, and early times, it was a whole tribe, or at least a wholly representative part of it, that moved together. Therefore, it was a total culture that moved' (1948:63).

Mobility, according to conservative critics such as Eliot, waters down tradition and leads to rootlessness and the erosion of culture. The value attached to tradition depends upon settling down and curing the disease of mobility among either individuals or small groups. Sedentism was initially a good upheaval in the Neolithic and continued to be so for Eliot's world of Modernism. Good upheavals in prehistory also arose from the movement en-masse of a people and their culture, the transposition of culture en-bloc rather than piecemeal. The arrival of farmers from Asia into Europe remains the classic archaeological statement of the good upheaval that benefited all. However, it is the primary metaphor of sending-down-roots rather than the data that need re-considering.

These are suggestions for further enquiry as the material basis for human identity is pursued, not through the familiar cast of characters such as hunter and farmer, but rather as all hominins made sense of their varied experiences of living through material proxies. For too long we have assumed, because Aristotle told us, that such experience is the preserve of language and texts. Future enquiries might like to consider that the epitome of civilised society owes more to the body and its material proxies and less to the triumph of the mind. And in those cultural histories the pre-literate past, and all our ancestors, will have a fundamental contribution to make.

Bibliography

Abramova, Z. A.
  1967 Palaeolithic art in the USSR. *Arctic Anthropology* 4:1–179.
  1993 Two examples of terminal Palaeolithic adaptations. In *From Kostenki to Clovis: Upper Paleolithic–Paleo-Indian adaptations*, edited by O. Soffer and N. Praslov, pp. 85–100. Plenum, New York.

Adler, D. (editor)
  1999 *Metric handbook: Planning and Design Data*. 2nd ed. Architectural Press, Oxford.

Adler, D., G. Bar-Oz, A. Belfer-Cohen and O. Bar-Yosef
  2006 Ahead of the game: Middle and Upper Palaeolithic hunting behaviors in the southern Caucasus. *Current Anthropology* 47:89–118.

Aiello, L. and R. Dunbar
  1993 Neocortex size, group size and the evolution of language. *Current Anthropology* 34:184–193.

Aiello, L. and P. Wheeler
  1995 The expensive-tissue hypothesis: the brain and the digestive system in human and primate evolution. *Current Anthropology* 36:199–221.

Aikens, M.
  1995 First in the world: the Jomon pottery of early Japan. In *The emergence of pottery: technology and innovation in ancient societies*, edited by W. K. Barnett and J. W. Hoopes, pp. 11–21. Smithsonian Institution Press, Washington.

Alexandri, A.
  1995 The origins of meaning. In *Interpreting archaeology; finding meaning in the past*, edited by I. Hodder, M. Shanks, A. Alexandri, V. Buchli, J. Carman, J. Last and G. Lucas, pp. 57–67. Routledge, London.

Allen, N. J.
  1995 The division of labour and the notion of primitive society: a Maussian approach. *Social Anthropology* 3:49–59.

Allen, N. J.
  1998   Effervescence and the origins of human society. In *On Durkheim's Elementary Forms of Religious Life*, edited by N. J. Allen, W. S. F. Pickering and W. Watts Miller, pp. 149–161. Routledge, London.
  2005   Tetradic theory and the origin of human kinship systems. Paper presented at The evolution of kinship, Gregynog, Royal Anthropological Institute.

Allen, J. and C. Gosden (editors)
  1991   *Report of the Lapita homeland project.* Department of Prehistory, Research School of Pacific Studies, Australian National University, Canberra.

Altuna, J.
  1979   La faune des ongulés du Tardiglaciaire en Pays Basque et dans le reste de la région Cantabrique. In *La Fin des Temps Glaciaires*, edited by D. de Sonneville-Bordes, pp. 85–95. CNRS, Paris.

Anderson, M. L.
  2003   Embodied cognition: a field guide. *Artificial Intelligence* 149:91–130.

Anderson, D. G. and J. C. Gillam
  2000   Paleoindian colonization of the Americas: implications from an examination of physiography, demography, and artifact distribution. *American Antiquity* 65:43–66.

Appadurai, A. (editor)
  1986   *The social life of things: commodities in cultural perspective.* Cambridge University Press, Cambridge.

Arqueológica, Z.
  2002   *Bifaces y elefantes: La investigación del Paleolótico Inferior en Madrid.* Museo Arqueológico Regional N.1, Alcalá de Henares.

Ascher, R.
  1961   Analogy in archaeological interpretation. *Southwestern Journal of Anthropology* 17:317–325.

Aurenche, O., J. Évin and J. Gascó
  1987   Une séquence chronologique dans le Proche Orient de 12,000 à 3,700 BC et sa relation avec les donées radiocarbone. *Chronologies du Proche Orient: relative chronologies and absolute chronology 16,000–4,000 BP*, edited by O. Aurenche, J. Evin and F. Hours. Oxford, British Archaeological Reports International Series 379: 21–37.

Bachelard, G.
  1964   *The poetics of space.* Orion Press, New York.

Bader, O. N.
  1978   *Sunghir.* Nauka, Moscow.

Bamforth, D. B.
  2002   Evidence and metaphor in evolutionary archaeology. *American Antiquity* 67:435–452.

Bar-Yosef, O.
1989   Geochonology of the Levantine Middle Palaeolithic. In *The human
        revolution*, edited by P. Mellars and C. Stringer, pp. 589–610. Edinburgh
        University Press, Edinburgh.
1998   On the nature of transitions: the Middle to Upper Palaeolithic
        and the Neolithic Revolution. *Cambridge Archaeological Journal*
        8:141–163.
2001   From sedentary foragers to village hierarchies: the emergence of social
        institutions. *Proceedings of the British Academy* 110:1–38.
2002   The Upper Palaeolithic revolution. *Annual Review of Anthropology*
        31:363–393.

Bar-Yosef, O. and A. Belfer-Cohen
1989   The origins of sedentism and farming communities in the Levant. *Journal
        of World Prehistory* 3:447–498.
1992   From foraging to farming in the Mediterranean Levant. In *Transitions to
        agriculture in prehistory*, edited by A. B. Gebauer and T. D. Price, pp.
        21–48. Prehistory Press, Monographs in World Archaeology 4, Madison
        (Wisconsin).

Bar-Yosef, O. and A. Gopher
1997   *An early Neolithic Village in the Jordan Valley. Part I the archaeology of
        Netiv Hagdud*. Peabody Museum of Archaeology and Ethnology, Harvard
        University, American School of Prehistoric Research 43.

Bar-Yosef, O. and S. Kuhn
1999   The big deal about blades: laminar technologies and human evolution.
        American Anthropologist 101:322–338.

Bar-Yosef, O. and R. H. Meadow
1995   The origins of agriculture in the Near East. In *Last hunters – first farmers:
        New perspectives on the prehistoric transition to agriculture*, edited by
        T. D. Price and A. B. Gebauer, pp. 39–94. School of American Research,
        Santa Fe.

Bar-Yosef, O. and F. R. Valla (editors)
1991   *The Natufian culture in the Levant*. International Monographs in
        Prehistory, Ann Arbor.

Bar-Yosef, O., B. Vandermeersch, B. Arensburg, A. Belfer-Cohen, P. Goldberg,
        H. Laville, L. Meignen, Y. Rak, J. D. Speth, E. Tchernov, A.-M. Tillier
        and S. Weiner
1992   The excavations in Kebara Cave, Mt Carmel. *Current Anthropology*
        33:497–550.

Bar-Yosef Mayer, D. E.
1991   Changes in the selection of marine shells from the Natufian to the
        Neolithic. In *The Natufian culture in the Levant*, edited by O. Bar-Yosef
        and F. R. Valla, pp. 629–636. International Monographs in Prehistory 1,
        Ann Arbor.

Bar-Yosef Mayer, D. E.
  1997   Neolithic shell bead production in Sinai. *Journal of Archaeological Science* 24:97–111.
  2000   The economic importance of molluscs in the Levant. In *Archaeozoology of the Near East IVA*, edited by M. Mashkour, A. M. Choyke, H. Buitenhuis and F. Poplin, pp. 218–227. ARC Publicatie 32, Groningen.

Barich, B. E. (editor)
  1987   *Archaeology and environment in the Libyan Sahara: the excavations in the Tadrat Acacus, 1978–1983.* British Archaeological Reports International Series 368, Oxford.

Barkan, E.
  1992   *The retreat of scientific racism: changing concepts of race in Britain and the United States between the world wars.* Cambridge University Press, Cambridge.

Barkow, J. H., L. Cosmides and J. Tooby (editors)
  1992   *The adapted mind: evolutionary psychology, and the generation of culture.* Oxford University Press, New York.

Barrett, L. and P. Henzi
  2005   The social nature of primate cognition. *Proceedings of the Royal Society of London B* 272:1865–1875.

Basalla, G.
  1988   *The evolution of technology.* Cambridge University Press, Cambridge.

Becker, A. E.
  1995   *Body, self, and society: the view from Fiji.* University of Pennsylvania Press, Philadelphia.

Belfer-Cohen, A.
  1988   The Natufian graveyard in Hayonim cave. *Paléorient* 14:297–308.
  1991   The Natufian in the Levant. *Annual Review of Anthropology* 20:167–186.
  1995   Rethinking social stratification in the Natufian culture: the evidence from burials. In *The archaeology of death in the ancient Near East*, pp. 9–16. Oxbow Books, Oxford.

Bellomo, R. V.
  1994   Methods of determining early hominid behavioral activities associated with the controlled use of fire at FxJj 20 main, Koobi Fora, Kenya. *Journal of Human Evolution* 27:173–195.

Bender, B.
  1978   Gatherer-hunter to farmer: a social perspective. *World Archaeology* 10:204–222.

Bermúdez de Castro, J. M. and M. E. Nicolás
  1997   Palaeodemography of the Atapuerca-SH Middle Pleistocene hominid sample. *Journal of Human Evolution* 33:333–355.

Bettinger, R.
  1991   *Hunter-gatherers: archaeological and evolutionary theory.* Plenum, New York.

Binford, L. R.

1962   Archaeology as anthropology. *American Antiquity* 28:217−225.

1968   Post-Pleistocene adaptations. In *New perspectives in archaeology*, edited by S. R. Binford and L. R. Binford, pp. 313−341. Aldine, Chicago.

1972   *An archaeological perspective*. Academic Press, New York.

1973   Interassemblage variability − the Mousterian, and the 'functional' argument. In *The explanation of culture change*, edited by C. Renfrew, pp. 227−254. Duckworth, London.

1977   Forty seven trips. In *Stone tools as cultural markers*, edited by R. V. S. Wright, pp. 24−36. Australian Institute of Aboriginal Studies, Canberra.

1978a   Dimensional analysis of behaviour and site structure: learning from an Eskimo hunting stand. *American Antiquity* 43:330−361.

1978b   *Nunamiut Ethnoarchaeology*. Academic Press, New York.

1979   Organization and formation processes: looking at curated technologies. *Journal of Anthropological Research* 35:172−197.

1980   Willow smoke and dogs tails: hunter-gatherer settlement systems and archaeological site formation. *American Antiquity* 45:4−20.

1981   *Bones: ancient men and modern myths*. Academic Press, New York.

1983   *In pursuit of the past*. Thames and Hudson, London.

1985   Human ancestors: changing views of their behaviour. *Journal of Anthropological Archaeology* 4:292−327.

1987   Searching for camps and missing the evidence? Another look at the Lower Palaeolithic. In *The Pleistocene Old World: regional perspectives*, edited by O. Soffer, pp. 17−31. Plenum, New York.

1988   Etude taphonmique des restes fauniques de la Grotte Vaufrey, couche VIII. In *La Grotte Vaufrey à Cenac et Saint-Julien (Dordogne), Paleoenvironments, chronologie et activités humaines*, edited by J.-P. Rigaud, pp. 535−564. Mémoires de la Société Préhistorique Française. vol. 19.

1989   Isolating the transition to cultural adaptations: an organizational approach. In *The emergence of modern humans. Biocultural adaptations in the later Pleistocene*, edited by E. Trinkaus, pp. 18−41. Cambridge University Press, Cambridge.

1993   Bones for stones: considerations of analogues for features found on the Central Russian Plain. In *From Kostenki to Clovis: Upper Paleolithic − Paleo-Indian adaptations*, edited by O. Soffer and N. Praslov, pp. 101−124. Plenum, New York.

2001   *Constructing frames of reference: An analytical method for archaeological theory building using ethnographic and environmental datasets*. University of California Press, Berkeley.

Bird-David, N.

1992   Beyond 'the original affluent society': a culturalist reformulation. *Current Anthropology* 33:25−47.

Bird-David, N.
  1994   Sociality and immediacy: or, past and present conversations on bands. *Man* 29:583–603.
  1995   Hunter-gatherers' kinship organisation: implicit roles and rules. In *Social intelligence and interaction: expressions and implications of the social bias in human intelligence*, edited by E. N. Goody, pp. 68–84. Cambridge University Press, Cambridge.
  1999   'Animism' revisited: personhood, environment, and relational epistemology. *Current Anthropology* 40(Supplement):67–91.

Björck, S., M. J. C. Walker, L. C. Cwynar, S. Johnsen, K.-L. Knudsen, J. J. Lowe and B. Wohlfarth
  1998   An event stratigraphy for the Last Termination in the North Atlantic region based on the Greenland ice-core record: a proposal by the INTIMATE group. *Journal of Quaternary Science* 13:283–292.

Blasco Sancho, M. F.
  1995   *Hombres, fieras y presas: estudio arqueozoológico y tafonómico del yacimiento del paleolitico medio de la Cueva de Gabasa 1 (Huesca) 38*. Monografías Arqueológicas, Zaragoza.

Bloch, M. E. F.
  1998   *How we think they think: anthropological approaches to cognition, memory, and literacy*. Westview Press, Boulder.

Bloom, P.
  2004   Children think before they speak. *Nature* 430:410–411.

Boas, F.
  1938   *The mind of primitive man*. Macmillan, New York.

Boëda, E.
  1994   *Le concept Levallois: variabilité des méthodes*. Centre Récherche Archéologique 9. CNRS Éditions, Paris.

Boëda, E., J. Connan, D. Dessort, S. Muhesen, N. Mercier, H. Valladas and N. Tisnerat
  1996   Utilisation of bitumen as hafting material on Middle Palaeolithic artefacts (around 40,000 BC) in Umm El Tlel (Syria). *Nature* 380:336–338.

Boëda, E., J.-M. Geneste and L. Meignen
  1990   Identification de chaînes opératoires lithiques du Paléolithique ancien et moyen. *Paléo* 2:43–80.

Boesch, C. and M. Tomasello
  1998   Chimpanzee and human cultures. *Current Anthropology* 39:591–614.

Boivin, N.
  2004   From veneration to exploitation: human engagement with the mineral world. In *Soils, stones and symbols: cultural perceptions of the mineral world*, edited by N. Boivin and M. Owoc, pp. 1–30. UCL Press, London.

Boivin, N. and M. Owoc (editors)
  2004   *Soils, stones and symbols: cultural perceptions of the mineral world*. UCL Press, London.

Bonsall, C. and C. Tolan-Smith (editors)
  1997   *The human use of caves*. S667. British Archaeological Reports, Oxford.
Bordes, F.
  1953   Essai de classification des industries 'Mousteriennes'. *Bulletin de la Société Préhistorique Française* 50:457–466.
  1968   *The old stone age*. Weidenfeld and Nicolson, London.
  1972   *A tale of two caves*. Harper and Row Bordes (1973), New York.
  1980   Le débitage Levallois et ses variants. *Bulletin de la Société Préhistorique Française*, 77:45–49.
Bosinski, G.
  1967   *Die Mittelpaläolithischen Funde im Westlichen Mitteleuropa*. 4, Koln/4, Koln.
  1979   *Die Ausgrabungen in Gönnersdorf 1968–76 und die Siedlungsbefunde der Grabung 1968*. Franz Steiner GMBH, Wiesbaden.
Bosinski, G. and G. Fischer
  1974   *Die Menschdarstellungen von Gönnersdorf der Ausgrabung von 1968*. Franz Steiner GMBH, Wiesbaden.
Bourdieu, P.
  1977   *Outline of a theory of practice*. Cambridge University Press, Cambridge.
Boyle, K. V.
  1990   *Upper Palaeolithic faunas from South-West France: a zoogeographic perspective*. British Archaeological Reports International Series 557, Oxford.
Brace, C. L.
  1964   The fate of the 'classic' Neanderthals, a consideration of hominid catastrophism. *Current Anthropology* 5:3–43.
  1979   Krapina, 'Classic' Neanderthals, and the evolution of the European face. *Journal of Human Evolution* 8:527–550.
Bradley, B.
  1977   *Experimental lithic technology with special reference to the Middle Palaeolithic*. Ph.D. dissertation, Cambridge University.
Bradley, R.
  2002   *The past in prehistoric societies*. Routledge, London.
Braidwood, R.
  1948   (1957). *Prehistoric men*. 3rd Edition. Chicago Natural History Museum Popular Series Anthropology, 37, Chicago.
  1960   The agricultural revolution. *Scientific American* 203:130–141.
Braidwood, R. and B. Howe
  1960   *Prehistoric Investigations in Iraqi Kurdistan*. Oriental Institute Studies in Ancient Oriental Civilization 31, Chicago.
Brain, C. K.
  1981   *The hunters or the hunted?* Chicago University Press, Chicago.
Brain, C. K. and A. Sillen
  1988   Evidence from the Swartkrans cave for the earliest use of fire. *Nature* 336:464–466.

Brantingham, P. J. and S. Kuhn
  2001   Constraints on Levallois core technology: a mathematical model. *Journal of Archaeological Science* 28:747–761.

Breasted, J. H.
  1926   *The conquest of civilisation*. Chicago University Press, Chicago.

Brooks, A., D. M. Helgren, J. M. Cramer, A. Franklin, W. Hornvak, J. M. Keating, R. G. Klein, J. Rink, H. Schwarcz, J. N. Smith, K. Stewart, N. E. Todd, J. Verniers and J. Yellen
  1995   Dating and context of three Middle Stone Age sites with bone points in the Upper Semliki Valley, Zaire. *Science* 268:548–553.

Brose, D. and M. Wolpoff
  1971   Early Upper Paleolithic man and Late Middle Paleolithic tools. *American Anthropologist* 73:1156–1194.

Brown, J. A.
  1893   On the continuity of the Palaeolithic and Neolithic periods. *Journal of the Royal Anthropological Institute* 22:66–98.

Brown, P., T. Sutikna, M. J. Morwood, R. P. Soejono, Jatmiko, E. Wayhu Saotimo and R. A. Due
  2004   A new small-bodied hominin from the Late Pleistocene of Flores, Indonesia. *Nature* 431:1055–1061.

Brumm, A.
  2004   An axe to grind: symbolic considerations of stone axe use in ancient Australia. In *Soils, stones and symbols: cultural perceptions of the mineral world*, edited by N. Boivin and M. Owoc, pp. 143–164. UCL Press, London.

Bunn, H. T.
  1981   Archaeological evidence for meat-eating by Plio-Pleistocene hominids from Koobi Fora and Olduvai Gorge. *Nature* 291:574–577.

Burke, A. M. (editor)
  2000   Reassessing evidence for Middle Palaeolithic hunting. *International Journal of Osteoarchaeology*. Special issue (3–4).

Busby, C.
  1997   Permeable and partible persons: a comparative analysis of gender and body in South India and Melanesia. *Journal of the Royal Anthropological Institute* 3:261–278.

Byrd, B.
  1989   The Natufian: settlement variability and economic adaptations in the Levant at the end of the Pleistocene. *Journal of World Prehistory* 3:159–197.
  1994   Public and private, domestic and corporate: the emergence of the southwest Asian village. *American Antiquity* 59:639–666.
  2005   Reassessing the emergence of village life in the Near East. *Journal of Archaeological Research* 13:231–290.

Byrd, B. and C. M. Monahan
  1995   Death, mortuary ritual, and Natufian social structure. *Journal of Anthropological Archaeology* 14:251–287.

Byrne, R. W. and A. Whiten (editors)
  1988   *Machiavellian intelligence: social expertise and the evolution of intellect in monkeys, apes and humans.* Clarendon Press, Oxford.

Callow, P., D. Walton and C. A. Shell
  1986   The use of fire at La Cotte de St. Brelade. In *La Cotte de St. Brelade 1961–1978: excavations by C.B.M. McBurney,* edited by P. Callow and J. M. Cornford, pp. 193–199. Geo Books, Norwich.

Cann, R., M. Stoneking and A. Wilson
  1987   Mitochondrial DNA and human evolution. *Nature* 325:31–36.

Capitan, L. and D. Peyrony
  1928   *La Madeleine, son gisement – son industrie, ses oeuvres d'art 2.* Publications de l'Institut International d'Anthropologie, Paris.

Carpenter, E.
  1973   *Eskimo realities.* Holt, Rinehart and Winston, New York.

Carrithers, M.
  1985   An alternative social history of the self. In *The category of the person: anthropology, philosophy, history,* edited by M. Carrithers, S. Collins and S. Lukes, pp. 234–256. Cambridge University Press, Cambridge.

Carrithers, M., S. Collins and S. Lukes (editors)
  1985.   *The category of the person: anthropology, philosophy, history.* Cambridge University Press, Cambridge.

Carroll, S. B.
  2003   Genetics and the making of *Homo sapiens. Nature* 422:849–857.

Carruthers, P.
  2002   The cognitive functions of language. *Behavioral and brain sciences* 25:657–726.

Carsten, J. and S. Hugh-Jones (editors)
  1995   *About the house: Lévi-Strauss and beyond.* Cambridge University Press, Cambridge.

Carver, M.
  1998   *Sutton Hoo burial ground of kings?* British Museum Press, London.

Cauvin, J.
  1978   *Les prémiers villages de Syrie-Palestine du IXème au VIIème Millénaire avant J.C.* Maison de l'Orient, Lyon.
  2000   *The birth of the gods and the origins of agriculture.* Cambridge University Press, Cambridge.

Chagnon, N. A.
  1977   *Yanomamo: the fierce people.* 2nd ed. Holt, Rhinehart and Winston, New York.

Chang, K. C.
  1962   A typology of settlement and community patterns in some circumpolar societies. *Arctic Anthropology* 1:28–41.

Chapman, J.
  2000   *Fragmentation in archaeology: people, places and broken objects in the prehistory of south-eastern Europe.* Routledge, London.

Chernysh, A. P.
  1961   *Palaeolitiginia Stoanka Molodova* 5. An. Ukr. SSR, Kiev.

Childe, V. G.
  1923   *How Labour governs.* Watts, London.
  1929   *The Danube in prehistory.* Oxford University Press, Oxford.
  1934   (1952) *New light on the most ancient East.* Routledge and Kegan Paul, London.
  1935a Changing methods and aims in prehistory. *Proceedings of the Prehistoric Society* 1:1–15.
  1935b Prehistory in the USSR. *Proceedings of the Prehistoric Society* 1:151–154.
  1936   *Man makes himself.* Watts and Co., London.
  1942   *What happened in history.* Penguin Books, Harmondsworth.
  1944   *Progress and archaeology.* Watts, London.
  1950   The urban revolution. *The Town Planning Review* 21:3–27.
  1958a *The prehistory of European society.* Penguin, Harmondsworth.
  1958b Retrospect. *Antiquity* 32:69–74.

Churchill, S. E.
  1993   Weapon technology, prey size selection, and hunting methods in modern hunter-gatherers: implications for hunting in the Palaeolithic and Mesolithic. In *Hunting and animal exploitation in the later Palaeolithic and Mesolithic of Eurasia*, edited by G. L. Peterkin, H. Bricker and P. A. Mellars, pp. 11–24. Archaeological Papers of the American Anthropological Association 4.

Clark, A.
  1997   *Being there: bringing brain, body and world together again.* MIT Press, Cambridge, MA.

Clark, G. A.
  1992a Continuity or replacement? Putting modern human origins in an evolutionary context. In *The Middle Paleolithic: adaptation, behaviour, and variability*, edited by H. L. Dibble and P. Mellars, pp. 183–207. The University Museum, University of Pennsylvania, Philadelphia.
  1992b A comment on Mithen's ecological interpretation of Palaeolithic art. *Proceedings of the Prehistoric Society* 58:107–109.

Clark, J.
  2003   *Our shadowed present: modernism, postmodernism and history.* AtlanticBooks, London.

Clark, J. D., Y. Beyenne, G. WoldeGabriel, W. K. Hart, P. Renne, H. Gilbert,
    A. Defleur, G. Suwa, S. Katoh, K. R. Ludwig, J.-R. Boisserie, B. Asfaw and
    T. D. White
  2003   Stratigraphic, chronological and behavioural contexts of pleistocene
          Homo sapiens from Middle Awash, Ethiopia. *Nature* 423:747−752.

Clark, J. G. D.
  1969   *World Prehistory a new outline* (Second edition). Cambridge University
          Press, Cambridge.

Clarke, D. L.
  1973   Archaeology: the loss of innocence. *Antiquity* 47:6−18.

Close, A. E.
  1995   Few and far between: early ceramics in North Africa. In *The emergence of
          pottery: technology and innovation in ancient societies*, edited by W. K.
          Barnett and J. W. Hoopes, pp. 23−37. Smithsonian Institution Press,
          Washington.

Cohen, M. N.
  1977   *The food crisis in prehistory: overpopulation and the origins of agriculture.*
          Yale University Press, New Haven.

Cole, S.
  1959   *The Neolithic revolution.* British Museum (Natural History), London.

Collins, S.
  1985   Categories, concepts or predicaments? Remarks on Mauss's use of
          philosophical terminology. In *The category of the person: anthropology,
          philosophy, history,* edited by M. Carrithers, S. Collins and S. Lukes,
          pp. 46−82. Cambridge University Press, Cambridge.

Conard, N. J.
  1992   *Tönchesberg and its position in the Palaeolithic prehistory of northern
          Europe.* RGZM Monograph 20. Habelt, Bonn.

Conard, N. J. and T. J. Prindiville
  2000   Middle Palaeolithic hunting economies in the Rhineland. *International
          Journal of Osteoarchaeology* 10:286−309.

Conkey, M. W. and S. H. Williams
  1991   The political economy of gender in archaeology. In *Gender at the
          crossroads of knowledge: Feminist anthropology in a post modern era,* edited
          by M. di Leonardo, pp. 102−139. University of California Press, Berkeley.

Conway-Morris, S.
  2003   *Life's solution: inevitable humans in a lonely universe.* Cambridge
          University Press, Cambridge.

Coon, C. S.
  1962   *The origin of races.* Cape, London.

Cosgrove, D.
  1999   Introduction: mapping meanings. In *Mappings,* edited by D. Cosgrove,
          pp. 1−23. Reaktion Books, London.

Cosgrove, R.
  1999   Forty-two degrees south: the archaeology of Late Pleistocene Tasmania. *Journal of World Prehistory* 13:357−402.

Count, E. W. (editor)
  1950   *This is race*. HenSchuman, New York.

Cresswell, T.
  2006   *On the move*. London: Routledge.

Cribb, R.
  1991   *Nomads in archaeology*. Cambridge University Press, Cambridge.

Dahlberg, F. (editor)
  1981   *Woman the gatherer*. Yale University Press, New Haven.

Damas, D. (editor)
  1984   *Handbook of North American Indians: Arctic*. 5. Smithsonian Institute, Washington.

Damasio, A.
  2000   *The feeling of what happens: body, emotion and the making of consciousness*. Vintage, London.

Dark, K. R.
  1998   *The waves of time: long-term change and international relations*. Continuum, London.

Darte, C., J. Mauricio, P. Pettitt, P. Souto, E. Trinkaus, H. Van der Plicht and J. Zilhao
  1999   The early Upper Palaeolithic human skeleton from the Abrigo do Lagar Velho (Portugal) and modern human emergence in Iberia. *Proceedings of the National Academy of Science USA* 96:7604−7609.

David, F. and C. Farizy
  1994   Les vestiges osseux: étude archéozoologique. In *Hommes et Bisons du Paléolithique Moyen à Mauran*, edited by C. Farizy, F. David and J. Jaubert, pp. 177−303. CNRS, Paris.

Davidson, I.
  1989   Freedom of information: aspects of art and society in western Europe during the last ice age. In *Animals into art*, edited by H. Morphy, pp. 440−456. Allen and Unwin, London.

Davidson, I. and W. C. McGrew
  2005   Stone tools and the uniqueness of human culture. *Journal of the Royal Anthropological Institute* 11:793−817.

Davidson, I. and W. Noble
  1993   Tools and language in human evolution. In *Tools, language and cognition in human evolution*, edited by K. R. Gibson and T. Ingold, pp. 363−388. Cambridge University Press, Cambridge.

Davis, T., Pa Tuterangi Ariki
  1999   *Vaka, saga of a Polynesian canoe*. Institute of Pacific Studies, Auckland.

Dawkins, R.
  1976   *The selfish gene*. Oxford University Press, Oxford.

Deacon, H. J.
  1989   Late Pleistocene palaeoecology and archaeology in the Southern
          Cape, South Africa. In *The human revolution: behavioural and
          biological perspectives on the origins of modern humans*, edited by
          P. Mellars and C. Stringer, pp. 547—564. Edinburgh University Press,
          Edinburgh.
  1995   Two late Pleistocene-Holocene archaeological depositories from the
          southern Cape, South Africa. *South African Archaeological Bulletin*
          50:121—131.

Deacon, J.
  1995   An unsolved mystery at the Howieson's Poort name site. *South African
          Archaeological Bulletin* 50:110—120.

Deacon, T.
  1997   *The symbolic species: the co-evolution of language and the human brain*.
          Penguin Books, Harmondsworth.

de Bie, M. and J.-P. Caspar
  2000   *Rekem: a Federmesser camp on the Meuse river bank. 2 volumes.* Leuven
          University Press (Archeologie in Vlaanderen 3), Leuven.

Delpech, F.
  1983   *Les faunes du Paléolithique supérieur dans le sud-ouest de la France*.
          CNRS, Cahiers du Quaternaire 6, Paris.

Delporte, H.
  1979   *L'image de la femme dans l'art préhistorique*. Picard, Paris.

de Lumley, H., A. Echassoux, S. Bailon, D. Cauche, M.-P. de Marchi, E.
  Desclaux, K. el Guennouni, S. Khatib, F. Lacombat, T. Roger and P.
  Valensi
  2004   *Le sol d'occupation Acheuléen de l'unité archéostratigraphique
          UA 25 de la Grotte du Lazaret, Nice, Alpes-Maritimes*. Edisud, Aix-en-
          Provence.

Denyer, S.
  1978.   *African traditional architecture*. Heinemann, London.

d'Errico, F.
  2003   The invisible frontier: A multiple species model for the origin of
          behavioural modernity. *Evolutionary Anthropology* 12:188—202.

d'Errico, F., C. S. Henshilwood, G. Lawson, M. Vanhaeren, A.-M. Tillier,
  M. Soressi, F. Bresson, B. Maureille, A. Nowell, J. Lakarra, L. Backwell
  and M. Julien
  2003   Archaeological evidence for the emergence of language, symbolism,
          and music: an alternative multidisciplinary perspective. *Journal of World
          Prehistory* 17:1—70.

d'Errico, F. and M. Vanhaeren
2002   Criteria for identifying red deer (*Cervus elaphus*) age and sex from their canines. Application to the study of Upper Palaeolithic and Mesolithic ornaments. *Journal of Archaeological Science* 29:211–232.

d'Errico, F., J. Zilhao, M. Julien, D. Baffier and J. Pelegrin
1998   Neanderthal acculturation in Western Europe?: a critical review of the evidence and its interpretation. *Current Anthropology* 39 Supplement: S1–S44.

Desbrosse, R. and J. Kozlowski
1994   *Les habitats préhistoriques des Australopithèques aux premiers agriculteurs*. CTHS Documents Préhistoriques 6, Cracow & Paris.

Dibble, H. and O. Bar-Yosef (editors)
1995   *The definition and interpretation of Levallois technology*. Prehistory Press. Monographs in World Archaeology 23, Madison.

Dietler, M.
2001   Theorizing the feast: rituals of consumption, commensal politics and power in African contexts. In *Feasts: archaeological and ethnographic perspectives on food, politics, and power*, edited by M. Dietler and B. Hayden, pp. 65–114. Smithsonian Institution Press, Washington.

Djindjian, F., J. Kozlowski and M. Otte
1999   *Le Paléolithique supérieur en Europe*. Armand Colin, Paris.

Dobres, M.-A.
2000   *Technology and social agency*. Blackwell, Oxford.

Dobres, M.-A. and C. R. Hoffman
1994   Social agency and the dynamics of prehistoric technology. *Journal of Archaeological Method and Theory* 1:211–258.

Dobres, M.-A. and J. Robb (editors)
2000a. *Agency in archaeology*. Routledge, London.
2000b. Agency in archaeology: paradigm or platitude? In *Agency in archaeology*, edited by M.-A. Dobres and J. Robb, pp. 3–17. Routledge, London.

Dominguez-Rodrigo, M., J. Serralonga, J. Juan-Tresserras, L. Alcala and L. Luque
2001   Woodworking activities by early humans: a plant residue analysis on Acheulean stone tools from Peninj (Tanzania). *Journal of Human Evolution* 40:289–299.

Donald, M.
1991   *Origins of the modern mind: three stages in the evolution of culture and cognition*. Harvard University Press, Cambridge MA.
1998   Mimesis and the executive suite: missing links in language evolution. In *Approaches to the evolution of language: social and cognitive bases*, edited by J. R. Hurford, M. Studdert-Kennedy and C. Knight, pp. 44–67. Cambridge University Press, Cambridge.

Douglas, M. and B. Isherwood
1978 *The world of goods: towards an anthropology of consumption*. Allen Lane, London.

Driver, F.
2004 Distance and disturbance: travel, exploration and knowledge in the nineteenth century. *Transactions of the Royal Historical Society* 14:73–92.

Drucker, D. G. and D. Henry-Gambier
2005 Determination of the dietary habits of a Magdalenian woman from Saint-Germain-la-Rivière in southwestern France using stable isotopes. *Journal of Human Evolution* 49:19–35.

Dunbar, R. I. M.
1992a Neocortex size as a constraint on group size in primates. *Journal of Human Evolution* 20:469–493.
1992b Time: a hidden constraint on the behavioural ecology of baboons. *Behavioural Ecology and Sociobiology* 31:35–49.
1993 Coevolution of neocortical size, group size and language in humans. *Behavioural and Brain Sciences* 16:681–735.
1996 *Grooming, gossip and the evolution of language*. Faber and Faber, London.
1998 Theory of mind and the evolution of language. In *Approaches to the evolution of language: social and cognitive bases*, edited by J. R. Hurford, M. Studdert-Kennedy and C. Knight, pp. 92–110. Cambridge University Press, Cambridge.
2003 The social brain: mind, language, and society in evolutionary perspective. *Annual Review of Anthropology* 32:163–181.

Dunnell, R. C.
1978 Style and function: a fundamental dichotomy. *American Antiquity* 43:192–202.

Earle, T.
1980 A model of subsistence change. In *Modeling change in prehistoric subsistence economies*, edited by T. Earle and A. L. Christenson, pp. 1–29. Academic Press, New York.

Earle, T. and A. L. Christenson (editors)
1980 *Modeling change in prehistoric subsistence economies*. Academic Press, New York.

Edmonds, M.
1999 *Ancestral geographies of the Neolithic*. Routledge, London.

Edwards, P.
1991 Wadi Hammeh 27: an early Natufian site at Pella, Jordan. In *The Natufian culture in the Levant*, edited by O. Bar-Yosef and F. R. Valla, pp. 123–148. International Monographs in Prehistory 1, Ann Arbor.

Efimenko, P. P.
1958 *Kostenki, I (in Russian)*. NAUKA, Moscow-Leningrad.

Elefanti, P.
> 2003   *Hunter-gatherer specialised subsistence strategies in Greece during the Upper Palaeolithic from the perspective of lithic technology.* British Archaeological Reports International Series 1130, Oxford.

Eliot, T. S.
> 1948   *Notes towards the definition of culture.* London: Faber and Faber.

Elston, R. G. and S. L. Kuhn (editors)
> 2002   *Thinking small: global perspectives on microlithization.* Archaeological papers of the American Anthropological Association 12.

Enfield, N. J.
> 2005   The body as a cognitive artifact in kinship representations: hand gesture diagrams by speakers of Lao. *Current Anthropology* 46:51–81.

Engels, F.
> 1884   (1902) *The origin of the family, private property and the State.* Charles H. Kerr, Chicago.

Evans, J.
> 1998   *The discovery of Aotearoa.* Reed, Auckland.

Fagan, B.
> 1987   *The great journey: the peopling of ancient America.* Thames and Hudson, London.

Fagan, B. (editor)
> 2004   *The seventy great inventions of the Ancient world.* Thames and Hudson, London.

Féblot-Augustins, J.
> 1990   Exploitation des matières premières dans l'Acheuléen d'Afrique: perspectives comportementales. *Paléo* 2:27–42.
> 1997   *La circulation des matières premières au Paléolithique.* ERAUL vol. 75, Liège.

Feinman, G. M. and J. Marcus (editors)
> 1998   *Archaic states.* School of American Research, Santa Fe.

Fladmark, K. R.
> 1979   Routes: alternate migration corridors for early man in North America. *American Antiquity* 44:55–69.

Flannery, K. V.
> 1967   Culture history versus cultural process: a debate in American archaeology. *Scientific American* 217:119–122.
> 1969   Origins and ecological effects of early domestication in Iran and the Near East. In *The domestication and exploitation of plants and animals*, edited by P. J. Ucko and G. W. Dimbleby, pp. 73–100. Duckworth, London.

1972a   The cultural evolution of civilizations. *Annual Review of Ecology and Systematics* 3:399–426.

1972b   The origins of the village as a settlement type in Mesoamerica and the Near East: a comparative study. In *Man, settlement and urbanism*, edited by P. J. Ucko, R. Tringham and G. W. Dimbleby, pp. 22–53. Duckworth, London.

2000   Comment on Stiner, Munro and Surovell. *Current Anthropology* 41: 64–65.

2002   The origins of the village revisited: from nuclear to extended households. *American Antiquity* 67:417–433.

Flood, J. M.

1990   *The riches of ancient Australia: a journey into prehistory*. University of Queensland Press and Australian Heritage Commission, Brisbane.

Floss, H.

1994   *Rohmaterialversorgung im Paläolithikum des Mittelrheingebietes*. Römisch-Germanishches Zentralmuseum, Forschungsinstitut für Vor- und Frühgeschichte 21. Habelt, Bonn.

Fodor, J.

1985   Precis of 'The modularity of the mind'. *The Behavioral and Brain Sciences* 8:1–42.

Foley, R. A.

1996   An evolutionary and chronological framework for human social behaviour. In *Evolution of social behaviour patterns in primates and man*. Edited by W. G. Runciman, J. Maynard-Smith and R. I. M. Dunbar, pp. 95–117. Oxford University Press, Oxford

2001a   In the shadow of the modern synthesis? Alternative perspectives on the last fifty years of palaeoanthropology. *Evolutionary Anthropology* 10:5–15.

2001b   Evolutionary perspectives on the origins of human social institutions. *Proceedings of the British Academy* 110:171–195.

Foley, R. A. and M. M. Lahr

1997   Mode 3 technologies and the evolution of modern humans. *Cambridge Archaeological Journal* 7:3–36.

Foley, R. A. and P. C. Lee

1989   Finite social space, evolutionary pathways, and reconstructing hominid behaviour. *Science* 243:901–906.

Fox, R.

1967   *Kinship and marriage*. Penguin Books, Harmondsworth.

Friedman, J.

1994   *Cultural identity and global process*. Sage, London.

Galanidou, N.

1997   *'Home is where the hearth is': the spatial organisation of the Upper Palaeolithic Rockshelter Occupations at Klithi and Kastritsa in Northwest Greece*. British Archaeological Reports International Series 687, Oxford.

Gambier, D.
  1992   Les populations Magdaléniennes en France. In *Le peuplement Magdalénien*, edited by CTHS, pp. 41–51. Actes du Colloque de Chancelade 10–15 Octobre 1988, Paris.

Gamble, C. S.
  1982a Leadership and 'surplus' production. In *Ranking, Resource and Exchange*, edited by C. Renfrew and S. Shennan, pp. 100–105. Cambridge University Press, Cambridge.
  1982b Interaction and alliance in Palaeolithic society. *Man* 17:92–107.
  1986   *The Palaeolithic Settlement of Europe*. Cambridge University Press, Cambridge.
  1993a *Timewalkers: the prehistory of global colonization*. Harvard University Press, Cambridge, Mass.
  1993b Exchange, foraging and local hominid networks. In *Trade and exchange in prehistoric Europe*, edited by C. Scarre and F. Healy, pp. 35–44. vol. 33. Oxbow Monograph, Oxford.
  1998   Palaeolithic society and the release from proximity: a network approach to intimate relations. *World Archaeology* 29:426–449.
  1999   *The Palaeolithic societies of Europe*. Cambridge University Press, Cambridge.
  2001   *Archaeology: The basics*. Routledge, London.
  2004   Materiality and symbolic force: a Palaeolithic view of sedentism. In *Rethinking materiality: the engagement of mind with the material world*, edited by E. DeMarrais, C. Gosden and C. Renfrew, pp. 85–95. McDonald Institute of Archaeological Research, Cambridge.

Gamble, C. S., W. Davies, P. Pettitt and M. Richards
  2004   Climate change and evolving human diversity in Europe during the last glacial. *Philosophical Transactions of the Royal Society Biological Sciences* 359:243–254.

Gamble, C. S., S. W. G. Davies, M. Richards, P. Pettitt and L. Hazelwood
  2005   Archaeological and genetic foundations of the European population during the Lateglacial: implications for 'agricultural thinking'. *Cambridge Archaeological Journal* 15:55–85.

Gamble, C. S. and S. Gaudzinski
  2005   Bones and powerful individuals: faunal case studies from the Arctic and European Middle Palaeolithic. In *The individual hominid in context: archaeological investigations of Lower and Middle Palaeolithic landscapes, locales and artefacts*, edited by C. Gamble and M. Porr, pp. 154–175. Routledge, London.

Gamble, C. S. and E. K. Gittins
  2004   Social archaeology and origins research: a Palaeolithic perspective. In *A companion to social archaeology*, edited by L. Meskell and R. Preucell, pp. 96–118. Blackwell, Oxford.

Gamble, C. S. and G. Marshall
  2001   The shape of handaxes, the structure of the Acheulean world. In
         *A very remote period indeed: papers on the Palaeolithic presented to
         Derek Roe*, edited by S. Milliken and J. Cook, pp. 19–27. Oxbow Books,
         Oxford.

Gamble, C. S. and M. Porr (editors)
  2005a *The individual hominid in context: archaeological investigations of Lower
         and Middle Palaeolithic landscapes, locales and artefacts*. Routledge,
         London.
  2005b From empty spaces to lived lives: exploring the individual in the
         Palaeolithic. In *The individual hominid in context: archaeological
         investigations of Lower and Middle Palaeolithic landscapes, locales
         and artefacts*, edited by C. Gamble and M. Porr, pp. 1–12. Routledge,
         London.

Gargett, R.
  1989   Grave shortcomings: the evidence for Neanderthal burial. *Current
         Anthropology* 30:157–90.

Garrard, A. N.
  1991   Natufian settlement in the Azraq Basin, eastern Jordan. In *The
         Natufian culture in the Levant*, edited by O. Bar-Yosef and F. R. Valla,
         pp. 235–244. International Monographs in Prehistory 1, Ann Arbor.
  1999   Charting the emergence of cereal and pulse domestication in South-west
         Asia. *Environmental Archaeology* 4:67–86.

Gathercole, P.
  1994   Childe in history. *Bulletin of the Institute of Archaeology*, London
         31:25–52.

Gaudzinski, S.
  1992   Wisentjäger in Wallertheim: zur taphonomie einer Mittelpaläolithischen
         Freilandfundstelle in Rheinhessen. *Jahrbuch des Römisch-Germanischen
         Zentralmuseums Mainz* 39:245–423.
  1995   Wallertheim revisited: A reanalysis of the fauna from the Middle
         Paleolithic site of the Wallertheim (Rheinhessen/Germany). *Journal of
         Archaeological Science* 22:51–66.
  1998   Knochen und Knochengeräte der Mittelpaläolithischen Fundstelle
         Salzgitter Lebenstedt (Deutschland). *Jahrbuch des Römisch-
         Germanischen Zentralmuseums Mainz* 45:163–220.
  1999   Middle Palaeolithic bone tools from the open-air site Salzgitter
         Lebenstedt (Germany). *Journal of Archaeological Science* 26:124–141.

Gaudzinski, S. and W. Roebroeks
  2000   Adults only. Reindeer hunting at the Middle Palaeolithic site Salzgitter
         Lebenstedt, Northern Germany. *Journal of Human Evolution*
         38:497–521.
  2003   Profile analysis at Salzgitter-Lebenstedt. A reply to Munson and Marean.
         Journal of Human Evolution 44:275–281.

Gaudzinski, S. and E. Turner
1996   The role of early humans in the accumulation of European Lower and Middle Palaeolithic bone assemblages. *Current Anthropology* 37:153–156.
1999   *The role of early humans in the accumulation of European Lower and Middle Palaeolithic bone assemblages.* 42. Römisch-Germanisches Zentralmuseum, Mainz.

Gebauer, A. B. and T. D. Price (editors)
1992   *Transitions to agriculture in prehistory.* Prehistory Press, Madison.

Gell, A.
1998   *Art and agency: towards a new anthropological theory.* Clarendon Press, Oxford.

Gellner, E.
1986   Soviets against Wittfogel: or, the anthropological preconditions of mature marxism. In *States in History*, edited by J. A. Hall, pp. 78–108. Basil Blackwell, Oxford.

Geneste, J.-M.
1988   Systemes d'approvisionnement en matières premières au Paléolithique moyen et au Paléolithique supérieur en Aquitaine. *L'Homme de Néandertal* 8:61–70.
1989   Economie des ressources lithiques dans le Moustèrien du sud-ouest de la France. In *La Subsistance*, edited by M. Otte, pp. 75–97. L'Homme de Néandertal. vol. 6. ERAUL, Liège.

Gerasimov, M. M.
1971   *The face finder.* J. B. Lippincott, New York.

Gerhardt, S.
2004   *Why love matters: how affection shapes a baby's brain.* Routledge, London.

Gero, G. and M. Conkey (editors)
1991   *Engendering archaeology: women and prehistory.* Blackwell, Oxford.

Gibson, J. J.
1979   *The ecological approach to visual perception.* Erlbaum Associates, Hillsdale.

Gibson, K. R.
1986   Cognition, brain size and the extraction of embedded food resources. In *Primate ontogeny, cognition and social behaviour*, edited by J. Else and P. C. Lee, pp. 93–105. Cambridge University Press, Cambridge.

Giddens, A.
1984   *The constitution of society.* University of California Press, Berkeley.

Gifford-Gonzalez, D.
1993   You can hide, but you can't run: representation of women's work in illustrations of Palaeolithic life. *Visual Anthropology Review* 9:23–41.

Gillespie, R.

2000 Age estimates for Willandra Lakes Human Bones. *http://www-personal. une.edu.au/~pbrown3/gillespi.htm.*

Gilman, A.

1984 Explaining the Upper Palaeolithic revolution. In *Marxist perspectives in archaeology*, edited by M. Spriggs, pp. 115–126. Cambridge University Press, Cambridge.

Goffman, E.

1959 *The presentation of self in everyday life*, Garden City NY, Anchor Books.

1963 *Behaviour in public places: notes on the social organisation of gatherings.* Free Press, New York.

1967 *Interaction ritual: essays on face to face behaviour.* Allen Lane, London.

Goodall, J.

1986 *The chimpanzees of Gombe: patterns of behaviour.* Belknap Press, Cambridge, Mass.

Goren-Inbar, N., N. Alperson, M. E. Kislev, O. Simchoni, Y. Melamed, A. Ben-Nun and E. Werker

2004 Evidence of hominin control of fire at Gesher Benot Ya'aqov, Israel. *Science* 304:725–727.

Goren-Inbar, N., C. Feibel, K. L. Verosub, Y. Melamed, M. E. Kislev, E. Tchernov and I. Saragusti

2000 Pleistocene milestones on the out-of-Africa corridor at Gesher Benet Ya'aqov, Israel. *Science* 289:944–947.

Goren-Inbar, N., G. Sharon, Y. Melamed and M. E. Kislev

2002a Nuts, nut cracking, and pitted stones at Gesher Benot Ya'aqov, Israel. *Proceedings of the National Academy of Science USA* 99:2455–2460.

Goren-Inbar, N., E. Werker and C. Feibel

2002b *The Acheulian site of Gesher Benot Ya'aqov: the wood assemblage.* Oxbow Books, Oxford.

Goretsky, G. I. and I. K. Ivanova

1982 *Molodova I: unique mousterian settlement in the middle Dniestr.* NAUKA, Moscow.

Goring-Morris, A. N.

1987 *At the edge: terminal Pleistocene hunter-gatherers in the Negev and Sinai.* British Archaeological Reports International Series 361, Oxford.

1988 Trends in the spatial organization of Terminal Pleistocene hunter-gatherer occupations as viewed from the Negev and Sinai. *Paléorient* 14:231–244.

Goring-Morris, N. and A. Belfer-Cohen

1997 The articulation of cultural processes and Late Quaternary environmental changes in Cisjordan. *Paléorient* 23:71–93.

Gormley, A.

2004a   Art as process. In *Substance, memory, display: archaeology and art*, edited by C. Renfrew, C. Gosden and E. DeMarrais, pp. 131–151. McDonald Institute Monographs, Cambridge.

2004b   Re-imagining the body. Paper presented at the Winchester festival of art and the mind, Winchester 6 March.

Gosden, C.

1994   *Social being and time*. Blackwell, Oxford.

1999   *Anthropology and archaeology: a changing relationship*. Routledge, London.

Gosden, C. and Y. Marshall

1999   The cultural biography of objects. *World Archaeology* 31:169–178.

Gosselain, O. P.

1999   In pots we trust: the processing of clay and symbols in Sub-Saharan Africa. *Journal of Material Culture* 4:205–231.

Gowlett, J. A. J.

1991   Kilombe – review of an Acheulean site complex. In *Approaches to understanding early hominid life-ways in the African savannah*, edited by J. D. Clark, pp. 129–136. vol. UISPP 11 Kongress Mainz 1987. Dr Rudolf Habelt, Bonn.

1996   The frameworks of early hominid social systems: how many useful parameters of archaeological evidence can we isolate? In *The archaeology of human ancestry; power, sex and tradition*, edited by J. Steele and S. Shennan, pp. 135–183. Routledge, London.

1998   Unity and diversity in the Early Stone Age. In *Stone age archaeology: essays in honour of John Wymer*, edited by N. Ashton, F. Healy and P. Pettitt, pp. 59–66. Oxbow Monograph 102, Oxford.

2000   Apes, hominids and technology. In *New perspectives on primate evolution and behaviour*, edited by C. Harcourt, pp. 111–135. Linnean Society, London.

2005   Seeking the Palaeolithic individual in East Africa and Europe during the Lower-Middle Palaeolithic. In *The individual hominid in context: archaeological investigations of Lower and Middle Palaeolithic landscapes, locales and artefacts*, edited by C. Gamble and M. Porr, 50–67. Routledge, London.

Gowlett, J. A. J., J. W. K. Harris, D. Walton and B. A. Wood

1981   Early archaeological sites, hominid remains and traces of fire from Chesowanja, Kenya. *Nature* 294:125–129.

Gräslund, B.

1987   *The birth of prehistoric chronology: dating methods and dating systems in nineteenth-century Scandinavian archaeology*. Cambridge University Press, Cambridge.

Graves, P. M.

1991   New models and metaphors for the Neanderthal debate. *Current Anthropology* 32:513–541.

Greene, K.
  1999   V. Gordon Childe and the vocabulary of revolutionary change. *Antiquity*
         73:97—109.

Gregory, C. A.
  1982   *Gifts and commodities*. Academic Press, London.

Gregory, D.
  2004   *The colonial present*. Blackwell, Oxford.

Griaule, M.
  1965   *Conversations with Ogotemmeli: an introduction to Dogon religious ideas*.
         Oxford University Press, Oxford.

Grigor'ev, G. P.
  1993   The Kostenki-Aveevo Archaeological Culture and the Willendorf-Pavlov-
         Kostenki-Aveevo Cultural Unity. In *Interdisciplinary Contributions to
         Archaeology: From Kostenki to Clovis: Upper Paleolithic-Paleo-Indian
         Adaptations*, edited by O. Soffer and N. D. Praslov. Plenum Press,
         New York.

Grimes, R. L.
  1992   The life history of a mask. *The Drama Review* 36:61—77.

Grimm, L.
  2000   Apprentice flintknapping: relating material culture and social practice
         in the Upper Palaeolithic. In *Children and material culture*, edited by
         J. Sofaer Deverenski, pp. 53—71. Routledge, London.

Grønnow, B.
  1988   Prehistory in permafrost: investigations at the Saqqaq site, Qeqertasussuk,
         Disco Bay, West Greenland. *Journal of Danish Archaeology* 7:24—39.

Grønnow, B., M. Meldgaard and J. B. Nielsen
  1983   Aasivissuit — the great summer camp: archaeological, ethnographical and
         zoo-archaeological studies of a caribou-hunting site in West Greenland.
         Meddelelser om Grønland, Man & Society 5.

Grün, R., C. Stringer, F. McDermott, R. Nathan, N. Porat, S. Robertson, L. Taylor,
         G. Mortimer, S. Eggins and M. McCulloch
  2005   U-series and ESR analyses of bones and teeth relating to the human
         burials from Skhul. *Journal of Human Evolution* 49:316—334.

Gudeman, S.
  1986   *Economics as culture: models and metaphors of livelihood*. RKP,
         London.

Gvozdover, M. D.
  1989   The typology of female figurines of the Kostenki palaeolithic culture.
         Soviet Anthropology and Archaeology 27(4):32—94.
  1995   *Art of the mammoth hunters: the finds from Avdeevo*. Oxbow Monograph
         49, Oxford.

Hamilakis, Y., M. Pluciennik and S. Tarlow (editors)
  2002a *Thinking through the body: archaeologies of corporeality*. Kluwer
         Academic/Plenum, New York.

Hamilakis, Y., M. Pluciennik and S. Tarlow
  2002b Introduction: thinking through the body. In *Thinking through the body: archaeologies of corporeality*, pp. 1–21. Kluwer Academic/Plenum, New York.

Hammond, M.
  1982 The expulsion of the Neanderthals from human ancestry: Marcellin Boule and the social context of scientific research. *Social Studies of Science* 12:1–36.

Hampson, N.
  1968 *The Enlightenment, an evaluation of its assumptions, attitudes and values.* Penguin, Harmondsworth.

Härke, H.
  1992 All quiet on the western front? Paradigms, methods and approaches in West German archaeology. In *Archaeological theory in Europe: the last three decades*, edited by I. Hodder, pp. 187–222. Routledge, London.

Harris, D. R.
  1996a Introduction: themes and concepts in the study of early agriculture. In *The origins and spread of agriculture and pastoralism in Eurasia*, edited by D. R. Harris, pp. 1–9. UCL Press, London.
  1996b (editor) *The origins and spread of agriculture and pastoralism in Eurasia.* UCL Press, London.

Harris, D. R. and G. C. Hillman (editors)
  1989 *Foraging and farming: the evolution of plant exploitation.* Unwin Hyman, London.

Harris, R. A.
  2005 A handbook of rhetorical devices. *http://www.virtualsalt.com/rhetoric.htm.*

Hayden, B.
  1990 Nimrods, piscators, pluckers and planters. *Journal of Anthropological Archaeology* 9:31–69.
  2000 On territoriality and sedentism. *Current Anthropology* 41: 109–112.
  2001 Fabulous feasts: a prolegomenon to the importance of feasting. In *Feasts: archaeological and ethnographic perspectives on food, politics, and power*, edited by M. Dietler and B. Hayden, pp. 23–64. Smithsonian Institution Press, Washington.

Hemingway, M. F.
  1980 *The initial Magdalenian in France.* British Archaeological Reports International Series 90 i and ii, Oxford.

Henderson, Z.
  1992 The context of some Middle Stone Age hearths at Klasies River Shelter 1B: implications for understanding human behaviour. *South African Field Archaeology* 1:14–26.

Henry, D. O.
  1985 Preagricultural sedentism: the Natufian example. In *Prehistoric hunter-gatherers: the emergence of cultural complexity*, edited by T. D. Price and J. A. Brown, pp. 365–384. Academic Press, Orlando.

1995 *Prehistoric cultural ecology and evolution: insights from southern Jordan.* Plenum, New York.

Henshilwood, C. S., F. d'Errico, C. W. Marean, R. G. Milo and R. Yates

2001 An early bone tool industry from the Middle Stone Age, Blombos Cave, South Africa: implications for the origins of modern human behaviour, symbolism and language. *Journal of Human Evolution* 41:631−678.

Henshilwood, C. S., F. d'Errico, M. Vanhaeren, K. van Niekerk and Z. Jacobs

2004 Middle Stone Age shell beads from South Africa. *Science* 304:404.

Henshilwood, C. S., F. d'Errico, R. Yates, Z. Jacobs, C. Tribolo, G. Duller, N. Mercier, J. Sealy, H. Valladas, I. Watts and A. G. Wintle

2002 Emergence of modern human behaviour: Middle Stone Age engravings from South Africa. *Science* 295:1278−1280.

Henshilwood, C. S. and C. W. Marean

2003 The origin of modern human behaviour: critique of the models and their test implications. *Current Anthropology* 44 : 627−651.

Henshilwood, C. S. and J. Sealy

1997 Bone artefacts from the Middle Stone Age at Blombos Cave, Southern Cape, South Africa. *Curent Anthropology* 38:890−895.

Henshilwood, C. S., J. C. Sealy, R. Yates, K. Cruz-Uribe, P. Goldberg, F. E. Grine, R. G. Klein, C. Poggenpoel, K. van Niekerk and I. Watts

2001 Blombos Cave, Southern Cape, South Africa: preliminary report on the 1992−1999 excavations of the Middle Stone Age levels. *Journal of Archaeological Science* 28:421−448.

Hespos, S. J. and E. S. Spelke

2004 Conceptual precursors to language. *Nature* 430:453−456.

Higgs, E. S. and M. R. Jarman

1969 The origins of agriculture: a reconsideration. *Antiquity* 43:31−41.

1972 The origins of animal and plant husbandry. In *Papers in economic prehistory*, edited by E. S. Higgs, pp. 3−13. Cambridge University Press, Cambridge.

Hill, C.

1986 The word 'revolution' in seventeenth-century England. In *For Veronica Wedgewood These: studies in Seventeenth-century history*, edited by R. Ollard and P. Tudor-Craig, pp. 134−151, Collins, London.

Hinde, R. A.

1976 Interactions, relationships and social structure. *Man* 11:1−17.

Hockett, C. F. and R. Ascher

1964 The human revolution. *Current Anthropology* 5:135−168.

Hodder, I.

1990 *The domestication of Europe: structure and contingency in Neolithic societies.* Blackwell, Oxford.

2001 Symbolism and the origins of agriculture in the Near East. *Cambridge Archaeological Journal* 11:107−112.

Hoffecker, J. F.
  2002   *Desolate landscapes: ice-age settlement in Eastern Europe*. Rutgers University Press, New Brunswick.

Holdaway, S. and N. Stern
  2004   *A record in stone: the study of Australia's flaked stone artefacts*. Victoria Museum, Melbourne.

Hollis, M.
  1985   Of masks and men. In *The category of the person: anthropology, philosophy, history*, edited by M. Carrithers, S. Collins and S. Lukes, pp. 217–233. Cambridge University Press, Cambridge.

Hoskins, J.
  1998   *Biographical objects: how things tell the story of people's lives*. Routledge, New York.

Howell, F. C.
  1965   *Early man*. Time Life Books, London.

Howells, W. W.
  1967   *Mankind in the making: the story of human evolution*. Mercury Books, London.

Hublin, J.-J.
  1984   The fossil man from Salzgitter Lebenstedt (FRD) and its place in human evolution during the Pleistocene in Europe. *Zeitschrift für Morphologie und Anthropologie* 75:45–56.

Hugdahl, F. P.
  1999   Poststructuralism: Derrida and Foucault. In *The Pimlico History of Western Philosophy*, edited by R. H. Popkin, pp. 737–744. Pimlico, London.

Hurcombe, L.
  1995   Our engendered species. *Antiquity* 69:87–100.

Imrie, R.
  2003   Architects' conceptions of the human body. *Environment and Planning D: Society and Space* 21:47–65.

Ingold, T.
  1993a   'People like us'. The concept of the anatomically modern human. Paper presented at the Pithecanthropus Centennial Congress, Leiden, the Netherlands.
  1993b   The temporality of the landscape. *World Archaeology* 25(2):152–173.
  1999   Comment on Bird-David. *Current Anthropology* 40(Supplement):82–83.
  2000   *The perception of the environment: essays in livelihood, dwelling and skill*. Routledge, London.
  2003   Comment on Proctor. *Current Anthropology* 44:232.

Irwin, G.
  1992   *The prehistoric exploration and colonisation of the Pacific*. Cambridge University Press, Cambridge.

Isaac, B. (editor)
  1990   *Change and continuity: The Hall of the North American Indian.* Peabody
         Museum Press, Cambridge, MA.

Isaac, G.
  1977   *Olorgesailie: archaeological studies of a Middle Pleistocene lake basin.*
         University of Chicago Press, Chicago.
  1978   The food sharing behaviour of proto-human hominids. *Scientific
         American* 238:90–108.
  1989   *The archaeology of human origins; papers by Glynn Isaac edited by
         Barbara Isaac.* Cambridge University Press, Cambridge.

Ivanova, I. K. and S. M. Tseitlin (editors)
  1987   *The multilayered Palaeolithic site of Molodova V. Stone Age men and
         environment.* NAUKA, Moscow.

James, S. R.
  1989   Hominid use of fire in the Lower and Middle Pleistocene. *Current
         Anthropology* 30:1–26.

James, W.
  2003   *The ceremonial animal: a new portrait of anthropology.* Oxford University
         Press, Oxford.

James, W. and N. J. Allen (editors)
  1998   *Marcel Mauss: a centenary tribute.* Berghahn Books, New York.

Janik, L.
  2000   The construction of the individual among North European fisher-
         gatherer-hunters in the Early and Mid-Holocene. In *Children and
         material culture*, edited by J. Sofaer Deverenski, pp. 117–130.
         Routledge, London.

Jaubert, J., M. Lorblanchet, H. Laville, R. Slott-Moller, A. Turq and J. Brugal
  1990   *Les Chasseurs d'Aurochs de La Borde* 27. Documents d'Archéologie
         Française, Paris.

Jelinek, A. J.
  1990   The Amudian in the context of of the Mugharan tradition at the Tabun
         Cave (Mount Carmel), Israel. In *The emergence of modern humans*,
         edited by P. Mellars, pp. 81–90. Edinburgh University Press, Edinburgh.

Jerison, H.
  1982   The evolution of biological intelligence. In *Handbook of human
         intelligence*, edited by R. J. Sternberg, pp. 723–792. Cambridge
         University Press, Cambridge.

Jochim, M. A.
  1976   *Hunter-Gatherer Settlement and Subsistence.* Academic Press, New York.
  1981   *Strategies for survival.* Academic Press, New York.

Johanson, D. C. and M. Edey
  1981   *Lucy: the Beginnings of Mankind.* Simon and Schuster, New York.

Johanson, D. C. and B. Edgar
  1996   *From Lucy to language.* Simon and Schuster, New York.

Johnson, A. W. and T. Earle
　　1987　*The evolution of human societies.* Stanford University Press, Stanford.
Johnson, G. A.
　　1978　Information sources and the development of decision-making organiza-
　　　　　tions. In *Social archeology: beyond subsistence and dating*, pp. 87—111.
　　　　　Academic Press, New York.
　　1982　Organizational structure and scalar stress. In *Theory and Explanation
　　　　　in Archaeology: the Southampton Conference*, edited by C. Renfrew,
　　　　　M. Rowlands and B. Segraves, pp. 389—422. Academic Press, New York.
Jones, A.
　　2002　*Archaeological theory and scientific practice.* Cambridge University Press,
　　　　　Cambridge.
Jones, A. and C. Richards
　　2003　Animals into ancestors: domestication, food and identity in Late
　　　　　Neolithic Orkney. In *Food, culture and identity in the Neolithic and
　　　　　Early Bronze Age*, edited by M. Parker-Pearson, pp. 45—52. British
　　　　　Archaeological Reports International Series 1117, Oxford.
Jones, P. R.
　　1994　Results of experimental work in relation to the stone industries of
　　　　　Olduvai Gorge. In *Olduvai Gorge Volume 5; excavations in Beds III, IV
　　　　　and the Masek Beds, 1968—71*, edited by M. D. Leakey and D. A. Roe,
　　　　　pp. 254—298. Cambridge University Press, Cambridge.
Jones, R. (editor)
　　1985　*Archaeological Research in Kakadu National Park.* 13. Commonwealth
　　　　　of Australia., Canberra.
Jones, R. and N. White
　　1988　Point blank: stone tool manufacture at the Ngilipitji Quarry, Arnhem
　　　　　Land 1981. In *Archaeology with Ethnography: an Australian perspective*,
　　　　　edited by B. Meehan and R. Jones, pp. 51—87. Department of Prehistory
　　　　　RSPacS, Australian National University, Canberra.
Jones, S.
　　1997　*The archaeology of ethnicity: constructing identities in the past and present.*
　　　　　Routledge, London.
Julien, M.
　　1992　Du fossile directeur à la chaîne opératoire. In *La Préhistoire dans le
　　　　　monde: nouvelle édition de La Préhistoire d'André Leroi-Gourhan*, edited
　　　　　by J. Garanger, pp. 163—193. Nouvelle Clio, Paris.
Kaufman, D.
　　1992　Hunter-gatherers of the Levantine Epipalaeolithic: the socio-
　　　　　ecological origins of sedentism. *Journal of Mediterranean Archaeology*
　　　　　5:165—201.
Keeley, L. H.
　　1980　*Experimental determination of stone tool use: a microwear analysis.*
　　　　　University of Chicago Press, Chicago.

Keep, J.
2005   Pots not pills. *Ceramic Review* 211:30–1. http://www.jkpottery. freeserve.co.uk.

Kelly, R.
1995   *The foraging spectrum: diversity in hunter-gatherer lifeways.* Smithsonian Institution Press, Washington and London.

Kirch, P. V.
1997   *The Lapita peoples.* Blackwell, Oxford.

Klein, R. G.
1969   *Man and culture in the Late Pleistocene: a case study.* Chandler, San Francisco.
1973   *Ice-age hunters of the Ukraine.* University of Chicago Press, Chicago.
1995   Anatomy, behavior, and modern human origins. *Journal of World Prehistory* 9:167–198.

Klejn, L. S.
1999   Gustaf Kossinna. In *Encyclopedia of Archaeology: The great archaeologists,* edited by T. Murray, pp. 233–246. ABC-Clio, Santa Barbara.

Klima, B.
1963   *Dolní Vestonice. V'yzkum táboriste lovcù mamutù v letech 1947–1952.* Academia, Prague.
1995   *Dolní Vestonice II.* ERAUL, Liège.

Knappett, C.
2005   *Thinking through material culture: an interdisciplinary perspective.* University of Pennsylvania Press, Pittsburgh.
2006   Beyond skin: layering and networking in art and archaeology. *Cambridge Archaeological Journal* 16:239–251.

Knecht, H. (editor)
1997   *Projectile technology.* Plenum, New York.

Knight, C.
1983   Lévi-Strauss and the dragon: Mythologiques reconsidered in the light of an Australian Aboriginal myth. *Man* 18:21–50.
1991   *Blood relations: menstruation and the origins of culture.* Yale University Press, New Haven.
1998   Ritual/speech coevolution: a solution to the problem of deception. In *Approaches to the evolution of language: social and cognitive bases,* edited by J. R. Hurford, M. Studdert-Kennedy and C. Knight, pp. 68–91. Cambridge University Press, Cambridge.

Kolen, J.
1999   Hominids without homes: on the nature of Middle Palaeolithic settlement in Europe. In *The Middle Palaeolithic occupation of Europe,* edited by W. Roebroeks and C. Gamble, pp. 139–175. University of Leiden and European Science Foundation, Leiden.

Kopytoff, I.

1986   The cultural biography of things: commoditization as process. In *The social life of things: commodities in cultural perspective*, edited by A. Appadurai, pp. 64–91. Cambridge University Press, Cambridge.

Kuhn, S. L.

1992   On planning and curated technologies in the Middle Palaeolithic. *Journal of Anthropological Research* 48:185–214.

1995   *Mousterian lithic technology: an ecological perspective*. Princeton University Press, Princeton.

Kuhn, T. S.

1962   *The structure of scientific revolutions*. University of Chicago Press, Chicago.

Kuijt, I.

1996   Negotiating equality through ritual: a consideration of Late Natufian and Prepottery Neolithic A period mortuary practices. *Journal of Anthropological Archaeology* 15:313–336.

2000   People and space in early agricultural villages: exploring daily lives, community size, and architecture in the Late Pre-pottery Neolithic. *Journal of Anthropological Archaeology* 19:75–102.

La Fontaine, J. S.

1985   Person and individual: some anthropological reflections. In *The category of the person: anthropology, philosophy, history*, edited by M. Carrithers, S. Collins and S. Lukes, pp. 123–140. Cambridge University Press, Cambridge.

Lahr, M. M. and R. A. Foley

1994   Multiple dispersals and modern human origins. *Evolutionary Anthropology* 3:48–60.

1998   Towards a theory of modern human origins: geography, demography, and diversity in recent human evolution. *Yearbook of Physical Anthropology* 41:137–176.

Lakoff, G. and M. Johnson

1980   *Metaphors we live by*. University of Chicago Press, Chicago.

Lambek, M. and A. Strathern (editors)

1998   *Bodies and persons: comparative perspectives from Africa and Melanesia*. Cambridge University Press, Cambridge.

Landau, M.

1986   Trespassing in scientific narrative: Grafton Elliot Smith and the temple of doom. In *Narrative psychology: the storied nature of human conduct*, edited by T. R. Sarbin, pp. 45–64. Praeger, New York.

1991   *Narratives of human evolution*. Yale University Press, New Haven.

Latour, B.
  1993   Ethnography of a 'high-tech' case: about Aramis. In *Technological choices: transformations in material cultures since the Neolithic*, edited by P. Lemonnier, pp. 372–398. Routledge, London.

Latour, B. and S. C. Strum
  1986   Human social origins: Oh please, tell us another story. *Journal of Social Biological Structure* 9:169–187.

Leach, E.
  1973   Concluding address. In *The Explanation of Culture Change*, edited by C. Renfrew, pp. 761–777. Duckworth, London.

Leach, H. M.
  2003   Human domestication reconsidered. *Current Anthropology* 44:349–368.

Leakey, M. D.
  1971   *Olduvai Gorge: excavations in Beds I and II 1960–1963*. Cambridge University Press, Cambridge.

Leakey, R., K. W. Butzer and M. Day
  1969   Early Homo sapiens remains from the Omo River region of south-west Ethiopia. *Nature* 222:1132–1138.

Lemonnier, P.
  1993   Introduction. In *Technological choices: transformations in material cultures since the Neolithic*, edited by P. Lemonnier, pp. 1–35. Routledge, London.

Le Mort, F. and D. Gambier
  1992   Diversité du traitment des os humains au Magdalénien: un exemple particulier le cas du gisement du Placard (Charente). In *Le peuplement Magdalénien*, edited by CTHS, pp. 29–40. Actes du Colloque de Chancelade 10–15 Octobre 1988, Paris.

Leroi-Gourhan, A.
  1957   *Prehistoric man*. Philosophical Library, New York.
  1968   *The art of prehistoric man in western Europe*. Thames and Hudson, London.
  1993   *Gesture and speech*. MIT Press, Cambridge.

Levinson, S. C.
  1995   Interactional biases in human thinking. In *Social intelligence and interaction: expressions and implications of the social bias in human intelligence*, edited by E. N. Goody, pp. 221–260. Cambridge University Press, Cambridge.

Lévi-Strauss, C.
  1966a   Introduction to the Raw and the Cooked. In *Structuralism*, edited by J. Ehrmann. Yale French Studies, Princeton.
  1966b   *The savage mind*. University of Chicago Press, Chicago.
  1969   *The elementary structures of kinship*. Beacon Press, Boston.

Lévêque, F., A. M. Backer and M. Gilbaud
    1993   *Context of a Late Neanderthal: implications of multidisciplinary research for the transition to Upper Paleolithic adaptations at Saint-Césaire, Charente-Maritime, France.* Monographs in World Archaeology 16. Prehistory Press, Madison (Wisconsin).

Lewis-Williams, D.
    2003   *The mind in the cave.* Thames & Hudson, London.

Lienhardt, G.
    1985   Self: public, private. Some African representations. In *The category of the person: anthropology, philosophy, history*, edited by M. Carrithers, S. Collins and S. Lukes, pp. 141–155. Cambridge University Press, Cambridge.

Linden, E.
    1976   *Apes, men and language.* Penguin Books, Harmondsworth.

Lindly, J. and G. A. Clark
    1990   Symbolism and modern human origins. *Current Anthropology* 31: 233–240.

Linnaeus, C.
    1800   *A General System of Nature (Translated by W. Turton from the last edition of the Systema Naturae published by Gmelin).* Lackington, Allen and Co., London.

LiPuma, E.
    1998   Modernity and forms of personhood in Melanesia. In *Bodies and persons: comparative perspectives from Africa and Melanesia*, edited by M. Lambek and A. Strathern, pp. 53–79. Cambridge University Press, Cambridge.

Lourandos, H.
    1997   *Continent of hunter-gatherers: new perspectives in Australian prehistory.* Cambridge University Press, Cambridge.

Lovejoy, C. O.
    1981   The origin of man. *Science* 211:341–350.

Lubbock, J.
    1865   *Pre-Historic Times, as illustrated by Ancient Remains and the Manners and Customs of Modern Savages.* Williams and Norgate, London.

Lyman, R. L.
    1994   *Vertebrate taphonomy.* Cambridge University Press, Cambridge.

Madsen, B. and N. Goren-Inbar
    2004   Acheulian giant core technology and beyond: an archaeological and experimental case study. *Eurasian Prehistory* 2:3–52.

Malafouris, L.
    2004.   The cognitive basis of material engagement: where brain, body and culture conflate. In *Rethinking materiality: the engaagement of mind with the material world*, edited by E. DeMarrais, C. Gosden and C. Renfrew, pp. 53–62. McDonald Institute of Archaeological Research: Cambridge.

Mania, D.
1990 *Auf den Spuren des Urmenschen: Die Funde von Bilzingsleben*. Theiss, Berlin.

Mania, D. and U. Mania
2005 The natural and socio-cultural environment of Homo erectus at Bilzingsleben, Germany. In *The individual hominid in context: archaeological investigations of Lower and Middle Palaeolithic landscapes, locales and artefacts*, edited by C. Gamble and M. Porr, pp. 98–114. Routledge, London.

Mania, D. and V. Toepfer
1973 *Königsaue*. Veröffentlichungen des Landesmuseums für Vorgeschichte in Halle Band 26, Berlin.

Manley, J.
1989 *Atlas of prehistoric Britain*. Phaidon, Oxford.

Marean, C. W.
1998 A critique of the evidence for scavenging by Neanderthals and early modern humans: new data from Kobeh Cave (Zagros Mountains, Iran) and Die Kelders Cave 1 Layer 10 (South Africa). *Journal of Human Evolution* 35:111–136.

Marean, C. W. and Z. Assefa
1999 Zooarchaeological evidence for the faunal exploitation behaviour of Neanderthals and early modern humans. *Evolutionary Anthropology* 8:22–37.

Marks, A. E.
1983 The Middle to Upper Palaeolithic transition in the Levant. *Advances in World Archaeology* 2:51–98.

Marks, A. E. and D. A. Freidel
1977 Prehistoric settlement patterns in the Avdat/Aqev area. In *Prehistory and palaeoenvironments in the central Negev, Israel. Volume 2 The Avdat/Aqev area, Part 2 and the Har Harif*, edited by A. E. Marks, pp. 131–159. Southern Methodist University, Dallas.

Marks, A. E., H. Hietala and J. K. Williams
2001 Tool standardization in the Middle and Upper Palaeolithic: a closer look. *Cambridge Archaeological Journal* 11:17–44.

Marks, A. E. and T. R. Scott
1976 Abu Salem: type site of the Harifian industry of the southern Levant. *Journal of Field Archaeology* 3:43–60.

Marks, J.
2002 *What it means to be 98% chimpanzee: apes, people, and their genes*. University of California Press, Berkeley.

Marlowe, F.
2005 Hunter-gatherers and human evolution. *Evolutionary Anthropology* 14:54–67.

Marshack, A.
1990   Early hominid symbol and the evolution of the human capacity. In *The emergence of modern humans: an archaeological perspective*, edited by P. Mellars, pp. 457–499. Edinburgh University Press, Edinburgh.

Marshall, G., C. S. Gamble, D. Roe and D. Dupplaw
2002   Lower Palaeolithic technology, raw material and population ecology. Archaeological Data Service, AHDS.http://ads.ahds.ac.uk/catalogue/specColl/bifaces/index.cfm, York.

Martin, P. S.
1973   The discovery of America. *Science* 179:969–974.

Maryanski, A. and J. H. Turner
1992   *The social cage: human nature and the evolution of society.* Stanford University Press, Stanford.

Mason, S., J. Hather and G. Hillman
1994   Preliminary investigation of the plant macro-remains from Dolní Vestonice II and its implications for the role of plant foods in Palaeolithic and Mesolithic Europe. *Antiquity* 68:48–57.

Mattelart, A.
1999   Mapping modernity: Utopia and communications networks. In *Mappings*, edited by D. Cosgrove, pp. 169–192. Reaktion Books, London.

Mauss, M.
(1936) 1979 Body techniques. In *Sociology and Psychology: essays. Translated by Ben Brewster*, pp. 97–123. Routledge and Kegan Paul, London.
1967   *The gift.* W.W. Norton, New York.
1979a   A category of the human mind: the notion of person, the notion of 'self'. In *Sociology and Psychology: essays. Translated by Ben Brewster*, pp. 59–94. Routledge and Kegan Paul, London.
1979b   *Sociology and Psychology: essays. Translated by Ben Brewster.* Routledge and Kegan Paul, London.

Mayr, E.
1950   Taxonomic categories in fossil hominids. *Cold Spring Harbor Symposium on Quantitative Biology* 15:109–117.

McBrearty, S. and A. S. Brooks
2000   The revolution that wasn't: a new interpretation of the origin of modern humans. *Journal of Human Evolution* 39:453–563.

McBryde, I.
1978   Wil-im-ee Moor-ring: or, where do axes come from? *Mankind* 11:354–382.
1988   Goods from another country: exchange networks and the people of the Lake Eyre basin. In *Archaeology to 1788*, edited by J. Mulvaney and P. White, pp. 253–273. Waddon Associates, Sydney.
1997   'The landscape is a series of stories'. Grindstones, quarries and exchange in aboriginal Australia: a case study from the Cooper/Lake Eyre Basin, Australia. In *Siliceous rocks and culture: Proceedings of the VI International Flint Symposium*, edited by A. Ramos-Millán and M. A. Bustillo. Madrid University, Granada.

McBurney, C. B. M.
   1967   *The Haua Fteah (Cyrenaica) and the stone age of the south east Mediterranean.* Cambridge University Press, Cambridge.

McDougall, I., F. H. Brown and J. G. Fleagle
   2005   Stratigraphic placement and age of modern humans from Kibish, Ethiopia. *Nature* 433:733−736.

McGhee, R.
   1996   *Ancient people of the Arctic.* University of British Columbia Press, Vancouver.

McGrew, W. C.
   1992   *Chimpanzee material culture: implications for human evolution.* Cambridge University Press, Cambridge.

McGuire, R. H.
   1992   *A Marxist archaeology.* Academic Press, San Diego.

McHenry, H. M.
   1988   New estimates of body weight in early hominids and their significance to encephalization and megadontia in 'robust' Australopithecines. In *The evolutionary history of the robust Australopithecines,* edited by F. E. Grine, pp. 133−148. Aldine, New York.

McNabb, J., F. Binyon and L. Hazelwood
   2004   The large cutting tools from the South African Acheulean and the question of social traditions. *Current Anthropology* 45:653−677.

McNairn, B.
   1980   *Method and theory of V. Gordon Childe.* Edinburgh University Press, Edinburgh.

Meek, R. L. (editor)
   1973   *Turgot: On Progress, Sociology and Economics.* Cambridge University Press, Cambridge.
   1976   *Social science and the ignoble savage.* Cambridge University Press, Cambridge.

Mellars, P. A.
   1973   The character of the Middle-Upper Palaeolithic transition in south-west France. In *The Explanation of Culture Change: Models in prehistory,* edited by C. Renfrew, pp. 255−276. Duckworth, London.
   1990   Comment on Lindly, and Clark: Symbolism and modern human origins. *Current Anthropology* 31:245−246.
   1996   *The Neanderthal legacy: an archaeological perspective from Western Europe.* Princeton University Press, Princeton.
   2005   The impossible coincidence: a single-species model for the origins of modern human behaviour in Europe. *Evolutionary Anthropology* 14:12−27.

Mellars, P. A. and C. Stringer (editors)
   1989   *The Human Revolution: behavioural and biological perspectives on the origins of modern humans.* Edinburgh University Press, Edinburgh.

Meltzer, D. J.
   1993 *Search for the first Americans.* Smithsonian Books, Washington.
Merleau-Ponty, M.
   1962 *Phenomenology of perception.* Routledge and Kegan Paul, London.
Merrick, H. V. and F. H. Brown
   1984 Obsidian sources and patterns of source utilization in Kenya and
         northern Tanzania: some initial findings. *African Archaeological Review*
         2:129–152.
Meskell, L.
   1999 *Archaeologies of social life.* Blackwells, Oxford.
   2004 Divine things. In *Rethinking materiality: the engagement of mind
         with the material world,* edited by E. DeMarrais, C. Gosden and
         C. Renfrew, pp. 249–259. McDonald Institute of Archaeological
         Research, Cambridge.
Meskell, L. and R. Preucell (editors)
   2004 *A companion to social archaeology.* Blackwell, Oxford.
Milardo, R. M.
   1992 Comparative methods for delineating social networks. *Journal of Social
         and Personal Relationships* 9:447–61.
Miller, D.
   1995a Consumption as the vanguard of history: a polemic by way of an
         introduction. In *Acknowledging Consumption: a review of new studies,*
         edited by D. Miller, pp. 1–57. Routledge, London.
   1995b Consumption studies as the transformation of anthropology. In *Acknowl-
         edging Consumption: a review of new studies,* edited by D. Miller,
         pp. 264–295. Routledge, London.
Mitchell, P.
   2002 *The archaeology of Southern Africa.* Cambridge University Press,
         Cambridge.
Mithen, S.
   1990 *Thoughtful foragers.* Cambridge University Press, Cambridge.
   1993 Individuals, groups and the Palaeolithic record: a reply to Clark. *Pro-
         ceedings of the Prehistoric Society* 59:393–398.
   1996 *The prehistory of the mind.* Thames and Hudson, London.
   2005 *The singing Neanderthal: the origins of music, language, mind and body.*
         Weidenfeld and Nicolson, London.
Montagu, A.
   1965 *The human revolution.* The World Publishing Company, Cleveland and
         New York.
   1972 *Statement on race.* 3rd edition. Oxford University Press, New York.
Moore, A. M. T.
   1995 The inception of potting in western Asia and its impact on economy
         and society. In *The emergence of pottery: technology and innovation in
         ancient societies,* edited by W. K. Barnett and J. W. Hoopes, pp. 39–53.
         Smithsonian Institution Press, Washington.

Moore, A. M. T. and G. C. Hillman

1992 The Pleistocene to Holocene transition and human economy in Southwest Asia: the impact of the Younger Dryas. *American Antiquity* 57:482−494.

Moore, A. M. T., G. Hillman and A. J. Legge (editors)

2000 *Village on the Euphrates: from foraging to farming at Abu Hureyra*. Oxford University Press, Oxford.

Moore, F. C. T.

1969 *The Observation of Savage Peoples by Joseph-Marie Degérando (1800)*. Routledge & Kegan Paul, London.

Moore, H.

1995 The problems of origins: poststructuralism and beyond. In *Interpreting archaeology; finding meaning in the past*, edited by I. Hodder, M. Shanks, A. Alexandri, V. Buchli, J. Carman, J. Last and G. Lucas, pp. 51−53. Routledge, London.

Morgan, L. H.

1877 *Ancient Society*. World Publishing, New York.

1881 *Houses and house-life of the American Aborigines*. Volume IV of Contributions to North American Ethnology. Government printing Office, Washington.

Morphy, H.

1989 From dull to brilliant: the aesthetics of spiritual power among the Yolngu. *Man* 24:21−40.

Morris, E. L.

1994 The pottery: In Excavations at a Late Bronze Age Settlement in the Upper Thames Valley at Shorncote Quarry near Cirencester, 1992. *Transactions of the Bristol and Gloucestershire Archaeological Society* CXII:17−57.

Morwood, M. J., R. P. Soejono, R. G. Roberts, T. Sutikna, C. S. M. Turney, K. E. Westaway, W. J. Rink, J.-X. Zhao, G. D. van den Bergh, R. A. Due, D. R. Hobbs, M. W. Moore, M. I. Bird and L. K. Fifield

2004 Archaeology and age of a new hominin from Flores in eastern Indonesia. *Nature* 431:1087−1091.

Moser, J.

1999 Recent cave dwellings in Southeast Asia: homes, domiciles or refuges? Explanation and interpretation of prehistoric archaeological structures. In *Ethno-analogy and the reconstruction of prehistoric artefact use and production*, edited by L. R. Owen and M. Porr, pp. 275−284. vol. Urgeschichtliche Materialhefte 14. Mo Vince Verlag, Tübingen.

Moser, S.

1992 The visual language of archaeology: a case study of the Neanderthals. *Antiquity* 66:831−844.

1998 *Ancestral images: the iconography of human origins*. Alan Sutton, Stroud.

Moser, S. and C. Gamble
   1997   Revolutionary images: the iconic vocabulary for representing human antiquity. In *The cultural life of images: visual representation in archaeology*, edited by B. L. Molyneaux, pp. 184–212. Routledge, London.

Moura, A. C. and P. C. Lee
   2004   Capuchin stone tool use in Caatinga dry forest. *Science* 5703:1909.

Movius, H. L.
   1966   The hearths of the Upper Perigordian and Aurignacian horizons at the Abri Pataud, Les Eyzies (Dordogne), and their possible significance. *American Anthropologist* 68:296–325.

Muheisin, M.
   1985   L'Épipaléolithique dans le gisement de Karaneh IV. *Paléorient* 11: 149–160.

Mulvaney, D. J.
   1976   'The chain of connection': the material evidence. In *Tribes and Boundaries in Australia*, edited by N. Peterson, pp. 72–94. AIAS, Canberra.

Mussi, M.
   1995   The earliest occupation of Europe: Italy. In *The earliest occupation of Europe*, edited by W. Roebroeks and T. v. Kolfschoten, pp. 27–49. University of Leiden and European Science Foundation, Leiden.
   2001   *Earliest Italy: an overview of the Italian Palaeolithic and Mesolithic*. Kluwer, New York.

Nadel, D.
   1994   Levantine Upper Palaeolithic-Early Epipalaeolithic burial customs: Ohalo II as a case study. *Paléorient* 20:113–122.
   2002   *Ohalo II − a 23,000 year old fisher-hunter-gatherers camp on the shore of the Sea of Galilee*. Hecht Museum, Haifa.
   2003   The Ohalo II brush huts and the dwelling structures of the Natufian and PPNA sites in the Jordan Valley. *Archaeology, Ethnology and Anthropology of Eurasia* 1:3448.

Nadel, D., I. Carmi and D. Segal
   1995   Radiocarbon dating of Ohalo II: archaeological and methodological implications. *Journal of Archaeological Science* 22:811–822.

Nitecki, M. H. and D. V. Nitecki (editors)
   1987   *The evolution of human hunting*. Plenum, New York.

Noble, W. and I. Davidson
   1996   *Human evolution, language and mind*. Cambridge University Press, Cambridge.

Oakley, K.
   1949   *Man the tool maker*. Natural History Museum, London.

O'Connell, J., K. Hawkes and N. G. Blurton Jones
   1999   Grandmothering and the evolution of *Homo erectus*. *Journal of Human Evolution* 36:461–485.

Odling-Smee, F. J.
  1993   Niche construction, evolution and culture. In *Companion encyclopedia
         of anthropology: humanity, culture and social life*, edited by T. Ingold,
         pp. 162–196.

Ortner, S. B.
  1973   On key symbols. *American Anthropologist* 75:1338–1346.

Owen, L. R.
  1988   *Blade and microblade technology. Selected assemblages from the North
         American Arctic and the Upper Paleolithic of Southwest Germany*. British
         Archaeological Reports International Series 441, Oxford.
  1996   Der Gerbrauch von Pflanzen im Jungpaläolithikum Mitteleuropas.
         Ethnographisch Archäologische Zeitschrift 37:119–146.

Owens, D. and B. Hayden
  1997   Prehistoric rites of passage: a comparative study of transegalitarian hunter-
         gatherers. *Journal of Anthropological Archaeology* 16:121–161.

Pagden, A.
  1986   *The fall of natural man: the American Indian and the origins of
         comparative ethnology*. Cambridge University Press, Cambridge.

Parker-Pearson, M.
  2004   Earth, wood and fire: materiality and Stonehenge. In *Soils, stones and
         symbols: cultural perceptions of the mineral world*, edited by N. Boivin and
         M. Owoc, pp. 71–90. UCL Press, London.

Parker-Pearson, M. and Ramilisonina
  1998   Stonehenge for the ancestors: the stones pass on the message. *Antiquity*
         72:308–326.

Parkington, J.
  1990   A critique of the consensus view on the age of Howieson's poort
         assemblages in South Africa. In *The emergence of modern humans: an
         archaeological perspective*, edited by P. Mellars, pp. 34–56. Edinburgh
         University Press, Edinburgh.

Parkington, J. and G. Mills
  1991   From space to place: the architecture and social organisation of Southern
         African mobile communities. In *Ethnoarchaeological approaches to
         mobile campsites: hunter-gatherer and pastoralist case studies*, edited
         by C. S. Gamble and W. A. Boismier, pp. 355–370. International
         Monographs in Prehistory, Ethnoarchaeological Series 1, Ann Arbor.

Pastoors, A.
  2001   *Die mittelpaläolithische Freilandstation von Salzgitter-Lebenstedt:
         Genese der Fundstelle und Systematik der Steinbearbeitung*. Salzgitter-
         Forschungen 3, Salzgitter.

Patrik, L. E.
  1985   Is there an archaeological record? In *Advances in Archaeological Method
         and Theory*, edited by M. B. Schiffer, pp. 27–62, vol. 8. Academic Press,
         New York.

Perlès, C.
1976   Le feu. In *La Préhistoire Française*, edited by H. deLumley, pp. 679–683. CNRS, Paris.

Perrot, J.
1966   Le gisement Natoufien de Mallaha (Eynan), Israël. *L'Anthropologie* 70:437–484.

Perrot, J. and D. Ladiray
1988   *Les hommes de Mallaha (Eynan) Israel, les sepulchures*. Memoires de Travaux du Centre de Recherche Française de Jerusalem, No. 7. Association Paléorient, Paris.

Pfaffenberger, B.
1988   Fetishised objects and humanised nature: towards an anthropology of technology. *Man* 23:236–252.
1992   Social anthropology of technology. *Annual Review of Anthropology* 21:491–516.

Pfeiffer, J. E.
1982   *The creative explosion*. Harper and Row, New York.

Pianka, E. R.
1978   *Evolutionary ecology*. 2nd edition. Harper and Row, New York.

Pichon, J.
1983   Parures natoufiennes en os de perdix. *Paléorient* 9:91–98.

Pigeot, N.
1987   *Magdaléniens d'Étiolles: économie de débitage et organisation sociale (l'unité d'habitation U5)* XXV supplement à *Gallia Préhistoire*. CNRS, Paris.
1990   Technical and social actors: flintknapping specialists at Magdalenian Étiolles. *Archaeological Review from Cambridge* 9:126–141.

Pike-Tay, A. and R. Cosgrove
2002   From reindeer to wallaby: recovering patterns of seasonality, mobility, and prey selection in the Palaeolithic Old World. *Journal of Archaeological Method and Theory* 9:101–146.

Pinker, S.
1997   *How the mind works*. Norton, New York.

Piperno, M.
1999   *Notarchirico: un sito del Pleistocene medio iniziale nel bacino di Venosa*. Edizioni Osanna, Venosa.

Pitt-Rivers, A. H. L. F.
1891   Typological museums. *Journal of the Society of Arts* 40:115–122.

Pitts, M. and M. Roberts
1997   *Fairweather Eden*. Century, London.

Pope, M.
2002   *The significance of biface rich assemblages: an examination of behavioural controls on lithic assemblage formation in the Lower Palaeolithic*. PhD thesis, Department of Archaeology, University of Southampton.

Pope, M. and M. Roberts
  2005   Observations on the relationship between Palaeolithic individuals
          and artefact scatters at the Middle Pleistocene site of Boxgrove, UK.
          In *The individual hominid in context: archaeological investigations of
          Lower and Middle Palaeolithic landscapes, locales and artefacts*,
          edited by C. Gamble and M. Porr, pp. 81–97. Routledge, London.

Poplin, F.
  1976   *Les grands vertébrés de Gönnersdorf. Fouilles 1968.* Gönnersdorf Band
          2, Wiesbaden.

Potts, R.
  1988   *Early hominid activities at Olduvai.* Aldine, New York.
  1991   Why the Oldowan? Plio-Pleistocene toolmaking and the transport of
          resources. *Journal of Anthropological Research* 47:153–176.
  1993   The hominid way of life. In *The Cambridge Encyclopedia of Human
          Evolution*, edited by S. Jones, R. Martin and D. Pilbeam, pp. 325–334.
          Cambridge University Press, Cambridge.

Potts, R., A. K. Behrensmeyer and P. Ditchfield
  1999   Palaeolandscape variation and early Pleistocene hominid activities:
          Members 1 and 7, Olorgesailie Formation, Kenya. *Journal of Human
          Evolution* 37:747–788.

Praslov, N. D.
  1993   Eine neue Frauenstatuette aus Kalkstein von Kostenki I 1 (Don,
          Russland). *Archäologisches Korrespondenzblatt* 23:165–173.

Praslov, N. D. and A. N. Rogachev (editors)
  1982   *Palaeolithic of the Kostenki-Borshevo area on the Don river, 1879–1979
          (In Russian).* NAUKA, Leningrad.

Price, T. D. and J. A. Brown (editors)
  1985   *Prehistoric hunters and gatherers: the emergence of cultural complexity.*
          Academic Press, New York.

Price, T. D. and A. B. Gebauer (editors)
  1995   *Last hunters – first farmers: New perspectives on the prehistoric transition
          to agriculture.* School of American Research, Santa Fe.

Proctor, R. N.
  2003   Three roots of human recency: molecular anthropology, the refigured
          Acheulean, and the UNESCO response to Auschwitz. *Current
          Anthropology* 44:213–239.

Quintero, L. A. and P. J. Wilke
  1995   Evolution and economic significance of naviform cores-and-blade
          technology in the southern Levant. *Paléorient* 21:17–34.

Radovanovic, I.
  1996   *The iron gates Mesolithic.* International Monographs in prehistory.
          Archaeological Series 11, Ann Arbor.

Rainbird, P.
  1999   Entangled biographies. *World Archaeology* 31:214–224.

Raposo, L. and M. Santonja
  1995   The earliest occupation of Europe: the Iberian peninsula. In *The earliest occupation of Europe*, edited by W. Roebroeks and T. v. Kolfschoten, pp. 7–26. University of Leiden and European Science Foundation, Leiden.

Renfrew, C.
  1972   *The emergence of civilisation: the Cyclades and the Aegean in the third millennium BC*. Methuen, London.

Renfrew, C. (editor)
  1973   *The explanation of culture change*. Duckworth, London.
  1996   The sapient behaviour paradox: how to test for potential? In *Modelling the early human mind*, edited by P. Mellars and K. Gibson, pp. 11–14. McDonald Institute for Archaeological Research, Cambridge.
  2001   Symbol before concept: material engagement and the early development of society. In *Archaeological theory today*, edited by I. Hodder, pp. 122–140. Polity Press, London.
  2003   *Figuring it out: What are we? Where do we come from? The parallel visions of artists and archaeologists*. Thames and Hudson, London.

Renfrew, C. and K. L. Cooke (editors)
  1979   *Transformations: mathematical approaches to culture change*. Academic Press, New York.

Renfrew, C., C. Gosden and E. DeMarrais (editors)
  2004   *Substance, memory, display: archaeology and art*. McDonald Institute Monographs, Cambridge.

Renssen, H., R. F. B. Isarin, D. Jacob, R. Podzun and J. Vandenberghe
  2001   Simulation of the Younger Dryas climate in Europe using a regional climate model nested in an AGCM: preliminary results. *Global and Planetary Change* 30:41–57.

Révillion, S. and A. Tuffreau (editors)
  1994   *Les industries laminaires au paléolithique moyen*. CNRS, Paris.

Rigaud, J.-P. and J.-M. Geneste
  1988   L'utilisation de l'espace dans la Grotte Vaufrey. In *La Grotte Vaufrey: paléoenvironement, chronologieet, activités humaines*, edited by J.-P. Rigaud, pp. 593–611. vol. 19. Mémoires de la Société Préhistorique Française, Paris.

Rigaud, J.-P., J. F. Simek and G. Thierry
  1995   Mousterian fires from Grotte XVI (Dordogne, France). *Antiquity* 69:902–912.

Robb, J.
  2004   The extended artefact and the monumental economy: a methodology for material agency. In *Rethinking materiality: the engagement of mind with the material world*, edited by E. DeMarrais, C. Gosden and C. Renfrew, pp. 131–140. McDonald Institute of Archaeological Research, Cambridge.

Roberts, M. B. and S. A. Parfitt
1999   *Boxgrove: a Middle Pleistocene hominid site at Eartham Quarry, Boxgrove, West Sussex*. English Heritage, London.

Roberts, M. B., C. B. Stringer and S. A. Parfitt
1994   A hominid tibia from Middle Pleistocene sediments at Boxgrove, U.K. *Nature* 369:311–313.

Roberts, M. B., S. A. Parfitt, M. J. Pope and F. F. Wenban-Smith
1997   Boxgrove, West Sussex: Rescue excavations of a Lower Palaeolithic landsurface (Boxgrove project B, 1989–91). *Proceedings of the Prehistoric Society* 63:303–358.

Roberts, R. G., R. Jones and M. A. Smith
1990   Thermoluminescence dating of a 50 000 year old human occupation site in northern Australia. *Nature* 345:153–156.

Rocek, T. and O. Bar-Yosef (editors)
1998   *Seasonality and sedentism: archaeological perspectives from Old and New World sites*. Peabody Museum Bulletin 6. Peabody Museum of Archaeology and Ethnology, Cambridge, Massachusetts.

Rodseth, L., R. W. Wrangham, A. Harrigan and B. B. Smuts
1991   The human community as a primate society. *Current Anthropology* 32:221–254.

Roe, D. A.
1968   British Lower and Middle Palaeolithic handaxe groups. *Proceedings of the Prehistoric Society* 34:1–82.
1994   A metrical analysis of selected sets of handaxes and cleavers from Olduvai Gorge. In *Olduvai Gorge Volume* 5; *excavations in Beds III, IV and the Masek Beds, 1968–71*, edited by M. D. Leakey and D. A. Roe, pp. 146–234. Cambridge University Press, Cambridge.

Roebroeks, W., J. Kolen and E. Rensink
1988   Planning depth, anticipation and the organization of Middle Palaeolithic technology: the 'archaic natives' meet Eve's descendants. *Helinium* 28:17–34.

Roebroeks, W., M. Mussi, J. Svoboda and K. Fennema (editors)
2000   *Hunters of the golden age: the mid Upper Palaeolithic of Eurasia 30,000–20,000 BP*. European Science Foundation and University of Leiden, Leiden.

Rogachev, A. N.
1957   Étude des vestiges de la colonie paléolithique de la société d'Avdeevo, sur le Seim. In *Paléolithique et néolithique de l'U.R.S.S.*, edited by A. P. Okladnikov, pp. 114–167. Louis Jean, Gap.

Rolland, N.
1995   Levallois technique emergence: single or multiple? A review of the Euro-African record. In *The definition and interpretation of Levallois technology*, edited by H. Dibble and O. Bar-Yosef, pp. 333–359. Prehistory Press. Monographs in World Archaeology 23, Madison.

Roux, V.
1999   Ethnoarchaeology and the generation of referential models: the case of Harappan carnelian beads. In *Ethno-analogy and the reconstruction of prehistoric artefact use and production*, edited by L. R. Owen and M. Porr, pp. 153–169. vol. Urgeschichtliche Materialhefte 14. Mo Vince Verlag, Tübingen.

Roveland, B.
2000   Footprints in the clay: Upper Palaeolithic children in ritual and secular contexts. In *Children and material culture*, edited by J. Sofaer Deverenski, pp. 29–38. Routledge, London.

Rowlands, M. J.
2004   The materiality of sacred power. In *Rethinking materiality: the engagement of mind with the material world*, edited by E. DeMarrais, C. Gosden and C. Renfrew, pp. 197–203. McDonald Institute of Archaeological Research, Cambridge.

Runciman, W. G.
2005   Stone age sociology. *Journal of the Royal Anthropological Institute* 11:129–142.

Sahlins, M.
1972   *Stone age economics*. Tavistock, London.

Said, E. W.
1978   *Orientalism: western conceptions of the Orient*. Penguin Books, London.

Santonja, M. and A. Peréz-González
2001   Lithic artefacts from the lower levels of Ambrona (Spain) – taphonomic features. In *Proceedings of the 1st International Congress, The world of elephants*, edited by G. Cavarretta, P. Gioia, M. Mussi and M. R. Palombo, pp. 592–596. Consiglio Nazionale delle Richerche, Rome.

Santonja, M., N. Lopez-Martinez and A. Perez-Gonzalez
1980   Ocupaciones Achelenses en el Valle del Jarama. *Arqueologia y Paleoecologia* 1:1–352.

Santonja, M. and P. Villa
1990   The Lower Paleolithic of Spain and Portugal. *Journal of World Prehistory* 4(1):45–94.

Sauer, C. O.
1952   *Seeds, spades, hearths, and herds: the domestication of animals and foodstuffs*. MIT Press, Cambridge MA.

Schick, K. D. and N. Toth
1993   *Making silent stones speak: human evolution and the dawn of technology*. Simon and Schuster, New York.

Schiffer, M. B.
1987   *Formation processes of the archaeological record*. University of New Mexico Press, Albuquerque.

Schlanger, N.

1994   Mindful technology: unleashing the chaîne opératoire for an archaeology of mind. In *The ancient mind: elements of cognitive archaeology*, edited by C. Renfrew and E. Zubrow, pp. 143–151. Cambridge University Press, Cambridge.

1996   Understanding Levallois: lithic technology, and cognitive archaeology. *Cambridge Archaeological Journal* 6:231–254.

2005   The chaîne opératoire. In *Archaeology: the key concepts*, edited by C. Renfrew and P. Bahn, pp. 25–31. Routledge, London.

Schmidt, K.

2006   *Sie bauten die ersten Tempel. Das rätselhafte Heiligtum der Steinzeitjäger*. Beck, Munich.

Schrire, C. (editor)

1984   *Past and present in hunter-gatherer studies*. Academic Press, London.

Scott, K.

1980   Two hunting episodes of Middle Palaeolithic age at La Cotte de Saint-Brelade Jersey (Channel Islands). *World Archaeology* 12:137–152.

1986   The bone assemblage from layers 3 and 6. In *La Cotte de St. Brelade 1961–1978. Excavations by C.B.M. McBurney*, edited by P. Callow and J. M. Cornford, pp. 159–184. Geo Books, Norwich.

Semaw, S., P. Renne, J. W. K. Harris, C. S. Feibel, R. L. Bernor, N. Fesseha and K. Mowbray

1997   2.5 million-year-old stone tools from Gona, Ethiopia. *Nature* 385(6614):333–336.

Shennan, S. J.

2000   Population, culture history, and the dynamics of culture change. *Current Anthropology* 41:811–835.

2002   *Genes, memes, and human history: Darwinian archaeology, and cultural evolution*. Thames and Hudson, London.

Sherratt, A.

1995   Reviving the grand narrative: archaeology and long-term change. *Journal of European Archaeology* 3:1–32.

1997a   Climatic cycles and behavioural revolutions: the emergence of modern humans and the beginning of farming. *Antiquity* 71:271–287.

1997b   *Economy and society in prehistoric Europe: changing perspectives*. Edinburgh University Press, Edinburgh.

Shipman, P. and J. Rose

1983   Evidence of butchery and hominid activitics at Torralba and Ambrona: an evaluation using microscopic techniques. *Journal of Archaeological Science* 10:465–474.

Simek, J.

1987   Spatial order and behavioural change in the French Palaeolithic. *Antiquity* 61:25–40.

Singer, R. and J. Wymer
    1982   *The Middle Stone Age at Klasies River Mouth in South Africa.* University of Chicago Press, Chicago.

Sklenár, K.
    1976   Palaeolithic and Mesolithic dwellings: problems of interpretation. *Památky Archeologické* 68:249–340.

Smith, E. A.
    1991   *Inujjuamiut foraging strategies: evolutionary ecology of an Arctic hunting economy.* Aldine de Gruyter, Hawthorne, N.Y.

Smith, G. E.
    1929   *The migrations of early culture.* Manchester University Press, Manchester.
    1930 (1934)   *Human history.* 2nd edition. Jonathan Cape, London.
    1933   *The diffusion of culture.* Watts, London.

Sofaer Deverenski, J.
    2000   Material culture shock: confronting expectations in the material culture of children. In *Children and material culture*, edited by J. Sofaer Deverenski, pp. 3–16. Routledge, London.

Soffer, O.
    1985   *The Upper Palaeolithic of the Central Russian Plain.* Academic Press, New York.
    1987   *Upper Palaeolithic connubia, refugia, and the archaeological record from Eastern Europe.* In *The pleistocene Old World: regional perspectives*, edited by O. Soffer, pp. 333–348. Plenum, New York.

Soffer, O., J. M. Adovasio and D. C. Hyland
    2000   The 'Venus' figurines: textiles, basketry, gender, and status in the Upper Palaeolithic. *Current Anthropology* 41:511–537.

Soffer, O., J. M. Adovasio, D. C. Hyland, B. Klima and J. Svoboda
    1998   Perishable technologies and the genesis of the Eastern Gravettian. *Anthropologie* 36:43–68.

Soffer, O. and N. D. Praslov (editors)
    1993   *From Kostenki to Clovis: Upper Palaeolithic–Paleo-Indian adaptations.* Plenum, New York.

Soffer, O., P. Vandiver, B. Klima and J. Svoboda
    1993   The pyrotechnology of performance art: Moravian venuses and wolverines. In *Before Lascaux*, edited by H. Knecht, A. Pike-Tay and R. White, pp. 259–275. CRC Press, Boca Raton.

Sökefeld, M.
    1999   Debating self, identity, and culture in anthropology. *Current Anthropology* 40:417–447.

Sollas, W. J.
    1911   *Ancient hunters and their modern representatives.* Macmillan, London.

Sperber, D.
    1996   *Explaining culture: a naturalistic approach.* Blackwell, Oxford.

Spicer, J.
  1991 The renaissance elbow. In *A cultural history of gesture*, edited by J. Bremmer and H. Roodenburg, pp. 84–128. Cornell University Press, Ithaca, New York.

Sterner, J.
  1989 Who is signalling whom? Ceramic style, ethnicity and taphonomy among the Sirak Bulahay. *Antiquity* 63:451–459.

Stiles, D.
  1998 Raw material as evidence for human behaviour in the Lower Pleistocene: the Olduvai case. In *Early human behaviour in global context*, edited by M. D. Petraglia and R. Korisettar, pp. 133–150. Routledge, London.

Stiner, M. C.
  1994 *Honor among thieves: a zooarchaeological study of Neanderthal ecology.* Princeton University Press, New Jersey.
  2002 Carnivory, coevolution, and the geographic spread of the genus *Homo*. *Journal of Archaeological Research* 10:1–64.

Stiner, M. C., N. D. Munro and T. A. Surovell
  2000 The tortoise and the hare: small-game use, the broad spectrum revolution, and Palaeolithic demography. *Current Anthropology* 41:39–73.

Stone, L.
  1965 *Social change and revolution in England 1540–1640.* Longmans, Green and Co., London.
  1966 Theories of revolution. *World Politics* 18:159–176.

Stout, D., J. Quade, S. Semaw, M. J. Rogers and N. E. Levin
  2005 Raw material selectivity of the earliest stone toolmakers at Gona, Afar, Ethiopia. *Journal of Human Evolution* 48:365–380.

Strathern, M.
  1988 *The gender of the gift: problems with women and problems with society in Melanesia.* University of California Press, Berkeley.
  1996 Cutting the network. *Journal of the Royal Anthropological Institute* 2:517–535.
  1998 Social relations, and the idea of externality. In *Cognitive storage and material culture: the archaeology of symbolic storage*, edited by C. Renfrew and C. Scarre, pp. 135–147. McDonald Institute, Cambridge.

Straus, L. G.
  2000 Coming out of the cold: Western Europe in Dryas I and beyond. In *Regional approaches to adaptation in Late Pleistocene Western Europe*, edited by G. L. Peterkin and H. A. Price, pp. 191–203. BAR International Series 896, Oxford.

Straus, W. E. and A. J. E. Cave
  1957 Pathology and posture of Neanderthal man. *Quarterly Review of Biology* 32:348–363.

Streeck, J.
1995   On projection. In *Social intelligence and interaction: expressions and implications of the social bias in human intelligence*, edited by E. N. Goody, pp. 87–110. Cambridge University Press, Cambridge.

Stringer, C. and P. Andrews
1988   Genetic and fossil evidence for the origin of modern humans. *Science* 239:1263–1268.

Stringer, C. and C. Gamble
1993   *In search of the Neanderthals: solving the puzzle of human origins.* Thames and Hudson, London.

Stringer, C. and E. Mackie
1996   *African exodus.* Cape, London.

Strum, S. C. and B. Latour
1987   Redefining the social link: from baboons to humans. *Social Science Information* 26:783–802.

Svoboda, J. (editor)
1991   *Dolní Vestonice II: western slope.* ERAUL, Liège.
1994   *Pavlov I: excavations 1952–53.* ERAUL, Liège.

Svoboda, J., V. Lozek and E. Vleck
1996   *Hunters between East and West: The Palaeolithic of Moravia.* Plenum Press, New York.

Taborin, Y.
1993   *La parure en coquillage au Paleolithique* XXIXe supplement à Gallia Préhistoire. CNRS, Paris.

Tactikos, J. C.
2003   A re-evaluation of Palaeolithic stone tool cutting edge production rates and their implications. In *Lithic analysis at the millennium*, edited by N. Maloney and M. J. Shott, pp. 151–162. Institute of Archaeology, UCL, London.

Tanner, N.
1981   *On becoming human.* Cambridge University Press, Cambridge.

Tarlow, S.
2000   Emotion in archaeology. *Current Anthropology* 41:713–746.

Tattersall, I.
1995   *The fossil trail: How we know what we think we know about human evolution.* Oxford University Press, New York.

Thieme, H.
1999   Altpaläolithische Holzgeräte aus Schöningen, Lkr. Helmstedt. Bedeutsame Funde zur Kulturentwicklung des frühen Menschen. *Germania* 77:451–487.
2005   The Lower Palaeolithic art of hunting: the case of Schöningen 13 II-4, Lower Saxony, Germany. In *The individual hominid in context: archaeological investigations of Lower and Middle Palaeolithic landscapes, locales and artefacts*, edited by C. Gamble and M. Porr, pp. 115–132. Routledge, London.

Thomas, J.
  1996   *Time, culture and identity: an interpretive archaeology.* Routledge,
         London.
  2004   *Archaeology and modernity.* Routledge, London.
Thomas, N.
  1991   *Entangled objects: exchange, material culture and colonialism in the
         Pacific.* Harvard University Press, Cambridge MA.
Tiles, M.
  2001   Philosophy of technology. In *A companion to the philosophy of science*,
         edited by W. H. Newton-Smith, pp. 483–491. Blackwell, Oxford.
Tilley, C.
  1996   *An ethnography of the Neolithic.* Cambridge University Press,
         Cambridge.
  1999   *Metaphor and material culture.* Blackwell, Oxford.
Tixier, J.
  1963   *Typologie de l'Epipaléolithique du Maghreb.* C.R.A.P.E. d'Alger, 2 Arts
         et Métiers Graphiques, Paris.
Tixier, J. and A. Turq
  1999   Kombewa *et alii. Paléo* 11:135–143.
Tode, A. (editor)
  1953   *Die Untersuchung der paläolithischen Freilandstation von Salzgitter-
         Lebenstedt Eiszeitalter and Gegenwart* 3. 144–220.
  1982   *Der Altsteinzeitlichen Fundplatz Salzgitter-Lebenstedt.* Bohlau Verlag,
         Koln.
Toren, C.
  1999   *Mind, materiality and history: explorations in Fijian ethnography.*
         Routledge, London.
Toynbee, A.
  1884   (1969). *Toynbee's Industrial revolution.* David and Charles, Newton
         Abbott.
Trigger, B. G.
  1980   *Gordon Childe: revolutions in archaeology.* Thames and Hudson,
         London.
Troeng, J.
  1993   *Worldwide chronology of fifty-three prehistoric innovations.* Acta
         Archaeologica Lundensia 21, Stockholm.
Tudge, C.
  1999   *Neanderthals, bandits and farmers: how agriculture really began.* Yale
         University Press, New Haven.
Tuffreau, A. (editor)
  1993   *Riencourt-les-Bapaume (pas-de-Calais).* Documents d'Archéologie
         Française, Paris.
Turgot, A. R. J.
  1751 (1973)   *On universal history*, edited by A. L. Meek, pp. 61–118. Cambridge
         University Press, Cambridge.

Turner, J. H.
1991   *The structure of sociological theory.* Fifth ed. Wadsworth, Belmont.

Turner, J. H. and A. Maryanski
1991   Network analysis. In *The structure of sociological theory,* edited by J. H. Turner, pp. 540–572. Wadsworth, Belmont.

Turq, A.
1990   Exploitation des matières prémières lithiques dans le Mousterien entre Dordogne et Lot. *Cahiers du Quaternaire* 17:415–427.

1993   L'approvisionnement en matières premières lithiques au Moustérien et au début du Paléolithique supérieur dans le nord-est du bassin Aquitain (France). In *El origen del hombre moderno en el suroeste de Europa,* edited by V. C. Valdes, pp. 315–325. Universidad de Educacion a Distancia, Madrid.

Ucko, P. J. and G. Dimbleby (editors)
1969   *The domestication and exploitation of plants and animals.* Duckworth, London.

Valla, F. R.
1975   La sepulture H104 de Mallaha (Eynan) et le problème de la domestication du chien en Palestine. *Paléorient* 3:287–292.
1988   Aspects du sol de l'abri 131 de Mallaha (Eynan). *Paléorient* 14:283–296.
1991   Les Natoufiens de Mallaha et l'espace. In *The Natufian culture in the Levant,* edited by O. Bar-Yosef and F. R. Valla, pp. 111–122. International Monographs in Prehistory 1, Ann Arbor.

Vanhaeren, M. and F. d'Errico
2001   La Parure de l'enfant de la Madeleine (Fouilles Peyrony). Un nouveau regard sur l'enfance au Paléolithique supérieur. *Paléo* 13:201–240.
2003   Le mobilier funéraire de la dame de Saint-Germain-La-Rivière (Gironde) st l'origine Paléolithique des inégalités. *Paléo* 15:195–238.
2005   Grave goods from the Saint-Germain-la-Rivière burial: evidence for social inequality in the Upper Palaeolithic. *Journal of Anthropological Archaeology* 24:117–134.

Vega Toscano, L. G., L. Raposo and M. Santonja
1999   Environments and settlements in the Middle Palaeolithic of the Iberian peninsula. In *The Middle Palaeolithic occupation of Europe,* edited by W. Roebroeks and C. Gamble, pp. 23–48. University of Leiden and European Science Foundation, Leiden.

Veit, U.
1989   Ethnic concepts in German prehistory: a case study on the relationship between cultural identity and archaeological objectivity. In *Archaeological approaches to cultural identity,* edited by S. J. Shennan, pp. 35–56. Unwin Hyman, London.

Verhoeven, M.
2004   Beyond boundaries: nature, culture and a holistic approach to domestication in the Levant. *Journal of World Prehistory* 18:179–282.

Verpoorte, A.
  2001   *Places of art, traces of fire: a contextual approach to anthropomorphic
          figurines in the Pavlovian (Central Europe, 29–24kyr BP)*. Faculty of
          Archaeology, University of Leiden, Leiden.

Villa, P.
  1991   Middle Pleistocene prehistory in southwestern Europe: the state of
          our knowledge and ignorance. *Journal of Anthropological Research*
          47:193–217.

Villa, P. and F. d'Errico
  2001   Bone and ivory points in the Lower and Middle Palaeolithic of Europe.
          Journal of Human Evolution 41:69–112.

Villa, P., E. Soto, M. Santonja, A. Pérez-González, R. Mora, J. Parcerisas and
C. Sesé
  2005   New data from Ambrona: closing the hunting debate. *Quaternary
          International* 126–128:223–250.

Vitelli, K. D.
  1995   Pots, potters, and the shaping of Greek Neolithic society. In *The
          emergence of pottery: technology and innovation in ancient societies*,
          edited by W. K. Barnett and J. W. Hoopes, pp. 55–63. Smithsonian
          Institution Press, Washington.

  1999   'Looking up' at early ceramics in Greece. In *Pottery and people: a dynamic
          interaction*, edited by J. M. Skibo and G. M. Feinman, pp. 184–198.
          University of Utah Press, Salt Lake City.

Vogelsgang, R.
  1998   *Middle Stone Age Fundstellen in Südwest-Namibia*. Heinrich-Barth-
          Institut, Köln.

Wadley, L.
  2001   What is cultural modernity? A general view and a South African
          perspective from Rose Cottage Cave. *Cambridge Archaeological Journal*
          11:201–221.

Wagner, R.
  1991   The fractal person. In *Big men and great men: personifications of power
          in Melanesia*, edited by M. Godelier and M. Strathern, pp. 159–173.
          Cambridge University Press, Cambridge.

Walker, A. C. and R. E. F. Leakey
  1978   The hominids of East Turkana. *Scientific American* 239:54–66.

Watkins, T.
  1992   The beginning of the Neolithic: searching for meaning in material
          culture change. *Paléorient* 18:63–76.
  2004a   Architecture and 'theatres of memory' in the Neolithic of Southwest
          Asia. In *Rethinking materiality: the engagement of mind with the
          material world*, edited by E. DeMarrais, C. Gosden and C. Renfrew,
          pp. 97–106. McDonald Institute of Archaeological Research,
          Cambridge.

Watkins, T.

2004b Building houses, framing concepts, constructing worlds. *Paléorient* 30:5–24.

Webb, S. G.

1989 *The Willandra lakes hominids*. Occasional papers in prehistory 16. Department of Prehistory, Research School of Pacific Studies, Australian National University, Canberra.

Weidenreich, F.

1943 *The skull of Sinanthropus pekinensis: a comparative study of a primitive hominid skull*. Palaeontologia Sinica (n.s.D) 10. Geological Survey of China, Beijing.

Wengrow, D.

1998 'The changing face of clay': continuity, and change in the transition from village to urban life in the Near East. *Antiquity* 72:783–795.

West, S.

1999 Social space and the English country house. In *The familiar past?*, edited by S. Tarlow and S. West, pp. 103–122. Routledge, London.

Westropp, H. M.

1872 *Pre-historic phases; or, introductory essays on pre-historic archaeology*. Bell and Daldy, London.

White, R.

1982 Rethinking the Middle/Upper Palaeolithic transition. *Current Anthropology* 23:169–192.

1989 Production complexity and standardization in early Aurignacian bead and pendant manufacture: evolutionary implications. In *The Human Revolution: behavioural and biological perspectives on the origins of modern humans*, edited by P. Mellars and C. Stringer, pp. 366–390. Edinburgh University Press, Edinburgh.

White, T. D., B. Asfaw, D. Degusta, H. Gilbert, G. D. Richards, G. Suwa and F. C. Howell

2003 Pleistocene *Homo sapiens* from Middle Awash, Ethiopia. *Nature* 423:742–747.

Whitelaw, T. M.

1994 Order without architecture: functional, social and symbolic dimensions in hunter-gatherer settlement organisation. In *Architecture and order: approaches to social space*, edited by M. Parker-Pearson and C. Richards. Routledge, London.

Whittle, A.

1996 *Europe in the Neolithic: the creation of new worlds*. Cambridge University Press, Cambridge.

2003 *The archaeology of people: dimensions of Neolithic life*. Routledge, London.

Williams, R.

1958 *Culture and society: 1780–1950*. Columbia University Press, London and New York.

1965   *The long revolution.* Penguin Books, Harmondsworth.

Wilmsen, E. N.

1989   *Land filled with flies: a political economy of the Kalahari.* University of Chicago Press, Chicago.

Wilson, P.

1988   *The domestication of the human species.* Yale University Press, New Haven.

Wilson, R. A.

2005   Collective memory, group minds, and the extended mind thesis. *Cognitive Process on line.*

Winterhalder, B. and E. A. Smith (editors)

1981   *Hunter-gatherer foraging strategies.* University of Chicago Press, Chicago.

Wobst, H. M.

1978   The archaeo-ethnology of hunter gatherers or the tyranny of the ethnographic record in archaeology. *American Antiquity* 43:303–309.

Wobst, H. M. and A. S. Keene

1983   Archaeological explanation as political economy. In *The socio-politics of archaeology*, edited by J. M. Gero, D. M. Lacy and M. L. Blakey, pp. 79–90. Department of Anthropology Research Report 23. University of Massachusetts, Amherst.

Wolpoff, M. A.

1988   Modern human origins. *Science* 241:772–773.

1989   Multiregional evolution: the fossil alternative to Eden. In *The human revolution: behavioural and biological perspectves on the origins of modern humans*, edited by P. Mellars and C. Stringer, pp. 62–109. Edinburgh University Press, Edinburgh.

Woodburn, J.

1991   African hunter-gatherer social organization: is it best understood as a product of encapsulation? In *Hunters and gatherers 1: history, evolution and social change*, edited by T. Ingold, D. Riches and J. Woodburn, pp. 31–64. Berg., New York.

Woolgar, S.

1987   Reconstructing man and machine. In *The social construction of technological systems*, edited by W. E. Bijker, T. P. Hughes and T. Pinch, pp. 311–328. MIT Press, Cambridge, MA.

Wright, K. I.

1994   Ground-stone tools and hunter-gatherer subsistence in Southwest Asia: implications for the transition to farming. *American Antiquity* 59:238–263.

Wright, K. I. and A. N. Garrard

2003   Social identities and the expansion of stone bead-making in Neolithic Western Asia: new evidence from Jordan. *Antiquity* 77:267–284.

Wylie, A.
   1985   The reaction against analogy. *Advances in Archaeological Method and Theory* 8:63–111.
   2002   *Thinking from things: essays in the philosophy of archaeology.* University of California Press, Berkeley.

Wynn, T.
   1993   Layers of thinking in tool behaviour. In *Tools, language and cognition in human evolution*, edited by K. Gibson and T. Ingold, pp. 389–406. Cambridge University Press, Cambridge.
   1995   Handaxe enigmas. *World Archaeology* 27:10–24.

Yellen, J. E.
   1977   *Archaeological approaches to the present. Models for reconstructing the past.* Academic Press, New York.

Zampetti, D. and M. Mussi
   1991   Segni del potere, simboli det potere: la problematica del paleolitico Superiore italiano. In *The archaeology of power: part 2*, edited by E. Herring, R. Whitehouse and J. Wilkins, pp. 149–160. papers of the fourth conference of Italian archaeology. vol. 2. Accordia Research Centre, London.

Zhou, W.-X., D. Sornette, R. A. Hill and R. Dunbar
   2005   Discrete hierarchical organization of social group sizes. *Proceedings of the Royal Society of London B* 272: 439–44.

Zilhão, J. and F. d'Errico
   1999   The chronology and taphonomy of the earliest Aurignacian and its implications for the understanding of Neanderthal extinction. *Journal of World Prehistory* 13:1–68.

Zohary, D. and M. Hopf
   2000   *Domestication of plants in the Old World: the origin and spread of cultivated plants in West Asia, Europe and the Nile Valley.* Third ed. Oxford University Press, Oxford.

Index

Compiled by Fiona Coward